MATTERS OF PRINCIPLE

AN INSIDER'S ACCOUNT OF AMERICA'S REJECTION OF ROBERT BORK'S NOMINATION TO THE SUPREME COURT

MARK GITENSTEIN

SIMON & SCHUSTER
NEW YORK LONDON TORONTO SYDNEY TOKYO SINGAPORE

SIMON & SCHUSTER
SIMON & SCHUSTER BUILDING
ROCKEFELLER CENTER
1230 AVENUE OF THE AMERICAS
NEW YORK, NEW YORK 10020

DESIGNED BY SONGHEE KIM
MANUFACTURED IN THE UNITED STATES OF AMERICA

1 3 5 7 9 10 8 6 4 2

LIBRARY OF CONGRESS CATALOGING-IN-PUBLICATION DATA
GITENSTEIN, MARK.
MATTERS OF PRINCIPLE : AN INSIDER'S ACCOUNT OF AMERICA'S REJECTION OF ROBERT BORK'S NOMINATION TO THE SUPREME COURT / MARK GITENSTEIN.
P. CM.
INCLUDES BIBLIOGRAPHICAL REFERENCES AND INDEX.
1. BORK, ROBERT H. 2. UNITED STATES. SUPREME COURT—OFFICIALS AND EMPLOYEES—SELECTION AND APPOINTMENT. 3. JUDGES—UNITED STATES—SELECTION AND APPOINTMENT. I. TITLE.
KF8742.G57 1992
347.73'2634—DC20
[347.3073534] 92-26149
CIP

ISBN: 0-671-67424-2

ACKNOWLEDGMENTS

I WOULD LIKE TO THANK MY FRIEND Senator Joseph Biden who had the confidence in me to make me Chief Counsel of the Senate Judiciary Committee so that I could participate in the events described in this book. Richard Ben Kramer convinced me that I had a story to tell. My agent, the irrepressible Flip Brophy, was always there when I needed her and helped me find Jim Silberman and Dominick Anfuso at Simon & Schuster who assisted me in turning this story into a book.

I was lucky to have the friendship and advice of Ted Kaufman, Ron Klain, and Chris Shroeder who read every page of this manuscript many times. I would also like to thank the dozens of individuals who participated in lengthy interviews with me. Space does not permit me to list them all. Many, like Tom Donilon, Jeff Peck, Ralph Neas, and Melanne Verveer, shared the battle with me as opponents of the nomination. I am particularly grateful to Robert Bork's friends and allies who were gracious enough to share their perspective with me: John Bolton, A. B. Culvahouse, Ken Duberstein, Terry Eastland, Tom Griscom, Tom Korologos, Patrick McGuigan and Brad Reynolds, among others. They could easily have decided not to help but instead spent countless hours with me.

There are many others, such as George LeMaistre of Mobile, Alabama, who researched portions of the book and deserve special thanks. I hope they will read this and know that they played some part in the great struggle and the telling of its story.

My wife, Libby, spent hours arguing over the tone of hundreds of pages of manuscript. Becky, my oldest daughter, not only researched parts of the book but gave me invaluable editorial assistance. My son, Ben, and my youngest daughter, Sarah, never waned in their enthusiasm for this project that took so many hours away from time we could have spent together. My mother-in-law, Sue Brown, transcribed hours of interview transcripts that were invaluable.

Both the publisher and I would like to gratefully acknowledge the permission granted us to publish excerpts from the following publications:

David Broder, columns appearing in the *Washington Post* on July 1 and October 6, 1987. © 1987, Washington Post Writers Group. Reprinted with permission.

David Broder, *Changing of the Guard* (New York: Simon & Schuster, 1980).

Reprinted from *Battle for Justice: How the Bork Nomination Shook America* by Ethan Bronner, by permission of W. W. Norton & Company, Inc. Copyright © 1989 by Ethan Bronner.

Lincoln Caplan, *Tenth Justice: The Solicitor General and the Rule of Law* (New York: Vantage, 1988).

Patrick Leahy, ''Judgment Days'' *Washingtonian Magazine,* April 1988.

Patrick McGuigan and Dawn Weyrich, *Ninth Justice* (Washington, D.C.: Free Congress Research and Education Foundation, 1990).

Michael Pertschuk and Wendy Schaetzel, *The People Rising: The Campaign Against the Bork Nomination* (New York: Thunder Mouth's Press, 1989).

THIS BOOK IS DEDICATED TO MY WIFE, LIBBY, AND MY THREE CHILDREN, BECKY, BEN, AND SARAH, WHO SHARED THESE DIFFICULT BUT IMPORTANT EVENTS WITH ME AND ENCOURAGED ME TO TELL THIS STORY.

CONTENTS

INTRODUCTION

ROBERT BORK AND HIS WIFE, Mary Ellen, entered the Roosevelt Room of the White House on Saturday morning, September 26, 1987, with a sense of angry determination. The previous two months had been a roller coaster ride for the sixty-year-old Court of Appeals judge.

On July 1, 1987, Robert Bork had been nominated by President Reagan to be a Justice on the Supreme Court, thus realizing his lifelong ambition. In the beginning he seemed tantalizingly close to achieving his dream. Pundits, liberal and conservative alike, predicted that the Democrats, led by Sen. Joseph Biden, the new, young chairman of the Senate Judiciary Committee, would be no match for the articulate, conservative Bork and his sponsor, Ronald Reagan.

By the third week in September, the tables had turned completely. The Administration's strategy for confirming Bork was in shambles. The plan, unbeknown to Bork, had been for Reagan, whose public standing was at its nadir because of Iran–Contra, to be kept in the background and for Bork to win the fight as the star witness in his own behalf in nationally televised hearings before the Senate Judiciary Committee. After a week of his testimony, with sharp and savvy questioning by Biden and his colleagues, three national polls showed devastating erosion in public support for the nomination.

In the week after his testimony, Bork had tried indirect approaches to the Administration, without success. At the end of the week Bork decided to make the case to Reagan political operatives face-to-face. Reagan's chief of staff, former Republican Sen. Howard Baker, and his deputy, Ken Duberstein, did not even attend the meeting.

Bork came to the meeting with a plan. He wanted the President to address the nation the next week on prime-time television on his behalf. Bork was blunt: "I've been trying to win this on my own. You guys aren't doing everything you can. I need the President. Unless there is a personal presidential effort, I am going to lose. I may lose anyway, but I can't win without the President."

Tom Griscom, the top political operative at the meeting, was designated to respond. He equivocated. The time was not ripe for the President to speak, he said. Bork was angry. "Are you all backing out? . . . I thought I had his commitment to make a speech."

Griscom would not budge. Besides, he explained, "We also have to be worried about the President himself. If this thing doesn't go, he is going to take a pretty big hit on it."

Three weeks later the President had still not delivered his address, and Administration representatives were quietly attempting to persuade Bork to abandon his hopeless dream and withdraw. They feared that, if Reagan did not put forward a new nominee soon, the struggle to fill the Powell vacancy would become increasingly difficult in 1988, a presidential election year.

Bork refused to slip quietly into the night. Not trusting his "friends" in the Administration, he insisted on seeing the President alone to tell him of his decision to stay in and force a Senate vote. Without even consulting Baker and his staff, Bork left the Oval Office, went directly to the White House press room, and delivered an eloquent speech about why it was important for him to insist upon a formal Senate vote. Bork felt a "crucial principle" was at stake. He felt he had been mistreated in the process, and he wanted to assure that no future nominee faced such a "public campaign of distortion."

At the time I was the chief counsel for the Senate Judiciary Committee and intimately involved in the effort to defeat the Bork nomination. His speech angered me: first, because I did not believe his allegations were accurate; second, because I wanted the ordeal to end.

Now, five years later, as I reflect on it, I recognize Bork's stand on principle as laudable. Although I still disagree with his accusation, it was important for this man of principle to make his stand once again on something in which he strongly believed. For so much of his struggle in 1987, he seemed to defer to the political experts, the handlers. He was at times bewildered and cautious. Finally, too late, the real Bork emerged, confident and forceful on behalf of a matter of principle.

Ironically, Bork's primary antagonist, Biden, had to undergo a similar metamorphosis that summer. Biden had not even sought the chairmanship of the Judiciary Committee. In the fall of 1986 he was on the verge of deciding to run for President, but with the Democrats winning back the Senate in November, he faced a difficult decision.

According to the seniority rules of the Senate, liberal Edward Kennedy could take the chairmanship of the Judiciary Committee, bumping Biden. The civil rights and women's groups pleaded with Kennedy to take it, over the iconoclast Biden. Biden's presidential campaign operatives wanted Biden to give up the chairmanship to devote himself entirely to the campaign. He refused.

On the eve of the hearings, Biden too seemed closer to his dream than he could imagine. Biden's pollster, Pat Caddell, showed him poll results suggesting that victory in the Iowa caucuses were within his grasp, a critical first step in the presidential nominating process. The weekend before the hearings began, Biden was sabotaged by his "friends"—in this case his fellow contenders for the Democratic presidential nomination, especially Michael Dukakis—who had all piously announced their opposition to Bork.

The Dukakis campaign, fearful of Biden's surge in the Iowa primaries and that success in the Bork hearings might make him unbeatable, fed *New York Times* reporter Maureen Dowd a story about Biden's unattributed use of quotes by a British politician in a campaign speech. Just as Biden was demonstrating intellectual agility in taking on the foremost judicial philosopher of the Reagan social revolution, he was being attacked by the press in a feeding frenzy abetted by his fellow Democrats, ultimately culminating in charges suggesting that Biden had been disciplined for cheating in law school.

Caddell insisted that the only way to answer the allegations was to go to Iowa and debate them, letting the voters decide in the caucuses. He was probably right. Many of the charges were inaccurate, and many voters thought them irrelevant, but Biden refused to abandon the task at hand. He felt a sense of duty to finish this battle of principle over the future of the Supreme Court.

He made the decision in a sad meeting on Tuesday evening, September 23, 1987. The next morning, as the staff struggled over the emotional letdown of organizing the funereal press conference to announce his withdrawal, Biden brought renewed zest and self-confidence to the hearings.

This was the day Bork's key witnesses were to appear, led off by former Chief Justice Warren Burger. What should have been a moment of tearful humiliation for Biden became a morning of deliberate and effective cross-examination.

There was a new crispness to Biden's questioning. A few minutes into his cross-examination, he politely pinned down the former Chief Justice: "With your indulgence, I would like to read an extended passage from one of your opinions."

He then read a passage in which Burger warned of the danger of too narrowly construing the expansive clauses of the Constitution—the central criticism Biden had made of Bork's writings.

Burger responded: "I see no problem about that statement, and I would be astonished if Judge Bork would not subscribe to it."

Obviously, Burger had no idea where Bork stood on the central issue of the hearings. The essence of Bork's jurisprudence was that the Constitution must be narrowly construed.

Biden then proceeded to drive the point home: "Let me ask you this, Mr. Chief Justice. Does the Ninth Amendment mean anything?"

The Ninth Amendment was put into the Constitution to guarantee a generous interpretation of the Bill of Rights. It reads, "The enumeration in the Constitution, of certain rights, shall not be construed to deny or disparage others retained by the people." Bork himself, in his many days on the witness stand, just concluded, had been almost flip in disregarding this provision of the Constitution, as if it had been added by mistake. By the date of Burger's testimony, it had become the central issue of the hearings: How broadly was the Ninth—and unenumerated rights generally—to be interpreted by the Supreme Court?

Burger fumbled around and tried to find the text of the Ninth Amendment in his copy of the Constitution, and as he looked, he began to mumble something about the importance of the word "persons" with special reference to the *Dred Scott* case. (This 1857 Supreme Court decision involved, in part, the question of whether blacks were "persons" entitled to protection under the due process clause of the Fifth Amendment.) Burger concluded, "It is hard to say which amendment is more important than any other amendment, but surely the matter of 'persons' becomes terribly important."

Biden respectfully ended his questioning by reading the text of the Ninth Amendment into the record. The word "persons," of course, does not appear in it, making it clear that one of the key witnesses in Bork's behalf had not understood what the hearings were all about. Thus Biden deftly and subtly discredited him.

The struggle over the Supreme Court in the summer of 1987 is much more than a story of Bork, Biden, and personal principle. It is also about scores of others who devoted the summer and fall of 1987 to this epic struggle, other Senators and their staff, young idealistic conservatives in the Reagan Administration, and dedicated members of the civil rights and civil liberties organizations in Washington, and members of the press who attempted to explain the battle to average Americans. More important, though, it is a story of a national debate over public principle—the direction of the Supreme Court and the United States as a nation of laws.

In 1990, almost three years after his nomination to be a Justice of the Supreme Court was rejected by the United States Senate, Robert Bork published his memoir of that experience. It is more than a sad and bitter version of what happened to him. It is a well written, indeed at times persuasive case for his jurisprudence.

Its title, *The Tempting of America: The Political Seduction of the Law,* suggests that for Robert Bork and his allies the struggle that began in July 1987 did not end with the 58–42 vote in October of that year that rejected the nomination. The struggle now is over the legacy. To Robert Bork his defeat was only one more battle in the war by the "ultraliberals" "for control of our legal culture." It was to him and his allies an illegitimate victory, a clever manipulation of public opinion that establishes no important, lasting, or worthy principle. The American people decided nothing with the defeat of Robert Bork or what he stood for.

For those, like myself, who devoted themselves to the defeat of the nomination, it was much more. Granted there were many times during those 115 days when we were troubled by the tactics and distortions that characterized both the pro- and anti-Bork efforts. There have certainly been times as we have pored over opinions written by Anthony Kennedy, who eventually filled the Powell vacancy, when we have wondered, "Would Robert Bork have been all that much worse?" As the months have turned into years, as I have struggled over this manuscript, there is one thing I have never doubted, however: Americans made a serious, principled decision in rejecting Robert Bork's jurisprudence that summer, a decision that will have a lasting impact on the Court and on America.

This book tells that story largely from my vantage point as chief counsel of the Senate Judiciary Committee. It makes the case that we undertook, as honestly as we could, to educate the American people as to the consequences of Robert Bork's jurisprudence on the Court and our country.

I have never met Robert Bork. His son, Robert Jr., made it clear to me on a number of occasions that the judge was simply not interested in talking to me. I can fully understand. So he still is to me, as he is to most Americans, an abstraction, an affable yet finally unconvincing witness in a hearing, the author of strident, often perplexing, sometimes threatening speeches.

The tragedy of nomination battles is that it is almost impossible to make the case against the nominee without rejecting the person as well as his or her views. I have spoken at length to many of his friends and allies, and they heavily influenced my perception of what happened. They have convinced me beyond a doubt that they, like Bork's opponents, were in pursuit of a principled vision of the Court, the Constitution, and the role of judges in our society. Robert Bork was the living embodiment of that vision, and I recognize, as one of his staunchest allies told me, that his defeat was a crushing personal disappointment, a wound that may never completely heal.

At the heart of the disagreement are two radically different visions of the Constitution and especially the Warren Court's interpretation of it. I have read no more articulate explanation of Robert Bork's vision than his own book.

As he explains in his book, the politicization of the law by the Left is intended to lead courts to judicial "results" that satisfy liberal ideological appetites. For many decades liberal lawyers, law professors, and Supreme Court Justices have rewritten Constitutional law to accomplish their agenda: legalized abortion, racial quotas, schools free of prayer, and police shackled with technical restrictions against violent criminals, to name a few.

Biden's reaction to Bork's ideas was instinctive. To him, "if Judge Bork had been Justice Bork during the past thirty years and had his view prevailed, America would be a fundamentally different place than it is today."

Bork was not simply taking on the Warren Court and Joe Biden, but a half-century of Constitutional law. In fact, if confirmed, Bork would have been the only Justice in history to espouse such a narrow vision of the Constitution.

To Bork, if a right was not explicitly written into the Constitution, it simply was not deserving of protection by the federal courts. "Bork just sees the Constitution as a lifeless contract," Biden told me late one night as we pored over the judge's speeches. Biden and those who opposed Bork looked to the Fourteenth Amendment's guarantee that no person would be deprived of "life, liberty or property, without due process" as an animating source of rights. The Constitution is not a limited codification of civil liberties. Instead, as one of our great jurists used to say, the Constitution protects rights "so rooted in the traditions and conscience of our people as to be ranked as fundamental."

If our Supreme Court had taken Bork's argument to its logical extreme, America would indeed be "a fundamentally different place." Because if the Fourteenth Amendment did not explicitly abolish segregation in the schools, segregation would simply remain;* if "one man one vote" were not implied by the Fourteenth Amendment, the federal courts would be powerless to reapportion state legislatures; if the Constitution did not specifically prohibit racially restrictive covenants, then they were enforceable; if it did not mention a generalized right to privacy, state legislatures could prohibit married couples from purchasing contraceptives or prohibit all abortions; if it specifically recognized no general right to educate your children as you wanted, states could prohibit sending your children to private schools or teaching them a foreign language. The above are all real cases. And every one except the desegregation cases were ones where, in Bork's mind, the Supreme Court had improperly "invented" a "fundamental" right.

Robert Bork believed that the American people sided with his vision of the Constitution, not Biden's. In fact, he was completely wrong about what the American people believe. They are not appalled by the work of the Supreme Court in the past thirty years. Indeed, for the most part they embrace it.

The nomination of Anthony Kennedy by Ronald Reagan and of David Souter by George Bush ratify a new conventional wisdom about Supreme Court nominees. Both deliberately distanced themselves from Bork's jurisprudence because they recognized that Americans do believe they have certain unwritten rights. The Senate will reject any nominee who does not embrace that philosophy or who suggests that the Warren Court was wrong in recognizing those fundamental rights.

That is not surprising or "dangerous," as Bork and some of his friends

*In fairness, Bork found a way around this logical trap and defended the *Brown* decision. However, he was troubled with the way the Supreme Court extended the *Brown* doctrine to the federal government and abolished school segregation in the District of Columbia.

would have us believe. Robert Bork was the first Supreme Court nominee to advocate such a narrow view, and he is likely to be the last.

In his book, as Bork describes his reactions the day of the final vote, he tells a touching story that gave me real insight into how he felt about the fight. One evening after the fight was over, as they were preparing to go out, his wife, Mary Ellen, showed him a new dress. She told him it was the dress she had bought to wear for his swearing-in. She had never doubted for a moment that it would happen. "The poignancy of that moment had nothing to do with my career but with her, and since I could not explain it, I said nothing and the moment passed."

As I have read his book and talked to his friends, I have become more and more convinced that he really could not "explain" what had happened to him. In fact, if anything dominated his approach to the process, it seemed to be bewilderment and a certain amount of naïveté. Although he did come across as arrogant at times in the hearings and in the press, I do not believe he is an arrogant man, just a man who espouses ideas that I find arrogant and elitist.

The real tragedy for Robert Bork, his allies, and the philosophy they espoused, however, is that their greatest champion let them down in the fight, a truth it must be very difficult to face. As several of Bork's friends and allies told me, Ronald Reagan deserves much of the blame.

For Bork to have had even a chance to win a fight like this, Ronald Reagan should have done what Franklin Roosevelt and Andrew Jackson did when they wanted to change the direction of the Supreme Court—personally wage a full-fledged national political debate. Instead, as one of Bork's allies told me, Ronald Reagan "stayed on the sidelines."

We argued a matter of fundamental principle to the American people. Ronald Reagan took the people and their attitudes for granted, and we won.

For me it is also a reassuring story. I believe that, even if Ronald Reagan had not stayed on the sidelines, we would have eventually won. For in rejecting Robert Bork, America reaffirmed a vibrant and expansive vision of personal liberty representing a deep and abiding trait of the American character. It is also satisfying to see that these two men, Robert Bork and Joseph Biden, who devoted so much to this great debate and despite these terrible personal setbacks in 1987, remain important figures in our national life largely because of what they did.

CHAPTER 1

A CHANGE OF PERSONNEL

IN THE LATE FALL OF 1971, Sen. James O. Eastland of Mississippi had been chairman of the Senate Judiciary Committee for well over a decade, running the committee like his own plantation. He had a reputation for fairness even with his ideological enemies, but he never let anything come to a final vote in his committee unless certain of an acceptable outcome. He was a conservative, a Southerner, and a Democrat, in that order.

When Lewis Powell, the courtly former president of the American Bar Association from Richmond, Virginia, came into Eastland's office on the second floor of the Dirksen Office Building, Powell and the supporters who accompanied him were, no doubt, expecting to be welcomed with opened arms. President Nixon had just announced his name along with William Rehnquist to fill two vacancies on the Supreme Court.

Eastland was determined to help the President put his conservative stamp on the Supreme Court, especially after the Haynesworth and Carswell fiascos, early in the Nixon term. In 1970 Nixon suffered two humiliating defeats at the hands of Senate liberals with the failed nominations to the Supreme Court of Clement Haynesworth and, immediately afterward, Harold Carswell (a seat eventually filled by Harry A. Blackmun). Eastland was confident the Senate would approve the Powell nomination. Indeed, he was probably a bit suspicious of a Southerner who had fought for desegregation and was an outspoken advocate of legal services for the poor. However, he could support Powell because he knew that Nixon had chosen him, in part, because of the new Justice's recent attacks on the ''radical left'' and support for electronic surveillance of domestic radicals.

The chairman's office was a spacious corner office adjacent to the committee's hearing room. It had a large walk-in safe, built especially for the chairman and his Internal Security subcommittee, so that he could have easy access to voluminous FBI files on nominees and subversives.

He sat at his desk puffing on a cigar as he did when he presided over committee business sessions, completely enveloped in smoke. Powell and his friends took their seats. Eastland informed them that Powell would undoubtedly be confirmed. Powell thanked him.

"Do you know why you're going to be confirmed?" Eastland asked.

No, he replied.

"Because," Eastland drawled, "they think you're going to die." Senate Democrats were confident that Powell, at sixty-two, would die or retire during the next Democratic Administration, which would surely begin in January of 1973. Powell, the cautious Southern moderate conservative, was perceived by liberals and conservatives, Democrats and Republicans, as a "safe" nominee who would have little, if any, impact on the Court and besides would have a very short tenure.

No one, least of all Lewis Powell, thought he'd serve fifteen and a half years on the Supreme Court. Powell had turned down Nixon immediately after the Carswell defeat, because he thought he was too old. Even in 1971 Powell only relented after a personal appeal by the President. He vowed to himself and his family to serve only ten years.

However, in 1982 as the Court approached the end of its term, the time when retiring justices usually announce their intentions, Powell hesitated. His family, especially his children, two of them lawyers, insisted that he stay on.

Certainly, neither Eastland nor Nixon expected Powell to play the pivotal role he did for fifteen years on the Supreme Court on civil liberties and civil rights issues. Within a year Powell wrote the Supreme Court decision that required, for the first time, court review of wiretapping of subversives, and within a few years he was the decisive vote in favor of the liberal position on a whole host of civil liberties and civil rights issues.

By June of 1987 Lewis Powell was labeled by the American Civil Liberties Union, "the most powerful individual in America" and by the Reagan Administration and its conservative allies as the single biggest roadblock to their judicial revolution.

On criminal law issues, his vote shifted the Court to the side of law enforcement, in favor of the death penalty, narrowing the *Miranda* rule requiring that police warn defendants of their rights or the exclusionary rule prohibiting prosecutors from using evidence seized in violation of the Court's complex rules limiting police searches. Although he voted the conservative line 80 percent of the time, in the remaining 20 percent he provided the critical fifth vote against weakening affirmative action, against overturning the controversial *Roe* v. *Wade* decision on abortion, and against permitting school prayer.

According to the American Civil Liberties Union, there were twenty major civil liberties decisions in the 1986–87 term of court on a 5–4 vote. Powell was in the majority on every one of them. However, nothing infuriated extreme conservatives any more than the fact that Republican-appointed justices, especially Justice Harry Blackmun, also appointed by Nixon, and Powell, provided the critical votes to uphold the *Roe* decision, as recently as June 1986.

The decades-old struggle by conservatives to end this judicial "tyranny" was to have succeeded at last with the opening of the new term of the Supreme Court in October 1986. President Reagan not only filled Chief Justice Warren Burger's vacancy with conservative Antonin Scalia but elevated the Court's most conservative member, William Rehnquist, to Chief Justice. The Reagan Administration, unlike its Republican predecessors, had engaged in a deliberate, indeed brilliant, strategy of carefully screening judicial nominees at all levels to implement its agenda in the courts. Never again would a Republican make the mistake of a Powell or a Blackmun.

Many conservative Court strategists, however, were disappointed with the Rehnquist Court. They had hoped that Rehnquist would use his position as Chief Justice more adroitly. The only real power the Chief Justice of the United States has to influence the development of the law is the authority to assign, either to himself or to another justice, the writing of the majority opinion of the Court, once the nine members have voted on a matter. The text of the opinion, joined in by the majority, can be as important as the result itself, because it becomes the authoritative statement of the law.

Under the practice of the Supreme Court, if the Chief Justice is on the losing side of the decision, the most senior member on the winning side determines who will write the majority opinion. Invariably then, on the controversial social issues that energized the conservatives—school prayer, affirmative action, abortion, or other civil liberties issues, where Powell swung the court to the Left—the Chief Justice of the United States was, for all practical purposes, not William Rehnquist but that nemesis of the far Right, William Brennan, the most senior liberal on the court.

Chief Justice Burger had been much more calculating than Rehnquist. He had deliberately voted with the majority so that he could control the opinion. Under Rehnquist, however, because Brennan either wrote the majority opinion or assigned it, liberals won even more sweeping victories than they had under the Burger regime.

Nothing was more galling to conservative movement lawyers. Bruce Fein of the Heritage Foundation furiously denounced the Court's trend and Rehnquist's inability to stem it: "If Rehnquist was a baseball manager, he'd have been fired in midseason. It's been Brennan's finest hour." And Ralph Neas, executive director of the Leadership Conference on Civil Rights, and a primary anti-Rehnquist lobbyist, smugly declared, "The [Edwin] Meese Justice Department has failed miserably."

But Supreme Court scholar, A. E. Dick Howard of the University of Virginia Law School, was prescient: "What this term shows" is that "over the next few years, without changes in personnel, it is going to take more than intellectual persuasiveness to alter the Court's decision."

A "change in personnel" was indeed about to occur the very next day. Potentially the most significant shift of power in recent jurisprudence was being discussed quietly over breakfast between Lewis Powell and his wife, Josephine. Powell explained that he would finally accede to her wishes and would tell the Chief Justice that he intended to resign.

On Thursday, June 25, Powell told the Chief he intended to announce his retirement the next day after the Court handed down its final opinions of the term. Rehnquist would respect the confidence and arrange for the President to be notified immediately before the public announcement in the morning.

On Friday morning the justices gathered in the anteroom adjacent to the courtroom to don their black robes. It is a tradition that they all shake hands each day before assuming the bench. Powell broke the news to his colleagues. Rehnquist had arranged for the President to be notified simultaneously. The justices solemnly took their seats to announce their final decisions of the term. At the end of the day's session, the Chief announced the retirement with a personal note. The justices "shall miss his wise counsel in our deliberations, but we look forward to being the continuing beneficiaries of his friendship."

The news spread quickly through Washington, both liberals and conservatives expressing concern over the next nominee. They knew the stakes would be high and the balance of the Court was the prize. As one conservative put it, "This is the last chance he [Reagan] has to leave any legacy whatsoever on social and civil rights issues."

Within minutes of the announcement, the network of young conservative lawyers in the large gray offices of the Department of Justice at 10th and Pennsylvania Avenue were on the phone with each other.

Steve Markman, assistant attorney general for the Office of Legal Policy, thought to himself, Finally we would have the chance to change the direction of the court. He found an immediate and enthusiastic meeting of the minds with Mike Carvin, deputy to the primary legal adviser to the Attorney General. Powell's successor, they agreed, should be Judge Robert H. Bork of the United States Court of Appeals for the District of Columbia.

Early in the Meese regime, a group had been established in the Justice Department for the purpose of screening potential Supreme Court nominees and formulating strategy for their selection. The group was chaired by William Bradford Reynolds of the Civil Rights Division and made up of many of the bright young conservative lawyers in the Department, including Markman, Carvin, Lee Lieberman, who later was to clerk for Scalia, and John Bolton, assistant attorney general for the Office of Legislative affairs, a former student of Bork's at Yale. The group was enthralled with Robert Bork.

"No one," explained Markman, "quite matched Bork in the pantheon of heroes of the conservative legal movement. [Liberals have] lots of Larry Tribes [liberal constitutional scholar Laurance Tribe of Harvard Law School], we've only got one Bob Bork."

Bolton spoke with the same reverence about Bork. Both agreed that, in June of 1987, there was a clear consensus that it was Robert Bork's turn. Bork had been passed over twice for the court by the Reagan Administration, in favor of Sandra Day O'Connor and Scalia—in part, according to Bolton, because of the political allure of nominating a woman and an Italian-American. Bolton and some of the others at Justice believed that Bork had been told by the White House that he would be next. That, of course, would only come to pass if President Reagan deferred to Reynolds and Meese, as he had in 1986 when Scalia and Rehnquist were chosen.

At the time Powell resigned, Reynolds and Meese were not in Washington, but in West Germany on official business. Bolton, Charles Cooper (Carvin's boss), and Carvin were concerned about what might happen in their absence. In the aftermath of the Iran–Contra controversy that had plagued the Administration for most of the previous eight months, former Sen. Howard Baker, a well-known moderate, had been named chief of staff in the White House.

Things began to happen quickly. Bolton and Cooper were not at all certain that the "pragmatic" White House staff brought in by Baker would appreciate the opportunity that had presented itself or were prepared to implement the Meese Supreme Court strategy.

Bolton and Cooper, knowing they had to seize the moment, called Reynolds and Meese in West Germany and told them they had better get back to the States immediately—"to save the Bork nomination," Bolton believed, "before the White House chickens out and names someone less controversial."

Just as Bolton and Cooper feared, it was Howard Baker who broke the news to the President. The Chief Justice's office had warned Baker to be ready for a call that morning. Baker was with the President in the Oval Office when the Chief called.

The White House issued a bland, noncommittal statement praising Powell for his service on the Court and stating that the President considered naming Powell's successor "one of the most significant duties of my office."

That night on the ABC evening news, a reporter summarized White House staff concerns that the President spend more time on nuclear détente, not on the Supreme Court nomination. It was a discouraging message to conservatives, precisely what many of them expected and feared from Howard Baker's White House staff. The "pragmatists" in the White House had the priorities in exactly the reverse order. To conservatives the Supreme Court was much more important than détente, and if Baker was not willing to recommend that the President invest his political capital on a controversial Supreme Court nomination, there was less chance that Bork would get the nod from Baker. Reynolds and Meese needed to get back in a hurry.

* * *

Three thousand miles away at Los Angeles International Airport, Continental Flight 905 was touching down. On board were Chairman Biden of the Senate Judiciary Committee and his wife Jill, along with a traveling party consisting of Tommy Vallely, a Boston pol who had become a feisty but reliable traveling companion for Biden, and Ruth Berry, whose job as head of advance was to be sure that everything ran smoothly. Biden, forty-four, was not simply chairman of the Judiciary Committee but was seventeen days into a presidential-nomination campaign. In a few months the Iowa caucus and the New Hampshire primary would be on him.

As the local campaign staff approached the gate, Vallely sensed something was wrong. One of the earnest young Los Angeles aides told him softly, "Biden needs to call his office immediately. Justice Powell has resigned."

Vallely turned to tell Biden. "I heard him," Biden said seriously. "Tom, use that pay phone and get the office. I want to talk to Mark." Vallely tried to get Biden into a private room, but the Senator refused.

Back in Washington, Larry Rasky, the campaign press secretary, and I were waiting for the call. The four hours between the Powell announcement and contact with Biden had been frustrating ones. We had been deluged with press calls, and we were certain he'd be ambushed by media at the airport. The implications of this for Biden's campaign seemed obvious. Biden was not interested in talking to the gaggle of political experts who were part of his primary campaign—the "gurus" as he called them—who crowded around the secretary as she answered the phone.

Biden had been dubious from the start about running for President and chairing the committee. It took months to make the decision to run. When the Democrats retook control of the Senate the previous November, Biden practically begged Sen. Edward Kennedy not to move to the Labor Committee, but to exercise his rights under the seniority rules and take the Judiciary Committee so that Biden could focus on his run for the presidency. Indeed, up to the week before his announcement for President on June 9, Biden gave serious thought to not declaring.

Perhaps we should have anticipated this particular development, but we did not. It was Biden's worst nightmare. The Supreme Court was closely divided 4–4 with one swing vote, Powell, especially on the issue of abortion. Biden would have to preside over the selection of his successor. Confirmation of Powell's successor would ultimately become the Number 1 domestic priority of the President of the United States. None of the other candidates faced a challenge or an opportunity like this. It would be the ultimate test of presidential leadership for Biden, a test that could make or break his candidacy.

Although there would be plenty of national attention, the process would be time-consuming and incredibly distracting from the campaign. Furthermore, as Biden recognized instantly, the opposition would seize on his presidential ambitions and portray everything he said or did on the nomination as political.

Biden, Rasky, and I quickly reviewed the situation on the phone.

"Hello Senator, great news, huh?" Rasky said.

"Yep, just what we needed," Biden responded ironically. "What's the press saying?"

"They want to talk to you, and you've got a press conference scheduled at the NEA convention in about an hour."

You could hear a discouraged sigh from Biden. "Great. What are they going to ask?"

"Everybody thinks Reagan's going to announce Bork," Rasky responded, "and they want to know about your endorsement of him in the *Philadelphia Inquirer*."

Biden seemed puzzled.

I began to read to him from an interview with *Inquirer* political reporter Larry Eichel in the fall of 1986: "Say the Administration sends up Bork and, after our investigation, he looks a lot like another Scalia, . . . I'd have to vote for him."

Biden interrupted: "I remember that now. I said 'after an investigation' and besides this is different."

Although the problem may have been what Eichel had in mind when he asked Biden the question, the Senator was not thinking of a circumstance in which the balance of the Court was at stake and Bork nominated to fill that slot. Furthermore, at the time, Biden viewed Bork as similar to Scalia, who simply did not have an extensive record of writings and appeared in his testimony to be similar to Burger, whom he was replacing. Biden had made these very points in August 1986 when he voted for Scalia. He said at the time that, on the basis of the Committee's hearing record and Scalia's public record, he saw little difference between Burger and Scalia. "Therefore," he pointed out, "I do not have undue concern about his impact and the impact of this appointment on the balance of the Court."

However, he warned, "We should . . . proceed with extreme caution before approving the nomination of any individual whose appointment would fundamentally alter in any direction the balance of the Court. . . ."

I read his statement on Scalia back to him on the phone.

You could hear the relief in his voice: "Good, but this *Inquirer* thing's still going to be a problem."

He asked me to set up a conference call immediately with Philip Kurland, conservative constitutional scholar at the University of Chicago, Walter Dellinger of Duke Law School, Washington lawyer Ken Bass, and Floyd Abrams, the top First Amendment litigator in the country and a partner in a prestigious Wall Street firm. "I want to be brought up to speed quickly on Powell and Bork.

"Now," Biden went on, "let me talk to whatever gurus are around, and you guys should hear this."

The Senator was short and firm. He did not need for them to explain the implications of the day's developments for his campaign. He wanted to deal with the matter at hand and did not want to talk about politics. It was absolutely essential that the campaign be segregated from the Supreme Court matter. Otherwise both efforts would be jeopardized.

The conference call took place later that afternoon. Bass summarized the last term and the role of Powell as the balance wheel. The ACLU had provided us with a list of twenty 5–4 decisions where Powell had made the difference. Bass and Dellinger explained the particular role Powell had played in frustrating the Reagan Administration's agenda on the social issues.

"It's not hard to figure out what's going on here," Biden said, "Meese and Reynolds want to win those cases, and they're going to find someone who is reliable."

"Tell me about Bork. You first, Phil."

Kurland was very complimentary. But Biden became more concerned, as he began to focus on Bork's attitude toward upsetting past decisions, his theory of *stare decisis* (the principle that Court decisions act as binding precedents). Bork would not be reluctant to reverse decisions with which he disagreed.

Dellinger and Abrams got into a long discussion of Bork's attitude toward *Roe* v. *Wade* and the constitutional right to privacy.

Biden interrupted: "Look, I don't think *Roe* is great constitutional law, but if this Administration is trying to put someone on the Court just to reverse that decision, they're going to tear this country apart. But to tell you the truth, what concerns me more is what you fellas are saying about his view on the right to privacy. It really concerns me more than abortion."

Bass responded: "Senator, we're all just talking from memory, and besides it may not be Bork."

Biden agreed and said that the only thing that was certain was that he had to be very careful what he said, that his statement should urge caution to the Administration.

Biden and Dellinger engaged in a lengthy discussion of the role of the Senate in the confirmation process. Biden kept pressing Dellinger about precedents in history in which the Senate had attempted to advise the President on nominees before they were sent to the Senate. Dellinger mentioned several, including one involving President Hoover, Sen. William Borah of Idaho, and Justice Cardozo.

"Look, we're not looking for a fight here. I'm going to call Howard Baker and ask for consultations on nominees, and here's what I want my public statement to say."

The statement he outlined focused primarily on the qualities he felt the President should seek in a successor to Powell. We felt that, without mentioning him, it excluded Bork. We did not realize it at the time, but we had stumbled upon a formulation which framed the debate over the nomination to our advantage.

The statement read in part:

> I hope that the President will nominate a man or a woman who is superbly qualified, who comes to the bench with an open mind—someone, in short, in the mold of Lewis Powell. . . .
>
> A major issue upon which this nomination could turn is whether the nominee would alter significantly the balance of the court. As I pointed out when the Committee considered the Scalia nomination last year, the balance issue is an important consideration. That is truer today than at any other time in recent history. For when we fill this vacancy, this one nominee—more than any other justice—could decide the course of our jurisprudence well into the next century.
>
> Justice Powell has been the decisive vote in a host of decisions in the past 15 years relating to civil rights and civil liberties. The scales of justice should not be tipped by ideological biases. I will resist any efforts by this Administration to do indirectly what it has failed to do directly in the Congress—and that is impose an ideological agenda upon our jurisprudence. . . .
>
> In light of the special role played with such distinction by Justice Powell as the deciding vote on so many issues of tremendous importance, I will examine with special care any nominee who is predisposed to undo long-established protections that have become part of the social fabric that binds us as a nation.

We were not prepared to distribute the statement to the press until around 6:00 P.M. Vallely had canceled the press conference in Los Angeles. The networks, which all had their cameras there, were furious. The print media was impatient. They almost all focused immediately upon the balance language, and the call to choose someone in the mold of Powell.

The ACLU had managed to get their list of twenty 5–4 decisions to every major media outlet. That, plus the fact that most of the legal correspondents had been in the midst of their wrap-up pieces on the last term of the Court, focused most of the stories on the implications of Powell as a swing vote being replaced by a Reagan nominee who might shift the balance.

The headlines the next day told the whole story. Almost every major daily saw the story just as the *New York Times* did: ''Powell leaves high court; Took key role on Abortion and on Affirmative Action; Opening for Reagan; President gains chance to shape the future of the courts.''

Once the national media focused on the balance question and whether it would be shifted, the next obvious question concerned the intentions of the

Administration and, more important, the views of the person to be nominated.

On June 27, many of Bork's allies must have read those headlines and thought to themselves, That's exactly what we want to do—in the words of the *Times,* to create a "new balance" on the court. But they realized they had one big hurdle to cross with their "friends" in the Administration, before the issue would even be drawn with their adversaries in the Senate.

Their choice, Robert Bork, might not yet be Ronald Reagan's choice, and he almost certainly was not yet Howard Baker's.

CHAPTER 2

IT WILL BE BORK

WITHIN AN HOUR of the Powell announcement, John Bolton was on the phone to me. As the Justice Department's primary lobbyist, it was his job to stay in close contact with the Senate Judiciary Committee through me. Usually Bolton is cautious, but not in this conversation: "It will be Bork. The only thing that's holding it up is that Meese is out of the country. As soon as he gets back, I'm sure we'll announce Bork."

I immediately thought of the *Philadelphia Inquirer* quote. "I hope you guys haven't misunderstood Biden's *Philadelphia Inquirer* statement. Don't assume he'll support Bork."

Bolton acted unconcerned.

I continued to press, "Look, the groups will pull out all the stops on this one, especially if it's Bork. It will be Armageddon. You ought to go slowly here."

Bolton hesitated, then he responded curtly: "Let's keep in touch."

Although Bolton acted confident on the phone, he knew that, "every day that passed without Bork being named worked against him."

Even with Meese back, Bork was going to face an uphill battle with "pragmatists" in the White House. As one Justice staffer pointed out, to the extent that Bork was identified with Meese, it hurt Bork's chances both in the White House and on the Hill. "Because of Iran–Contra and various conflict-of-interest charges, Meese was considered a liability."

Indeed, Meese was aware of the risk of any candidate becoming too closely identified with him. For example, on Sunday June 28, Meese addressed a gathering at Chautauqua, New York, and was confronted with laughter when he said the Administration would use no ideological litmus test in the selection of Powell's successor. He was cautious in not speculating on individual names when he appeared on the Brinkley show on Sunday, in part, so as not to identify any candidate as his. Meese would become angry early in the week when Bork was increasingly portrayed as his choice.

Besides, as the Justice staffer pointed out, "Meese was not the best bureaucratic infighter, although he had a better average on [pushing through conservative] judicial nominations. We were really concerned about the Bork situation.''

They had reason to be.

Howard Baker was troubled about what he, and others who knew the Senate better than Meese, called ''confirmability.'' As one White House aide put it to the *New York Times* on Sunday, ''For the first time, a nominee will have to go before a body not controlled by your party, so you have to take extra-special care that the appointment is confirmable.'' On Sunday Senate Republican Whip Alan Simpson, a loyal proponent of Reagan judicial nominees, made it clear on CBS's ''Face the Nation,'' where he came out on the confirmability issue.

Simpson warned young conservatives in the Administration to be realistic. They ought to ''consider the issue of confirmability through a Democratically controlled Senate. That's called real life in Washington—that is real life.''

By Sunday morning, the struggle within the Administration over who would control the selection process was front-page news in the *New York Times*. Justice Department spokesman Terry Eastland announced, ''The Attorney General is the President's chief adviser in this area.'' However, according to the same reporter, a senior White House official ''maintained that . . . [Howard Baker] would take personal charge of the selection of a nominee to succeed Justice Powell. . . .''

The White House made it clear that Mr. Baker as a moderate probably would seek a like moderate such as Mr. Powell or Justice Harry A. Blackmun.'' By the end of the weekend, ''Whispers spread [presumedly from the White House] about Bork's age [sixty], weight and heavy cigarette smoking.''

In Los Angeles on Saturday, Chairman Biden attempted as best he could to maintain his campaign schedule—a tight round of fund-raising and political meetings with key California supporters. But the Supreme Court nomination was beginning to take over his campaign.

He had two goals for the day; one was to learn as much as he could about Bork, and the other was to get in touch with Baker as soon as possible to persuade him to consult about Powell's successor. It was essential to head off a confrontation, especially on a Bork nomination.

When Tommy Vallely placed the call for Biden on Friday afternoon, Baker's White House office knew immediately Biden was calling about the Powell resignation. Baker had already left for his home in Tennessee, but his staff would track him down for Biden. When Biden and Baker finally connected the next day, Biden spoke comfortably and candidly with his old colleague. Baker was immediately receptive to the notion of consultations. Biden made it clear that he hoped that the President would use Powell as a model for selection of his successor. Baker and he did not specifically speak of Bork.

Biden was determined not only to send a confidential message through Baker but to continue to hone his public message—the essence of his first statement on the Powell resignation on Friday afternoon. Sunday morning on ''Face the Nation,'' and in an interview with Garrick Utley on the ''NBC Nightly News'' that evening, Biden said that the advice he was giving the President was ''to try to pick someone in Justice Powell's mold—to pick a conservative who is open-minded and moderate in [his] instincts, one who is a persuader, one who is not an ideologue.''

We had no conscious strategy at the time, but the formulation Biden had stumbled upon in his first statement on Friday night was beginning to take hold in the national media. On Saturday and Sunday, the editorial pages of the *New York Times* and the *Washington Post* gave the same advice to the White House. The President should be seeking someone in the mold of Justice Powell.

Biden added on ''Face the Nation'' that if the President rejects this advice and chooses ''someone who has a predisposition on every one of the major issues, the social issues, and wished to move the Court in a direction where it was twenty or twenty-five years ago,'' the Senate would resist. The *Los Angeles Times* agreed in an editorial that same day.

Biden's performance on ''Face the Nation'' enraged the Right. Monday morning's headline in the conservative *Washington Times* said it all: ''CONSERVATIVES ERUPT AS BIDEN SETS PURITY TEST.''

One called upon Democrats to consider removing him as chairman because he was imposing ''an ideological litmus test.'' The conservative strategy was to take the ''mold of Powell'' argument and make Bork critics appear silly, shallow, and politically partisan.

Patrick McGuigan, at the conservative Free Congress Foundation, complained, ''What do they want to do, clone Lewis Powell? That's silly. It will be up to liberals to explain what their justification is for opposing a qualified man or woman who seeks merely to apply the law.'' The *Wall Street Journal,* in the first of many scathing editorials, condemned Biden for seeking personal and partisan advantage for the benefit of his presidential campaign. White House spokesman Marlin Fitzwater made similar charges.

Republicans also sought to create a little political heat at home in Biden's Delaware. An old Delaware political rival of Biden's, Republican former Delaware governor Pete Dupont, also a candidate for President, would be the most frank: ''Joe has clearly made confirmation a part of his presidential campaign and that's not right. I hate to see a job so important as this being used as a pawn in a presidential campaign.''

Meanwhile activists on the Left were also beginning to gear up. Much of what they would do helped Biden's ultimately unsuccessful effort to seek a moderate choice by Reagan. Some of it damaged that and much of what the anti-Bork Senators attempted to do for the next four months. During this period the activists were not consulting with Biden or his staff.

By Sunday, Ralph Neas, who as executive director of the Leadership Conference on Civil Rights had coordinated civil rights group opposition to Rehnquist the year before, toughened his stand on the selection of a successor to Powell. The White House was drifting toward Bork, and Neas, hoping to head that off, sought to make it clear that in doing so they were heading toward a collision with the civil rights community. "The Bork nomination, or that of anyone who would jeopardize the civil rights accomplishments of the past 30 years, would most likely precipitate the most controversial and confrontational legislative battle of the Reagan years."

By the end of the weekend, journalists recognized that a Bork nomination was almost inevitable. Neas and the rest of the civil rights activists in the city were fighting a determined but uphill battle against Bork in the press. Neas seized upon a 1963 article by Bork in the *New Republic,* criticizing the Kennedy Administration's legislation to desegregate public accommodations.

Some elements of Neas's coalition were not nearly so diplomatic in their pronouncements. They intended not only to threaten the White House but to take on Biden as well. Kate Michelman of the National Abortion Rights Action League (NARAL) continued to focus on abortion and threatened "an all-out frontal assault to knock the nomination out of the water" if Bork was named.

Although Michelman bragged that she was sending the same message to Biden, there was actually little, if any, direct communication between those groups and Biden before Bork was selected. Neas had seen a copy of Biden's statement upon the Powell resignation, and listened to him on "Face the Nation," where he made it clear that he did not feel bound by the *Philadelphia Inquirer* quote. Neas was satisfied that Biden was doing all in his power to head off a Bork nomination.

Kate Michelman was obviously not satisfied. Nor was Estelle Rogers, director of the Federation of Women Lawyers. On the day Powell resigned, she had condemned Biden for his *Inquirer* quote, called on him to retract the statement, and, she added sarcastically, to "take time from his busy schedule to exercise the kind of leadership we expect from the chairman of the Senate Judiciary Committee. If he can't, he'd be wise to think carefully about resigning the chairmanship."

By Sunday the Supreme Court had almost completely enveloped the Biden campaign. Biden's chief fund-raiser, Ted Kaufman, was traveling with Biden in California and was intending to take him to Wisconsin for important meetings on Sunday. "We barely made the fund-raising events in California, and the Senator insisted on canceling the whole Wisconsin trip to do 'Face the Nation' and the other press events."

Kaufman was more than just a fund-raiser for Biden. He had been his closest political confidant for over a decade and agreed with Biden that his highest priority was the Supreme Court controversy and that his next most important was preparing for the Democratic candidates' debate in Houston on

Wednesday. "The candidates had been slugging it out in Iowa and New Hampshire for six months to a year. Outside of a few big-time activists and money people . . . no one knew about these candidates. Houston was the first nationally televised event in the [primary] campaign. It was critical that Biden do well there."

Paul Tulley, the political director for the Dukakis campaign, agreed: "It's the most important event since Gary Hart dropped out of the race." A spokesman for the Public Broadcasting System estimated that over 10 million households would tune in on Wednesday night.

Biden, a student of past presidential campaigns, had insisted in strategy meetings during the past two years that he would carefully prepare for his debates. He pointed out that one reason that Kennedy had "won" the Kennedy–Nixon debates in 1960 was that Nixon had not taken time to rest before the debate after an exhausting campaign swing to Alaska and the Northwest.

The plan was for Biden to go to Chicago for two days after the Wisconsin trip, to have substantive briefings in a hotel, to arrive in Houston on Tuesday afternoon and relax there for a full twenty-four hours before the debate the next evening. What Biden faced in the next few days made Nixon's challenge in 1960 seem tame by comparison.

First, Biden and his staff was almost completely distracted by stratagems for heading off the Bork selection and avoiding a confrontation with the White House over the Supreme Court. Staff briefings for the debate had hardly begun on Monday morning in a hotel in Chicago when Sen. Strom Thurmond, the ranking Republican on the Judiciary Committee, called. It was "essential" that he talk to Biden about the Powell vacancy.

Thurmond and Biden had an excellent working relationship. It is hard to imagine two men of more divergent style and political philosophy. Thurmond was almost twice Biden's age, and his conservatism made the moderate Biden look like an extreme liberal. But in his own way Thurmond was a pragmatist, like Biden. There was genuine affection between the two men, which had contributed no small part to the smooth running of the committee for the previous six and a half years and the enactment of hundreds of pages of legislation in the criminal justice field, which they had coauthored.

Thurmond immediately got Biden's attention: "Joe, you and I can name the next Supreme Court Justice."

"You can bet I'd like to do that, Strom. I'm not looking for a fight with the Administration."

"I know that, Joe. I've heard about your conversation with Howard [Baker]. He wants to talk to both of us." Biden could almost anticipate the pitch. "Joe, you and I should get behind Judge Wilkins for the Court. You remember he helped you out on the death penalty at the Sentencing Commission."

''I remember, Strom.''

Judge William Wilkins, a former Thurmond staffer, was a member of the United States Court of Appeals for the Fourth Circuit. He had been named chair of the federal sentencing commission, created to propose uniform sentencing guidelines for federal judges. In early 1987, in a clever move to outwit death penalty opponents in the Senate, the Meese Justice Department had persuaded several members of the commission to propose capital punishment as one of the sentences. Death penalty legislation—Thurmond's and Meese's Number 1 legislative priority—had been stalled for years by liberal filibusters. Wilkins, an advocate of the death penalty, recognized, however, that such a move was clearly contrary to the intent of the commission's charter. He courageously cast the decisive vote against the proposal.

Thurmond continued to press: ''Joe, we need a Southerner on the Court. Powell was a Southerner, and Wilkins is perfect.''

''Strom, I'll have to have my staff quickly check out his background, but I'm interested in pursuing it. . . . Let me have Diana [Huffman, the committee staff director] talk with Dennis [Shedd, the minority staff director], and get some background material on Wilkins.''

The staff was enthusiastic—maybe we could dodge this bullet. But Biden warned us, ''Look, if this guy really is like Powell, a Southern moderate . . . it may not be enough to convince Reagan to let down Meese and the conservatives.''

Dennis Shedd was very forthcoming, and the material he gave Huffman was benign. A quick review of his judicial opinions demonstrated that Wilkins's action in the death penalty controversy was very much in character. He was indeed a conservative, but one who was moderate in demeanor, a pragmatist who sought the consensus position. Shedd agreed. He was exactly what we were looking for, but when pressed, Shedd acknowledged that Biden was probably right. Even with Thurmond supporting him, Wilkins would not be acceptable to Meese and therefore Reagan.

After the Thurmond call, the staff and Biden settled back into an intensive, substantive discussion of the issues. Biden was a fast study and quickly absorbed what he needed from the staff that afternoon. However, the next morning, when the staff's political pollster and strategist, Pat Caddell, began to discuss the campaign message, Biden became visibly angry. He resisted Caddell's idea of basing the campaign on aggressive populism. This argument over the direction of the Biden campaign message had been ongoing for a month, and the candidate was getting impatient with such disagreements barely twenty-four hours before his first national debate.

The argument was interrupted by a call from Howard Baker: ''Joe, this thing's moving pretty fast. You'd better get down here.''

''Howard, I thought we were going to talk first.''

''We are, but we better do it this afternoon.''

"I'll be there in a few hours."

Biden hung up and turned to Vallely. "We'll have to charter, and I'll just continue the briefing on the plane."

It was not even worth raising the Wilkins possibility. Clearly "things are moving quickly" meant the Bork juggernaut was out of Baker's control, assuming he even wanted to control it.

The press consistently listed other candidates—Clifford Wallace, a member of the Ninth Circuit Court of Appeals, and Sen. Orrin Hatch, a conservative Republican member of the Judiciary Committee—but they, like Wilkins, were not real contenders. The only real candidate was Bork.

Bork's partisans at the Justice Department saw the process of consultations with Biden and Thurmond as an effort by Baker to kill the Bork nomination. One Justice official explained, "We saw the consultation process as a means by which Baker could make the case against Bork that there was too much opposition on the Hill."

Dennis Shedd agreed with his friends at Justice. Every delay hurt Bork's chances and assuming Wilkins was not going to make it, Bork should. Through staff he urged several conservative Senators to call the White House and insist that Baker not give in to Biden.

Sen. Charles Grassley, a conservative member of the committee, warned the President not to be "turned around by the Democrats," and Sen. Gordon Humphrey cautioned the White House against "preemptive capitulation."

Conservative activist Richard Viguerie put the onus directly on Baker: "The eyes of all conservatives are on Howard Baker. If conservatives lose the Supreme Court, we will hold Baker responsible, and he will bear that mark on his forehead for the rest of his life."

Many inside and outside the White House saw the Powell vacancy as presenting more than just an opportunity for President Reagan to implement his social agenda in the Supreme Court. In the wake of the Iran–Contra controversy, pundits in Washington were beginning to look seriously upon Reagan as a lame duck. On Sunday a lengthy story appeared on the front page of the *New York Times,* which openly discussed that prospect. However, many in Washington argued that a successful battle against liberal Democrats to fill the Powell vacancy could significantly rehabilitate the President's fading image. It was an issue on which Reagan needed to win.

Senator Humphrey predicted, "If Ronald Reagan is looking for an issue to regain the initiative—and he's dead in the water because of the Iran–Contra business—this is it. He's either going to get a conservative on the Court or the Republicans will cream the Democrats in 1988 because of the political fallout."

Although it is not surprising that Gordon Humphrey should make such enthusiastic predictions, it is surprising, in retrospect, that many of the most respected journalists seemed to share this optimistic view of Bork's prospects. David Broder, the *Washington Post*'s premier political reporter, concluded that "the Powell vacancy is sheer bliss for Reagan. . . ." The *Detroit Free Press* predicted "There is little evidence that Democrats will mount a major fight against [Bork]." James Reston of the *New York Times* suggested that almost "any respectable conservative on Mr. Meese's short list will undoubtedly be confirmed."

Baker and Meese spoke over the weekend and agreed to meet on Monday. Meanwhile White House counsel A. B. Culvahouse would compile a list of ten names, which Meese, Baker, and Culvahouse would cull down to five names to present to the President.

When they finally met on Monday morning, Baker professed "bewilderment" at news reports of his "displeasure" with a Bork nomination. Baker was not going to attempt to block the Bork nomination. At that point the effort to name Bork literally became, as conservative political columnists Evans and Novak described it, the Bork Express.

Perhaps Baker believed the predictions made by many in the national media that Reagan could win any nomination fight, especially if the only issue was ideology. The only serious ethical allegations against Bork concerned his role in the Saturday Night Massacre.

In 1973, as Nixon's Solicitor General and third ranking member of the Justice Department, Bork had agreed to execute the president's order to fire Watergate Special Prosecutor Archibald Cox over the so-called White House tapes. He did so after the top two ranking officials, Attorney General Elliot Richardson and his deputy, William Ruckelshaus, refused to carry out Nixon's order and resigned.

Elliot Richardson was at the White House on Monday, the day Meese and Baker were to meet. Richardson reassured Baker's staff that he would defend Bork's action. With Richardson's statements and subsequent testimony on the judge's behalf, the Saturday Night Massacre allegations were essentially mooted.

By the end of that meeting, Bork was the next nominee to the Supreme Court unless he met determined and effective opposition on the Hill. Baker and Meese would take a pro forma list of nominees up to share with Biden and the Senate leadership.

As he flew from Chicago to Washington, Biden continued with intensive debate preparation for Houston. Tom Donilon and David Rubenstein, two Democratic Washington attorneys with extensive experience gained in preparing Pres. Jimmy Carter and 1984 Democratic nominee Walter Mondale for debates, discussed substantive answers and debate strategy with Biden and his chief domestic policy aide, Liz Tankersley, and chief foreign policy aide, John Ritch.

When he landed, Biden was met by a police escort. He was already late for the meeting. It was impossible to talk with the noise of the siren blasting as we raced for the Capitol. We were deep in our own thoughts. This was the last chance to head off a confrontation with the President, which no one in the Biden organization desired, least of all Biden.

The meeting was in Majority Leader Robert Byrd's ornate conference room immediately adjacent to the Senate floor. It was to be a "principals only" meeting. Staff waited anxiously outside the room with a small group of reporters.

In the meeting, Meese and Baker presented Biden and Byrd with a list of ten nominees, appropriately sprinkled with blacks and women. Some names were included only to make the list appear bipartisan. Carter Administration Solicitor General Wade McCree, a black, and Democratic Sen. Howell Heflin were on the list but neither was being seriously considered by the Administration.

Biden and Byrd went down the list one by one. For the most part, Byrd deferred to Biden while Meese listened passively. Biden did not recognize some of the names. In each case Baker pressed Biden for a response. When they got to Bork, it was clear they had reached the real purpose of the meeting. Baker kept drawing Biden out.

"What's the problem with Bork, Joe?"

"I just don't understand why the President would want to raise the Watergate issue in the aftermath of this Iran–Contra thing."

Meese responded quickly, "The Saturday Night Massacre's not a problem. He'll be able to handle that."

"You're not going to have a problem from me on that score. If that was going to be the issue, I would have voted against him for the Court of Appeals. But you don't seriously believe that other Democrats will hang back on that issue?"

Meese responded again: "We can handle that."

Baker pressed on: "What is the problem, Joe?"

"His views. I'm worried about where he will take the Court."

Neither Meese nor Baker responded. Baker turned to Byrd: "Bob, will you oppose him?"

"No."

Biden was angry at Byrd. He interrupted, "If you go ahead with Bork, it's going to be a long summer."

Meese and Baker were satisfied as the meeting broke up. They had not asked Biden directly about what he would do on Bork, but it should have been obvious. But then again it did not seem to matter to them, for surely the most important piece of intelligence they picked up was that Biden was essentially on his own. Byrd did not intend to be part of any effort to block a Bork nomination. Byrd surely represented enough Democratic votes to deny Biden a majority against Bork.

From that moment on, the die was cast for a Bork nomination. Biden sensed it, but he thought he would have at least forty-eight hours to make it through the Houston debate the next night. Once Bork was the nominee, it would be difficult to concentrate on anything else.

At 11:30 P.M. on Tuesday night, Biden campaign manager Tim Ridley called me at home. He often got the earliest version of the next morning's *Post*. He read me David Broder's Wednesday column word for word:

> Biden is really under the gun, facing a test he cannot afford to lose. If Reagan sends up a first-rate conservative, Biden can conceivably choose to play the statesman and escort that person to confirmation, while making it clear he does not endorse the nominee's views. But, if Biden sets out to defeat the president's choice, he had better line up his votes. He has drawn some criticism for inept generalship on the 1986 Manion nomination. [Biden's effort to defeat extreme conservative Daniel Manion to serve on the Court of Appeals fell one vote short after several Republicans changed their vote when pressured by the White House.] To have a Democratic Senate confirm a Supreme Court justice he had vowed to defeat would leave Biden hanging out to dry.
>
> That's a fight the president will enjoy. . . .

Ridley cleared his throat nervously. "Nothing like a high stakes game, huh, Mark?"

"God, let's hope it's not Bork. Joe hasn't said a thing to me, but you and I both know that he'll oppose him." In a classic case of wishful thinking, I assured Ridley that they would not announce anything for another day or so.

"Well, let's worry about this after the debate."

For the second time in less than a week, Biden's future was being decided while incommunicado in an airplane, this time en route to Houston. The White House courtesy call came to the Biden staff a mere hour before the public announcement.

It was a madhouse in Houston, where campaign Press Secretary Larry Rasky and Tommy Vallely awaited Biden. They were already deluged with press requests. Rasky and Vallely agreed with Tom Donilon, who was playing an increasing role in the Bork strategy, that Biden had to meet with the press when he got to Houston.

Instead of a full day in advance to rest and relax, Biden was arriving a mere five hours before the biggest event thus far in the campaign. The last thing Biden would want to do would be to meet with scores of reporters a few hours before the debate.

Tommy Vallely watched the President's announcement of the Bork nomination on the TV in the limousine as he went to the airport to pick up Biden. He was not prepared for Biden's angry reaction.

Vallely took Biden into a holding room as soon as his plane landed: "You've got to meet with the press."

''Says who?'' snapped Biden.

''Rasky and Donilon.''

''Didn't you arrange for me to go to a gym so I can work out?''

Vallely was confused. ''Yes, but . . .''

''Well, I'm going to the gym.''

Vallely wanted to keep talking, but Biden started for the door. Vallely and the rest of the advance party followed.

Biden eventually relented, spending hours of precious debate prep and relaxation time with endless press interviews.

That night and the next morning, the pundits gave Biden only moderate grades for his performance in the debate.

There seemed to be a consensus among the ''experts'' over who ''won'' the debate. Apparently oblivious to what was going on with the nomination and Biden's role in it, the experts decided that for some reason Biden seemed distracted.

As I watched the debate that evening with Ridley and the campaign staff, I had trouble concentrating as well. I kept thinking about an incident a few days earlier.

Early Monday morning, June 29, I was standing in the kitchen of my house, taking one last look at the *Post* before going to the office. The phone rang. Marianne Baker, Senator Biden's personal secretary, got right to the point: ''The Senator just called. He's on the road, and he wants you to return a call from Dean Guido Calabresi from Yale Law School.''

Calabresi was gracious and eloquent. After the small talk about mutual friends on the Yale faculty, he began to talk about his friend and former colleague Robert Bork. He made a persuasive case for Bork. He hoped Biden would keep an open mind and not veto the name if consultations with the Administration did take place.

He focused on the Saturday Night Massacre. I agreed that, contrary to conventional wisdom, Bork's involvement in the incident should not, and probably would not, play a major role in his confirmation but that his judicial philosophy would. I warned him, though, that a Bork nomination and a fight over judicial philosophy was not necessarily good news for his friend.

Calabresi did not respond.

Then with a sense of sadness, indeed dread, I realized that a Bork nomination was just as bad for Biden. Although I could not tell him exactly how, or why, I told Calabresi, ''A Bork nomination is going to be bad for your friend Bork and my friend Biden.''

CHAPTER 3

POLITICS IN THE ARISTOTELIAN SENSE

■

IN 1981 RONALD REAGAN faced the prospect of filling his first vacancy on the Supreme Court. With the resignation of Justice Potter Stewart, Reagan decided to fulfill his campaign promise to place the first woman on the Supreme Court. By July 1, 1981, the Justice Department had narrowed the list down to four women.

The President was immediately charmed by the fifty-year-old Sandra Day O'Connor when he interviewed her in the White House. Forces on the Left and Right were focused almost entirely upon the impact she would have on the *Roe* decision. At that point the Pro-Choice majority on the court was a reasonably comfortable 6–3. Reagan asked the prospective nominee how she felt about abortion. O'Connor responded that, although she deplored the practice, she would not let her personal views influence her vote. Apparently hers was not unlike the position that Biden and Kennedy took on the question, opposing the practice personally but not wanting to impose their views on others.

O'Connor's response clearly did not bother Reagan, for he nominated her on July 7 without even interviewing the other three candidates. Although they probably did not know of her conversation with Reagan, O'Connor, as an Arizona state senator, had sponsored legislation which seemed to Reagan's right wing allies as proabortion. Moral Majority president Jerry Falwell warned that "good Christians" should be wary and along with the National Right to Life Committee opposed the nomination.

Reagan's support of a constitutional amendment to reverse the *Roe* decision had been critical in gaining right wing support in the 1980 election. However, his opposition to abortion was obviously not the central animating vision of his presidency. Early in his governorship of California, he had signed one of the most liberal abortion laws in the country, and once he became President, although he did address the annual Pro-Life national rally in Washington, he would only do so by telephone to avoid appearing on television with antiabortion leadership.

Despite his obvious personal ambivalence about abortion, to Reagan's allies on the Right, the presidential election of 1980 and especially Reagan's reelection in 1984 were victories for a new, more conservative jurisprudence, especially a reversal of *Roe*. The 1980 Republican Party platform called for the appointment of judges who "respect traditional family values and the sanctity of innocent human life . . . [and] who share our commitment to judicial restraint."

Bruce Fein, who had served in Reagan's Justice Department, explained that "judges wedded to the doctrine of judicial restraint" were judges "who reject the idea underlying the Supreme Court's decrees on abortion, school prayer, civil rights and criminal law: that the judicial power of interpretation is not confined to carrying out the intent of our constitutional authors."

Reagan's stated objective was to reverse Supreme Court decisions outlawing school prayer and legalizing abortion. Although Reagan may not have seen it as good policy upon which he would stake his presidency, he definitely saw it as good politics.

In calling for a school prayer constitutional amendment in his State of the Union address in 1983, Reagan argued that "God should never have been expelled from America's classrooms in the first place." In his 1984 State of the Union address, he called for a "positive solution to the tragedy of abortion," by which he meant a constitutional amendment overturning the Supreme Court's decision in *Roe* v. *Wade*. He continued his case for a school prayer constitutional amendment: "If members of Congress can begin each legislative day with prayer, then why cannot the freedom to acknowledge God be enjoyed again by children in every school across this land?"

Five days later he opened his 1984 reelection campaign with a speech to conservative religious leaders calling for antiabortion legislation. In August at a prayer breakfast, he argued that "politics and morality are inseparable—and as morality's foundation is religion, religion and politics are necessarily related." He went on to accuse school prayer opponents of "attacking religion." "They are doing it in the name of tolerance, freedom and open-mindedness. Question: Isn't the real truth that they are intolerant of religion?"

He did not dampen his rhetoric in the second term. In January of 1986 he told an antiabortion rally that he would "work together with members of Congress to overturn the tragedy of *Roe* v. *Wade*." On February 5 in his State of the Union, he made a dramatic case for his constitutional amendment: "We are a nation of idealists, yet today there is a wound in our national conscience. America will never be whole as long as the right to life granted by our Creator is denied to the unborn. For the rest of my time, I shall do what I can to see that this wound is one day healed."

Despite the florid rhetoric and the high expectations, most important legislative initiatives on the social agenda died in Congress during the Reagan years. In August of 1982, Sen. Jesse Helms of North Carolina abandoned his effort to pass antiabortion and school prayer legislation in the face of a filibuster. In June of the next year, the Republican-controlled Senate defeated a constitutional amendment on abortion 49–50, eighteen votes short of the necessary two thirds of the Senate. In March 1984 the Senate voted down a proposed constitutional amendment to allow organized, recited prayer in the public schools 54–44, thirteen votes shy of the necessary two thirds.

By the spring of 1984 conservative activists were publicly expressing their disappointment. James McClellan, a former key Judiciary Committee staff aide to the late John East, an extreme conservative Republican from North Carolina, commented, "It is a melancholy fact that, in spite of the campaign rhetoric and the Republican Party platform of 1980, which held out hope of judicial reform, nearly all of the Supreme Court doctrines and decisions which brought us to our present state of affairs remain securely intact." They increasingly began to blame the pragmatists in the Congressional Affairs office in the White House. Paul Weyrich argued that senior White House aides were simply not committed to Ronald Reagan's social agenda. Of course, the real question was whether Ronald Reagan was committed to Ronald Reagan's social agenda.

In the first term, even conservative Reagan political strategists, like Lyn Nofziger and Patrick Buchanan, believed it would be a mistake for the President to expend political capital on what they considered a hopeless cause. Nofziger argued that "people forget that Ronald Reagan is a practical politician, as well as a zealot, on some issues. And he knows you're not going to shove that stuff through Congress no matter how much he wants it, certainly not with the makeup of Congress today. Other things, like taxes, the budget and summits, have superseded the social agenda, and they always will."

Moderate Republicans agreed. For example, then Congressman, now Secretary of Defense, Richard Cheney of Wyoming observed, "I can't think of anything that would have been more divisive up here or created more difficulty for other parts of the program than for the Administration to push repeatedly, for example, on abortion."

There was a consensus among conservatives and moderates alike that the absence of direct White House, indeed presidential, involvement helped opponents to defeat Reagan's legislative program on the social agenda. Sen. Richard Lugar, a moderate Republican from Indiana, explained, "Clearly nothing beats calls coming from the President and his own hands-on intervention." That simply did not happen on the important votes on the social agenda legislation. The President saved the personal lobbying, a task he enjoyed and excelled at, for his tax, budget, and defense initiatives.

By March 1986, well into the second Reagan term, the Administration was beginning to lose its credibility with the conservative community. Richard Viguerie, conservative direct mail wizard, remarked, "Our expectations were dashed early in the first Reagan Administration. Pat Buchanan had said, 'Boy, wait 'til we get by the reelection, we're gonna really hump for those issues,' but we didn't really believe that song and dance." Other conservatives had been more willing to see the defense buildup, and cutting taxes had a higher priority but a promise had been made that with the reelection the priorities would be switched.

During Ronald Reagan's first term, White House counselor Edwin Meese was the "major point of contact" for the conservative groups in the White House. So his nomination by Reagan to be Attorney General in 1984 was not warmly received by many Democrats and other progressives in the Senate. His confirmation was delayed for over a year because the Judiciary Committee's initial investigation had uncovered alleged ethics violations, and an independent counsel was appointed to resolve the charges.

Once confirmed in early 1985, however, Meese embarked on an ambitious program to break the stalemate on the conservative social agenda. Recognizing that the legislative approach was probably stalled, the Meese strategy consisted of three elements: First, as Attorney General he would advocate a new philosophical framework for the conservative agenda, which he would label the jurisprudence of "original intent." Second, this new jurisprudence would provide the framework for the department's advocacy of conservative law reform in the federal courts at all levels, especially at the Supreme Court, through the Solicitor General's office. Third, the Department of Justice would continue to spearhead the careful judicial selection process begun early in the first term to assure that Reagan Administration nominees adhered to this jurisprudence of original intent.

Meese first articulated his jurisprudence of original intent in a speech to the American Bar Association in July 1985: "A Jurisprudence of Original Intention . . . reflects a deeply rooted commitment to the idea of democracy. . . . It has been and will continue to be the policy of this Administration to press for a Jurisprudence of Original Intention. In the cases we file and those we join as *amicus,* we will endeavor to resurrect the original meaning of constitutional provisions and statutes as the only reliable guide for judgment."

In this and subsequent speeches, he went on to explain that this new jurisprudence required a reexamination of such fundamental jurisprudential notions as the "incorporation doctrine." Since 1925, the Supreme Court has been engaged in a process of applying each of the Bill of Rights to state and local governments by "incorporating" them into the due process language of the post-Civil War Fourteenth Amendment. Obviously, if that doctrine could be abolished, the Right's social agenda could be accomplished immediately, because the Bill of Rights protections would not apply to state and local government.

As to the incorporation doctrine, Meese complained, "Nothing can be done to shore up the intellectually shaky foundation upon which the doctrine rests. . . . [It is] politically violent and constitutionally suspect." Meese soon backed off his critique of the incorporation doctrine, saying that he has no "particular quarrel at this stage of the game with what the Court has done in the intervening [years since 1925]."

However, Justice Department spokesman Terry Eastland conceded that the department might well decide in a particular case to reopen the argument. All conservatives did not go quite as far as Meese would, in applying the original intent argument to a rollback of the incorporation doctrine, but all agreed that original intent meant that all of the Supreme Court cases that prompted the social agenda of the Right should be reexamined.

Some critics argue Meese modeled his ABA speech, almost phrase for phrase, after an address by Bruce Fein to the conservative American Enterprise Institute. However, the real father of this new conservative doctrine was Robert Bork.

Bork described the fundamental principle of the original intent jurisprudence in a lecture at the American Enterprise Institute in 1984: "It is necessary to establish the proposition that the framers' intentions with respect to freedoms are the sole legitimate premise from which constitutional analysis may proceed." Although Bork did not endorse Meese's application of original intent to overturn the incorporation doctrine, Bork had, since a classic 1971 law review article, advocated a significant reexamination of numerous decisions of the Warren Court and its predecessors.

The Meese ABA speech provoked the unprecedented spectacle of two sitting justices of the Supreme Court, Brennan and Stevens, delivering speeches specifically rebutting the Attorney General's new jurisprudence. Biden also responded in a lengthy address at Georgetown Law School.

Until the Reagan Administration, the Solicitor General of the United States held a position of unique stature and independence in our system of justice. Although the SG was housed in the Department of Justice and is charged by statute with representing the interests of the Executive Branch before the Supreme Court, he has had a special "dual responsibility," as Justice Powell used to say, to both the Executive and Judicial Branch. Because of this unique responsibility, the SG was sometimes known as the Tenth Justice.

The Reagan Administration's politicization of the office did not begin with the ascension of Edwin Meese to the office of Attorney General. One notorious case involving fundamentalist Bob Jones University took place at the very beginning of the Reagan Administration. The question was whether the Constitution and federal statutes permitted a tax exemption for Bob Jones University, despite the fact that it practiced racial discrimination. The Administration exerted pressure on career attorneys in the SG's office to side with Bob Jones. According to Lincoln Caplan in his book on the SG's office, Meese had been instrumental in constructing the Administration's support of the tax exemption for Bob Jones in 1981. "When lawyers at the Justice Department said they felt pressure from the White House to take a position in a case, they invariably meant from Meese."

Harvard Law professor Charles Fried became Solicitor General in the fall of 1985. As one lawyer who worked for Fried told Caplan confidentially, "Fried is completely in tune with Meese and company, who have a radical vision of the law. He has a very good sense of how far to go in pushing the agenda, so this office has become a tool of the Administration rather than the legal conscience of the government." Fried, working with Brad Reynolds and Meese, led the office, for example, to argue unsuccessfully that summer for reversing *Roe* v. *Wade* and for a substantial narrowing of the recently enacted extension of the Voting Rights Act of 1965.

Of the three elements of the Meese strategy, the most successful was the program for screening all Reagan Administration judicial nominations. Indeed, this process began in the first Reagan term well before Meese became Attorney General. It simply became more public once Meese took office.

Bruce Fein explained that the failures of the first term required a new approach. "It became evident after the first term that there was no way to make legislative gains in many areas of social and civil rights. The president has to do it by changing the jurisprudence." Although initially the Administration denied that such a screening process was underway, Sheldon Goldman, a scholar who specializes in judicial selection, pointed out, "Political and policy considerations have never before been so systematically taken into account [by an administration]." A former senior Reagan official conceded that "The emphasis is almost totally toward philosophy and disregards almost everything else, including a willingness to approach issues with an open mind."

Bruce Fein was equally candid: "The administration is being more meticulous in its concern about judicial philosophy than other presidents. . . . A president who fails to scrutinize the legal philosophy of federal judicial nominees courts frustration of his own policy agenda. . . . It is thus imperative that President Reagan scrupulously examine the philosophies of his nominees to vindicate many of the pledges he made to the American people in 1980 and 1984."

By 1986 Reagan was himself making the case for changing the jurisprudence by changing the composition of the federal judiciary, especially the Supreme Court. In June, Reagan conceded that Congress had failed to respond to his agenda on the social issues. Earlier, Reagan's communication director, conservative journalist Patrick Buchanan, had argued, "The appointment of two justices to the Supreme Court could do more to advance the social agenda—school prayer, antipornography, antibusing, right-to-life, and [ending] quotas in employment—than anything Congress can accomplish in 20 years."

Three months later President Reagan embraced the comments of his communications director without equivocation. By the summer the argument in favor of remaking the federal judiciary more in his own image became a full-blown campaign theme for the off-year congressional elections. For example, in a speech to the Knights of Columbus in August, the President predicted, "In many areas—abortion, crime, pornography, and others—progress will take place when the federal judiciary is made up of judges who believe in law and order and a strict interpretation of the Constitution." As the November elections approached, his rhetoric became more strident and more overtly political.

In November he bragged about his Administration's judicial selection project and promised more of the same, especially if the Senate remained Republican. "We don't need a bunch of sociology majors on the bench. What we need are strong judges who will aggressively use their authority to protect our families, communities and our way of life. . . . And since coming to Washington we've been putting just such people on the bench."

In specific races, such as the Georgia Senate race, where a Reagan stalwart, Mack Mattingly, was being challenged by Democratic moderate Wyche Fowler, Reagan made a specific pitch, one he repeated in almost every Southern Senate race: "Without him [in this case Mattingly] and the Republican majority in the Senate, we'll find liberals like Joe Biden and a certain fellow from Massachusetts [Kennedy] deciding who our judges are." Fowler ultimately won.

What Ronald Reagan was trying to do in November 1986, to build a national constituency to change the direction of the Supreme Court, was by no means unprecedented in our history. Indeed, two of our most dynamic Presidents—Andrew Jackson and Franklin Roosevelt—undertook similar campaigns and succeeded in creating a true political climate for change in the Court.

The difference between them and Reagan is the zest and commitment they brought to the endeavor. Although Reagan was quite willing to see lieutenants like Meese, Reynolds, and Fried carry his banner, Jackson and Roosevelt made reshaping the Supreme Court to their liking a personal crusade. In both cases that personal crusade triggered an angry and vigorous response from the United States Senate, but it was that personal presidential commitment that brought Jackson and Roosevelt ultimate change.

As Biden and his advisers struggled with how the Senate ought to respond to Reagan's nomination of Bork, Dellinger and Kurland kept reminding us of how the Senate had reacted to similar initiatives by Jackson and Roosevelt. Recent history suggests a more compliant role for the Senate, but in the full span of 200 years a much more tumultuous relationship existed between a President trying to change the Court and a Senate that sought to defend the Supreme Court's independence.

Finally, Biden became convinced that, although Reagan might have the right to reshape the Court, the Senate had the right and obligation to oppose the President if it disagreed with where the President would take the Court. The history of what Jackson and Roosevelt undertook and the Senate did in response convinced Biden that the Senate could properly resist Reagan if he was attempting to reshape the Court with the Bork nomination.

As I reviewed the history of the Jackson and Roosevelt struggles with Biden, I was reminded of my conversation with Yale Dean Calabresi. When a President and the Senate do battle over a matter of principle involving the Supreme Court, the conflict is likely to be bitter and personal. I became increasingly fearful of what that history portended for the summer of 1987.

McCullough v. *Maryland* was the *Roe* v. *Wade* of the 1820s and 30s. In that 1819 case, the Supreme Court struck down a Maryland tax on the Bank of the United States, arguing that "the power to tax is the power to destroy." The case is one of the pillars of our jurisprudence because Chief Justice Marshall wrote a classic opinion on the authority of Congress under the so-called necessary and proper and supremacy clauses of the Constitution.

The political significance of the case at the time was every bit as inflammatory as the 1973 decision that legalized abortion. The Bank of the United States (BUS) had been chartered in 1816 for a twenty-year period. By the late 1820s the Federalists and their successors the Whigs saw the BUS as a seminal achievement bringing financial stability to the young nation.

State banking interests, especially in Jackson's native South, resented the interference by an essentially private institution that boasted a federal charter. The Jacksonians favored local currency and local banks and were suspicious of a large central banking system. The *McCullough* decision sustained the supremacy of the bank over state and local banks.

Jackson believed that the bank was a dangerous political institution, which sought to elect its friends and punish its enemies. Jackson believed that the bank and its allies had actively opposed his election in 1828.

It extended interest-free loans to members of Congress. It had prominent journalists and even Daniel Webster on its payroll while he was a member of the Senate.

Jackson successfully thwarted an effort to recharter the bank in 1828 in his famous Bank Veto message. It had been a long, bitter, and intensely personal struggle for the President. To Jackson, the BUS was a monster that he intended "to kill" before it "killed" him.

Roger Taney was an important ally to Jackson in that struggle. Taney had managed Jackson's 1828 campaign in Maryland and became Attorney General at the end of Jackson's first term and played a prominent role in helping the President draft his famous veto message. It was the first time a President was vetoing a bill primarily because he disagreed with its policy goals instead of just its constitutionality.

The message was a populist tract in which Jackson described the BUS as "the prostitution of our Government to the advancement of the few at the expense of the many." It sounded the opening shot of the 1832 presidential campaign in which Jackson and his allies would be lined up against the financial establishment of the nation, men like Francis Biddle, the chairman of the BUS, and the Whigs in the Senate, men like Daniel Webster and Henry Clay.

He not only succeeded in sustaining his veto, but with his reelection in 1832 Jackson believed that he had the monster "chained." But he wanted a more permanent solution. The lifeblood of the bank was its U.S. Government deposits. When his Secretary of the Treasury defied his order to remove the deposits, Jackson fired him and named Taney to the position. Taney promptly complied with the President's request.

The Whigs in the Senate were furious. They rejected the Taney nomination and as one pro-Administration paper later put it, "No man, we believe, ever had more falsehoods invented and propagated against him in a short space of time, than Mr. Taney has since he removed the deposits."

The Webster–Taney struggle, personal as it was, was really not about Webster and Taney but about the Bank and President Jackson. Indeed, it was about even deeper philosophical issues that split our fledgling republic—a struggle between debtors and creditors, between agrarians and the Philadelphia bankers whom they distrusted, between the Legislative and Executive branches, between the new Federalists—the Whigs—and the new Jeffersonians represented by Jackson.

The Treasury nomination was not the last opportunity the Whigs in the Senate would have to take out their ire on Jackson by rejecting Taney, then a symbol of his presidency.

By 1835, Jackson had made three appointments to the Supreme Court, and although arch-Federalist John Marshall was still Chief Justice, the court was shifting in favor of the states, much to Jackson's liking. On January 14, 1835, octogenarian Gabriel Duval of Maryland resigned from the court.

The next day Jackson nominated Taney for the Duval seat. The Whig-dominated Senate would have nothing of it. The Senate delayed action on the nomination until March 3, the last day of its short session. It not only indefinitely delayed the nomination, tantamount to killing it, but passed legislation abolishing the vacancy on the Supreme Court. Fortunately, the House of Representatives refused to go along.

Jackson would, of course, have the last laugh. On July 6, 1835, the great John Marshall died, ending a thirty-four-year stint as Chief Justice. He had been as important as any of the framers in giving life to the Federalist philosophy, and he was revered by the Whigs in the Senate. For months Jackson tantalized friends and foes alike as he took under advisement various names to fill the two vacancies and create his own majority on the court.

Most attention, though, was on whom he would choose to fill Marshall's slot.

It was clear what was at stake. As Biddle wrote a friend three weeks after Marshall's death, "General Jackson says the Bank is unconstitutional. . . . Will the judges—his officers, dare to decide otherwise. . . ?" Webster best summarized the sentiments of his Whig colleagues in a letter to his daughter-in-law as he relayed a conversation with one of the few Federalist justices still on the court, Joseph Story: "[Story] thinks the Supreme Court is gone, or seems rapidly going."

On December 28, Jackson announced his decision. He would nominate Taney to Marshall's position and Philip Barbour of Virginia to Duval's vacancy. The reaction surprised no one. A fierce debate raged on the nation's editorial pages. One Federalist paper viewed Taney as "a supple, cringing tool of power" nominated by Jackson to vindicate "the President's pet measure" (the end of the BUS). A pro-Administration paper warned that "all the venom of the Bank cabal, and the ambitious, electioneering rancor and influence of Whig Senators and the vile Machinations" of the Whigs won't defeat Taney.

In early 1836 the Senate was composed of twenty-two pro-Administration Senators, twenty-four anti-Administration Senators and two swing votes. To win the fight this time, Jackson knew he had to move with much greater care. He could not force a vote in the Senate until he had a reliable majority. That year the spring elections had gone well for the Democrats. New Democrats were elected in North Carolina and Virginia; three more pro-Administration Senators were selected in Connecticut, Illinois, and Louisiana and two opposition Senators died, giving Jackson another opportunity.

On March 14 the Federalist Senator from Virginia, John Tyler, resigned and a loyal Jacksonian Democrat was appointed in his place. Now Jackson felt he had the margin he needed. He instructed his friends in the Senate to move the nomination the next day. Taney won on a 29–15 vote after the Whigs failed in a last-ditch effort to delay the vote.

The victory represented not only a victory of the President and his party but of the Jacksonian view of government. Jackson was the ultimate majoritarian and in that sense was the enemy of the republicanism that had characterized the early years of the republic. He identified himself completely with the majority will of the people, and he wanted a Supreme Court that did the same. It could not be that "four men who form a majority of the Supreme Court" should have "dominion . . . over the rights of the majority of the people of the United States."

It had been a bitter and personal debate in the Senate and the nation at large over whether Jackson would have his way in shaping a majority on the Supreme Court against the Bank of the United States. It was a debate not unlike what Reagan sought over the Supreme Court and the social issues in 1987 and like what Franklin Roosevelt sought more than fifty years earlier over the constitutionality of his New Deal program.

Roosevelt raised the prospect of a conservative Supreme Court standing in the way of progress in his first campaign, in a speech in October of 1932. He reminded voters that the Republicans had been in control of all three branches of government—including the Supreme Court—for four years. He wanted there to be no question as to who was to blame for their economic woes. President Hoover assailed Roosevelt, warning that, if elected, the governor would "reduce the tribunal to an instrument of party policy."

In the early years of the first term, the Administration avoided Supreme Court tests out of fear of what the conservative court would do with the legislation. For years progressives had looked with dismay upon the Supreme Court's consistent opposition to state reform measures similar to the New Deal legislation. The Court had constructed a doctrine, later to be called the "substantive Due Process" doctrine, which held that the due process clauses of the Fifth and Fourteenth Amendments to the Constitution prohibited such reforms.

As early as January of 1934, there were reports of the Administration inner circle considering ways to "reconstitute" the Supreme Court. However, those efforts were held in abeyance, awaiting the Court's review of certain New Deal statutes. The first real crisis did not occur until a year later, when the Supreme Court, in the *Panama Refining Co.* case, for the first time struck down part of a New Deal statute—critical provisions of the National Recovery Act.

The Republican *New York Herald-Tribune* was ecstatic. For years the New Dealers had "brushed aside the Supreme Court as they brushed aside Congress and the Constitution. . . . The President paid perfunctory lip-service to the nation's charter of liberty." The Supreme Court in its 8–1 decision had thrown "this revolutionary nonsense into the Potomac where it belongs."

According to historian William Leuchtenburg, the Administration still held out hope for the Court. Although contingency planning was underway, out of fear that this was the beginning of a trend, FDR restrained his Brain Trust. They drafted a hard-hitting radio address attacking the Court, to be delivered if the Court were to invalidate Administration monetary reform legislation. The Administration won the case. So FDR did not use the speech or go forward with legislative proposals to deprive the Supreme Court of jurisdiction to hear New Deal cases.

Black Monday came on May 27, 1935, when the Supreme Court handed down three cases that shook the Administration to its core. In *Schechter Corp.* v. *United States* and *Louisville Bank* v. *Radford* the Court invalidated the National Industrial Recovery Act, the heart of FDR's industrial recovery effort and the Frazier–Lemke Act. In *Humphrey's Executor* v. *United States,* the Court severely limited the power of the President to remove members of independent regulatory commissions.

Four days later, the President discussed the opinions at length in a press conference. "We have got to decide one way or the other . . . whether in some way we are going to . . . restore to the Federal Government the powers which exist in the national governments of every other Nation in the world." He went on to conclude that, "We have been relegated to the horse-and-buggy definition of interstate commerce."

Republican Sen. Arthur Vandenberg spoke for many of his conservative colleagues when he responded: "I don't think the President has any thought of emulating Mussolini, Hitler, or Stalin, but his utterance as I have heard it is exactly what these men would say."

According to Leuchtenburg, FDR at this point was focused on a constitutional amendment purporting to reverse many of the Court's recent decisions. However, it was in the period immediately after Black Monday that the notion surfaced that something might be done to affect the current membership of the Court. For example, the *Washington Post* carried a story in May 1935 about Administration plans to ask Congress for authority to expand the membership of the court—"packing the court."

According to historian Arthur Schlesinger, FDR's plan at this point was to keep the public focused on the Supreme Court. His theory was that, if the Court upheld the legislation, the problem would fade away. If the Court continued to frustrate the New Deal recovery program, there would be "marching farmers and marching miners and marching workingmen throughout the land."

On January 6, 1936, the Supreme Court dealt another blow to the next most important part of the New Deal program, the AAA processing tax. Despite public outcry, especially by farmers who were now denied $2 billion in benefit checks, FDR continued to remain mute, to keep the focus on the Court itself.

He confided to his Cabinet that he was planning a showdown with the Court, and he had his Department of Justice working quietly on various reform options. In his reelection campaign that year, he resisted efforts to make it an explicit issue and indeed refused to allow the Democratic Party to make it an issue in the party platform. Just as Jackson had decided to take the issue of the Bank to the people, FDR would do the same. However, Roosevelt lived in a more sophisticated age, and it was important that he not appear to politicize the issue and that he keep the focus of the people's outrage on the Court. Therefore, Roosevelt waged the 1936 campaign on the successes of the New Deal program and won a resounding endorsement of himself and his program.

Having received his mandate on the New Deal philosophy, he resolved to move ahead with removing the last remaining roadblock to realizing the New Deal program, the Supreme Court. Six days after the election and his first day back in Washington, he summoned Attorney General Cummings to the White House. He instructed Cummings to have a set of recommendations for him to review on his forthcoming trip to South America. Cummings, whose staff had been working for most of the past few months on the project, provided the President with volumes of background reading and a sixty-five-page memorandum summarizing the various options.

The memorandum to the President did not recommend a specific option. However, by the end of December, the department was resolved to support what came to be known as the "court packing" plan. In the name of "efficiency" and increasing the vitality of the "nine old men," the President would be permitted under the proposed legislation to add one federal judge to any court, including the Supreme Court, for each judge over the age of seventy who had served at least ten years.

Roosevelt decided to proceed but not to announce the plan until after a February 2 White House dinner for members of the Court.

Senator Borah's description of FDR at that party is of a President who approached the struggle with relish, reminiscent of Jackson's stratagems and melodramatic statements about "killing" the Bank of the United States before it "killed him." Borah, who only later found out what the President was up to, reflected back on the high spirits with which FDR engaged in conversation with Chief Justice Hughes and Justice Van Devanter, who were solid anti-New Deal votes on the Court: "That reminds me of the Roman Emperor who looked around his dinner table and began to laugh when he thought how many of those heads would be rolling in the morrow."

Despite all the time and energy the President put into the project and the tremendous margin of support he enjoyed in the Congress, the proposal was one of the biggest political disasters of the FDR Administration. First and foremost, he failed to consult with his allies in the Congress, and for the most part, the proposal, which had been shrouded in secrecy, came as a complete surprise. When public reaction backfired on the President, his allies abandoned him. House Judiciary Committee Chairman Hatton Sumners probably spoke for many of his colleagues, New Dealers and non-New Dealers alike: "Boys, here's where I cash in my chips."

Vice President John Nance Garner was so angry about not being consulted, and not wanting to have to defend the plan, that he left Washington. House Speaker Bankhead confessed to a colleague that the President did not consult with his friends in Congress because "he knew that Hell would break loose."

In the Senate, opposition came not only from conservatives but from strong New Dealers like Joseph O'Mahoney of Wyoming, Tom Connally of Texas, and Burton Wheeler of Montana. In the end, Roosevelt's allies in the Senate would hand the President a humiliating defeat. In large measure the defeat would, ironically, be fueled by the action of the Supreme Court itself.

The President had announced the plan on February 5. On March 29, in a 5–4 decision, the Supreme Court reversed itself on minimum-wage legislation. Two weeks later that same 5–4 majority upheld the Wagner act. Justice Owen Roberts had changed sides in the debate, and a new pro-New Deal majority had been created on the Court. On May 18, Justice Van Devanter, at the prodding of progressive Senator Borah, announced his resignation.

FDR had the potential of a one-, perhaps two-, vote margin on the Court, but he continued to press on. Since he had lost some cases on 6–3 votes, he was not satisfied.

The next blow would be landed by his friends on the Senate Judiciary Committee. The committee was controlled by the Democrats. On June 14, they issued the committee's report on the legislation. They concluded that the President's proposal demonstrated "the futility and absurdity of the devious." The committee viewed it as an effort to "punish the justices" because of their position on the New Deal and was "an invasion of judicial power such as has never before been attempted in this country."

The report detailed its hearing record, including a letter from the Chief Justice, which revealed the President's argument that the Court was overworked for the sham that it was. The Chief Justice made a compelling case that having more justices would create greater delay.

The report concluded with a warning to the President and the nation that Executive attempts to intimidate the Judiciary were "the very thing against which the American Colonies revolted, and to prevent which the Constitution was in every particular framed." The last sentence of the report was quoted in hundreds of newspapers across the land within hours of its release: "It is a measure which should be so emphatically rejected that its parallel will never again be presented to the free representatives of the free people of America."

The legislation was reported to the Senate with a negative report. The report was the kiss of death. When combined with the Roberts switch and the Van Devanter resignation, there seemed no reason to forge ahead.

Ultimately, the Senate permitted the President to transform the Court to his liking, but it insisted he do so by traditional means, through the filling of vacancies. Since the majority in the Senate clearly shared the President's goals, they were not troubled by the pro-New Deal views of all his nominees. Within two and a half years, he would have appointed a majority on the court. Indeed before he died, President Roosevelt would have appointed eight Justices and one Chief Justice, a legacy unrivaled by any President.

Despite the Court-packing disaster, Roosevelt ultimately succeeded in changing the Court because he had skillfully made the "nine old men," not himself, a national issue. The court-packing plan was a terrible political mistake. His determination to pursue the idea even after the Roberts switch, the Van Devanter resignation, and the Senate committee report illustrates the passion and determination which Roosevelt, like Jackson, brought to his cause.

In large measure because of this passion, Jackson and Roosevelt were much more successful than Reagan in garnering support in the 1832 and 1936 elections for their campaigns against the Supreme Court. Reagan's pitch in the 1986 elections was too little too late. It was not effective in the races in the South in particular, where he had raised the question of Democrats controlling who would serve on the Supreme Court. The Democrats won the Senate back by a margin of 55–45, making Joe Biden the chairman of the Judiciary Committee. As *Newsweek* pointed out, "It turned out to be [Reagan's] most resounding political defeat since he lost the presidential nomination to Gerald Ford in 1976."

The gloom in the White House and the conservative movement intensified with the revelations of the Iran–Contra affair, which surfaced by Thanksgiving. By early 1987 ominous leaks were coming from within the White House about the President's detachment. *Newsweek* reported in January from an insider that "[Reagan] seemed more like a somnambulist feeling his way through unfamiliar rooms. Before a friendly audience of businessmen, he apparently lost his train of thought. . . . We're looking at six months [before the crisis ends] if we're lucky."

By the summer, prominent political reporters were warning that Reagan might be a lame duck, and conservatives, inside and outside the Administration, were worried that time was running out for them to gain control of the Supreme Court.

All of that appeared to change on June 26, 1987. The Powell resignation was like a new dawn for the conservatives. Richard Viguerie, conservative direct-mail wizard: "Conservatives have waited for almost 30 years for this day. . . . This is the most exciting news for conservatives since President Reagan's reelection." Dan Popeo, founder of the Washington Legal Foundation: "We have the opportunity now to roll back 30 years of social and political activism by the Supreme Court." Pat McGuigan of the Free Congress Foundation: "Bork has a constituency that will be easy to activate. This is very exciting."

Within hours of the President's nomination of Robert Bork, skeptical liberals and enthusiastic conservatives began to debate what standard the Senate should apply in evaluating the nomination. Was it appropriate to consider Judge Bork's views on issues that could easily swing the court decidedly to the Right? If they did not want to see Ronald Reagan's nominee take the Court in that direction, did they have a duty to oppose the Bork nomination?

The language of Article II, Section 2 of the Constitution is simple and direct but opaque. The President "shall nominate, and by and with the Advice and Consent of the Senate, shall appoint . . . Judges of the Supreme Court." Since Biden's colleagues were deluging him with questions about the appropriate standard, he decided that his first speech on the Bork nomination would not be about Bork but about Advice and Consent.

Ironically the Whig Senate in the 1830s did not question for a moment their right to attempt to stop Jackson. However, the prevailing view in

Washington in 1987 was that such inquiry was partisan, political, and wholly inappropriate. Minority Leader Robert Dole warned of the danger of the Senate requiring "that judicial candidates pledge allegiance to the political and ideological views of particular senators or interest groups."

Bork's opponents argued, as one columnist put it heavy-handedly, that the Administration apparently believes that "the Senate's job is limited to determining whether the candidate is breathing and speaks English."

Constitutional scholar Paul Freund notes that "The history of unsuccessful nominations has suggested that, although politics in the partisan sense has never ceased to be a factor, it has been increasingly outweighed by politics in the larger, Aristotelian sense—a perception that an individual's identity is conditioned by his or her associations, inclinations, and sympathies, concomitant with a heightened awareness of the Supreme Court's role in the social, economic and political life of the nation."

Professor Freund need not have limited his comments to unsuccessful nomination struggles but to controversial struggles in general. In both the cases of Jackson and Roosevelt, the Senate ultimately acquiesced to the President's wishes. In both cases, the struggle appeared superficially partisan at times but actually involved much deeper Aristotelian questions about the President's vision for the nation and a Supreme Court that he sought to enlist in that quest, in part because of the Court's increasingly vital role in setting the course of our nation.

In the summer of 1987, similar forces were unleashed. Ronald Reagan's campaign to place Robert Bork on the Supreme Court faced a determined Senate controlled by the Democrats, which in the end had to determine whether it shared Reagan's jurisprudence. The outcome would depend upon whether Reagan could commit to the battle the same zest and determination that Jackson and FDR had and whether the Senate in 1987 would respond as it had fifty and one hundred fifty years earlier.

Harvard constitutional scholar Bruce Ackerman summarized the ultimate question for the Senate in the summer of 1987: "Should President Reagan, like President Roosevelt, be granted the constitutional authority to make transformative appointments? . . . to insist that the Senate endorse a radical break with the constitutional achievements of the last generation."

As with the Bank of the United States and the New Deal, the social issues that were at the crux of these "constitutional achievements" were highly volatile questions. To answer the question of whether Reagan should be entitled to have this transformative power, Americans would not only want to know more about Robert Bork but about those who supported and opposed his nomination. As with the earlier battles over the Supreme Court, each side initially sought tactical advantage by questioning the other's motives. And just as Biden feared, his presidential ambitions and the close ties between the civil rights community and the Democrats provided easy first targets.

CHAPTER 4

WILL DEMOCRATS SELF-DESTRUCT ON BORK?

ON JULY 1, within a few hours of the President's announcement of the Bork nomination, Sen. Edward Kennedy strode up to his desk at the back of the Senate chamber. He sought and obtained recognition to speak. He spoke in his characteristic Bostonian accent, and his voice boomed through the chamber. He was angry, and he spoke without equivocation.

"The man who fired Archibald Cox does not deserve to sit on the Supreme Court of the United States. He stands for an extremist view of the Constitution.

"Robert Bork's America is a land in which women would be forced into back-alley abortions, blacks would sit at segregated lunch counters, rogue police could break down citizens' doors in midnight raids, schoolchildren could not be taught about evolution."

There are many different theories as to why Kennedy delivered such an unqualified attack on Bork. Linda Greenhouse of the *New York Times* speculated that "[Biden's] leeway was narrowed by the vituperative attack on Judge Bork that Senator Edward M. Kennedy unleashed within moments of the nomination. . . . [Kennedy], with his unquestioned liberal credentials, set a standard against which liberal interest groups—a vital part of the Democratic constituency—are likely to measure all other senators' words."

Ironically Biden's basic political approach was to condemn just such coercion by the "liberal interest groups." He was first propelled upon the national political stage with a speech he delivered in the New Jersey State Democratic Convention in September 1983. In the speech he specifically criticized the Democratic Party for being swayed by the "pleadings of special interests." Before he was finished, Biden attacked civil rights organizations, teachers' unions, farmers' groups, and the women's movement, and called on all to seek "a sense of shared sacrifice and mutual responsibility, and a set of national priorities that emphasized what we had in common."

For years Biden built his national reputation among party elites and activists with this kind of message. His reviews were surprisingly positive, especially in light of the fact that it was a criticism of the audience. To the chagrin of the leadership in the liberal community, he had continued the attack on the special interests as he geared up for his presidential campaign.

Biden's refusal to march to the civil rights community's drum had been a source of serious tension, especially in his role as Democratic leader on the Senate Judiciary Committee. The civil rights groups looked with great suspicion upon his joining the Judiciary Committee in 1977 because of his outspoken opposition to court-ordered busing. However, in 1981, when he became ranking Democrat on the committee, he took a leadership role in fighting Reagan nominees who had questionable civil rights records.

Biden was successful in leading the committee to defeat Brad Reynolds to be associate attorney general in 1985. Reynolds's career as assistant AG for the Civil Rights Division had made him the nemesis of the civil rights coalition. In 1986, Biden led the effort to defeat Jefferson Sessions in 1986 for the district court in Alabama, amid allegations of racist comments. However, Biden's caution in the nomination struggles over whether Ed Meese should have been Attorney General or William Rehnquist Chief Justice had angered the civil rights community. Indeed, many in the civil rights movement clearly preferred Kennedy to Biden as chair of the Judiciary Committee and had tried to persuade Kennedy to exercise his seniority and bump Biden out of the chairmanship after the Democrats regained the majority in 1986.

The Bork fight would for the first time propel Biden into the national spotlight beyond that closed circle of party and liberal activists. If past nominations struggles were any precedent, Biden would succeed only if he, rather than the groups, controlled the strategy. It was critical that he and his staff not be portrayed as puppets of the civil rights community and the women's movement.

Kennedy's July 1 speech was looked upon with some trepidation by those who had serious questions about the nomination, important swing votes we had to get to beat Bork. Sen. Richard Shelby of Alabama, a conservative Southern Democrat whose opposition to Bork would be critical in the end, spoke for many of his colleagues: "With Senator Kennedy against him, that puts a lot of Southern Democrats in bed with Bork." Even some in the civil rights community saw the tone of the Kennedy speech as "risky."

Biden arrived back in his office from Houston late in the afternoon of July 2. Upon hearing of Kennedy's remarks, Biden's reaction was instinctive: "If we're going to win this thing, we better take control of the message." Implicit in what he said was that Kennedy's rhetoric was not the way to the hearts of the Richard Shelbys of the Senate. Without their support a Bork defeat was hopeless.

There is little evidence that the civil rights community had encouraged Kennedy to deliver his blistering attack on Bork. In fact, civil rights leaders were worried about such extreme rhetoric.

Ralph Neas, the executive director of the Leadership Conference on Civil Rights (LCCR), knew before Bork had been nominated that Biden was right—message was critical. He was not concerned about Biden's position on the nomination. Himself a consensus builder, he had been reassured by the caution with which Biden had approached the Powell vacancy the weekend before. Neas's problem was with his friends in the civil rights community, not with his occasional ally on the Hill, the chairman of the Judiciary Committee.

On the afternoon of the Bork nomination, Neas worried that he had to develop a "unified position" in the coalition. Although Neas would never say it, those who understood how the civil rights coalition worked worried about an Estelle Rogers of the Federation of Women Lawyers or Nan Aron of the Alliance for Justice. Both tended to speak first and think later. Frequently quoted in the national media, their visceral reactions often created just the kind of rhetoric that can be used by opponents to make the groups the issue rather than Bork.

Each time a representative of the civil rights community spoke off the cuff in anger, it tended to limit the effectiveness and flexibility of moderates like Biden. Just as the strong rhetoric of the Kennedy speech dampened the ardor of a Shelby, so a strong or threatening comment by a member of the civil rights community tended to be counterproductive with Biden. The political press covering the Bork fight would interpret anything Biden did as if it were a reaction to political pressure.

The impulsive and angry reaction of Estelle Rogers illustrates the point; the day of the Powell resignation, she called on Biden to resign over the *Philadelphia Inquirer* quote. So do the comments of Nan Aron: "There will be a mass mobilization."

Rogers' and Aron's language was almost gratuitous and seemed to serve no tactical purpose. They would hardly affect an Administration that had gone out of its way to alienate the civil rights community, and besides neither represented a group with any real clout in Washington.

The strongest language came from Kate Michelman, executive director of the National Abortion Rights Action League. In her case though, it was clear from the outset that the very issue around which her organization was built—abortion—would be at stake with the Powell announcement.

Michelman would later tone down her rhetoric and with great finesse work very effectively within the coalition, but her initial statements were not helpful: "We're going to wage an all-out frontal assault like you've never seen before on this nominee, assuming it's Bork."

And when asked by a reporter for *USA Today* whether Biden got the message, Michelman was blunt, " 'Biden got it today. All day.' "

Of course, as of July 1, 1987, neither Nan Aron, Estelle Rogers, Kate Michelman, nor any representative of the civil rights community had any communication with Biden about his position on the Bork nomination. Ralph

Neas and the rest of the leadership of the civil rights coalition deliberately avoided any appearance of pressuring Biden, and for the first week there was no such communication.

Neas's concern in those initial meetings of the LCCR was not simply with avoiding outbursts of this kind but with reaching consensus over three strategic goals: to ''freeze the Senate'' (keeping Senators from endorsing Bork), to obtain a delay in the hearings, and to keep the fight off single issues like abortion.

When Neas convened the membership of the Leadership Conference on Thursday afternoon, July 2, even he was surprised by the response. It was the biggest meeting in the history of the organization. Representatives of eighty groups met in the conference room of the stately old mansion that served as their headquarters near Dupont Circle in Northwest Washington. Stalwarts of the liberal community, like Ralph Nader, had to stand in the hall. The group swiftly adopted the most urgent item on Neas's agenda. Neas and the executive committee of the LCCR would ask for an immediate meeting with Biden to make one simple request: a delay in the beginning of the hearings until the fall.

In case Neas and his allies needed an explicit message on the danger of single-issue high-pressure tactics in their campaign to defeat Bork, they needed only to read conservative George Will. In his nationally syndicated column for that same day, Will delivered a vicious personal attack on Biden, characterizing him as having ''forfeited'' ''his reputation for seriousness,'' ''the incredible shrinking presidential candidate.'' Will based his attack on the Rogers intemperate call for Biden to ''retract his endorsement'' of Bork.

In Will's words, ''Suddenly Biden . . . began to position himself to do as bidden. Either Biden changed his tune because groups were jerking his leash or worse, to prepare for an act of preemptive capitulation.''

Almost as if to fulfill the Will scenario, the civil rights activists proceeded to give the columnist more ammunition. That weekend the NAACP convention in New York adopted a strongly worded resolution opposing the nomination. The executive director, Rev. Benjamin Hooks, announced that his organization would go ''all out'' to defeat the nomination. In light of Bork's civil rights positions, especially an article appearing in the *New Republic* in 1963 opposing the Kennedy Administration's civil rights legislation, the NAACP's position was hardly surprising or impolitic.

However, Hazel Dukes, NAACP board member and Democratic National Committeewoman from New York, delivered a line that would make even Estelle Rogers blush. Introducing Sen. Daniel Moynihan to the convention, she announced that he would surely oppose the Bork nomination. Moynihan himself, however, was noncommittal. When told of the Senator's caution, Dukes responded angrily, ''I have the votes in New York to defeat him . . . when I get with his staff in New York, I'll get what I want. It's strictly politics.''

Dukes's impulsive comment became the pretext, along with the Kennedy speech, for another Will column condemning Biden. Biden, "who has used Bork to establish himself firmly as the flimsiest presidential candidate, is courting liberal interest groups." Will then proceeded to expand his attack beyond Kennedy and Biden to the whole Democratic party, "battered by the public's belief that the party is servile toward imperious interest groups." To Will, the Dukes–Moynihan exchange epitomized the problem.

The real direct pressure on Biden was coming not from the civil rights groups but from the Biden presidential campaign, pressure which he resisted. On July 6 the campaign hierarchy met in an unsuccessful attempt to persuade Biden to join Kennedy in blasting Bork.

Lowell Junkins, who served as the honorary chair of the Iowa campaign, had flown in from Des Moines specifically for the meeting. He clearly came with a mission from the Iowa campaign staff. The two primary Iowa operatives—David Wilhelm and Mike Lux—felt strongly that Biden should move quickly to oppose Bork.

It did not take long for Junkins and me to get into debate on the issue. He argued as a former state senator: "In the Iowa senate, when a strong chair wants to accomplish something, he makes it absolutely clear to his members where he comes out, and he tells them. That's what leadership is all about."

I responded impatiently: "Lowell, this is not the Iowa senate. This is not a piece of legislation we're talking about. This is a nomination to the Supreme Court. I am certain Joe is not going to come out with a formal statement today."

Junkins then got more explicit: "David [Wilhelm] and Mike [Lux] feel very strongly about this. Gephardt, Dukakis, even Babbitt are going to come out against Bork at the NAACP convention. Everybody's asking, 'Where's Biden?' "

I responded: "Biden's not going to the convention. And besides, if we were going to take a position, that's the last place he should take it. Joe's built his whole campaign around not pandering to the groups."

In retrospect it's easy to see the bind the Iowa caucus campaign felt itself in. As Donilon explained it, "It was in the interest of the other candidates to position Joe as neutral so that he would take a lot of heat from the liberals. [Meanwhile] they were demagoguing it. That is, other candidates were coming out against Bork at the NAACP convention and with the other liberal groups.

When Biden joined the meeting, he made it clear that, although he was leaning toward opposition, he would not take a public position immediately and did not want Junkins or anyone in Iowa taking a position for him. After he had made this clear to Junkins, he quickly focused the meeting on the logistical nightmare presented by the Bork nomination.

Donilon summarized the concerns of the campaign operatives: "My concern was how much time this was going to take to prepare and ultimately conduct these hearings and how much time this was going to take away from the presidential campaign. What was it going to mean in time not spent in Iowa and New Hampshire.''

After poring over scheduling documents for an hour, Biden decided that the optimum time for him was as soon as he felt he could be ready. It would be impossible to have the requisite number of briefings by the time the Senate left for its August recess, but I felt that Biden could be ready for hearings during the recess. He agreed.

Biden proceeded to contact his Democratic colleagues on the committee. Most members deferred to Biden as chairman to set the date, but Kennedy and especially Metzenbaum were adamant for delay. Metzenbaum argued for hearings in October at the earliest. As campaign aides pored over scheduling documents on the side porch, Biden walked out and announced the results of his telephone conversations: ''It's clear what the liberal strategy is—to get as much delay as possible.''

Biden next talked with Thurmond.

''Joe, we should have these hearings next week,'' the Senator insisted.

''Strom, you know we can't do that. We waited almost a month to do the Rehnquist hearings when you were the chairman. This nomination is even more important.''

Thurmond became a little indignant. ''Well, that's because you insisted on the delay. I would have started 'em earlier.''

Biden responded quickly: ''O.K. What if we had them in August?''

Thurmond hesitated. ''Well, I don't know if we could get our members back in August. I don't want to do that.''

''Well, let's shoot for when we return from the August recess after Labor Day. I'll still have to clear this with the Democrats.''

Thurmond agreed reluctantly.

Moments later, I received a call at Biden's house from Ralph Neas. The LCCR wanted to meet with Biden about scheduling. I did not tell him about Biden's conversations with Thurmond but said that Biden would meet with them. I made it clear that Biden would not talk about his position on the nomination. Neas understood.

Biden agreed to meet with the Leadership Conference at 12:30 on Wednesday. It was to be a hectic day. Bork had asked for a private meeting with the chairman, and it was scheduled for 10:00 A.M. Immediately thereafter Biden would meet with an advisory committee of distinguished lawyers and academics who would advise him on the nomination: Ken Bass, a former Hugo Black law clerk; Washington superlawyer Clark Clifford; Prof. Walter Dellinger of Duke Law school; and Prof. Philip Kurland of the University of Chicago. Biden would meet with his Democratic colleagues on the committee at 1 P.M., and at 4:00 Sen. Alan Cranston, the Democratic Whip, wanted to meet with him about the nomination.

The Bork meeting went just as planned. It took place in Biden's hideaway office on the third floor of the Capitol. Biden was generally reluctant to have private off-the-record meetings with prospective nominees, but in this case he felt it was important to accommodate Bork's request. Biden had never had his opinion of a nominee affected by one of these private sessions, but he appreciated Bork's apparent strategy in the meeting: to convince Biden that he was a decent human being. By then it was apparent the hearings would be heated, and the two men would be sitting across from each other for hours with the television cameras watching their every move. Both men used the meeting to take the measure of the other.

Biden let Judge Bork know that he was likely to oppose him, but would not announce his position immediately and would attempt to be as fair as possible in the hearings. "Indeed," Biden offered, "you can have any witness you want in the hearings on your behalf."

"Mr. Chairman, I understand you are inclined to oppose me, but I hope that you will give me a chance to change your mind in the hearings. I intend to answer your questions as candidly as I can, and I hope you will stay open-minded about my answers."

"Judge Bork, I intend to be scrupulously fair about this. I hope to run these hearings like the Rehnquist hearings were conducted. Both sides will get equal numbers of witnesses. I will engage in no personal attacks."

Biden explained the structure of the hearings. He encouraged Bork to invite his family. Bork said he would.

John Bolton, representing the Department of Justice, explained that he had once been a student of Bork's.

Biden laughed. "So this is all your fault."

And the meeting concluded.

It was a short meeting, and the only time the two men were ever in a small private group—two men whose actions and reactions in the coming weeks would have untold impact on each other.

Biden rushed from the hideaway back to his conference room in the Russell Building, where the meeting with Clifford, Kurland, Dellinger, and Bass was already underway. It was an intense and productive meeting, in which Biden described a speaking schedule he intended to undertake. First, within two weeks he would deliver a lengthy speech on the Senate floor making the case that, in circumstances like the Bork nomination, it was appropriate for the Senate to consider the nominee's judicial philosophy. Second, sometime thereafter, hopefully before the Senate recessed in early August, he would deliver a formal statement on his assessment of Bork's judicial philosophy and his reasons for opposing the nomination. This speech would not be delivered until early August in San Francisco at the American Bar Association Convention.

Biden enjoyed the give-and-take of the meeting. Nothing challenged Biden more than the notion of taking a complex issue and converting it into a matter that lay people could understand. That was the essence of his task in the coming months. The next meeting with the civil rights groups would not be the kind of intellectual exchange he enjoyed, and he kept Neas and his colleagues waiting for forty-five minutes.

When he came into the civil rights meeting, he still had the speech ideas and schedule on his mind. Ralph Neas was joined by Elaine Jones, an articulate and strong-willed lawyer with the NAACP Legal Defense Fund, Nan Aron, Judy Lichtman, one of the senior feminist lawyers in Washington representing the Women's Legal Defense Fund, Mario Marino of the Mexican American Legal Defense Fund, and Susan Liss of People for the American Way.

Biden had one major goal for the meeting. He wanted to make it clear that he would give the Bork nomination the time it deserved, even at the risk of his campaign. He was still sensitive to insinuations by Estelle Rogers and others in the civil rights community that he would not take sufficient time from the campaign for the Bork effort.

Ralph Neas and Joe Biden were friends. Indeed Biden had once approached Neas about working for him. But over the years they had argued frequently about tactics.

Biden began with characteristic candor:

''I don't know the rest of you, but Ralph and I know each other pretty well. I want to speak bluntly to you all, and I want it understood that everything that goes on in these meetings [is] confidential for the time being.

''First, I want to make it clear that I view this nomination as of historic importance. I am prepared to devote as much time as necessary to this effort. I have met with my campaign staff and made it clear to them that I will sacrifice the whole campaign if necessary to work on this nomination.''

Ralph spoke for the group: ''Senator, we don't doubt that for a minute. We're not concerned about that. We want to talk about when the hearings will begin. That's our concern today.''

Elaine Jones interrupted and began to describe how she and lawyers in the civil rights community were analyzing Bork's record and how it was going to take weeks to complete.

Biden would not let her finish:

''Look, Ralph, your people are taking shots at me about this. [I've made] it clear that I'm going to put in the [necessary] time on this, but I want to make something else clear . . . I want to decide what the strategy is for those of us who have concerns about Bork.''

Determined to get control over the direction of the effort, especially control over the message, Biden reiterated the public statement he made when the Bork nomination was announced that he had ''grave doubts.''

"But if I lead this fight, it will not be a single issue campaign. That's not how we beat Sessions or Reynolds, and it won't work here."

At that point, Judy Lichtman volunteered, "We know that we can't fight this over abortion. We will look to you for a way to frame this fight on broader issues."

The tension eased immediately.

The meeting finally moved to the topic of the hearing date. Biden explained that he was going to try to get consensus with Democrats on the committee over an early September hearing. Jones wanted more time, possibly October (Biden made it clear that that was not likely), but Neas seemed relieved. Then Biden got up to leave for the Capitol and his meeting with the Democratic members of the committee.

Just as he was starting down the hall, Marianne Baker called him back. Strom Thurmond was on the phone. There was a glitch in their agreement for a September 15 start date for the hearings. He wanted a commitment that the committee would vote by October 1 on the nomination.

"Look, Strom, assuming the hearings are over, that's fine by me. I want to do a good job but also to get this over with. But I'm not sure I can get this by my members."

He was right. Senators Metzenbaum and Kennedy did not even want to start the hearings until October. The other members, although they would defer to Biden, were not willing to go on record with a commitment for a vote by a specific date. The consensus was to announce a September 15 starting date and to make no commitment on a vote.

Biden called Thurmond and then stepped before the press awaiting him outside the meeting room on the second floor of the Capitol. He announced the September hearing date and the "overwhelming prospect" that he would oppose the nomination.

I stood at the back of the crowd of reporters. Carolyn Osolinik, Senator Kennedy's savvy chief counsel, turned and said to me, "Biden's doing a good job on this." I agreed. So far so good.

The euphoria did not last long. When I returned to my office in the Dirksen Building, Pete Smith, the committee's press secretary, came in with his characteristic grim expression.

"Ken Noble of the *Times* is on the phone. He's got the whole story about the civil rights meeting. He's going with the story that Biden's going to lead the fight against Bork."

I told Smith that I could not believe Neas would have talked to the press. "Somebody else must have leaked it. Pete, this is bad. We don't want that. Besides, that's not what he said. He didn't announce his position to them." Before I could finish, Ralph Neas was on the phone telling me that Noble was trying to get him to confirm the story. He assured me that neither he nor anyone at the meeting was the source. I later learned that no one at the meeting was the immediate source but that someone at the meeting must have talked to someone who spoke to the *Times*. The person who gave Noble the story told me that his information came from the civil rights community.

"Ralph, I need to talk to Joe. We've got to be saying the same thing."

He agreed.

Diana Huffman, the committee's staff director and a former reporter herself, agreed with Pete Smith and me: We should confirm that Biden had met with the groups, because it was a mistake to look like we were saying something privately to the groups and something else publicly. Biden agreed.

We were focusing on the wrong problem. We were so concerned about being consistent and avoiding another *Philadelphia Inquirer* type quote (pro-Bork) that we did not cover the opposite situation (anti-Bork). We failed to point out to Biden that it might appear that he had discussed his position with the groups before making it public—as if they had coerced him into taking a stand. We terribly compounded his problem without even knowing it.

Further, we induced Biden to approve a statement that went beyond what had actually occurred in the meeting. Smith was authorized to say to Noble that Biden "intends to oppose the nomination and to lead the effort against it in the Senate." In addition Smith would say that Biden did not plan to announce his opposition formally until he had a chance to spell out his reasons in detail in a series of speeches, which he planned to begin the next week.

Actually the statement that Neas read to us and to Noble was much closer to the truth: "He [Biden] made it very clear to us that he knows what he's going to do, and that he considers the confirmation fight so important that he's willing to work on this, and not on the presidential campaign."

Although both Smith's and Neas's statements appeared in the *Times* and *Washington Post* articles, the clear implication was that Biden actually told the groups first as part of a strategy to placate them. Noble pointed out that the groups had been unhappy with his reticence in the Rehnquist fight, and a story in the *Post* related Biden's alleged private commitment to the groups directly to the presidential campaign: "Biden told the activists, whose constituencies are important to his presidential campaign, that he will detail his reasons for opposing Bork in his upcoming statement, the sources said."

As soon as Biden saw the story the next morning, he realized that we had made a serious mistake. It only took one day for the full impact to be felt. First came a blistering editorial from the *Washington Post*.

Under the heading "Judge Bork and the Democrats," the *Post* aimed directly at Biden: "While claiming that Judge Bork will have a full and fair hearing, Sen. Joseph Biden this week has pledged to civil rights groups that he will lead the opposition to the confirmation. As the Queen of Hearts said to Alice, 'sentence first—verdict afterward'."

Reminding the reader of the *Inquirer* interview, the *Post* accused Biden of swinging "reflexively to the other side of the question at the first hint of pressure, claiming the leadership of the opposition, doesn't do a whole lot for the senator's claim to be fit for higher office." Bork deserved a fair and thorough hearing but "How can he possibly get one from Sen. Biden, who has already cast himself in the role of a prosecutor instead of a juror in the Judiciary Committee? If there is a strong, serious case to be argued against Judge Bork, why do so many Democrats seem unwilling to make it and afraid to listen to the other side?"

The most damaging allegation—that Biden had been somehow pressured by the groups or acted in anticipation of their pressure—simply was not true. However, because of our missteps, we had clearly given the *Post* and our opponents reason to believe their worst fears.

As bad as the *Post* editorial was, nothing wounded like a column that next day by Mark Shields, a liberal columnist in the *Post*. Shields was prepared to write the obituary for the Biden presidential campaign. In a column headed "Will the Democrats Self-Destruct over Bork?" Shields argued, almost in Bidenesque language, that the Democrats need a leader "with vision who is independent, tough and can effectively define the national interest." Biden had seemed to many to be that leader, but as a "patsy of liberal pressure groups, neither Biden nor anyone else will fill that bill of leadership for change."

For the next ten days the problem compounded itself. On Saturday, July 11, Biden went to Portsmouth, Seabrook, and other New Hampshire stops. He met with local activists who opposed the nuclear plant, but instead of getting publicity for his speech in opposition he was photographed conversing with Pro-Life demonstrators carrying large signs condemning his position on the Bork nomination.

A photograph of Biden surrounded by placards that asked, "Joe, why is there time to visit N.H. but not for Hearings?" appeared in papers across the nation. Usually it was attached to Sunday think pieces on the wisdom of his taking an early position on the nomination. A piece in the *Post* summarized the week's events and the reaction among political operatives as to whether Biden would benefit politically.

A similar article appeared in the *Baltimore Sun* with the same photograph, and the *Delaware State News* pointed out that the demonstrators were not simply Pro-Life demonstrators but part of the presidential campaign of Jack Kemp. The *Sun* article quoted a civil rights activist who had been in the Wednesday meeting speculating on how Biden's early opposition would help his campaign. That sort of gratuitous speculation, especially by someone who was in the meeting, simply added to the impression that Biden was just posturing for the electorate in Iowa or New Hampshire rather than trying to take control of the nomination struggle.

During the next week Biden packed his days with substantive briefings on

Bork's record, and what little campaigning he was doing was crammed into day trips on the weekends. That next Saturday Biden flew to Cleveland for a meeting of the Democratic Party state chairs. At the meeting he performed superbly in a presentation on his foreign policy, but in a question-and-answer he said he made "the biggest mistake of my political career in coming out against Bork the way I did."

The fact that Biden had "admitted he had made a mistake" became a standard part of the litany of the Biden missteps during the early days of the Bork struggle.

As he explained the next week, it was "more of a public-relations mistake than a substantive mistake." He meant that it was not a mistake to come out against Bork—only to do so in the context of a meeting with the groups. But the press simply portrayed it as another example of "inconsistency."

Early in the afternoon the following Tuesday, Biden and I spoke quietly as we waited for Rasky and Donilon to arrive for a strategy session. They had both privately criticized his admitting he made a mistake. Biden was reliving the past few weeks. "I have absolutely no doubt that we had to come out like this to get control of the debate. But it was a mistake to do it the way we did it."

I winced when he said it. He would never confront me about it, but the "we" was me. I still was defensive that I had advised him to release the statement to Noble.

"The thing that's so galling to me," he said, "was that I've worked so hard to develop positions independent of the groups but which I believe represent the values we share. The way I'm being portrayed is as if I'm their tool. That's not me."

I agreed.

As Donilon and several Judiciary Committee staffers walked into the room, we turned to the business at hand, a final review of a speech he was drafting on the Senate's role in reviewing the qualifications for Supreme Court nominees.

After several rewrites dictated by Biden, he was finally happy with the draft.

"Now we can get to what we like doing best. With this speech we can start to frame the debate. We can 'draw our line in the dust.' When we start doing that, none of this criticism of the last few weeks will matter."

He was referring to a refrain from his Atlantic City speech about the importance of Democrats not blindly following the machinations of various interest groups but making their own principled arguments in favor of liberal values, drawing "a line in the dust around our past accomplishments" and daring Reagan to cross it. The defensiveness of the first month—for taking an early position—would dissolve if we pursued that kind of strategy: a critique of Bork, based upon principled disagreement with his philosophy.

Joe Biden's dilemma had been how to gain control of the anti-Bork effort by indicating early opposition before he had formulated a well-refined rationale. Howard Baker and his White House staff faced a similar dilemma—how to gain control of the volatile conservative alliance and at the same time create a rationale for support for Robert Bork, which might be at odds with what conservatives thought Bork stood for.

In a sense both men faced a similar problem—how to frame a principled argument that would persuade average Americans, at the risk of offending and even alienating partisans of the extreme Left and Right. In the end Biden would fare much better than Baker in that difficult exercise.

CHAPTER 5

HOWARD BAKER AND THE BUDDY SYSTEM

IN THE SECOND MONTH of the Reagan Administration, the *Conservative Digest* published an open letter to its hero, the President. The letter was written by the *Digest*'s editor John Lofton: "Your mandate for change is in danger of being subverted. The very real possibility that this catastrophe could occur is the result of your personnel operation being run by individuals who are politically naive and, worse still, individuals whose backgrounds reveal a hostility to almost everything for which you have so strongly stood over the years. . . ." At that time, the conservative establishment was concerned about moderates, such as James Baker and Michael Deaver, running the new White House staff.

To Lofton and his friends on the right, Howard Baker was even worse. The affable, statesmanlike Tennessean had demonstrated his "hostility" to Reaganite positions during the Carter Administration, when he, as Minority Leader of the Senate, supported the Panama Canal treaty. That treaty, and its return of the Canal Zone to the Panamanians, was a rallying call for the Right and especially Ronald Reagan.

Baker was vilified by the Right for his role in that effort, and it contributed to the failure of his own presidential campaign in 1980. The fact that Ronald Reagan turned to Baker to restore the credibility of his presidency, in the aftermath of the Iran–Contra scandal in early 1987, was a particularly bitter pill for early Reagan loyalists.

Ronald Reagan had spoken often of the danger of the "clubby" "buddy system [in Washington] . . . the forces that have brought us our problems: the Congress, the bureaucracy, the lobbyists, big business and big labor." To Lofton and other conservatives like F. Clifton White, Ronald Reagan had hired "boys to do a man's job." Ronald Reagan had done it again, this time reaching into the heart of the Washington establishment, a high-powered Washington law firm, where Baker, in semiretirement from the Senate, was paid to lobby the Congress and the bureaucracy on behalf of big business. So the man who planned Ronald Reagan's every move in July of 1987 was in

Lofton's words "the 'buddy system' incarnate . . . a dedicated lifelong anti-Reaganite mushy moderate."

As was often the case with the New Right, the rhetoric was sharp and personal. Despite its enthusiastic beginnings, the pro-Bork effort was shrouded in an atmosphere of suspicion and distrust. In the Washington of Ronald Reagan's buddy system, this atmosphere manifested itself in petty but often fierce struggles for control of the effort—or, in the jargon of the Capitol, "turf battles."

Although Baker did not control the decision to choose Bork, once President Reagan nominated him, Baker moved quickly to take control of the Administration's strategy to secure confirmation. He immediately placed the pragmatic White House staff firmly in charge of the citadel of the New Right in Ed Meese's Justice Department. However, delivering that message to the United States Senate, the real battleground for the Bork nomination, was entirely another matter. Indeed, the process of persuading the Senate to follow the White House lead simply created a new arena for the turf battles between the pragmatists and the true believers.

At 2:00 P.M. on Wednesday, July 1, the day that President Reagan nominated Robert Bork, Terry Eastland, Department of Justice spokesman, released a press packet. It contained a résumé on Judge Bork, several of his Court of Appeals decisions (one holding that there was no constitutional right to privacy for homosexual activity, balanced with a First Amendment decision that was viewed as pronewspaper) and some of his more renowned conservative treatises, in particular the 1971 *Indiana Law Review* article. Eastland acted on his own, because he could detect no White House strategy.

White House spokesman Marlin Fitzwater did not want Eastland or anyone at the Department of Justice briefing on Bork's record. Eastland was informed that Leslie Arsht in Fitzwater's office would be the point person on press calls on Bork. The White House intended to maintain tight control over what the Administration had to say about Robert Bork.

The White House had good reason to be concerned. Will Ball, director of the White House legislative operation, had conducted a preliminary vote count on the nomination soon after Bork was named. He and Howard Baker immediately began calling Senators and focusing in particular on Southern Democrats who had sided with the Administration in the fight a year earlier to confirm William Rehnquist as Chief Justice. The results were disquieting. According to Ball, "We knew by the end of the week that the Southern Democrats were going to be a problem."

Without delay the White House addressed the question of whether to activate the Right and to introduce to the Senate and the American people the Robert Bork who had so captivated conservatives. Ball had strong feelings about which approach would work: "We had huddled about this. I felt very strongly about this, but if you looked at the Democratic votes you had to have, it was a matter of cold political reality. If you were going to get these Southerners, it was not going to be with those kind of tactics. You ran the risk of losing. Our role was to show [Bork] wasn't an extremist, [that he was] open-minded and enjoyed intellectual integrity.''

Conservatives in the Justice Department were annoyed by Fitzwater's effort to gain immediate control of the media, but the Administration was united in dealing with the first two tactical issues presented to it—Kennedy's opening salvo the day the Bork nomination was announced and Thurmond's agreement a few days later to delay the hearings until September 15.

The Kennedy speech was viewed in the Administration the same way that Biden and his staff viewed it—as an extreme statement that undermined the ability of the moderate Democrats and Republicans to join in the anti-Bork effort. John Bolton recognized that, if Kennedy led the charge, the anti-Bork effort would fail. According to Reynolds, Kennedy was viewed as "a joke, . . . a non-player.'' The thinking at the time was that ''Kennedy would get his headline, a snicker and a laugh.''

Culvahouse and Will Ball now agree that no one from any camp of the conservative movement sought to have the President respond to Kennedy. Reynolds concedes that the President ''was never asked to respond'' and that he agreed at the time that it would have been wrong for the President "to dignify'' Kennedy's speech with a response.

There was little disagreement within or without the Administration that Kennedy did speak for the civil rights–civil liberties community. The anti-Bork coalition was angry, and Robert Bork's friends in the Administration understood that they were going to face a determined attack from the Left. Those who had been involved in the past struggles—for example, the effort to make William Rehnquist Chief Justice the year before—understood that such opposition from the Left can make a difference. However, in 1986, opposition to Rehnquist, expressed in much the same voice and led by Kennedy, failed, and for the most part Baker and his staff and those in Justice were hardly panicked by Kennedy's statement on behalf of the Left.

As Reynolds explained it, ''I lived through Rehnquist and Scalia. There were people on Rehnquist and Scalia doing something that sounded like this. . . .'' As measured against the mild opposition to Sandra Day O'Connor's nomination in 1981, Rehnquist and Scalia had faced stiff objections, but the nominations had survived. "We were able to overcome it with Rehnquist,'' Reynolds said, ''and he was perceived to be probably more conservative than Bork.''

However, there was not total satisfaction with the role that Thurmond and his staff had played in that battle, and in particular Administration strategists were concerned about delay between the announcement of the nomination and the commencement of the hearings. In 1986, Biden, as ranking Democrat on the committee, had negotiated, with then Chairman Thurmond, a lengthy delay between the announcement of the nomination and the commencement of the hearings. The civil rights community used that time to organize opposition to the Rehnquist nomination. Bolton was prepared for a similar tactic by the Left with the Bork nomination.

As soon as Thurmond got off the phone with Biden on July 6, having agreed to delay the beginning of the Bork hearings until early September, his staffers knew that the announcement would not be welcomed by other Republicans on the committee—or by the Administration. As one Republican staffer characterized it, "Thurmond seemed to be avoiding a fight. Thurmond needed to realize that there were others in this fight and should have consulted with his colleagues."

Bolton was not so charitable. He went "ballistic" when he found out what Thurmond had agreed to. He was particularly angered when he learned that Howard Baker had also agreed to the Thurmond–Biden arrangement. He knew that the month of August could be critical to the success of the Bork nomination.

Hatch, Gordon Humphrey, and other Republicans, though concerned about the delay, never attacked Thurmond or Baker publicly about the schedule. Instead Biden became the focus of their ire. For example, Gordon Humphrey regularly attacked him on the floor of the Senate and in the press. He prepared charts to show that Biden was taking more time to prepare for hearings on Bork than on any of his predecessors. He combined the attack on delay with calls for Biden to "put aside his campaign" and predicted a "witch hunt" in committee.

The weekend after Bork was nominated, Duberstein, deputy chief of staff at the White House, had summoned Tom Korologos, a former White House lobbyist, with a reputation for being skilled in the handling of difficult presidential nominations. He and Korologos met with Ball and A. B. Culvahouse to begin to develop a strategy. Korologos had already spoken to Bork and asked him for the names of prestigious members of academia and the bar, especially Democrats, who would speak out in his behalf. One of the first goals would be to broaden Bork's base of support.

The next day Duberstein convened a meeting in his office of the principal staff and officials in the Reagan Administration who would wage the battle on behalf of Judge Bork. Will Ball, director of communications Tom Griscom, and A. B. Culvahouse were in attendance. The Department of Justice was represented by Brad Reynolds, who was Meese's point man on the nomination, and John Bolton, assistant attorney general for legislative affairs.

The meeting's agenda ranged from the mundane to the strategic. Bolton, Culvahouse, and others were assigned prominent members of the bar and academia to contact on behalf of Bork, but Bolton was also told to call Morris Liebman, a prominent conservative, who was calling Bork at home with unsolicited advice and tell him "to get on board," which presumedly meant to work through the Administration. Justice Department staff was to prepare an answer to Biden's "balance" argument and a series of one-minute speeches for Republican Senators to use on the floor the next day.

As a result of the meeting, several things became clear. The White House through this apparatus would manage the Bork effort, and the White House intended to maintain tight control of the public definition of Robert Bork—the so-called message. Just as Biden had to be sure that he—not Kennedy or the civil rights groups—controlled the anti-Bork message, Howard Baker was determined that he—not the Justice Department or the Right Wing groups—controlled the pro-Bork message.

One name Bork had given Korologos as likely to help was Lloyd Cutler, a prominent Democrat, President Carter's White House counsel and a liberal who had been active in civil rights causes. In the meeting A. B. Culvahouse was assigned to "call Lloyd Cutler for the purpose of seeing what he was willing to do, and re: a possible op-ed piece."

According to Reynolds, two strategic goals were agreed upon at the July 6 meeting. First, the group would seek out people on the outside to leap to Bork's defense—academics, judges, justices, lawyers, politicians close to Senators, and state officials like attorneys general. The idea "was to build to a crescendo right before the hearings," with each person "saying substantial things about Bob." The first success in that strategy was Lloyd Cutler.

Cutler and other prominent lawyers joined Bork and Ray Randolph, a friend of Bork and his former deputy at the Solicitor General's office, for a meeting with other prominent members of the bar at the White House a week later on July 13. It was decided that Randolph and Lee Lieberman, a former Justice Department employee, a former clerk to Justice Scalia, and a founder of the conservative Federalist Society, would work from Randolph's office to contact prominent members of the bar around the country to ask them to write to members of the Senate. Dean Gerhard Casper of the Law School at the University of Chicago would do the same for academics.

The second goal was to begin to assemble all of Bork's writings and to summarize them into a series of white papers. Originally there were going to be sets of white papers, one for the press and one for staffers on the Hill, but it was determined that it was too "dangerous" to have two separate reports on Bork's writings. Reynolds and Culvahouse divided up responsibility for assembling these materials between Department of Justice and White House lawyers. These materials would be assembled in blue notebooks and would become known in the Administration as the Blue Book on Bork.

Later that week, Howard Baker met with the Republican Senate leadership and the Republican members of the Senate Judiciary Committee. The meeting took place in Howard Baker's old Republican leader's office on the second floor of the Capitol adjacent to the Senate floor. It was hosted by Baker's successor, Robert Dole. Both were political rivals, both still harbored ambitions to succeed Ronald Reagan.

Baker came up to the Senate to send one simple message: ''The White House will take charge of this fight.'' Turning to Will Ball, Baker indicated, ''Will is to be the point man at the White House. And I have asked Tom Korologos to come help us on this. John [Bolton] will be the point at Justice.''

Tom Korologos moved quickly to try to assert the White House leadership role. He called several Republican staffers, including Randy Rader, to follow up on planning for the fight. Rader was reluctant to attend a meeting without Thurmond's staff present. He induced Korologos to invite Duke Short and Dennis Shedd, Thurmond staffers. Shedd was unwilling to have a meeting unless all of the Republican staff of the committee was included.

Bolton thought a broader meeting was a mistake. First, he much preferred to work with Rader than with Short, Thurmond's chief investigator. ''Duke could give you fifteen reasons why something couldn't be done.'' In other words Short was Thurmond's man first, a Republican loyalist second. Naturally the more doctrinaire Justice staffers, like Mike Carvin, did not get along with Short. Furthermore, a broad meeting of all Republican staffers would include moderate Republican Arlen Specter's staff, Neal Manne, his chief of staff, and Jeff Robinson, a counsel who had just left Biden's staff to head up Specter's Judiciary Committee staff. Both Manne and Robinson had close ties to the Democrats and the civil rights movement.

Bolton was convinced that, with Manne and Robinson in attendance, everything that happened would be passed on to the Democrats and the liberal groups. Shedd understood the risk, but as minority chief counsel he felt that all Republican staffers needed to be included, at least initially.

The meeting took place in the third week of July. Every Republican on the committee was represented.

It was Shedd's meeting, but he turned immediately to Korologos. Korologos began by introducing the White House staffers, Nancy Kennedy and Pam Turner, both of whom were already familiar to the committee staff. He then proceeded to explain the White House strategy—basically repeating what Baker told their bosses in Minority Leader Dole's office, a few days later. He then explained committee procedure to the staff, in an almost condescending tone of voice.

Bolton sensed that Korologos had crossed the line in lecturing the staffers. ''Shedd and Short knew as much about Judiciary Committee nomination fights as Korologos did.'' The tension began to build.

Shedd pressed Korologos on the need for a sophisticated vote count. Korologos responded quickly, ''Dennis, why don't you leave that to me?''

Shedd had already conducted a vote count with Markman and Carvin, and the results were disturbing, but he did not press it further with Korologos.

Korologos proceeded to explain the laissez-faire strategy: ''The committee really isn't that important. Biden has already committed to allow the nomination to go to the floor.'' In a statement the first week, Biden had reached an agreement with the Republican leadership not to "bottle up" the nomination in committee. "Our only concern is that Bork not make any public commitments on how he will vote on the Supreme Court."

Bolton disagreed. "Well, I think the committee is important. Bork should respond to every charge."

Korologos wasn't so sure. "I think Bork needs work as a witness."

Bolton responded indignantly, "The first time Biden, or one of those Democrats who thought he knew something about Bork, takes him on, Bork will pound him into the dust."

Korologos shot back, "That's exactly what the problem is. This [the Senate hearing] isn't Yale Law School. That won't work."

The obvious tension between the two points of view prompted an embarrassed silence among the Republican staffers. Korologos tried to break the pall with bravado:

"I've got some good news. The White House is well prepared on this one, better prepared than ever."

Shedd couldn't resist the comeback: "No matter how well prepared you [at the White House] are, they're [the opposition] going to be better prepared."

The mood was becoming very gloomy.

Korologos pleaded for Republican unity: "Well, at least we can all work together to get the nomination through. Well, I guess almost all of us." He looked at the Specter contingent, the moderate staffers.

Manne grinned. Everyone else shifted uncomfortably.

Korologos quickly tried to change the subject, but he stumbled into a most volatile subject—access to Robert Bork and information about him. Obviously, staffers attempting to prepare Senators for the hearings were desperate for that kind of access. And no one felt more strongly about it than Duke Short.

Korologos looked at Manne. "Well, does anyone's boss need to meet with Bork?"

Manne quickly indicated that Specter would want to meet several times with Bork.

Korologos announced that all contacts with Bork would be channeled through him, because that's the way the White House wanted it, and an appointment would be set immediately for Bork to meet with Specter.

Korologos's comment was directed primarily at Short. Short, as Thurmond's representative, saw it as his prerogative to deal directly with Bork. He reacted angrily: "I'll talk to Judge Bork whenever I want to. I don't work for Ronald Reagan. I work for the United States Senate."

It was not turning out to be the kind of meeting that any proponent of the nomination could have wished for. The meeting demonstrated clear tension not only within the Administration but between the White House and the committee leadership, especially Thurmond's senior staff.

Dennis Shedd was probably the most talented conservative staffer on the Hill, a mastermind in several anticivil-rights efforts in past years. However, Shedd was virtually eliminated from any significant role in pro-Bork strategy because of the meeting. White House senior officials let Shedd know that they were not happy with how Korologos was treated at the meeting, and after that Will Ball dealt directly with Thurmond and practically ignored Shedd.

Shedd was about to leave the Thurmond staff to practice law in Columbia, South Carolina, and was planning a long-deserved vacation. Korologos managed a sarcastic closing directed at Shedd to end the meeting: "Dennis, have a nice vacation. Don't worry. We've got everything in hand."

This meeting, in addition to sowing confusion as to who would control the strategy within the Administration, significantly undercut Thurmond's leadership. The more Thurmond's role was questioned, the more the leadership vacuum drew in Dole and Simpson. Dole's staff made the case in the meeting that it was a Senate issue and that Dole should take the lead. Simpson's staff argued that he should take the lead. The only explicit questioning of Thurmond's role came from staffers who argued that judicial philosophy would be the focus of the battle and that Thurmond was vulnerable on that question.

They correctly anticipated that Biden would argue that it was legitimate for the Senate to consider Bork's judicial philosophy in determining whether he should be confirmed. Thurmond could not question that proposition, because it is precisely what he had argued when he fought the nomination of Abe Fortas to be Chief Justice in 1968. The argument only served to further anger the Thurmond staffers.

Perhaps worst of all, the meeting did not serve to resolve the most fundamental question. How would staffers get access to pro-Bork materials. Korologos, Culvahouse, and Ball insisted that every piece of information on Bork supplied by the Administration be cleared by the White House staff.

By the third week in July, Howard Baker's White House staff was firmly in control of the pro-Bork strategy. It was hardly the kind of principled defense of Robert Bork's conservative philosophy that John Lofton and his conservative allies would have wanted. Ronald Reagan had turned over the strategy to Howard Baker and the buddy system, the Washington establishment, headed by Lloyd Cutler, a Jimmy Carter liberal with close ties to the civil rights community.

The next step in the Administration's strategy was the development of the Blue Book on Bork—a briefing book on Bork's views modeled after Cutler's op-ed. It was no simple exercise, for it required the conservatives in the Justice Department, the pragmatists at the White House, and the buddy system to agree on who Robert Bork was and what he stood for.

CHAPTER 6

WHO IS THE REAL ROBERT BORK?

IN 1981, ROBERT BORK joined the Washington office of the Chicago law firm, Kirkland & Ellis, for which he had worked in the 1950s. This was to end an important phase of his career. For almost two decades Bork had made a significant financial sacrifice so that he could be a part of the world of ideas in academia and public service.

The money at the law firm was good, reportedly $400,000 per year, and Bork immediately bought a new BMW sedan and a nice house in a fashionable neighborhood. The day he moved into his new home, he got a call from then Attorney General William French Smith, informing him that President Reagan would like him to fill a vacancy on the United States Court of Appeals for the District of Columbia.

He had just left the modest salaries and intellectual pursuits of academia. However, the 75 percent pay cut from law practice to the Court had to be balanced against the fact that the Court of Appeals was considered a steppingstone to Bork's ultimate ambition—the Supreme Court. In Bork's own words, ''I was made to feel that the train was leaving the station.''

The Supreme Court could be the culmination of a career of intellectual pursuits. Professor Bork was described with a combination of admiration and some discomfort by his colleagues and students at Yale Law School. Although some would ''cringe'' at some of Bork's views on civil liberties and civil rights, they all seemed to agree on his wit and his intellect, his restless intellect.

Intellectual dialogue was an essential part of his upbringing. ''My mother and I used to argue far into the night about all kinds of things. My father would yell down at us from the bedroom: 'This is not a debating society. Go to sleep!' ''

It was in that cerebral environment that young Robert Bork began his intellectual odyssey. Oddly, he began as a Socialist. ''Socialism sounded to me like a swell idea, and rebellion sounded like a swell idea, too.'' He even attended Communist Party meetings. A neighbor and childhood friend pointed out, ''We weren't concerned about women's rights and abortion, but we wanted to put food on tables and find jobs for people. . . . Bob liked to provoke, especially the people who were so self-satisfied, like the people of [his middle-class Republican neighborhood].''

Bork entered the University of Chicago Law School in the late 1940s, ''somewhere between a follower of Eugene V. Debs and Franklin Roosevelt. I don't know, New Deal.

''In 1952, I was out on a street corner with my wife, passing out leaflets for Adlai Stevenson. It was the years '52 to '54 when I had this experience that changed my mind.''

The experience, in his words, ''a little bit like a conversion experience'' from liberalism to free-market conservatism, came at the hands of an émigré economist at the University of Chicago, Aaron Director. To Bork the principal revelation was that, ''A free economy, within obvious limits, produces greater wealth for people in general than a planned economy does.''

Bork joined Kirkland & Ellis in 1955, rising quickly to partner. He worked mainly on complex commercial, especially antitrust, litigation. After seven years in practice, Bork was restless. He rejected an offer in journalism and joined the Yale Law faculty at less than half his salary as a partner. ''I realized I was going to be doing the same kind of thing [at the law firm] over and over again. . . . I really hadn't gone into law with that sort of thing in mind. I had gone into it with a rather more intellectual interest. . . .''

Bork came to Yale to teach antitrust law, but in 1964 he sought his wife Claire's opinion on what to teach as a second specialty. ''What's the biggest field in the law, the most exciting, intellectual field?'' his wife asked.

''Constitutional law.''

''Then teach that,'' she responded.

When Bork went to Yale, concluded two reporters for the *Washington Post,* he embarked on ''an intellectual odyssey in search of his core beliefs. To test an idea, he insisted, one must write it down, or teach it. In short, one must stick out one's neck.''

Little did he know how far out he would stick his neck to make a point in the coming years.

One of the most important arenas for testing these ideas was with his students, especially in a class which he cotaught with Alexander Bickel, a liberal and probably the preeminent constitutional scholar of his day.

Bickel became a dear personal friend and mentor. He advised Bork to ''wreak yourself upon the world.'' And Bork did.

''I thought it was possible to work out a theory of when governmental regulation of humans is permissible, and on the other hand when individual freedom is required.''

He began as a libertarian, one who believes in the primacy of free thought and action. A natural outgrowth of the free-market notions that dominated his antitrust teachings, the philosophy sounded harsh, even inhumane, when applied to social policy.

In 1963 in the *New Republic* he condemned the Kennedy Administration's civil rights legislation. It was simply wrong to impinge upon white people's freedom of association by telling them they must serve blacks in their places of business. The principle upon which the Kennedy legislation was based was, according to Bork, one of "unsurpassed ugliness."

In 1968 he further elaborated his libertarian notions in a lengthy article in *Fortune* magazine. In it he defended the Supreme Court's controversial decision in the 1965 case of *Griswold* v. *Connecticut,* in which the Court struck down the Connecticut state law banning the use of contraceptives by married couples. He sought a libertarian jurisprudence, which could support this inherent right to marital privacy even though a generalized right to privacy is nowhere mentioned in the Constitution.

By 1971, a sabbatical in England and his continued debates with Bickel led Bork to an almost opposite political philosophy. In a 1971 article in the *Indiana Law Review,* he completely reversed fields on *Griswold* v. *Connecticut.* He condemned the decision as "unprincipled" and "intellectually empty." In the article he articulated a philosophy that was to become the intellectual foundation for what, in the Reagan era, would come to be known as the original intent jurisprudence. He reasoned that if a right—like the right to privacy in the *Griswold* case or, better yet, the right to an abortion, which was to come later in the *Roe* case—was not specifically mentioned in the Constitution, then it simply did not exist.

The 1971 article, which is his most complete explanation of his constitutional philosophy, was a sweeping and scathing attack on the jurisprudence of the Warren Court and its immediate predecessor. He attacked everything from the one-man–one-vote decision to decisions outlawing poll taxes, racially restrictive covenants, striking down state statutes that prohibited the teaching of German or ruling unconstitutional statutes that prohibited private school education. In every case, Bork argued, the justices based their opinions more on personal whim than on explicit provisions of the Constitution. That to Bork represented indefensible judicial activism.

The next year Bork was asked by President Nixon to serve as his Solicitor General, the Administration's advocate in the Supreme Court. With the election of Jimmy Carter and a new regime at the Department of Justice, Bork returned to Yale in 1977. It was not a happy time. His friend and colleague, Alex Bickel, had died of cancer, and Bork's wife Claire was herself waging a losing battle with the disease. As one student who studied under him during this period explained, "He just read his lecture notes. It was very boring and very sad. The last day of class he did not even return after the break. I think his wife died a few days later."

His writings became even more strident. One profile in the *Washington*

Post described his *Antitrust Paradox,* published in 1978, as having "an embattled tone, with a vehement attack upon liberalism." He was particularly critical of the "intellectual class" and adopted the rhetoric of the neoconservatives and the so-called New Right, which would provide the manpower for Ronald Reagan's victory in 1980.

In Bork's words, "Intellectuals as a class have distinctive interests and tastes, and are disproportionately able to move law in the direction of their interests and tastes. The intellectuals' preference for government economic regulation is attributed to a desire to shift power and prestige from the business class to themselves."

He began to increase his off-campus speaking schedule, especially with conservative groups like the American Enterprise Institute, the conservative Washington think tank. Even after joining the Court of Appeals, Bork continued to speak out, especially to the conservative law students' association, the Federalist Society. Indeed, by the time of his nomination to the Supreme Court, *USA Today* in a profile described Bork as the "unofficial philosopher king of the conservative legal movement."

On occasion he did anger his friends on the Right, for example, his opposition in a 1979 op-ed in the *Wall Street Journal* to a constitutional amendment to balance the budget, and his 1981 testimony before the Senate Judiciary Committee against legislation that purported to deny federal courts jurisdiction to enforce the Supreme Court's *Roe* decision. For the most part, however, his speeches and writings followed the structure laid out in the 1971 *Indiana Law Review* article.

However, by July 1987, when reporters for the *New York Times* and the *Washington Post* were conducting extensive interviews with Bork, he was calling himself a "Burkean." Like Alex Bickel, who ended his career enamored with the philosophy of the eighteenth century British philosopher Edmund Burke, Bork was no longer confident of broad intellectual frameworks. Bork explained, "I mean by Burkean, highly suspicious of sweeping, abstract principles as a way of organizing society, because they tend to be highly coercive; respect for community, tradition, constitutional structure; a willingness to look at a law and ask 'will it do more good than harm?' "

Bork's was a dramatic intellectual journey—from Socialist to Communist, to New Dealer, to free-market advocate, to libertarian, to strict constructionist, to statist, to Burkean. Most scholars are identified with one major philosophical school during their careers. Bork was identified with several. He never gives a truly convincing explanation for his change of position. Indeed Bork only devotes a footnote in his recent book to the most dramatic change in position from his 1968 *Fortune* article, in which he embraces *Griswold,* to his 1971 *Indiana Law Review* article, in which he repudiates it.

Bickel's suggestion to Bork that he "wreak himself upon the world" led Bork to fashion his own distinctive approach to intellectual discourse. It was an approach that "pushes him," as a profile in the *Washington Post* noted, "to be a force in public debate and never to cower before public disapproval."

As his friend Ray Randolph pointed out, "He does not sugar-coat things. He is not a person that is looking to be accepted. His mind works for the purpose of trying to find what the truth is, whatever that may be, whatever the correct solution may be to a particular problem. And he will state it regardless of whether the dead cats will begin to sing."

Some of Bork's most controversial statements seemed to verge on hyperbole. He had served in the Marines during the Korean War, and in a sense he brought the tough, determined, almost belligerent demeanor of a marine to intellectual debate. At times he brandished a macho and sarcastic tone in his utterances.

For example, in condemning the *Griswold* decision in the 1971 *Indiana Law Review* article, he argued that the desire of "a husband and wife to have sexual relations without unwanted children" was indistinguishable, for constitutional purposes, from the desire of an electrical utility company to "void a smoke pollution ordinance. The cases are identical." It was an extremely controversial position not just because he failed to recognize the right to privacy but it seemed insensitive to equate the regulation of private marital acts with the regulation of public acts of pollution.

Randolph explained that the 1971 article was originally a speech. Indeed, he pointed out, except for his treatise on antitrust, *The Antitrust Paradox,* nearly every single one of Bork's controversial writings was a speech. "And in speeches one does not deal with subjects in the kind of depth that one does in the law review-type article, heavily laden with footnotes, exceptions, qualifications, etc. When you give a speech, you try to do it with words that try to carry in the wind and they are much more punchy than in a typical law review article."

As for the sentence from the 1971 law review article equating marital privacy and pollution control, Randolph agreed that, if you were writing a scholarly piece from scratch, it was not the kind of line you would use. "His speeches entertain and his speeches provoke people to think and that was a provocative line."

His numerous statements and articles were not just entertaining to members of the Senate Judiciary Committee in 1987 but provocative. It was a kind of provocation that the White House staff would have a hard time explaining away in their Blue Book.

They had decided that, if Bork was going to make it to the Supreme Court, he had to be portrayed as a moderate in the image of Lewis Powell, Potter Stewart, and John Harlan. A. B. Culvahouse, White House counsel and one of the architects of the Administration's strategy to win the Bork nomination, agreed that Biden and other Bork critics had made the balance of the Court the issue. The first weekend after Powell's resignation, the test advanced by Biden and adopted by the national media was "to find someone in the mold of Powell." To Culvahouse, "It was natural for the White House to say, 'Yes, he's like Powell'." The goal was "to put Bork in the mainstream." To White House strategists, Bork was a Burkean. He really did not have an ideology.

One White House official intimately involved in the effort was much more crass: "It was pretty clear where we needed to get the votes [to win]. They weren't [from] the Right but from the Middle." The Right was not happy with that strategy, but according to the aide was willing to play along if it worked.

The first Administration attempt to peddle Robert Bork as Lewis Powell was the July 16 op-ed by Lloyd Cutler in the *New York Times,* which A. B. Culvahouse was instructed to solicit. It became the blueprint for the Administration's portrayal of Bork: "Judge Bork is neither an ideologue nor an extreme right-winger. . . ." Cutler argued that Bork believes in judicial restraint and would be a Justice in the tradition of Holmes, Brandeis, Frankfurter, Stewart, and Powell.

He conceded that Bork was a leading critic of the *Roe* decision, "but this does not mean that he is a sure vote to overrule *Roe v. Wade;* his writings reflect a respect for precedent that would require him to weigh the cost as well as the benefits of reversing a decision deeply imbedded in our legal and social systems (Justice Stewart, who had dissented from the 1965 decision in *Griswold v. Connecticut,* on which *Roe v. Wade* is based, accepted *Griswold* as binding in 1973 and joined the *Roe v. Wade* majority)."

"I predict that if Judge Bork is confirmed, the conventional wisdom of 1993 will place him closer to the middle than to the right, and not far from the Justice whose chair he has been nominated to fill."

Phil Kurland called me as soon as he read Cutler's column. "Mark, this is an outrage. I've got to do something." He wanted Biden to say something. I responded defensively, "Look, Phil, we're being attacked for being unfair. We have to establish our credentials by lying low for a while." Kurland reacted impatiently: "Well, I'm going to write a letter to the editor." I encouraged him: "You're the most prominent conservative constitutional scholar in the country. You *do* have the credentials, and you certainly know [Bork's] writings."

Kurland not only wrote to the *Times,* but to every major daily in the country. He wielded a wicked pen: "Bork is either the moderate, restrained New Deal-type jurist that he is depicted to be by some of his recent advocates in the press. Or he is the Meeseian, 'original intent,' constitutional revisionist, as he has depicted himself to be in his talks to 'the Federalist Society' and in other forums throughout the country. In either case, the Senate is entitled to have the real Robert Bork presented to it for its advice and consent on the nomination."

Bork's opponents hoped to take on the "real Bork." The Administration could not have it both ways. He could not be both Lewis Powell and the "philosopher king" of the Right. It was becoming obvious that one way to kill the Bork nomination was with Bork's own words. Ralph Neas circulated Kurland's letter extensively in the press and used the same approach in his public statements: "There is a 25-year body of articles, testimony, statements, speeches, and judicial decisions that will demonstrate conclusively why Judge Bork has been the legal champion of the far right for so many years."

Conservative staffers in the Justice Department knew that Kurland was right.

As Culvahouse, Carvin, and Markman exchanged drafts of the Blue Book, two different portraits of Bork began to emerge. For the most part Carvin and Markman had acquiesced in the White House mandate and drafted a moderate document, but in a few areas—especially general statements about Bork's jurisprudence and how it differed from the Warren Court and his views on criminal law—they sought to highlight Bork's more conservative views. Carvin had also written a strong attack on Biden for the report.

Carvin was not happy with the White House effort to meet the Biden-inspired test to make Bork "fit the mold of Powell." He set about immediately to analyze all of the 5–4 opinions in the last term of the Supreme Court to determine quite literally where Powell had been the swing vote, and it was obvious to him that Bork was not the same as Powell. Clearly the pendulum was going to swing back to the Right.

"My attitude was let it swing back to the Right," Carvin said. "The White House's was to mute it."

"The Left was going to have their parade of horribles—civil rights. We should have had ours. Ours are more current than the Left. Why should five old men decide questions like abortion, affirmative action, and homosexual rights? Ours were the questions for the future, and the Left would be defending the past."

Carvin and Markman, each with staffs of a half dozen bright young conservative Justice lawyers, were charged with preparing the Blue Book. To Carvin, the "muted message" was not going to work. Earlier, Steve Markman, Dennis Shedd, and Mike Carvin had done their own vote analysis and come to the same conclusion as Will Ball. Not only could they "not find the sixty votes necessary to break an anti-Bork filibuster, but we were not even sure there were fifty votes for Bork." Again, "the problem was the new Southern Democrats." Their solution was very different from Ball's, whose strategy depended on wooing moderates with a moderate Bork. Markman, Shedd, Rader, and Carvin believed that only a confrontational approach would work with the Southerners and moderates.

"You can't make the conservative jurisprudence points without specific examples [like its impact on homosexual rights, affirmative action, and abortion]. But Korologos and the White House wouldn't let us make those points.''

The undecided Senators should be forced to choose between two visions of the Supreme Court—their conservative vision or the vision expressed by the American Civil Liberties Union, the feminist women's groups, and the rest of the Left. In Carvin's words, ''The real issue should have been the future of the Supreme Court. . . . But the White House conceded that argument by saying nothing would change [with Bork].''

Carvin had written a very strong attack on Biden (based specifically on the *Philadelphia Inquirer* quote) and on other moderates and liberals for what Carvin called ''flip-flops'' on the standard the Senate should use in reviewing Supreme Court nominees and on the Bork nomination. The White House felt it was too strong and unnecessary. Culvahouse felt it was ''gratuitous.''

The White House insisted that there be a section in the book emphasizing that Bork would be a tough law-and-order judge. White House pollster Dick Wirthlin apparently felt that the Democrats were vulnerable on the crime issue, and to the extent that Bork seemed to expose that vulnerability it would help his chances. According to Reynolds, Frank Donatelli, the White House director of political affairs, and Will Ball felt that ''politicians would respond to the death penalty'' and Bork's support of it.

Not only did law-and-order become a bone of contention between the Justice lawyers and the White House, but Bork was apparently unhappy about using it as well. The Justice Department lawyers wrote a very strong section, which simply could not be supported by Bork's record, and Culvahouse rejected it. Bork had simply not spoken out on these issues.

Reynolds pointed out, ''He was pretty skinny in that area. He had some views, but he was not a criminal law expert. To portray him that way was . . . playing to Bob's weaknesses, not his strengths. . . . Bob felt quite uncomfortable about it. He was not going to the Court with that portfolio.''

According to Reynolds, Bork only reviewed part of the briefing book, the part dealing with his judicial record. Although he was not intimately involved in the preparation of the document, he would certainly have to live with its consequences. For as a practical matter, the book set in stone the Administration's strategy for how he would be portrayed.

When Markman saw how Culvahouse had edited their draft, he went to Reynolds to complain. Reynolds understood what the White House was doing. The White House ''was trying to do as much as possible to remove controversy from the nomination, therefore modulating some of Bob's opinions. . . . They were trying to make him a 'kinder gentler candidate'.''

However, Reynolds was unwilling to challenge Culvahouse on them. Throughout the process Reynolds sided with the White House on tactical considerations of this kind. In fact Reynolds and Culvahouse were in general agreement on the thrust of the paper.

Bolton went directly to the Attorney General, but he deferred to Reynolds as well. Meese made it clear that it was a fait accompli.

Reynolds's attitude was a matter of great frustration to Bork loyalists in the Justice Department, especially because, except for Meese, Reynolds was the only Justice official to whom the White House staff listened.

As one senior Bork loyalist in the Department put it, "Reynolds always thought things were going great, even when you brought him bad news. He was a lone wolf. He kept things to himself. Sometimes I felt that he did not even pass on our concerns to Meese or the White House."

Some of those involved in the process of developing the Blue Book regret it now, but they admit that they deferred to the White House in its basic thrust. Carvin recalls that "once we were locked into the 'Bork is the same as Powell' notion and that we couldn't change the approach, we became loyal implementers." However, he called it the "Bork as a Liberal" book and fully expected it to be followed by a "Bork as a Conservative" book.

The Administration was having a hard enough time getting out one book, not to mention two. Besides, the White House would never formally authorize a conservative version. Time was running out. Senate staffers wanted materials from the Administration, before the August recess, to use on Bork's behalf when expected attacks on him began in the Senate. By the last week of July the Blue Book had still not been released.

The civil rights community had lost all patience with Biden as well. Kennedy had given his speech on July 1. Neas visited me at least once a week, asking, "Where is Biden's speech?" He was visibly shaken when I insisted that Biden would not speak out on the merits of the nomination before August. Neas did not think it enough simply to address the question of whether it was appropriate for the Senate to consider Bork's views without also condemning them at the same time.

On July 23 Senator Biden went to the floor of the Senate and delivered an hour-long scholarly address on the role of the Senate in exercising its advice and consent function. To Neas's great disappointment, the speech contained no specific attack on Bork's judicial views. Biden carefully reviewed the history of the provision in the constitutional convention and writings of the framers in the Federalist Papers. He concluded that the original intent of the drafters was clear that the Senate was to play an important role in checking a President who, like Reagan, sought to change the direction of the Court.

In drafting the Constitution, the framers assumed a dominant role for the Senate. Originally the selection of judges was to be made exclusively by the Senate, and only on the fifth attempt at the close of the convention in Philadelphia did the delegates even agree to a role for the President in the selection of judicial nominees. The ratification debates suggest that our forefathers assumed the Senate would defend the independence of the judiciary, and the advice and consent clause would give the Senate the power to prevent the President from appointing Justices to be "the obsequious instruments of his pleasure."

In reviewing that history and the precedents of the Senate, Biden concluded that there was little doubt that the tradition of the Senate was to consider the nominee's views—especially in cases where the President has chosen the nominee because of his views. After summarizing the history of similar struggles in the past—in particular the Jackson and FDR examples—Biden concluded, "We are once again confronted with a popular President's determined attempt to bend the Supreme Court to his political ends. No one should dispute his right to try. But no one should dispute the Senate's duty to respond."

Biden explained to the *New York Times* why the speech was necessary: "Only if they can persuade the public on that point can the Democrats go on to make their case that a person with Judge Bork's views on a range of constitutional issues should not be confirmed."

Actually the public was already on the side of Biden and the Bork opponents. That same day, the *New York Times* released a nationwide poll on the Bork nomination, which specifically asked whether the Senate should consider a nominee's substantive views. According to the poll, 62 percent of Americans felt that Senators should give "a lot" of consideration to a nominee's views. The fact that the poll was released that day was not fortuitous. The Biden staff had advertised his intention to speak on the subject that day and persuaded the *Times* to release the poll to coincide with Biden's speech.

The speech had some impact on skeptics in the Senate, especially moderates who had not made up their minds on Bork. Republican Sen. Arlen Specter stopped me on the street a few days later to compliment the Senator's speech. Although he did not tell me so that day, his staff later remarked that he found the speech very persuasive.

Armed with the Biden speech and the new poll, Bork opponents, like the anti-Bork People for the American Way, began to launch a campaign in newspaper ads: Was the Bork nomination part of the Reagan social agenda? The public and the rest of the Senate should be prepared to learn the answer.

Biden's speech did not go unnoticed at the Department of Justice and among Senate Republicans. Sen. Alan Simpson, the Republican Whip and also a member of the committee, immediately asked the Department of Justice to prepare a point-by-point rebuttal to Biden's speech.

Assistant attorney general Steve Markman, who had once served in the Senate as Hatch's chief Judiciary Committee staffer, recognized that Biden had "laid down the intellectual foundation for the opposition." He "knew [the proponents] were in for a serious fight and that Biden took it seriously."

It would not be the half-hearted, last-minute opposition that characterized Biden's position on the Rehnquist nomination a year earlier. He was carefully and methodically building the case against Bork, and his sentiments were a reflection of uneasiness among moderates about Bork. For example, when Biden took the Senate floor again two weeks later to discuss the advice-and-consent question, he was joined by two moderate Southern Democrats, Sen. Wyche Fowler of Georgia and Sen. Terry Sanford of North Carolina. Both were newly elected Senators and both expressed their agreement with Biden's argument in favor of a more aggressive role for the Senate in reviewing Supreme Court nominees.

It was no coincidence that Biden had persuaded Fowler and Sanford to join him on the floor, and although no one else in the Administration seemed to notice the Fowler–Sanford presence on the floor, John Bolton recognized it as further evidence that the "new Southern Democrats were going to be a problem."

Meanwhile Justice staffers were sharing their frustrations, over disagreements within the Administration about the Blue Book, with Rader and other Republican staffers on the committee. Senate staffers were getting impatient for materials to use on Bork's behalf. Rader and his friends in Justice came up with an idea to "smooth the waters." Rader went to Korologos, his good friend, with the idea: "Why don't we choose neutral ground, like the Heritage Foundation [the conservative think tank with offices adjacent to the Capitol grounds]. We can arrange a peace conference between representatives of the Senate, the White House, and Justice."

Edwin Feulner, president of the foundation, agreed to host the meeting. In Bolton's words, "The purpose of the meeting was to 'kiss and make up'."

In attendance were the following: from the White House, Korologos, Will Ball, Ken Cribb (a former Meese adviser with close ties to all of the conservative groups), and Tony Dolan (a speech writer with equally strong conservative credentials); from Justice, Reynolds and Bolton; and from the Senate only Rader and Senator Humphrey. Conspicuous by their absence were Short and Shedd. Not only were no other Senate staffers in attendance, but Thurmond's staff was not even aware the meeting was taking place.

Feulner opened the meeting: "Let's get things out on the table and discuss our differences."

Will Ball and Korologos insisted that "everything's OK."

Ball said that he had not gone to the meeting to argue with anyone. He wanted to listen to their concerns. He made it clear, however, that "This is the top of the President's list. It's his top priority. He will spare no effort."

Dolan, a close friend of Bolton's, called on Bolton for the Justice perspective. Bolton was reluctant to be the first to discuss the disagreements: "I don't want to be critical, but we've let July go by. Let's get things going, the other side is. We need grass-roots activities [during the upcoming recess], town meetings, etc."

Sen. Gordon Humphrey agreed. It was important to get more information out on Bork. The clear message from Humphrey was "This should be all-out war.'' There was discussion of whether to do television commercials and radio spots, and several participants wanted assurance that the President would get personally involved in the fight.

Ball and Cribb reiterated the President's commitment to Bork, but Ball pointed out, ''The President is at the ranch [the President's ranch in California where he would vacation for most of August] over the recess, and that's a fact of life.'' In other words, the President would not be personally involved in the fight over the August recess.

Rader was very disappointed. He had hoped that Bolton and others at Justice would air their concerns about the White House approach to the Blue Book, which they had shared with Rader privately. As Reynolds explained over a year later, reflecting on the Heritage Foundation meeting, ''It was a round-table discussion. There was some grumbling that there was not enough being done here, and it was not clear who was doing what. But again here, people who were at that meeting were not about to point fingers at anybody. What should have been said was not really said. . . . The problem was there was an underlying turf battle going on . . . the meeting . . . was helpful but it didn't come to grips with the problem.''

An honest effort by allies from the outside to resolve fundamental differences within the Administration was papered over with pep-rally rhetoric about how ''we all needed to work together.''

The Blue Book, in the form of a lengthy white paper, entitled ''Materials on Judge Robert H. Bork,'' was released to the press, Hill staff, and outside groups on August 3. The thrust of the book was to portray Judge Bork as in the ''mainstream tradition'' of Justices Lewis Powell and John Harlan.

The paper encouraged the Senate to focus on the nominee's judicial record, not his academic record. It pointed out that his criticism of the ''reasoning of Supreme Court opinions'' is just something that ''law professors do'' and was not something the Senate should be concerned about. Bork was described as one of the ''most eloquent and principled proponents of judicial restraint.'' According to the White House, Bork ''has never wavered in his consistent and principled protection of . . . civil liberties . . . that can actually be derived from the Constitution and federal law,'' and that he has ''opposed what he views as impermissible attempts to overturn'' the right-to-privacy decisions. It claimed that his ''record indicates he would be a powerful ally of First Amendment values on the Supreme Court.''

The paper summarized an extensive statistical analysis of Judge Bork's voting record as a judge, pointing out that none of his majority opinions had been reversed by the Supreme Court. There was ''no basis . . . in judge Bork's record'' that he would ''seek to 'roll back' many existing precedents'' and that he ''believes in abiding by precedent.''

President Reagan summarized the essence of the Blue Book a few days before it was released: ''If you want someone with Justice Powell's detachment and statesmanship, you can't do better than Judge Bork.'' *USA Today* summarized Reagan's speech to the National Law Enforcement Council as ''hailing Bork as all but an ideological clone of . . . [Justice] Powell.''

One reporter, after having reviewed the report, called John Bolton: ''If he's really the way this briefing book portrays him, why did you guys nominate him?''

Bolton did not have a ready answer.

The Right reacted with anger and denial. To Richard Viguerie, their powerful direct-mail czar, ''It was a disaster the way they repackaged Bork. It's hard to get people to go out and fight, bleed, and die for Lewis Powell.'' Conservative constitutional scholar Bruce Fein said exactly what Carvin thought but was prohibited from writing: ''Judge Bork, even if he's portrayed as a moderate and is confirmed, is not going to alter his vote that way. . . . I think when you try to be a little too cute as the President is being I believe, that no one is deceived. . . . They chose Bob Bork because they wanted him to make changes in the law.''

Terry Eastland, then the Justice Department's spokesman, was candid a year and a half later when asked to assess the report. ''The portrayal was disingenuous. It was a disaster. It didn't work on the inside, and it didn't work on the outside.'' Eastland meant that it did not help with Bork's allies in the Senate or the conservative interest groups, and it didn't help with the press and the general public.

Bolton was blunt and a little bitter. ''The briefing book was a clear signal to the Right: 'Your issues are not the issues we're going to fight this on.' ''

Bolton, Viguerie, and Eastland were right. The Administration had committed a terrible blunder. Worst of all, they opened themselves and Bork to the charge that Robert Bork of the briefing book was not the real Robert Bork.

CHAPTER 7

IF JUDGE BORK HAD BEEN JUSTICE BORK

IN THE BEGINNING OF AUGUST, Biden and his allies were largely unaware of the Administration's problems and were very much preoccupied with problems of their own. Indeed, Monday, August 3, was a low point for Joe Biden in the Bork struggle. The headline on the front page of the Wilmington paper said it all: "HASTE IN CONTESTING BORK'S NOMINATION MAY DAMAGE BIDEN." William Schneider, a Washington political commentator, who was close to Biden at the time, was quoted as saying, "He is ridiculed and discounted as politically maladroit and inept. People are already talking about the collapse of the Biden campaign. I don't think it was as devastating . . . [but] he's made defeat of Bork more difficult, and galvanized the GOP."

Tom Donilon, Vince D'Anna, a Biden political adviser, and I waited on the side porch of Biden's comfortable Wilmington home as he took a last-minute swim in his pool with his daughter. He had spent the weekend on the campaign trail in Iowa and was exhausted. As he came onto the porch still wet from the pool, he flopped down onto one of the white wicker chairs. He had a dour, almost bedraggled, expression on his face.

The Wilmington paper was on the coffee table with the headline in plain view. He looked down at the newspaper. "It was the worst mistake of my political career." He was referring to the awkward way in which his opposition to Bork had been made public.

I tried to defuse the tension: "Look, we all share the blame for this."

He bristled. "Yeah, Mark, but I have to live with it every day out there."

Now that he had unloaded a bit, he sighed. "Look, we've got to get beyond this."

We then began one of the most fruitful meetings of the whole nomination struggle. We had brought an agenda of a half-dozen basic decisions that had to be made:

"How should we respond to Republican pressure in committee to move up the hearing date?"

"How can we get more Democrats out there taking some of the heat on this thing?"

"Should we be pursuing a strategy of defeating the nomination in committee?"

"Should we be considering a filibuster strategy?"

"What sort of field strategy should the various outside groups be pursuing?"

"Now that we have laid down the marker on advice and consent [in the July 23 speech on the Senate floor], when and where should we begin to say something substantive about the reasons for opposing the Bork nomination? Should we begin to lay out some of the case against the nomination in your speech next week to the American Bar Association?"

The meeting went on for hours, and the more he became engaged in the decisions, the more he relaxed. Some issues he responded to almost instinctively:

"We cannot agree to move the hearing date up. It might be good politics to look like we're giving in to them to blunt the unfairness issue. But the fact is that neither we nor they can be ready any earlier than the middle of September. The fact is, this is the most important nomination in recent memory. [Bork] will sit for life. He can wait a few more weeks. I've seen enough to know I'm against the guy, but I haven't even read all those speeches."

He decided to meet with sympathetic Democrats as soon as he got back to Washington. Senators Kennedy, Inouye, Cranston, and Sanford had asked to meet with him the week before. He would take them up on their suggestion. The subject of the meeting would be what could they do to help in the effort.

The Senate majority leader, Robert Byrd, had made it clear that he did not want to see the nomination bottled up in committee, so any committee strategy was probably hopeless. After hearing us give a preliminary vote count, Biden became convinced that any further talk of a filibuster was counterproductive. There were actually more votes to defeat the nomination than there were to sustain a filibuster. This was in large measure because moderates and Southerners had made it clear to Biden that it was easier to vote against the nomination than it was to appear to be stalling it.

After looking at the vote count, he listened to our recommendation about where the outside groups should target their efforts. Biden seemed less interested in the targeting than in making it very clear about what he didn't want the groups to do. "I care a lot less about who they target than in what they say. If we have any more threatening of Senators, like they did Pat Moynihan, we're dead. With friends like that, we don't need enemies."

Most of the meeting was spent arguing over when and how to frame the debate against the nomination. Donilon felt strongly we had to move to making the case against Bork. "We cannot simply depend on the advice and consent argument''—that it was appropriate for the Senate to consider Bork's philosophy.

D'Anna agreed: ''We have to say what it is we don't like about his philosophy.''

''I know what I don't like,'' Biden said. ''We can begin with all the landmark Supreme Court decisions he has criticized, but I don't know how to say that without further complicating the fairness issue.''

The risk was obvious. As soon as Biden began to make the case against Bork, the Administration would jump on us not only for delaying the hearing and coming out against the nomination but for attacking their nominee.

Biden concluded the meeting: ''I'm willing to revisit this issue when we meet on Friday to go over the draft of the ABA speech.'' He was scheduled to give a major address on the Bork nomination to the American Bar Association on August 11 in California. He had made it clear that he wanted this speech to be based in large part upon his earlier address to the Senate on advice and consent. ''We ought to see if there is some way to do what Tom suggests without being unfair.''

The rest of that week Biden followed through on the strategy we agreed to on Monday. On Tuesday, he announced that he would not change the hearing date for the reason he had discussed with us. He made it clear, however, that he set early October as a date for the committee to report the nomination to the floor. He met twice with Cranston, Kennedy, and Inouye. They agreed with Biden's assessment of the committee strategy and the notion of discouraging any further talk of a filibuster.

In addition to these political chores, Biden had decided to spend the bulk of July and August learning as much as he could about Robert Bork. He did so through a series of intensive briefings with outside experts.

Once he had determined the issue areas, he directed staff director Diana Huffman and Ken Bass, a Washington attorney who headed up his group of outside advisers, to assemble the best experts for a meeting. A briefing notebook was prepared in advance, and the materials and the experts were made available to other members of the committee after the Biden meeting was finished.

By the first week in August, briefings had been concluded with such eminent scholars as Philip Kurland of the University of Chicago on Bork's view of the role of precedent and Floyd Abrams on the judge's view of the First Amendment and freedom of expression. Similar briefings were conducted on antitrust, privacy, and the Saturday Night Massacre.

Biden, like Bork, was a conversationalist. He benefited most from the spirited exchange of ideas as a means of honing his own approach to a problem. Biden had clearly not settled on his ''approach'' to the Bork nomination. The briefings were conducted like a seminar in which Biden, as the instructor, called on the experts and then cross-examined them.

On August 6 a briefing was scheduled for a discussion of the Law and Economics movement and Bork's jurisprudence. The briefing was to be conducted by Robert Litan, a lawyer and economist at the Brookings Institution, and Chris Schroeder, a professor at Duke Law School. Litan was a friend of Biden, who had advised him on economic policy issues for several years. Schroeder was a consultant to the committee, who had been brought on to advise the committee on the nomination of Bernard Seigan to the U.S. Court of Appeals for the Ninth Circuit. Seigan, a friend of Meese, was a controversial nominee because his jurisprudential views were even more conservative than Bork's. Seigan apparently supported a view of the due process clause of the Fourteenth Amendment that was not unlike that of the "nine old men" who had frustrated Roosevelt's New Deal legislation: namely, the due process clause prohibited Congress from passing economic reforms that interfered with the constitutional right of employers and employees to contract with one another.

Schroeder had prepared a lengthy memorandum explaining the Law and Economics movement, the so-called Chicago School and its relationship to Seigan's views. Biden wanted to explore the same issues with respect to Bork.

Litan briefly explained the free market economic theories espoused by Aaron Director and the other members of the Chicago School. Schroeder moved directly into their application to Law and Economics and Bork's views. Biden was using this briefing as he had used the others—to try to translate Bork's writings on the subject into something that "average people could understand."

He interrupted: "Does Bork have an ideology?"

Schroeder quoted from a memorandum he had prepared: "If 'ideology' connotes a coherent set of beliefs and preferences that both shape the way questions about the world are framed and what answers are given, Law and Economics fully qualifies as ideology.

"Bork describes his exposure to Aaron Director, one of the founders of the Law and Economics movement at the University of Chicago, as a 'kind of conversion experience.' "

Biden was taken by the phrase: "A conversion experience? What did he mean by that?"

"Well, I don't think he meant it strictly in a religious sense, but in Bork's own words, he discovered 'a social science which suddenly begins to give [him] an organizing way of looking at the world that [he'd] never seen before, and it does make a deep impression, and it does have the effect of making you see the world just differently, altogether differently.' "

Schroeder proceeded to elaborate on Director's philosophy: "Law and Economics adherents believe that providing the widest possible range of individual choice is the best way to run society. Some in the Chicago

School—for example, Seigan—go so far as to argue that the Constitution restricts what Congress can do in this sphere. This is essentially the position the Court took in striking down the New Deal legislation. Bork rejects this view. He believes, as long as Congress acts within its sphere, it can restrict the market."

Biden was familiar with Seigan. "But they do agree on the role of the courts?"

"Correct. Bork and the rest believe courts have a very limited role in enforcing the contract that the legislature has made—the statute or deal made with the American people in the Constitution."

Biden pressed Schroeder: "Every legislative act is simply a contract or deal made by the people's representatives at one particular point in time and, like a business contract, must be read literally?"

"Correct!" Schroeder responded.

"Therefore, the Constitution or the Civil Rights Law of 1965," Biden continued, "are no different from, say, a public works bill. They have no animating spirit."

Schroeder paused. "True, but it's really more fundamental than that, because of the Law and Economics School view of human nature."

Litan broke in: "You mean because they view human actions like you would expect economists to?"

Schroeder agreed, because for these practitioners of the dismal science "individual choice is protected, because human ends and aspirations are held to be essentially subjective and arbitrary matters. To quote Bork, 'There is no principled way to prefer any claimed human value to any other.'

"All that consumers, or citizens, can possibly have is 'wants,' because there are no values, ends, or aspirations that deserve respect independently of someone wanting them, because all such entitlements are merely subjective and arbitrary. There can be no 'needs,' no 'merit considerations,' no 'inherent human dignity'."

The safest thing for a judge to do is to look at the Constitution or a statute and interpret the bare bones of the document as if it were a contract. A judge must not attempt to choose between or impose any of those values.

Biden seized on the notion that a judge could not recognize "inherent human dignity." "Where do notions of condemning prejudice or extolling human dignity fit in?"

"They don't, unless they are incorporated in a specific reference in a statute or the Constitution, and if they don't, the rights simply cannot be enforced by the courts. Discriminatory prejudices, animus toward immigrants, tolerance for dissenting views, compassion for victims of poverty all stand on a par as arbitrary."

Biden winced. "It sounds pretty cold and inhuman."

Schroeder continued to elaborate: "In his *Indiana Law Review* article, he found it impossible to distinguish between the freedom of a husband and wife 'to have sexual relations without fear of unwanted children' from the desire of an electric utility company to be free of a smoke pollution ordinance. He writes, 'Freedom cannot be created (courts creating new constitutional rights against government or expanding old ones); it is merely shifted from a larger group to a smaller group'."

Biden translated, "Taking away rights from the majority and giving them to the minority."

"Correct."

"And judges would just arbitrarily impose their [personal] values of human dignity on the majority."

Schroeder explained that, according to Bork, "In order to draw a sharp line between judicial power and democratic authority" the judge must adhere strictly to the original intent of the drafters of the statute or the Constitution. Bork believes that "an observer must be able to say whether or not the judge's result follows fairly from premises given by an authoritative, external source and is not merely a question of taste or opinion."

In an op-ed by Schroeder published in the *Los Angeles Times* a week later, he explained that Bork believed that "we need something to prevent judges from tyrannizing the rest of us with *their* arbitrary values. . . . He has remained a firm adherent of the Chicago School of Economics . . . that posits the ability of *laissez-faire,* with minimal governmental regulation, to provide maximum 'consumer want satisfaction.' This idea is epitomized in a Latin phrase *De gustibus non est disputandum*—taste cannot be debated."

Bork's views were austere, to say the least, but his view of the judicial function was by no means unique or even extreme. As other opponents of Bork's views were quick to point out, it was from a very respectable school of jurisprudence. For example, Thomas Grey of Stanford, in a 1975 article with the revealing title "Do We Have an Unwritten Constitution," pointed out that Bork's views and New Deal liberal Hugo Black's were similar in that "constitutional doctrines based on sources other than the explicit commands of the written constitution" were illegitimate.

Grey quotes scholar Hans Linde to the effect that "The judicial responsibility begins and ends with determining the present scope and meaning of a decision that the nation, at an earlier time, articulated and enacted into constitutional text. . . ."

Biden continued to try to bring Schroeder's abstractions down to something lay people could understand. "So to Bork and his friends there are just two choices for a judge when he decides a case: external sources, which are the literal words of a statute or the Constitution, on the one hand, and his prejudices on the other. He should only choose the former."

Schroeder finished the thought: "And all external sources are ultimately compressed into exactly one type. Wills, contracts, statutes, and Constitutions are basically the same."

Biden's eyes brightened. He was beginning to develop a potent line of attack. "So the Constitution is essentially a contract that should be narrowly construed—nothing more, nothing less. It has no spirit, it is not a reflection of the hopes and aspirations of the American people."

Schroeder added a little historical color: "The idea of Chief Justice Marshall, in *McCullough* v. *Maryland,* that Supreme Court Justices must remember that it is 'a constitution they are expounding,' becomes at best a meaningless statement and at worst a dangerous one for someone with Bork's views."

"Chris, how does he deal with *Brown* v. *Board*?"

"I'm sure he supports *Brown,* but he does it because he believes that the original intent of the drafters of the Fourteenth Amendment intended that result."

"But they didn't!" Biden interrupted.

"I don't know, but I'm sure that he would not explain his support for *Brown* because of some ennobling notion of the Constitution or because the values of our country require it. To Bork any such vision is mere taste or opinion."

Biden saw the irony of the Borkian view of the Constitution—on its Bicentennial in September 1987. "So the Constitution is just a lifeless contract."

Schroeder got the drift. "The great phrases of the document, 'due process,' 'equal protection of the law,' 'privileges and immunities,' are read devoid of any animating power or sense of purpose."

Biden brought the thought down to earth: "A Constitution without life or spirit."

Biden was enthusiastic as we ended the briefing. For the first time he was genuinely warming to the subject of Robert Bork and his judicial philosophy. Biden and I were constantly haunted by the experience of the Rehnquist fight, when Biden attempted to engage Rehnquist on jurisprudential issues and lost the public's attention in the process. At the end of this briefing with Litan and Schroeder, Biden was beginning to see a line of attack that might resonate with lay people.

As we stood up to leave, I explained to him that the White House had that week released its Blue Book on Bork. Chris Schroeder explained, "It attempts to take Bork's judicial decisions and an analysis of Powell, Harlan, Black, and Frankfurter, and show that he is in that tradition."

"How can that be?"

"Well, it's a stretch," I pointed out.

Jeff Peck, a young Washington lawyer who had just joined our staff, set out a few specific inaccuracies in the Blue Book, including a quote from a news story in the *Los Angeles Times* that made it appear as if the newspaper endorsed the nomination when actually it had editorialized against Bork that same day.

"I want a response to this prepared immediately," Biden said. He proceeded to talk for almost ten minutes about what he wanted in the report, referring back to several of the briefings he had had with experts during the past two weeks.

As he was leaving, he smiled at me. "This may be exactly what we've been waiting for. They've finally made a mistake. They have given us a very legitimate opening to begin to make the case against Bork. Robert Bork is *not* Lewis Powell."

After Biden left, I turned to Schroeder and Peck to announce the obvious: "You guys are going to have to write this thing."

As Peck recalls that moment years later, "I came into the meeting thinking we would write a ten-page memo and ended the meeting, after Biden dictated what he wanted in the response, realizing that he wanted a book."

Peck, along with Schroeder, became the real workhorses for Biden in the Bork effort, in the end never leaving Biden's side during the hearings. At this point they hardly knew each other, much less Biden. Peck was absolutely tireless, even-tempered and with a delightful sense of humor.

As the three of us stood alone in Biden's conference room, Peck reminded me of an incident the week before when I had reviewed a memorandum he had done summarizing Bork's criticism of Supreme Court decisions: "Geez, Jeff, this is amazing. I didn't know he'd said all these things. Why don't you reorganize this memorandum into subject areas—you know, 'civil rights,' 'privacy,' etc., and just include a sentence with the holding in the case and a copy of Bork's quote about the case."

The list was astonishing. Under the heading "Race & Voting" Bork criticized a 1948 decision forbidding enforcement of racially restrictive covenants; the 1962 and 1964 decisions establishing the doctrine of one-man-one-vote, and the 1966 decision upholding the constitutionality of the 1966 Voting Rights Act. Under "Privacy" Peck listed the 1965 *Griswold* decision, *Roe* v. *Wade,* and the 1942 *Skinner* decision, in which the court prohibited sterilization of certain criminals. Under "Religious and Ethnic Minorities in public education," he listed *Pierce* v. *Society of Sisters,* the 1925 decision striking down an Oregon statute, which in effect prohibited private education and *Meyer* v. *Nebraska,* a 1922 decision striking down a Nebraska law prohibiting the teaching of German.

The next morning, Donilon, D'Anna, and I again met Biden at his home in Wilmington to work on the ABA speech. When we arrived, he was on the phone with Caddell, using Schroeder's memo to explain Bork's jurisprudential views.

As we started into the draft of what we had prepared for his speech to the ABA, he was in a totally different frame of mind from earlier in the week. He kept cutting back on the advice and consent portion of the speech.

"I agree with Tom and Vince now. I want to make room in this speech to say something about Bork's jurisprudence. I just read Peck's memo. Let's use some of that.''

We pored over Peck's memo. Biden was also taken by Kurland's briefing on Bork's attitude about overturning old precedents. Kurland pointed to testimony by Bork before the Senate Judiciary Committee in 1981, when he had suggested reconsidering ''dozens of cases'' in which the Court had wrongly applied the Constitution. Biden kept asking whether we thought the cases in Peck's memo were the ''dozens of cases'' that Bork wanted to reconsider when he was on the court. By the time it was over, Biden was on the phone with Peck, carefully summarizing the actual holding (decision) in these and in other landmark cases and the precise quotes from Bork. With each case, Biden's face brightened. By the time it was over, Biden had turned Peck's dry legal memorandum into a rhetorical gem.

Three thousand miles away and four days later, he delivered the speech to almost a thousand lawyers in a hotel ballroom in San Francisco. Ted Kaufman, Biden's brother Jim, and his son Beau stood at the back of the room. The speech went on for almost an hour, and a few in the room seemed to be getting restless. But as the Senator went through the Supreme Court decisions and Bork's comments, the stunned silence was punctuated by gasps. Biden had carefully constructed the language so that all that he gave was the holding in the case and Bork's comment:

''One. *Griswold* v. *Connecticut,* 1965.

''The Court struck down a state law making it a crime for a doctor to advise married couples about the use of birth control.

''Judge Bork has described it as an 'unprincipled decision' and stated that there is nothing in the Constitution to distinguish between the desire of a husband and wife to be free 'to have sexual relations without fear of unwanted children' and the desire of an electric utility company to be free of a smoke-pollution ordinance.

''Two. *Skinner* v. *Oklahoma,* 1942.

''The Court struck down a law authorizing the involuntary sterilization of criminals.

''Judge Bork has said that *Skinner* was 'as improper and as intellectually empty as *Griswold.*'

''Three. *Shelley* v. *Kraemer,* in 1948.

''The Court held that the Fourteenth Amendment forbids state courts from enforcing racially restrictive covenants.

''Judge Bork has written that he 'doubted' that it was possible to find a 'neutral principle' which would 'support' such a decision by the Supreme Court.

''Four. *Baker* v. *Carr,* in 1962, and five, *Reynolds* v. *Sims* in 1964.

''The Court adopted the one-man-one-vote principle. Judge Bork concluded that 'on no reputable theory of constitutional adjudication was there an excuse for the doctrine' of one-man-one-vote 'imposed' by the Warren Court.''

By the time Biden got to one-man-one-vote, the reaction was a louder murmuring in the audience. These lawyers were as surprised as any of us when they heard all of Bork's comments on landmark decisions listed together. Biden went on to list thirteen more cases.

He concluded:

''The right of married couples to buy contraceptives, one-man-one-vote, the Voting Rights Act . . . Is it true, as Judge Bork suggests, that the Constitution does not protect them?

''Racially restrictive covenants, the sterilization of criminals . . . Is it true, as Judge Bork has written, that the Constitution does not forbid them?

''We cannot be certain that these are among the dozens of precedents that Judge Bork might vote to overturn. But we can be certain that if Judge Bork has meant what he's written for the past thirty years—that had he been Justice Bork during the past thirty years and had his view prevailed—America would be a fundamentally different place than it is today. We would live in a very different America than we do now.''

It was the high point of the speech and a powerful catch line, which caught the fancy of the crowd.

Kaufman recalls, ''The last time I had seen anything like this was at Atlantic City. The crowd rose spontaneously and burst into a long-standing ovation.'' The press swarmed around him after the speech, demanding that press secretary Larry Rasky supply them with copies, because, as usual, Biden had tinkered with the prepared text. Rasky snapped back, ''Didn't they teach you to take notes in journalism school?''

Even without the text the coverage the next day was excellent. The *Washington Post* covered the speech in a front-page piece. It led off with Biden's catch line about America being a very different place had Judge Bork's views prevailed. It was the first unabashedly positive piece for Biden in the Bork struggle.

Finally, forty days after the nomination and almost a month after he had let his opposition be known, Biden had settled on a formulation of his opposition that resonated at least with lawyers and the *Washington Post*. He was finally beginning to frame the national debate on whether Robert Bork should be confirmed. Of course, it was one thing to convince a crowd of upper middle class lawyers; it was quite another to make the case to average Americans who had never read a law case in their lives.

The next day President Reagan was scheduled to address the nation. Although Joe Biden had begun August with the burden of considerable negative press on his *Philadelphia Inquirer* quote, the leak from the meeting with the civil rights groups, and the controversy over the delay in the hearings, Ronald Reagan had an even greater burden. The Iran–Contra scandal had severely damaged his standing in the polls. That day the *Wall Street Journal* reported that the President was "deeply troubled by the persistent finding in polls that most Americans don't think he is telling the whole truth about his role in the Iran–Contra scandal." His own pollster told him that 60 percent of Americans did not believe him.

White House communications director Tom Griscom was in charge of crafting the message for the speech that evening. He explained his thinking at the time: "We've got to get the President's message for Iran–Contra and put that to bed and get on with the program."

As Griscom worked on the speech, "we really looked at the Bork nomination as a plus. . . ." He and his colleagues in the White House felt Reagan would win that fight in the fall and that the fight would actually help pull the President out of the doldrums in the national polls. In his speech, the President was supposed to admit some mistakes in the Iran–Contra scandal but to look to the future. In Griscom's words, "Here's where we go from here."

The speech would announce three major initiatives for the fall: two foreign—democracy in Nicaragua and a new arms control treaty with the Russians—and one domestic, confirming Robert Bork. So the idea behind the speech was "This President is back in charge. . . ."

It was a short speech and over half of it was devoted to Reagan's goals for the remainder of his term. The Bork nomination was the first item on his agenda. Put simply, his message was that Robert Bork was the best and the brightest. It was to be a battle over the judge's credentials, and on those terms he would win hands down.

The President never mentioned any of Bork's positions. He was a "brilliant scholar." Borrowing directly from the Blue Book, Reagan pointed out that Bork had never had a single opinion reversed by the Supreme Court on appeal. He would be "an important intellectual addition to the Court."

By August 12, the Bork lines had become "boiler plate," rote. Reagan's address to the nation as it related to the nomination was a distillation of what he had said in announcing the nomination on July 1 and in later speeches that summer. The July 29 speech to the National Law Enforcement Council was a good example of how Griscom was marketing the message and especially relying on the Blue Book. Not only was Bork "brilliant" and an apostle of "judicial restraint," but (quoting Lloyd Cutler) the President predicted Bork would be a judge in the tradition of Holmes, Brandeis, Frankfurter, Stewart, and, of course, Powell. "If I could appoint a whole Supreme Court of Felix Frankfurters, I would," Reagan boasted. "And I've taken a step, I think, with Robert Bork."

For Will Ball, the strategy and the message were quite simple and straightforward: "Our role was to show [Bork] wasn't an extremist [but] open-minded, that he enjoyed intellectual intensity. . . . The idea was to set forth

Bork's record, not to engage in a political battle.'' By ''Bork's record,'' Ball undoubtedly meant the record laid out in the Blue Book, which was essentially his judicial record, not his speeches and articles.

Tom Korologos's goals were a bit more stylistic. He wanted to ''humanize'' Bork, to show he ''didn't have horns,'' to show he wasn't ''a right-wing kook.'' So Korologos acquiesced in Bork's desire to meet extensively with the press in interviews. ''But we had two criteria: he was not to talk about anything specific as far as legal issues or cases; he was to talk about his life and times and his favorite color. . . .''

Although pleased with Biden's speech, Ralph Neas and the civil rights groups still preferred a more direct attack on Bork's jurisprudence. They intended to spend August preparing detailed reports on Bork, to be released on the eve of the hearings in early September—at the same time Senator Kennedy delivered another more specific attack. Biden viewed the Peck and Schroeder response to the Blue Book as *our* report, to be prepared independently from what the groups and Senator Kennedy were doing. The Administration plan was that neither the White House nor Bork himself would respond to charges until the hearings.

Brad Reynolds was a part of that strategy, although he now regrets it. ''We did not perceive the political debate going on in the July–August time frame as having the kind of impact that would carry over into the hearings.'' He now concedes that what the Administration did in August to counter the substantive debate that Biden began at the ABA, ''was too little, too late. We did not use the brunt of the White House on the matter. One, because there was a miscalculation as to how serious the problem was, and, two . . . as we saw it, the strategy that was most effective was to save our big guns until later.''

One ''big gun'' was, of course, Bork himself. The White House and Reynolds were not too concerned about what they were hearing from Biden, the groups, and Kennedy. ''Part of the mind-set is that all of this is going to fall away when you have the candidate up there, and he's going to say what he's going to say. The White House was very confident about it. . . . I was [only] somewhat confident about it. Bob thought that if they just get a chance to hear him. Remember, we all looked at it as prime-time TV, not just news bites, so there was a sense that you would be able to reach the mass audience that was being bombarded with the man himself in the hearings, and in the final analysis that would be the best offensive.''

Griscom probably spoke for many in the White House when he referred to the August period, not as a time when a very calculated message was being communicated, but as a time of relaxation for the President and his staff. ''I was mentally and physically exhausted after having lived through the Iran–Contra stuff. And my mind at that point was only peripherally focused on

Bob Bork, and I think we had basically decided we needed a little time to catch our breath. This is a September problem.''

Furthermore, Culvahouse and other staffers at the White House were not focused solely on Bork, either. They were implementing what was known as Baker's grand or ''geopolitical'' strategy for 1987 and 1988:

- Survive the Iran–Contra hearings without impeachment proceedings;
- Conclude a major arms control agreement with the Soviets, ultimately the INF (Intermediate Nuclear Force) Treaty; and
- Elect a Republican President.

''There was a very conservative notion that we had to put the President back to where he had been (before Iran–Contra). Anything that got in the way of that was a problem.''

In early August Bork looked winnable to Culvahouse, despite the ''turf battles'' in the Administration. Their strategy seemed to be working. Besides, the White House was confident that Bork would be a good witness in the hearings. It was clear to Culvahouse then, and even more so two years later, that neither the Bork nomination nor anything else should be allowed to put the overall strategy at risk. ''The closer we tied the President to Bork (through personal speeches or personal lobbying) in an uphill battle, the more dangerous it was for the President.'' In short, ''The timing was poor for Bob Bork.''

There was some uneasiness about the President taking off August, but no one was calling upon him to speak out in Bork's behalf during the recess. Granted, there was grumbling in the troops, but on the whole things looked pretty rosy to Reynolds and Culvahouse.

The President, the Great Communicator, would take off August. It's not what Andrew Jackson or Franklin Roosevelt did when they decided to shape the future of the Supreme Court, but perhaps this was a different age. Besides, in this battle, Ronald Reagan was not the main protagonist. Robert Bork was.

Skeptics and those who already opposed Bork were not about to take August for granted. Skeptics on the committee, Republican Arlen Specter of Pennsylvania, Democrats Patrick Leahy of Vermont, and Dennis DeConcini of Arizona intended to spend that month trying to get to know ''the real Bob Bork'' and square what they learned about him with the portrait the Administration painted of him in the Blue Book. Biden, although happy with the ABA speech, wanted to spend August trying to figure out how to explain Robert Bork and his views to ordinary Americans.

CHAPTER 8

YOU KNOW IT'S AN UNWRITTEN RIGHT

ON AUGUST 24 Biden was to have a briefing by Charles Abernathy of Georgetown Law School, an expert on civil rights law. I had warned him that Biden, however, might be more interested in the deeper jurisprudential questions raised by the Administration's Blue Book. Was Bork's philosophy really similar to that of Lewis Powell, Felix Frankfurter, and John Harlan?

The due process clauses of the Fifth and Fourteenth Amendments state that no person shall "be deprived of life, liberty, or property without due process of law." Abernathy explained that to understand how Bork compares to men like Frankfurter and Harlan one has to understand how the Court and in particular these two men interpreted those majestic words.

Biden now regularly included Vince D'Anna in our meetings. D'Anna, a nonlawyer, had worked with Biden since Biden first entered politics in 1970 on the New Castle County Council. Biden found him valuable in meetings of this kind because his practical, down-to-earth approach to politics assured that the discussions would not get so abstract as to lose meaning to average Americans. In short, D'Anna, bright and politically savvy as he was, was critical to Biden's overall goal of translating what Bork stood for into something average Americans could understand.

Abernathy understood that and pitched his briefing to a layman's level: "The Supreme Court has created two due process doctrines under the Fifth and Fourteenth Amendments.

"*Substantive due process* sets out [basic] liberty and property rights upon which the state may not infringe—for example, the right to privacy. *Procedural due process* means that no matter what the property right or liberty, whatever its source, the government may not take away or limit the right unless it does so in a procedurally correct manner. For example, there must be notice and a hearing.

"The controversy with Bork is over substantive due process not procedural. His views on the latter are conventional."

Between 1905 and 1937 the Supreme Court relied upon the substantive due process doctrine to identify certain rights as individual, but, as Abernathy pointed out, to "in effect protect entrenched economic interests." It was this doctrine that bedeviled Franklin Roosevelt's New Deal legislation. Wage and hour legislation and other social welfare legislation was struck down because they interfered with the employees' "right to work" or the employer's "right to contract." The theory was that an employee had the right to work for as little per hour as he wanted.

Liberals in those years were using the Borkian argument that judges were making up rights and imposing their own arbitrary values to stop the democratic process. At the forefront of that movement was Hugo Black, a Roosevelt appointee to the Supreme Court. Abernathy explained, "That's why so much of Bork's writing is steeped in Black."

D'Anna got the picture immediately. "So Bork can just say, 'I'm using the argument you liberals used in the 1930s, why aren't you guys consistent, why don't you want a very narrow role for the court'?"

"That's right."

D'Anna continued, "But how could there be this massive expansion of rights in the 1940s, 50s, and 60s largely brought about by the FDR appointees if they were enemies of substantive due process?"

For one thing, Abernathy explained, except for Black, Felix Frankfurter and the other Roosevelt appointees did not totally reject substantive due process, and even in Black's case it is not entirely clear that he totally rejected the doctrine. In the early part of this century, while the Court was using the substantive due process doctrine to strike down progressive legislation because it interfered with "rights to employment" and "rights to contract," it was also articulating other individual rights.

For example, in 1922 the Supreme Court, in the decision of *Meyer* v. *Nebraska,* struck down a state law that made it a crime to teach any foreign language in a public or parochial school. The Court held that there was also a substantive "right of the individual . . . to acquire useful knowledge, to marry, establish a home and bring up children . . . and generally to enjoy the privileges long recognized at common law as essential to the orderly pursuit of happiness by free men."

Three years later in *Pierce* v. *Society of Sisters* the Supreme Court struck down a state law that required all children between the ages of eight and sixteen be sent to a public school. The Court reasoned that the statute "unreasonably interferes with the liberty of parents and guardians to direct the upbringing and education of children under their control. . . . The child is not the mere creature of the state; those who nurture him and direct his destiny have the right, coupled with the high duty, to recognize and prepare him for additional obligations."

These decisions predated the Roosevelt revolution on the Court, but they were well-accepted precedents even after Black and his brothers joined the

Court. Indeed there is no evidence that they would have agreed with Bork that *Meyer* and *Pierce* were "wrongly decided." The Supreme Court had, in effect, decided that the state could not deny parents the right to make fundamental decisions about how to raise their children—whether they could be taught a foreign language or whether they could attend a private school of their choice.

D'Anna understood the political implications immediately. "This is powerful stuff. You mean that Bork doesn't believe the Supreme Court was right in protecting these rights of parents?"

Abernathy agreed. Biden smiled.

In 1942 in the case of *Skinner* v. *Oklahoma,* the Supreme Court was faced with the question of whether the state could decide whether someone could have children at all. Now with the new Roosevelt appointees, Black and Frankfurter on board, the Court had to decide whether substantive due process was violated by an Oklahoma statute that mandated involuntary sterilization for any person convicted of three or more crimes "amounting to felonies involving moral turpitude."

The Court struck down the statute, explaining, "We are dealing here with legislation which involves one of the basic rights of man. Marriage and procreation are fundamental to the very existence and survival of the race. The power to sterilize, if exercised, may have subtle, far-reaching, and devastating effects. In evil or reckless hands it can cause races or types which are inimical to the dominant group to wither and disappear."

In light of what was going on in Nazi Germany at that very moment, the language was powerful and unforgettable. Black and Frankfurter were joined in the opinion by Justice Douglas.

Bork found *Skinner* "intellectually empty."

Abernathy explained it was these three cases that formed one of the doctrinal underpinnings for a significant expansion of individual liberties during the next few decades. In each case the Supreme Court found in the substance of the liberty protected by the due process clause certain "fundamental rights":

- The right to stop a government from outlawing the use of birth control by married couples in 1965 in the case of *Griswold* v. *Connecticut*;
- The right to an abortion in 1973 in *Roe* v. *Wade*;
- The right to stop the city of Cleveland from using its zoning power to exclude children from certain areas and thereby prevent a grandmother from taking an orphaned grandson into her home, in *Moore* v. *City of East Cleveland*. That 1977 opinion was authored by Justice Powell.
- The right to marry, when states interfered with that right: for poor people in 1976, in the case of *Zablocki* v. *Redhail*, and for prisoners in 1987, in an opinion written by Reagan appointee Sandra Day O'Connor in the case of *Turner* v. *Safley*.

D'Anna focused immediately on the *Griswold* case. "So he doesn't believe there is a right to privacy that protects a married couple to buy contraceptives?"

Biden took over: "Remember we used some of these cases in the ABA speech. But Bork particularly loves to criticize the *Griswold* case. I guess because, if you don't have *Griswold,* you can't get to *Roe*. You see, the Supreme Court bases its decision in *Roe* on *Griswold.* Without even getting into the abortion issue, listen to what he says about the contraceptive issue."

After the ABA speech, he had asked Jeffrey Peck to get him every statement Bork had ever made against Griswold. He read them to D'Anna as if he were reading an indictment:

"*Griswold* . . . is an unprincipled decision, both in the way in which it derives a new constitutional right and in the way it defines that right, or rather fails to define it. . . . The truth is that the court could not reach its result in *Griswold* through principle."

The result in *Griswold* could not "have been reached by interpretation of the Constitution."

"I don't think there is a supportable method of constitutional reasoning underlying the *Griswold* decision."

All the "sexual freedom cases"—that is, *Roe* and *Griswold*—represent the Supreme Court imposing "upper middle class, college education, east-west coast morality" on the rest of us. By implication sexual freedom was an upper middle class value that the rest of America did not share.

D'Anna reacted viscerally: "Bingo! This guy really doesn't think the Court should protect middle class couples from buying birth control."

Biden laughed. "Could you imagine what would happen if I went down to Gerardo's [a middle-class restaurant in Wilmington D'Anna and Biden liked to frequent] and told a group of couples there after a softball game that I was taking away their right to use birth control?"

D'Anna responded, "They'd go crazy." Then he paused. "This guy's in trouble."

Biden concluded, "I agree."

It wasn't simply that Bork was tampering with rights of child rearing, procreation, and birth control that average Americans had come to take for granted. Bork's jurisprudence impinged upon fundamental notions of liberty deep in our national psyche. This became more obvious as we delved deeper into how Justices Frankfurter and Harlan handled this difficult question of whether the Supreme Court could recognize expanded individual liberties under the Constitution.

Frankfurter and Black had a long-standing disagreement about how the Supreme Court should extend individual liberties. Black was, like Bork, preoccupied with how to avoid judges arbitrarily imposing their own values upon the country when interpreting the due process clause. Bork, unlike Black, lambasted the earlier substantive due process decisions, which expanded individual liberties and were unrelated to the New Deal—for example, *Meyer, Pierce,* and *Skinner*. But the most important difference was that Black did have an aggressive theory for expanding individual liberties without risking judicial abuse. Black believed that all of the Bill of Rights, the first ten amendments to the Constitution, should be applied to the states and local governments as well as to the federal government.

Black reasoned that by including the due process clause in the Fourteenth Amendment, the drafters intended that the whole Bill of Rights, originally written as a restriction on the federal government, were intended to restrict the state and local governments as well. He would "incorporate" those rights into the Fourteenth Amendment. So, for Black, the "liberty" clause of the Fourteenth Amendment had a precise meaning. It meant the Bill of Rights.

Black and Justice Douglas, another Roosevelt appointee, agreed that "liberty" under the due process clause meant the Bill of Rights, except that Douglas did not view the explicit rights mentioned in the first ten amendments as an exclusive list, whereas Black did. Douglas in his majority opinion in *Griswold* said the right to privacy "emanated" from the "penumbras" cast by the Bill of Rights. Said another way, he implied the right from the Bill of Rights. Black saw the literal words of the ten amendments as an exclusive list which did not include a generalized right to privacy, and he dissented.

Frankfurter and Harlan had a less wooden approach to the meaning of "liberty" under the Fourteenth Amendment. Frankfurter did not simply transplant the ten amendments into the Fourteenth Amendment. He looked to another giant of our jurisprudence in determining what the word "liberty" meant—Benjamin Cardozo. In 1934, Cardozo had written of those rights as being ones "so rooted in the traditions and conscience of our people as to be ranked as fundamental" and three years later as rights "implicit in the concept of ordered liberty."

It was Cardozo's notion of "fundamental rights" that Bork found most troublesome: "The choice of 'fundamental values' by the Court cannot be justified. Where constitutional materials do not clearly specify the value to be preferred, there is no principled way to prefer any claimed human value to any other. The judge must stick close to the text and the history, and their fair implications, and not construct new rights."

Cardozo's and Frankfurter's notion that the due process clause has "independent potency," was anathema to Robert Bork. It was much too unpredictable.

Biden interrupted Abernathy's presentation: "Bork has a point though. The standards are vague?"

"Yes, but as Frankfurter pointed out, it is the essence of what it is to be a judge to make some decisions of this kind. Judges are not some kind of automaton. They have to judge."

I later found language in a Frankfurter opinion that made just that point and sent it to Biden in a memo: "[t]o believe that this judicial exercise of judgment could be avoided by freezing 'due process of law' at some fixed stage of time or thought is to suggest that the most important aspect of constitutional adjudication is a function for inanimate machines and not for judges. . . ."

Harlan also based his notions of what the due process clause meant on Cardozo's notions of "fundamental rights" and rights "implicit in the concept of ordered liberty." Ironically, Harlan's most dramatic exposition on inherent or unenumerated rights was addressed to the same Connecticut anticontraceptive statute that Bork felt so adamantly was outside the province of the Supreme Court to strike down.

Griswold was not the first case in which the Supreme Court considered the constitutionality of the Connecticut antibirth-control statute. In 1961, four years earlier, the Court had rejected for procedural reasons a challenge to the statute in the case of *Poe* v. *Ullman.* Harlan dissented from the rejection of the appeal, arguing that the statute was "an intolerable and unjustifiable invasion of privacy in the conduct of the most intimate concerns of an individual's personal life."

His dissent in that case stands today as one of the most eloquent expressions of the notion of fundamental rights, rights nowhere specifically enumerated in the Constitution—the very opposite of Bork's jurisprudence. Listen to how Justice Harlan would have responded to Bork:

> Due process has not been reduced to any formula; its content cannot be determined by reference to any code. The best that can be said is that through the course of this Court's decisions it has represented the balance which our Nation, built upon postulates of respect for the liberty of the individual, has struck between that liberty and the demands of organized society. . . . That tradition is a living thing. A decision of this Court which radically departs from it could not long survive, while a decision which builds on what has survived is likely to be sound. No formula could serve as a substitute, in this area, for judgment and restraint . . . there is no 'mechanical yardstick' no 'mechanical answer'."

Are Cardozo, Frankfurter, and Harlan right? What are the sources of these rights? Bork is what is known as an originalist. He insisted on finding the source of any right in the explicit language of the Constitution or the original intent of the framers in some more vague or open-ended language of the Constitution.

As Professor Grey explained, for Cardozo, Frankfurter, and Harlan, where a case arises under the due process clause, "the broad textual provisions are seen as sources of legitimacy for judicial development and explication of basic shared national values. These values may be seen as permanent and universal features of human social arrangements—natural law principles—as they typically were in the eighteenth and nineteenth centuries."

Biden was thumbing a copy of the Constitution as Abernathy discussed Bork's view of the due process clause. "So you're suggesting that if Bork is concerned about original intent of the framers, he would have to be an advocate of natural law?"

"Correct, the framers were all steeped in natural law."

Then Biden turned to the Bill of Rights. "How does Bork deal with the Ninth Amendment?" He read from the Constitution for D'Anna's benefit: " 'The enumeration in this Constitution of certain rights'—in other words, Vince, the Bill of Rights—'shall not be construed to deny or disparage others retained by the people.' So the framers made it clear that they never intended the Bill of Rights to be an exclusive list. Didn't they?"

Abernathy explained that Bork's view is that the framers' intent with respect to the Ninth Amendment is so obscure that judges should ignore the provision. "When the meaning of a provision . . . is unknown, the judge has in effect nothing more than a water blot on the document before him . . . and his proper course is to ignore it."

The framers' intent is simply not ambiguous. The Constitution drafted in Philadelphia in 1787 did not contain a Bill of Rights. Opponents of the Constitution in the ratifying conventions based their opposition primarily upon its absence. George Mason, the author of Virginia's Declaration of Rights in 1776, opposed the Constitution for that reason. John Adams and Thomas Jefferson both had similar concerns.

Within months after they left Philadelphia to secure ratification in the states, the Federalists realized they had made a critical error in omitting a Bill of Rights from the Constitution. It was rapidly becoming a powerful argument in the states against ratification. How could these demigods have made such a mistake? Ironically it was because of what both the Federalists and anti-Federalists agreed upon about the relationship of the individual to the government. They were all firm believers in natural law and inalienable rights.

Jefferson's words in the Declaration of Independence united both the proponents and opponents of the new Constitution: "We hold these truths to be self-evident, that all men are created equal, that they are endowed by their Creator with certain unalienable rights, that among them are life, liberty and the pursuit of happiness."

One longtime critic explained how differently Bork and the framers viewed individual rights. "When conservatives like Bork treat rights as islands surrounded by a sea of government powers, they precisely reverse the view of the founders as enshrined in the Constitution, wherein government powers are limited and specified and rendered as islands surrounded by a sea of individual rights."

Federalists argued, in the natural-rights vein, that to enumerate rights in a Bill of Rights was dangerous. For example, Madison contended at the Virginia ratifying convention, "If an enumeration be made of all our rights, will not it be implied that everything omitted is given to the general government?" He argued that "an imperfect enumeration" . . . "is dangerous."

Another Federalist, James Iredell, at the North Carolina ratifying convention, seemed to be anticipating a future Bork when he warned of the danger of enumerating specific rights. He posited a hypothetical government lawyer, at some future date, challenging the assertion of a right not enumerated:

> "We live at a great distance from the time when this Constitution was established [his hypothetical lawyer says]. We can judge of it much better by the ideas of it entertained at the time, than by any ideas of our own. The bill of rights, passed at that time, showed that the people did not think every power retained which was not given, else this bill of rights was not only useless but absurd. But we are not at liberty to charge an absurdity upon our ancestors, who have given such strong proofs upon their good sense, as well as their attachment to a liberty. So long as the rights enumerated in the bill of rights remain unviolated, you have no reason to complain. This is not one of them."

"Thus," warned Iredell, "a bill of rights might operate as a snare rather than a protection." So to Iredell's future Bork, because the framers did not enumerate a right to privacy in the Constitution, they must not have intended that we have that natural right. As the real Bork explained in 1986 "[t]he Constitution specified certain liberties and allocates all else to democratic processes"—in other words, to the government elected by the express will of the majority.

How could a Bill of Rights be drafted that did not become a snare? Madison came up with the solution—the Ninth Amendment. Madison changed his position on a Bill of Rights as it became clear the Constitution would not be ratified without one. Indeed, Madison ran for the new House of Representatives with a commitment to support a Bill of Rights in the Congress when he got there.

Madison drafted the Bill of Rights and introduced the constitutional amendments in Congress on June 8, 1789. He explained the Ninth of those amendments as follows: "It has been objected also against a bill of rights, that, by enumerating particular exceptions to the general grant of power, it would disparage, those rights which were not placed in that enumeration; and it might follow by implication, that those rights which were not singled out, were intended to be assigned into the hands of the General Government, were consequently insecure. This . . . may be guarded against. I have attempted it [in the Ninth Amendment]."

These powerful natural rights notions—that we have certain God-given rights which no one, no government, can take away from us—predate the framers. They can be traced back to well before the Declaration of Independence, to the Bible, to Cicero, to John of Salisbury in the Middle Ages but at a minimum to the Magna Charta.

The Magna Charta's Article 39 was one of the inspirations for our due process clause and the Ninth Amendment: "No free man shall be taken, or imprisoned, or dispossessed, or outlawed, or banished, or in any way destroyed, nor will we go upon, nor will we send upon him, except by the legal judgment of his peers or by the law of the land." It is the only part of the Magna Charta that is still on the English statute books. Yet in its original draft "free man" only applied to landed gentry, not to men of common stock. Over the centuries the words, like our due process clause, had a generative life of their own and expanded to protect many rights never anticipated by the barons and King John at Runnymede nearly eight centuries ago.

By the early seventeenth century Lord Coke invoked the long-dormant words of Article 39 in his struggle with the autocratic Stuart monarchs. When Coke recited the Magna Charta, he spoke of natural law "written with the finger of God in the heart of man." He reminded his compatriots, as they took on the powerful British monarchs, that when their forebears, the barons at Runnymede, crafted the words of the Magna Charta, they did not believe they were inventing new rights. They believed they were only reminding King John that they, as Anglo-Saxons, had certain God-given rights, encompassed in the words "law of the land," which the Norman kings could not take away from them.

Just as Coke invoked that tradition to rally his countrymen against the Stuart tyranny, so did John Adams and his followers against King George in the 1760s.

The Founders were steeped in Coke, a giant of English jurisprudence in the seventeenth and eighteenth centuries. So when they were making the case against the Stamp Act, the writs of assistance, and other repressive legislation imposed upon the colonies, they turned to the Magna Charta and the English Common Law, which grew out of it, as the authority for their arguments. John Adams argued that the Stamp Act was unconstitutional because it violated the right to a jury trial under Article 39 of the Magna Charta and natural rights: "Rights antecedent to all earthly government—Rights that cannot be repealed or restrained by human laws—Rights derived from the great legislator of the universe. . . . British liberties are not the grants of princes or parliaments, but original rights, conditions of original contracts . . . coequal with government. . . . Many of our rights are inherent and essential, agreed on as maxims, and established as preliminaries, even before a parliament existed."

It is inconceivable that the founders intended to reverse that tradition a few years after the revolution with the new Constitution. So Robert Bork's idea that the Constitution establishes a democratic government with an exclusive list of limitations on the powers of that government is deeply at odds not only with Harlan, Frankfurter, and Cardozo but with our founders, English Common Law, and with our whole jurisprudence.

By August of 1987 liberal intellectuals were beginning to make many of the same points in print that professors Schroeder and Abernathy were making to Biden in their private meetings. Renata Adler wrote a blistering attack on Bork in the "Talk of the Town" column of *New Yorker* magazine.

Adler pointed out that "Bork dismisses" the notion of rights inhering in humans "as some new, modish rhetorical development" but that the notion was "held so firmly by the founders of the republic" that it was "incorporated in the Declaration of Independence." She relayed how Bork "brushes aside" the Bill of Rights "as a 'hastily drafted document upon which little thought was expended' " and of "the 'men who put the [Fourteenth] Amendment in the Constitution' that 'many or most of them had not even thought the matter through'."

As to the right of privacy, "Bork believes quite simply that no such right exists: that it is a 'court-created right.' . . ." She reminds the reader of Bork's position on the 1942 sterilization case, *Skinner* v. *Oklahoma,* and then explained the consequences of Bork's philosophy in graphic terms. "So there is nothing to prevent a majoritarian preference from being expressed, for instance, in a statute requiring everyone, of every race, to be blond. And nothing—perhaps this is more serious—to prevent the State from enforcing a majoritarian preference that all single mothers should be sterilized. Or all women with an I.Q. below 130. Or all mothers under eighteen."

On August 18, Ronald Dworkin, a professor at New York University Law School and an old academic sparring partner of Bork's, unleashed a strong attack on the nominee in the *New York Review of Books,* employing the acrid language that Bork himself loved to use. In speaking of Bork's assertion in the *Indiana Law Review* article that there is "no principled way to decide that one man's gratifications are more deserving of respect than another's," Dworkin wrote, "Taken at face value, that means that no one could have a principled reason for preferring the satisfactions of charity or justice, for example, to those of racism or rape. A crude moral skeptic is an odd person to carry the colors of moral fundamentalists."

His strongest attack concerned Bork's fascination with the overriding importance of Majoritarianism. "His writings show no developed political philosophy, however, beyond frequent appeals to the truism that elected legislators, not judges, ought to make law when the Constitution is silent. . . . He flirts with the radical populist thesis that minorities in fact have no moral rights against the majority at all. . . . But populism of that form is so plainly inconsistent with the text and spirit of the Constitution, and with the most apparent and fundamental convictions of the framers, that anyone who endorses it seems unqualified, for that reason alone, for a place on the Court.''

Proponents of Judge Bork were not particularly troubled by an attack from liberal intellectual journals in New York City. That is exactly where they would expect it to come from. They felt they had in Robert Bork the advocate of a politically potent argument that would reach well beyond the exclusive salons of the elite to the middle-class suburbs of America where the votes were. The argument would go something like this: ''Senator Biden, why are you concerned about a right to privacy and the right to purchase contraceptives or the right of woman to have an abortion? Why don't you, as a legislator, just enact those things rather than have the courts do it for you?''

The political instincts of Biden and Vince D'Anna were that the other side of the argument had as much, if not more, potency. They believed that Americans believed they had certain inalienable rights, especially a right to privacy. And that Americans not only were not upset with a Supreme Court that recognized these rights in the face of a runaway legislature, but they expected as much of the Court. Many of Biden's allies in the anti-Bork movement and their advisers were not quite so sure he was right.

Early in the effort to organize the anti-Bork coalition, the key strategists of the LCCR determined that they would do something they had never done before in one of these nomination struggles. They would turn to sophisticated national polling and focus groups, the high-tech wizardry of modern election campaigns. A national poll could help strategists understand how a large statistically random group of Americans felt about various issues in the Bork fight. A focus group could go one step farther. A focus group is a carefully selected unit of voters who are exposed, through a moderator, to a variety of arguments to determine which arguments are the most powerful and why.

Coalition strategists met with Bill Galston, an experienced liberal public policy analyst who had served as Walter Mondale's issues director in his 1984 presidential campaign. Galston was summarizing the results of focus group studies he had just completed; these were held with Southern voters on a variety of issues, not specifically the Bork nomination. By then the anti-Bork strategists knew what Will Ball and others in the Administration had already figured out—if the Southern Democrats swung against Bork, the nomination was dead—so Southern voters were the key to the Bork fight.

The leaders summarized their conclusions after listening to Galston: ''The message of this campaign, it was agreed, must be that advice-and-consent is the duty of the Senate, ideology is an appropriate concern, and that the notion of a balanced court must be maintained. *The focus cannot be issues considered leftish such as abortion and privacy* [emphasis added].''

Although there was little disagreement about the rather abstract notions of advice-and-consent and balance, Galston and the strategists in the civil rights movement seemed to be very much at odds with Biden. Biden agreed that abortion should not be the argument. Indeed the whole purpose of his meeting with them on July 8 was to relay that message. However, unbeknownst to them, by early August Biden was swiftly coming to the conclusion that he would base much of his attack on Bork on privacy and unenumerated rights.

As a result of the Galston and similar meetings, the anti-Bork strategists decided to conduct their own polls and focus groups specifically on the issues raised by the nomination. With the help of $40,000 from the American Federation of State, County, and Municipal Employees, the anti-Bork coalition hired the polling and media firm of Marttila & Kiley. Tom Kiley was to do a nationwide poll on the nomination. John Marttila, Kiley's partner, was already working for the Biden primary campaign. Kiley was not, but Biden political strategist Tom Donilon, who was by then heavily involved in the Bork strategy, and I did have a lengthy conversation with Kiley as to how the poll should be constructed.

Donilon and I were anxious for Kiley to oversample for Alabama and Pennsylvania, which means to deliberately poll more voters from these particular states. We were convinced conservative Democrat Howell Heflin from Alabama and moderate Republican Arlen Specter from Pennsylvania were going to be important swing votes on the committee and bellwethers as to how Southern Democrats and moderate Republicans in the rest of the Senate might vote. We did not tell Biden, but we were also concerned that the privacy issue be thoroughly plumbed to determine whether his instincts were correct.

Kiley's poll was of over 1,000 Americans during a four-day period—August 13, 14, 16, and 17. The poll was carefully constructed to determine which of a number of basic anti-Bork arguments were the most effective. Kiley moved very quickly, but his report was not ready until August 28, well after Biden was committed to the privacy argument. By then he was constructing a witness strategy, an opening statement, and an opening line of questions based almost entirely on the argument that Bork did not believe in a constitutional right to privacy and another argument related to the threat that Bork would reopen old civil rights wounds in the South.

Biden was not interested in being briefed by Kiley. He sent Donilon and me back from a meeting in Wilmington to Washington to review the results. The survey turned out to be generally encouraging as to the vulnerability of Bork, or at least the fact that undecided voters could be moved against him, but Kiley's memorandum summarizing the results debunked the privacy argument just as Galston had. It advocated a line of attack that Biden was unlikely to pursue.

Kiley argued, "*It is our conclusion that those who form the moderate center will move toward a rejection of Bork only if they find in his background and record a pattern of insensitivity that suggests he may harbor a predetermined attitude against certain causes and issues, if not classes of people* [emphasis Kiley's].'' It might be an effective argument, but it was not one Biden would use. He did not believe Bork was a racist, and Biden was not comfortable hurling that epithet at anyone, much less a potential member of the Supreme Court.

Kiley did not argue he was a racist either. He believed that one way to make that case would be his ''*civil rights record [which], more than anything else in his background, will raise questions in the public mind about his fairmindedness* [emphasis Kiley's].'' The problem was that Bork might be effective in disowning his past positions.

Worst of all from our perspective, Kiley gave short shrift to the privacy argument: ''Along with arguments dealing with *Watergate,* the *Reagan–Meese judicial agenda,* and *balance-of-court arguments,* the *privacy theme* appears from our results to be somewhat obtuse and limited in its potential for broad-based communication.'' Kiley did think that, if the argument was recast into one of personal autonomy and government infringements upon the right to choose, it might have some potential. At the end of the small section on privacy, there was a curious sentence about public reaction to the *Griswold* case: ''(Not surprisingly, voters strongly objected to Bork's disagreement with *Griswold.*)''

Tom Donilon and I met immediately after the presentation. Donilon was insistent: ''If Biden is wrong about this privacy argument, we've got to tell him immediately. But before we do you've got to get the cross-tabs from Kiley.''

''You mean so Caddell can look at them?''

''Yes.''

''Well, I'll have to tell Kiley what we're doing. He might not like it.''

''I'm not going to tell Biden he's wrong,'' Donilon persisted, ''unless Caddell can back us up with numbers.''

The cross-tabs on a poll are the raw numbers cross-indexed by various criteria, usually demographic. For example, for each question the numbers are divided by sex, race, income, domicile, etc. A good analyst, like Biden's pollster, Pat Caddell, would insist on seeing those numbers before drawing any firm conclusions. Usually pollsters do not share those numbers, especially with another pollster.

Kiley was gracious. He would have to get permission from his clients, but he had no problem with Caddell looking at the cross-tabs. Within a few days Caddell had them and was back to me and Donilon from his retreat in California.

''Biden is absolutely right. These numbers support his case completely.''

Donilon and I looked at each other across the room and sighed in relief.

Caddell then proceeded to make a forty-five-minute convincing analysis of the poll.

Caddell could be arrogant, but when it came to polls and political strategy, his analyses bordered on genius. Today he was being very patient. "Look, Mark, in a poll like this, what you're trying to understand is why the undecideds move your way. And remember here the problem we're trying to solve is how to move the Southern Democrats and the moderate Republicans, the Alabamans and Pennsylvanians, the Heflins and the Specters."

"That's why we oversampled in Alabama and Pennsylvania," Donilon added.

Caddell laughed. "Gee, Tom, I didn't think you were that smart."

"Fuck you, Pat." Caddell and Donilon loved to pick at each other, but in this case it was purely jocular. They respected each other, and it was clear that Biden was gaining respect for Donilon as an equal to Caddell in both political savvy and substantive knowledge in the presidential campaign and especially in the Bork fight.

Caddell continued in a back-to-business tone of voice: "The important thing in this poll is that between the beginning and the end of this poll the anti-Bork vote grows from seventeen percent to fifty-one percent. Why does that happen and where does it happen?"

Caddell went on to explain that we did not care about general changes in the undecideds nationwide, because we were not engaged in a national referendum but in a state-by-state battle. The states we were most interested in were Alabama and Pennsylvania and also voter groups in the states where the other Southern Democrats and moderate Republicans resided.

"When you look at the cross-tabs for Alabama and Pennsylvania, you find that the only argument other than privacy that works as powerfully in both states is Bork's position in the *New Republic*." Caddell was referring to Bork's twenty-three-year-old article condemning the Kennedy Administration's civil rights bill, a less-than-impressive argument since it was so long ago, and Bork had changed his mind since. "I agree with Joe that [Bork's] comeback is effective on that. So the best argument with them is privacy."

Caddell then turned to what he thought was even more important: "Getting beyond Alabama and Pennsylvania, look at the numbers for Southern whites and women less than forty. The Southern whites are the numbers that are not only going to move Heflin but all the Southerners, and the women under forty are what moderate Republicans look at. Privacy's the most powerful argument for Southern whites and next to the most powerful for the women."

In a subsequent memorandum that Cáddell prepared for distribution to Southern Democrats in the Senate, he made these points:

- 71% of white Southerners are LESS inclined to support Bork after hearing that he does not believe that "the Constitution specifically recognizes a right to privacy";
- 75% of white Southerners are LESS inclined to support Bork because he "disagrees with the 1965 Supreme Court decision which struck down a state law preventing the availability of birth control devices even for married couples."

Donilon and I never even raised the issue with Biden after Caddell's call, other than to say to him that the poll generally supported his approach. What we did not know at the time is that the civil rights groups had in their possession other extremely compelling information supporting the privacy, unenumerated-rights approach. Indeed the results of a focus group conducted by the Peter Hart polling company in Atlanta, Georgia, on August 26 was never studied by anyone in the Biden camp until almost two years later, when I reviewed the transcripts as I researched this book.

A poll is cold statistics. A focus group literally brings alive public opinion and the arguments that can shape it. Hart's focus group was with eleven people—six who called themselves middle of the road, three conservative, and two liberal—roughly representative of the Southern electorate.

The moderator explained to the group Bork's position on the right to privacy: "He believes that the right to privacy is not guaranteed by the Constitution and argues that the Court should not protect citizens from government intrusion into personal affairs and private family matters.

"For example, he has criticized the Supreme Court when it overturned a state law that would have made it a crime for married couples to use contraceptives. The law was in Connecticut in 1965. It said couples couldn't use contraceptives in the privacy of their own home. . . .

"Is that something that disturbs you, with that position?"

VOICE ON THE TAPE: (I'm) Very concerned about that.

MODERATOR: About the right to privacy?

VOICE: And prevention of government intrusion. They could come in here right now and arrest us for having this meeting and formulating opinions if we didn't have our privacy."

The moderator wants to be sure that the participants understand Bork's position and that it is not exaggerated: "If the state wants to outlaw contraceptives, the Supreme Court can't stop them. . . ."

VOICE: He has to be basing this on some kind of precedent?

MODERATOR: Well, he is saying that the word "privacy" never appears in the Constitution. . . . He is saying the word "privacy" never appears in the Constitution, so the Supreme Court can't have rulings to protect the right of privacy, because there is no constitutional right to privacy. That is his reasoning. It doesn't make that much sense to you?

VOICE: No.''

At the end, the moderator attempts to determine what is the most powerful argument against Bork. When he finds out it is privacy, he tries again to be sure the group understands Bork's position and his rationale:

MODERATOR: The privacy thing really comes up a lot. Why is that so important to you? I mean, there [are] a lot [of] things on the list [of arguments provided the group to rank in importance]. Why does the Privacy matter [come up] so much? . . .

VOICE: They don't have a right to pry into my business. I don't go in their bedroom and stay all night.

MODERATOR: But know [what] Bork said—you know, everybody talks about strict construction in the Constitution, and Bork is factually accurate when he says the word ''privacy'' never appears in the Constitution. I mean, what makes you think you have got a right to privacy? Where is it written that you have got that right?

SIMULTANEOUS VOICES.

VOICE: You know, it is an unwritten right.''

Biden and D'Anna were clearly right. The American people would have no trouble understanding the notion of an unenumerated right to privacy and the fact that Robert Bork does not believe it exists.

CHAPTER 9

THE BLOODY CROSSROADS

WHILE BIDEN WAS ABSORBED with Bork's views on privacy and unenumerated rights that August, two other members of the Judiciary Committee, Arlen Specter and Patrick Leahy, were bothered by another area that concerned the "real Bob Bork." To understand Bork's views on freedom of speech and dissent is to understand the turbulent 1960s in the urban ghetto, on college campuses, especially the Yale campus, and Bork's relationship with his mentor, Alexander Bickel. Specter and Leahy would match Bork's views against their own experience as young district attorneys faced with maintaining order in the face of the violence that characterized the era.

The Supreme Court was, as it has often been in our history, at the center of the generational, cultural, racial, and ethnic conflict that engulfed that turbulent period. Three other men were to play bit roles in that drama—firebrands, troublemakers, who tested the limits of permissible dissent during two of the most violent years, 1968 and 1970. Clarence Brandenburg, Paul Robert Cohen, and Gregory Hess all forced the Supreme Court to draw that delicate line between liberty and order, the line that separates the rule of law from the rule of men, that guarantees rational discourse in the face of the hysteria of the mob.

In 1968 Clarence Brandenburg telephoned a reporter at a Cincinnati television station and invited him to a Klu Klux Klan "rally" to be held at a nearby farm. With the cooperation of Brandenburg (a leader of the group), the reporter and a cameraman filmed the rally. The films were later broadcast both locally and nationally.

Viewers saw twelve hooded armed figures gathered around a large burning cross. The cameraman and the reporter were the only observers. Although the viewers could not make out most of what the Klansmen were saying, some words were unmistakable. They were clearly racist and anti-Semitic:

"How far is the nigger going to—yeah."

"This is what we are going to do to the niggers. . . ."

"Send the Jews back to Israel. . . ."

"Bury the niggers. . . ."

"Nigger will have to fight for every inch he gets from now on."

A subsequent scene showed Brandenburg in full Klan regalia making a threatening speech: "If our President, our Congress, our Supreme Court, continues to suppress the white, Caucasian race, it's possible that there might have to be some revengeance [*sic*] taken." Brandenburg predicted a march, 400,000 strong, on Washington the following July 4 and additional marches in the South.

A local prosecutor charged and convicted Brandenburg under the Ohio criminal syndicalism statute, which makes it a crime to "advocate the duty, necessity, or propriety of crime, sabotage, violence, or unlawful methods of terrorism as a means of accomplishing industrial or political reform" and for "voluntarily assembl [ing] with any, society, group, or assemblage of persons formed to teach or advocate the doctrines of criminal syndicalism."

Brandenburg was fined $1,000 and sentenced to one to ten years in prison. He appealed his conviction to the Supreme Court of the United States.

That same year Paul Robert Cohen entered the Los Angeles County courthouse wearing a jacket bearing the words "Fuck the Draft." He wore the jacket "as a means of informing the public of the depth of his feelings against the Vietnam War and the draft." There is no evidence that he spoke in a loud voice or attempted to threaten anyone.

Once in a courtroom, he "removed his jacket and stood with it folded over his arm." A policeman who had seen Cohen with the jacket on sent a note to the presiding judge suggesting that he be held in contempt. The judge refused. As soon as he left the courtroom, the officer arrested Cohen.

Cohen was convicted in Los Angeles Municipal Court of violating a provision of the California Penal Code, which prohibits "maliciously and willfully disturb [ing] the peace or quiet of any neighborhood or person . . . by . . . offensive conduct. . . ." He was given thirty days imprisonment. He also appealed his conviction to the Supreme Court.

In May 1970 the Bloomington, Indiana, police department was called in by Indiana University officials to help clear approximately 200–300 antiwar demonstrators blocking doorways to a university building. Two demonstrators were arrested. As a result 100–150 students gathered in front of the building and the patrol car containing the two arrestees. The sheriff and his deputies asked the crowd to disperse. When it did not, the police officers dispersed the demonstrators by walking up the street directly into the crowd.

Gregory Hess, standing on the curb and facing the crowd, said, "We'll take the fucking street later [or again]." Hess spoke in a loud voice but "no louder than statements by other demonstrators'' and ''did not appear to be exhorting the crowd.''

Hess was arrested and convicted of violating the state's disorderly conduct statute, a statute similar in purpose and effect to the California statute under which Robert Cohen had been convicted. Hess appealed his conviction to the Supreme Court as well.

Robert Bork and his best friend and colleague, Alexander Bickel, followed these cases in the Supreme Court with great interest and concern. They viewed them through the lens of their beloved Yale, for the most disturbing aspect of domestic disorder for them was what it was doing to academia.

In April 1970, the threat of violence came to Yale. Black Panther Bobby Seale had been charged with murder in the criminal courts of New Haven, Connecticut. Campus revolutionaries had organized a campus strike at Yale premised on the assertion that Seale and his codefendants could not get a fair trial anywhere in the United States. Groups off-campus threatened violence, according to Bickel, ''to bring Yale to its knees''. . . . ''Over this trumped-up crisis of the trial hundreds upon hundreds of students whipped themselves to a pitch of hysteria, finally voting to strike.''

On April 23, the Yale faculty met to hear the president of Yale express his general agreement with the assertion. The faculty voted to countenance the strike. Bickel wrote of the experience a few months later in the *New Republic:* ''I was at the meeting and so voted, and did not really feel ashamed until I walked out through the crowd of students who we had known were out there, whom we had heard, and who now cheered us. . . . If we had said what is true, that the trial was no crisis . . . that there is no reason to equate the police in Chicago [at the tumultuous 1968 Democratic convention] with the courts in New Haven . . . we would have been denounced as rigid and unresponsive . . . we have listened and talked ourselves into the situation we are in. We have listened—quietly, even solemnly, as if it were rational—to incredibly loose talk about the obsolescence and rottenness of our society and all our institutions, and have come to parrot it, in order to propitiate a sizable number of young.''

Four days after the faculty's decision, a headline appeared in the *New Haven Register:* ''YALE LAW LIBRARY HIT BY SUSPICIOUS BLAZE.'' According to Ethan Bronner in his book on the Bork nomination controversy, ''A photograph above [the headline] shows hundreds of charred lawbooks piled upon the sidewalk across from the neo-Gothic facade of the law library. Police barriers close off the street. A couple of people are examining the books. A short distance away from them, briefcase in one hand, whiskered face held by the other, is a lone and worried figure, Robert Bork. Although unidentified by the newspaper, it is unmistakably he. It is a telling tableau. What the newspaper termed a suspicious fire had damaged the library and the books, holy implements in the temple of learning.''

In his own book, *The Tempting of America,* Judge Bork devotes the final third to a bitter memoir of his nomination experience. The title of that final section is "The Bloody Crossroads." He takes the title from Lionel Trilling, who was writing about the "bloody crossroads" where politics and literature meet. Bork means by it the "even bloodier crossroads where politics and law meet." Underlying the whole section of the book is Bork's contempt for the "authoritarian character" of the Left, which he holds responsible for his defeat. So Bork's "bloody crossroads" in the summer of 1987 was not his first. Almost two decades earlier, he had been at another such crossroads on the campus at Yale, and it undoubtedly colored how he viewed his experience in 1987 *and* the proper limits on domestic dissent.

Bork and his mentor Bickel were shaken by the events at Yale that spring. For Bork, Bickel's reaction was probably as important as the events themselves. It is hard to overstate the importance of Bickel to Bork's own thinking. Bork's eloquent and touching elegy at Bickel's funeral in 1974 describes an intimate and robust relationship. "It is rare to have a friend with whom one shares every level of experience, from drinking and joking, to intensely personal concerns, to discussions of law and legal theory, and speculations about the order of things. It is true that, as the activity ascended in the intellectual scale, my share tended to shrink, mostly because of his flow of words."

Bickel's first thoughts about campus unrest in 1969 were reasonably conciliatory, suggesting that the solution was to increase student representation on faculty and administration decision-making bodies. By the violent spring of 1970 his "shame" was turning to anger. "The University is full of slogans painted and stenciled all over it. These stenciled and spoken slogans and threats are called dissent. But they are in truth vandalism, a kind of transgression almost physical, in content most often a series of curses which do not pretend any attempt at persuasion." He openly condemned the universities' complicity: "We observe it and listen to it respectfully, and thus legitimate it. Nothing is unspeakable, and hence nothing is really undoable."

Bickel compared the "ideological orthodoxy" to Joe McCarthy and concluded with a slogan of his own. "No more vandalism; no more assaultive, vicious speech; no more incitement to violent action; no more bullying, simulated or actual."

By October of 1970 Bickel observed that the "guilt-ridden" "liberals and intellectuals are intimidated by" the revolutionaries on campus and off. He was outraged not just with the indulgences on college campuses but in the "establishment's own newspapers and magazines and books. . . ."

He concluded with fear of a "dictatorship of the self-righteous." "To be revolutionary in a society like ours, is to be totalitarian, or not to know what one is doing."

By the fall of 1970 and the spring of 1971, Bickel was beginning to think and write about the broader implications of the recent developments. So was his friend Robert Bork. Both began to focus increasingly on the First Amendment to the Constitution and the Supreme Court's interpretation of its freedom of speech protections.

In the spring of 1971, Bork delivered the lecture at the Indiana University School of law that would later be published in the *Indiana Law Journal.* Although Joseph Biden had focused on the article's attack on the unenumerated rights case, "Neutral Principles and some First Amendment Problems" was focused primarily on a critique of the Supreme Court's recent First Amendment decisions.

Although he conceded the First Amendment a "central place in our society," Bork embraced the writing of Prof. Harry Kalven, Jr., that in Bork's words, "Constitutional protection should be accorded only to speech that is explicitly political." "Political speech is not any speech that concerns government and law, for there is a category of such speech that must be excluded." Specifically, "There should be no constitutional obstruction to laws making criminal any speech that advocates forcible overthrow of the government or the violation of any law."

When it came to those who fell beyond the pale of constitutional protection under Bork's theory, there was little ambiguity. Clarence Brandenburg, Robert Cohen, Gregory Hess, and those who advocated lawlessness at Yale a year earlier, beware.

In November of 1972 Bickel, writing in *Commentary* magazine, made many of the same points about the proper interpretation of the First Amendment, especially in the context of the domestic unrest that plagued America at the time. Bickel spoke, not as a doctrinaire conservative, but as one of the foremost constitutional scholars of his day, one clearly identified with liberal, Democratic politics. In 1969 he had served as a consultant to Sen. George McGovern's Democratic Party Commission on Party Reform. In 1971, he had served as chief counsel to the *New York Times* in its case before the Supreme Court, successfully challenging the Nixon administration's effort to suppress the publication of the Pentagon Papers in the *Times.*

Bickel explained that for most of the nineteenth century a generous interpretation of the First Amendment was an "unquestioned assumption." There was the notorious Alien and Sedition Act period in our history, when Federalists had stifled dissent from Jeffersonians and others in the early nineteenth century, and there had been repression of abolitionists in midcentury, but "there were no systemic, and certainly no nationwide legal constraints." This was largely because the free speech protections only applied to the federal government and did not constrain states and localities.

Quoting the first great First Amendment scholar, Zachariah Chaffee, Bickel explained, however, that " 'freedom of speech was a cherished tradition, but remained without specific [legal] content'." The First Amendment's "legal career in court decisions is a matter, essentially, of the past half century."

The robust notions of free expression which are now commonly accepted in America did not reach full flower until the civil rights and antiwar movements of the 1960s. However, it was the social unrest of the labor movement and the international turbulence in the early twentieth century that gave rise to the legal controversies that finally began to force the Supreme Court to give specific content to the First Amendment. It was a period of social unrest similar to, if not even more tumultuous, than what we experienced in the 1960s.

One of the first important cases was *Schenck* v. *United States* in 1919. The case involved a conspiracy to violate the federal espionage statutes in June of 1917. The defendants circulated a pamphlet designed to discourage young men from cooperating with the military draft.

Oliver Wendell Holmes, in the opinion of the Court affirming the convictions, explained that "in many places and in ordinary times the defendants . . . would have been within their constitutional rights. But the character of every act depends upon the circumstances in which it is done. The most stringent protection of free speech would not protect a man in falsely shouting 'Fire!' in a theatre and causing a panic."

Holmes next expressed a test or formula, which was to dominate the Supreme Court's thinking, if not a majority of the Court, for the next five decades—a doctrine that was the target of Bickel and Bork's critique of the Supreme Court half a century later: "[The] question in every case is whether the words used are used in such circumstances and are of such a nature as to create a clear and present danger that they will bring about the substantive evils that Congress has a right to prevent. It is a question of proximity and degree. When a nation is at war, many things that might be said in time of peace are such a hindrance to its effort that their utterance will not be endured so long as men fight. . . ."

Holmes was prepared to construe his clear-and-present-danger test strictly to the detriment of the government even in time of war. Later that same term, in the case of *Abrams* v. *United States,* Holmes distinguished the above case from the efforts of Russian immigrants to keep America from interfering in the Russian Revolution. The leaflets in question called upon "workers" not to help make military equipment that would be used in such an intervention.

Holmes explained that, even in time of war, "Congress certainly cannot forbid all efforts to change the mind of the country." With respect to one passage of the pamphlets, he concluded "that the only object of the paper is to help Russia and stop American intervention there against the popular government—not to impede the United States in the war that it was carrying on." In this case, however, a majority of the Supreme Court was not willing to go along with Holmes's clear-and-present-danger analysis. Holmes and Brandeis were in the minority. The Court did not explicitly disown the test, but it certainly was not prepared to see it reverse the Abrams conviction.

However, six years later, in 1925, the Court did abandon the clear-and-present-danger test in the case of *Gitlow* v. *United States*. By 1925, the United States was well beyond the World War I era, and the Court was applying the First Amendment to the states through the Fourteenth Amendment. In this case the defendant, Benjamin Gitlow, was engaged in left-wing, antigovernment organizing.

He was convicted of two counts of violating the New York criminal anarchy statute—a statute similar in purpose and effect to the Ohio criminal syndicalism statute under which Klansman Brandenburg was convicted almost fifty years later. In June of 1919, Gitlow had been elected to the National Council of the left wing section of the Socialist Party in New York. The council had adopted a Manifesto, and Gitlow was in charge of publishing it in the Party's magazine, the *Revolutionary Age*. The manuscript was, for the most part, a dry essay on the merits of radical Socialist and Communist ideology.

The Court, however, seized on language in the paper calling for a mobilization of the " 'power of the proletariat in action' through mass industrial revolts developing into mass political strikes and 'revolutionary mass action'." The goal was to destroy the democratic process and put in its place a "revolutionary dictatorship of the proletariat."

The Court found that the New York statute did not penalize the discussion of "abstract 'doctrine'," but the Court interpreted the Manifesto as advocating "in fervent language mass action." So the Court did apply the restrictions of the First Amendment, but concluded that "this freedom does not deprive a State of the primary and essential right of self-preservation." It then proceeded, in so many words, to abandon Holmes's clear-and-present-danger test. Actually, it decided that the test simply did not apply to the "class" of cases represented by *Gitlow,* where the legislature had been much more specific in crafting the statute.

The majority slammed the clear-and-present-danger test: "The State cannot reasonably be required to measure the danger from every such utterance in the nice balance of a jeweler's scale. . . . It cannot reasonably be required to defer the adoption of measures for its own peace and safety until the revolutionary utterances lead to actual disturbances of the public peace or imminent and immediate danger of its own destruction. . . ."

Brandeis joined Holmes in dissent, arguing that "there was no present danger of an attempt to overthrow the government by force on the part of the admittedly small minority who shared the defendant's views." To Holmes, there was no chance that the Manifesto would start a present conflagration.

Ironically what the Court took with the right hand in *Gitlow*—by its narrow reading of the First Amendment—it gave with the left—by applying the federal Bill of Rights to the states through the Fourteenth Amendment. This was a truly revolutionary expansion of civil liberties protection. No longer was the Constitution simply a limitation on the federal government but the due process language of the Fourteenth Amendment meant that at least parts of it (in this case the First Amendment) applied to every state, city, and hamlet in America.

Two years later, the radical wing of the Socialist Party was again forcing the Supreme Court to determine whether seditious activity was protected by the First Amendment. In *Whitney* v. *California,* the Supreme Court was examining advocacy growing out of the creation of another radical Socialist splinter group in meetings the same year as in the *Gitlow* case, 1919.

In this case, Miss Anita Whitney was involved in a meeting of disaffected Radical Socialists in Oakland, California. The group adopted a Platform and Program, not tremendously different from the Manifesto that had gotten Benjamin Gitlow into so much trouble that same year in New York. She also attended meetings of the newly formed Communist Labor Party in Oakland. Again the purpose was to align Whitney and her group more closely with more radical forms of world Communism.

Justice Sanford, writing for the majority, upheld her conviction under the California syndicalism act: "That a State in the exercise of its police power may punish those who abuse this freedom by utterances inimical to the public welfare, tending to incite to crime, disturb the public peace, or endanger the foundations of organized government and threaten its overthrow by unlawful means is not open to question."

Brandeis and Holmes concurred in the result, but they specifically applied the clear-and-present-danger test to the case. They pointed out that the Court had still not formulated a specific standard by which to determine when a danger was clear, how remote it had to be, and the "degree of evil" substantial enough to justify an abridgment of free speech. Both Brandeis and Holmes were clearly dissatisfied with the opinion and the way issues were presented in the case. Much of the behavior of Whitney, which the majority was prepared to criminalize, Brandeis and Holmes found to be protected speech. However, they found sufficient evidence of a conspiracy by others to commit "present serious crimes" and the fact that what Whitney was doing would further the conspiracy that they would uphold the convictions.

As Bickel pointed out in his 1972 article in *Commentary,* the clear-and-present-danger test has evolved over the years. Bickel was satisfied that it "makes room for what used to be called seditious speech, and for a measure of necessary in-system civil disobedience." However, Bickel feared that "it places a bit more reliance in the discretion . . . of judges . . . than judicial conservatives find altogether comfortable."

In his article he picked apart Holmes's reasoning in his classic opinions on the doctrine. For example in *Gitlow,* Holmes took the notion of the free market of ideas to its extreme. Bickel quotes one particularly strong passage: " 'If in the long run the beliefs expressed in the proletarian dictatorship are destined to be accepted by the dominant forces of the community, the only meaning of free speech [Bickel interjects *the only*] is that they should be given their chance and have their way'."

Bickel observes sardonically, "If in the long run the belief, let us say, in genocide is destined to be accepted by the dominant forces of the community, the only meaning of free speech is that it should be given its chance and have its way. Do we believe that? Do we accept that?"

Continuing with the same theme, Bickel takes on Holmes's eloquent dissent in *Abrams,* where Holmes argues, "When men have realized that time has upset many fighting faiths they may come to believe even more than they believe the very foundations of their own conduct that the ultimate good desired is better reached by free trade in ideas—that the best test of truth is the power of the thought to get itself accepted in the competition of the market, and that truth is the only ground upon which their wishes safely can be carried out."

Again Bickel questions whether "the idea of proletarian dictatorship, or segregation or genocide" are appropriate for the marketplace. "A marketplace without rules of civil discourse is no marketplace of ideas, but a bullring. . . . The theory of the truth of the marketplace, determined ultimately by a count of noses—this total relativism cannot be the theory of our Constitution, or there would be no Bill of Rights. . . ."

For Bickel the most dangerous consequence of the marketplace notion was that "to listen to something on the assumption of the speaker's right to say it is to legitimate it." To illustrate his point Bickel again turned to campus unrest. On one college campus a crowd gathered around an ROTC building. Faculty joined the crowd of students and participated in a debate on whether to set fire to the building: "The matter was ultimately voted upon and the affirmative lost—narrowly. But the negative taken by the faculty was only one side of a debate which the faculty rendered legitimate by engaging in it. Where nothing is unspeakable, nothing is undoable."

Beginning with his *Indiana Law Review* article, Bork repeated many of Bickel's themes, but in almost every case he was willing to go one step further. For example, while Bickel was not totally persuaded by Brandeis and Holmes's "rhetoric" in their famous dissents in *Abrams* and *Gitlow,* he was never prepared to reject outright the clear-and-present-danger test. Indeed, Bickel makes it clear in his *Commentary* article that he is not totally unhappy with the various "procedural compromises" that characterize the Supreme Court's attempt to accommodate different interests under the First Amendment.

Bork, on the other hand, goes right to the heart of the matter and adopts Justice Sanford's position in the majority in the *Gitlow* and *Whitney* decisions. He was taken with Sanford's assertion that, "It cannot be said that the state is acting arbitrarily or unreasonably when in the exercise of its judgment as to the measures necessary to protect the public peace and safety, it seeks to extinguish the spark without waiting until it has enkindled the flame or blazed into the conflagration.''

So for Bork the real offense of the clear-and-present-danger test was that ''it erects a barrier to legislative rule where none should exist.''

On June 6, 1969, the Supreme Court handed down its opinion in the *Brandenburg* case. On a 9–0 vote the Court struck down the Ohio syndicalism statute and reversed the Brandenburg (Ku Klux Klan) conviction. The Court explicitly overruled the *Whitney* decision in which Justice Sanford had, forty years earlier, upheld the California syndicalism statute, which was quite similar to the Ohio statute.

The Court found that Brandenburg had been convicted of ''mere advocacy'' and implied that the only activity falling outside the First Amendment's protection was ''incitement to imminent lawless action.'' Although the Court did not explicitly revive the clear-and-present-danger test, the effect was the same. Justices Douglas and Black joined in a concurring opinion, but they condemned the clear-and-present-danger test as being an inadequate protection of First Amendment rights.

On June 7, 1971, the Supreme Court reversed Robert Cohen's conviction under the California disturbing-the-peace statute for wearing a coat with the antidraft slogan in the Los Angeles County Courthouse. The most prominent conservative on the court, Justice Harlan, wrote for the majority: ''At least so long as there is no showing of an intent to incite disobedience to or disruption of the draft, Cohen could not . . . be punished for asserting the evident position on the inutility or immorality of the draft his jacket reflected.''

Two and a half years later, in November 1973, the Court reversed Gregory Hess's conviction under the similar Indiana statute, because of his statement in the middle of an antiwar demonstration at Indiana University. The Court concluded that Hess's statement (''We'll take the fucking street later [or again]'') ''at worst . . . amounted to nothing more than advocacy of illegal action at some indefinite future time.''

These decisions, especially when read with *Brandenburg,* infuriated Bork. In three critical speeches given in 1977, 1979, and 1984, Bork went well beyond Bickel's critiques, although he clearly sounded some of the very same themes.

First, Bork found *Hess* and *Brandenburg* ''fundamentally wrong interpretations of the First Amendment.'' In a speech at the University of Michigan in 1979, he went back to his *Indiana Law Review* analysis of the First Amendment, that the only protection should be for political speech. ''Speech advocating the forcible destruction of democratic government or the frustration of such government through law violation has no value in a system whose basic premise is democratic rule.''

As to *Cohen,* Bork concluded that the Court had ''articulated no better grounds . . . than the dangers of the slippery slope and moral relativism as a constitutional command.'' He picked apart Harlan's reasoning in the case as illustrating the Court's slide into moral relativism, especially as it related to the slogan ''Fuck the Draft.''

Justice Harlan: ''The principle contended for by the State seems inherently boundless. How is one to distinguish this from any other offensive word?''

Robert Bork: ''One might as well say that the negligence standard is inherently boundless, for how is one to distinguish the utterly reckless driver from the safe one. The answer in both cases is by the common sense of the community. Almost all judgments in the law are ones of degree, and there is no warrant in that fact to prevent communities from exercising any control whatever over what may be said or written in public.''

Justice Harlan: ''One man's vulgarity is another's lyric.''

Robert Bork: ''On that ground, it is impossible to see how law on any subject can be allowed to exist.''

To Bickel, and even more so to Bork, the First Amendment and the Supreme Court's interpretation of it right down to the *Cohen* case involved the most fundamental questions of public philosophy. As Bork remarked in his 1979 speech at the University of Michigan, ''It is not surprising that the contest between views of the proper relationship between the individual and the society should come to the fore in First Amendment cases. That Amendment is pivotal; it both reflects the current balance of opposing philosophies and, in turn, strongly influences the movement of that balance.''

Bork continued his analysis of the decisions in the Michigan speech in terms of the ''core value'' of the First Amendment being ''protection of democratic political speech,'' the point he had developed at Indiana. Specifically he was concerned about the Court's ''extraordinary and, in my view, unjustified tenderness, indeed solicitude, for the well-being and vigor of subversive advocacy.''

However, his real concern was about these deeper philosophical and cultural issues. He was still fighting the 1960s battles a decade later. He found that the Court's ''work in this area seems both a reflection and a contributor to very disquieting intellectual, moral, and social trends.'' He saw the Court as ''writing into the First Amendment a current social trend. . . . The law increasingly protects the individual's desire for self-expression and gives progressively less importance to the social forms and institutions that hold us together and make us a community.''

The spirit of the age, as he saw it, was ''obsessive'' ''narcissistic concern with self,'' the Me Decade as Tom Wolfe describes it, an ''individualistic hedonism'' characterized by the *Playboy* philosophy. His critique of the First Amendment philosophy of the Supreme Court not surprisingly extended beyond protection of subversives to protection of pornography as well.

The consequences for our society were grim. "Both in the society and in the law we see a corresponding distrust of government; distrust of private centers of power; disdain for what may be called conventional or bourgeois values; moral relativism; tenderness, if not fascination, with radical, violent politics. . . ."

At Carlton College in 1977, Bork described to the graduating class the social consequences. "It is now apparent that for the past twenty years [the] health of our institutions has been in decline. It is hard to find any that have the moral authority they had twenty years ago. And it is hard to find any not under attack, any whose legitimacy is not questioned. Universities, elementary and secondary schools, corporations, the military services, the intelligence agencies, the presidency, the Congress, the churches, the family—all have experienced loss of respect within the past two decades." All of this took place at least in part in the "atmosphere created by Vietnam and the protest movement."

He continued, "Some powerful force has been unleashed which seems capable of flattening the American institutional landscape. Indeed, it is apparent that force is gathering power in all of the western liberal democracies.

"Many people welcome that flattening and hasten to help it along. They think it means greater freedom for the individual. They are quite wrong. The decline of multiple power centers is a threat to the safety and the freedom of the individual."

Bork was prepared to place a large share of the blame squarely on the shoulders of the Supreme Court. As he said at Michigan, "What is troublesome is that the Court, by misunderstanding a crucial part of the Constitution, has put the First Amendment largely on the wrong side of the struggle." The Court, Bork continued, "is an active agent in our culture as in our polity, and its intellectual and moral weight has influence both obvious and subtle throughout our lives."

Keying off Justice Harlan's comment in *Cohen* that "one man's vulgarity is another's lyric," Bork at a speech at the Judge Advocate General's School in 1984 remarked that "that is moral relativism with a vengeance." At its heart the problem was that the Court had taken the notion of self-expression too far. "The approach of individual self-expression, when it carried to the lengths of moral relativism, brings constitutional law into conflict with the common sense and the common morality of the community."

Again Bork was not alone in these and similar opinions. By the time of his death in 1974, Alexander Bickel was a darling of the Right for expressing similar sentiments. As George Will pointed out in a column that year, Bickel believed that the lawlessness of Watergate was presaged by the notion of civil disobedience advocated by the civil rights and antiwar movements and right-wing groups like the Klan. "Bickel's most acute—and acutely resented—perception was this: the impatient, righteous, anti-institutional impulse that helped produce Watergate had been much in evidence—and much applauded—in Government itself, since the midfifties.'' The agency of government to which Bickel and Will were referring was, of course, the Supreme Court of the United States.

At Michigan, Bork attacked the philosophical underpinnings of liberal tolerance of dissent. ''Almost unlimited personal autonomy is defended in this area by the shopworn slogan that the individual should be free to do as he sees fits so long as he does no harm to others. The formula is meaningless. . . . This strain of liberalism holds that only physical or material injury is entitled to be noticed by the law.'' The fact that liberals cited John Stuart Mill for authority provided a ''spurious air of philosophic certainty by an arbitrary and indefensible definition of what people are entitled to harm.'' Bork believed that liberals misread Mill, who he argued was no moral relativist.

The immediate harm that had galvanized Bickel and Bork's attention was the survival of the democratic state. That is why Bork, like Bickel, was so upset with Holmes's line in *Gitlow* that ''If in the long run the beliefs expressed in proletarian dictatorship are destined to be accepted by the dominant forces of the community, the only meaning of free speech is that they should be given their chance to have their way.'' To Bork that meant that ''according to the fundamental law of our nation, the theory of Marxist dictatorship imposed by force is at least as legitimate as the idea of a republican form of government. That political relativism was certainly foreign to the Founders' thought, and ought to remain foreign to ours.''

Bork was taken with Justice Sanford's warning in *Gitlow*: ''A single revolutionary spark may kindle a fire that, smoldering for a time, may burst into a sweeping destructive conflagration.''

But to Bork, the danger was there even if the spark did not ignite a conflagration. As he warned at Michigan, ''Speech of that nature, moreover, poses obvious dangers. If it is allowed to proliferate and social or political crisis comes once more to the nation, so that there really is a likelihood of imminent lawless action, it will be too late for law. Aside from that possibility, it is well known that such speech has been and is used to recruit persons for underground activity, including espionage, and for terrorist activity.''

Other patriotic and thoughtful Americans had a very different view of the threat of seditious speech than did Justice Sanford, or Alexander Bickel or Robert Bork. Justice Harlan, for example, spoke to this in the *Cohen* case: ''To many, the immediate consequence of this freedom may appear to be only verbal tumult, discord, and even offensive utterance. These are, however, within established limits, in truth necessary side effects of the broader enduring values which the process of open debate permits us to achieve. That the air may at times seem filled with verbal cacophony is, in this sense, not a sign of weakness but of strength.''

John Harlan, like his predecessors Holmes and Brandeis, simply was not afraid to let people hear these "subversive" words. He would agree with Holmes that "time has upset many fighting faiths" and that "the best test of truth is the power of the thought to get itself accepted in the competition of the market, and that truth is the only ground upon which their wishes safely can be carried out."

There simply could not be a more fundamental difference than there was between Bickel and Bork on the one hand and Harlan, Holmes, and Brandeis on the other. Bickel and Bork were not trusting enough of the people and secure enough in the strength of our republic to leave seditious rhetoric free in the land. Harlan, Holmes, and Brandeis had more faith in America's government and its people. Indeed, they believed that it was this free and robust debate that was the source of our strength as a society.

Bork was right to attack John Stuart Mill, because he indeed was the father of this approach to free expression. To Mill, "The only freedom which deserves the name, is that of pursuing our own good in our own way, so long as we do not attempt to deprive others of theirs, or impede their efforts to obtain it." To these men suppression of ideas and speech was much more dangerous than the "dangerous" ideas themselves.

In 1989, a little over two years after he first sat down to study Bork's writings and especially these speeches, in preparation for the confirmation hearings, Arlen Specter reflected back on his thoughts during August of 1987. As he reminisced about that provocative and exciting moment in his life, he spoke with zest and conviction—as if he were at that very moment leaning over the table, sitting at the edge of the chair, and pressing Bork on his views.

He spoke at the week that the Berlin Wall was crumbling and irrepressible freedom in eastern Europe was shredding the Iron Curtain. "Our country was not in jeopardy in the 60s. I was on the front lines. . . . Judge Bork was . . . at the university, at Yale Law School in 67–68. . . ."

"I was district attorney of Philadelphia in 1965. We had the problems of 1967 and 1968—Detroit, Pittsburgh, Newark burned up. Martin Luther King was assassinated. Philadelphia was in tremendous turmoil. I was the chief law enforcement officer of the city and county of Philadelphia. I worked with Frank Rizzo. We used to drive the streets on Friday nights, worried about what was going to happen in the town. And that year, 1968, I published a little booklet, [on the] rights and limitations on speech and assembly because of the importance of recognizing constitutional rights. I put out a little booklet for the police. . . .

"I saw [protection of free speech] as very important. The mayor issued a proclamation in Philadelphia that precluded twelve or more from gathering on street corners. And I refused . . . to uphold it. I said it was unconstitutional. It was a bad thing to limit the number of people. It's like stopping the people from going out of East Germany. The easiest way to stop them is to let them go."

Arlen Specter served as district attorney in Philadelphia for eight years, overseeing the prosecution of over 250,000 cases. He was not simply a good prosecutor, but a dogged politician who once conceded he had a ''rocky road getting'' to the Senate.

His confrontation with Mayor Tate over the constitutionality of how to control the riots was only one of many such clashes. Indeed as one profile points out, Specter developed a reputation as one who ''thrived on confrontation.''

When he was finally elected to the Senate in 1980, he brought his prosecutorial approach to public life with him. He came into the Senate with the Reagan landslide. The Senate changed hands from Democratic to Republican control. The Judiciary Committee's new chairman, Strom Thurmond, had trouble finding Republicans who wanted to serve on the committee, because of the controversial agenda of social issues and nominations that were routine fare for the committee.

Specter had no such reluctance. ''When I came in 1980, no one wanted the Judiciary Committee. I got it because I was the lowest in seniority. You had all the tough votes. I was ready for Judiciary. I wanted the Judiciary Committee.''

He immediately saw the nominations process of the committee as one of the most important functions of the Senate, especially Supreme Court nominations. ''I don't think that legislation can compare with the importance of the calendar of the Supreme Court. I don't think there is anything else the Senate does that compares with the importance of that. The Supreme Court has become the most powerful instrumentality of government.''

Neal Manne was Specter's chief of staff in the summer of 1987. A tough but soft-spoken lawyer from Texas, he was the perfect alter ego to Specter during the Bork fight. He was fiercely loyal but not afraid of Specter, who can be quite intimidating with staff. Manne explained, ''Specter has always given heightened interest to nominees. People always get him more worked up than abstract propositions. Maybe because he's more confrontational. I would hope it's because he sees potential in any particular individual to have a big impact on the society. He respects the extent to which one individual can have a huge impact. Nowhere can that be more true than in confirming someone for high office.''

Specter had become deeply involved in several of the controversial nomination fights in the committee in his first term. Indeed, his opposition to Reagan's efforts to pack the Civil Rights Commission with nominees who shared his conservative civil rights agenda, his pivotal opposition to Brad Reynolds to be associate attorney general because of those civil rights policies, and his opposition to other right-wing judicial nominations had greatly angered conservatives in the Administration.

Specter's independence on these fights, when matched with his opposition to Contra funding, school prayer, cuts in abortion funding, his reluctance to support the MX, and the fact that he voted against the Reagan Administration more than any Senate Republican made him a perfect target for conservatives in his 1986 reelection bid. The stalking horse for the conservatives that year was his old nemesis, Pennsylvania Republican governor Richard Thornburg, who considered but finally dropped the idea of challenging Specter.

The Bork fight was a "personal crucible" for Arlen Specter, Manne explained. The problem in 1986 had not been the Democrat, Congressman Bob Edgar, whom Specter beat handily, but the Thornburg threat in the primary. Thornburg's machinations were to Manne "a calculated effort by the conservatives in Pennsylvania and at the higher levels of the Meese Justice Department to pay Specter back."

According to Manne, "[Specter] was convinced that voting against Bork was going to hurt him. He thought it might very well get him defeated. He thought that voting for Bork was a politically safe thing to do. It would endear him to his party."

As one observer noted, however, Specter is not a "natural politician." Although he certainly recognized the political risks, it is entirely believable that Specter did not view the Bork controversy as a political fight.

Specter can get so wrapped up in the issue itself that he literally loses sight of the political ramifications. Manne points out that "Specter is often described as one of the better lawyers on the committee. I would describe him as the one on the committee who loves the law the best, enjoys the law, and thinks of everything in lawyers' terms. That's not always for the best. . . . Sometimes its a disadvantage, especially in an institution built on compromise."

Specter had been an editor of the *Yale Law Journal* when he attended the school in the 50s and considered himself somewhat of a constitutional expert from his eight years as a prosecutor. Specter viewed the nomination struggle as "a lawyer's issue. Who was going to be on the Supreme Court? . . . He faced a candidate who, just like himself, viewed the whole world through lawyers' eyes, who took a legalistic approach to questions which were not necessarily lawyers' questions." In that sense Bork had an ironic similarity to Arlen Specter.

As someone close to Specter pointed out, "The Bork hearing itself and the preparation for it was for Arlen Specter . . . a rare occasion in his career as a politician when he could justify basically taking three months reading the law and reading philosophy, and struggling with law review-type issues."

Specter plunged into the effort in July and August. He authorized Manne to recruit every lawyer on his staff to collect and summarize all of Bork's writings and opinions. The focus was to be on the doctrine of original intent, judicial review, equal protection, and Bork's views on the First Amendment. In the First Amendment area, he was interested in the judge's views on censorship of art and literature and subversive speech. Increasingly, though, he focused that summer on Bork's view on the clear-and-present-danger test.

Specter insisted on reading everything in its original form and to reread the classic Supreme Court decisions, *Schenck, Abrams, Gitlow,* and *Whitney* on the clear-and-present-danger test. He spent, all told, several hours in personal meetings with Bork, discussing his positions. Specter spent the month of August at his beach house in New Jersey, poring over all of the materials gathered for him by the staff. Manne sat by the phone in Washington, processing daily requests for more materials to satisfy Specter's insatiable appetite. According to Manne, it was like a ''spider web,'' because one request led to another, but it was also like a ''black hole.'' Manne and his staff ''Fedexed boxes of articles, nothing ever came back except 'Send me more'.''

On August 6 Floyd Abrams briefed Chairman Biden on the implications of Bork's First Amendment positions. Abrams is the foremost First Amendment litigator in the United States. He had joined Bickel in defending the *New York Times* in the Pentagon Papers case and was frequently consulted by his media clients and members of Congress on matters relating to the First Amendment.

Reflecting on Bork's position in his writings on the clear-and-present-danger test, Abrams told Biden, ''It is difficult to overstate how radical that position is. Holmes and Brandeis are recalled in American folklore as perhaps our two most revered judges because of the very opinions Bork disagrees with—opinions affirming the right of our people to have the widest range to oppose governmental action and (up to a point) to urge people to disobey unjust laws. That, after all, is what Martin Luther King did when he counseled disobedience. To say that such speech should receive *no* protection under the First Amendment is to stand the last sixty years of constitutional history on its head.''

Abrams praised Bork's position in the case of *Ollman* v. *Evans,* in which Judge Bork had written an opinion for the D.C. Circuit Court of Appeals. The court had dismissed a libel action against newspaper columnists Robert Novak and Rowland Evans, because of the threat to a free press. ''His opinion in the *Ollman* libel case shows commendable sensitivity to the risk that libel law can too easily chill both speech and press. But his views when the contest is not between individuals and the press but the government and the press are consistently underprotective of First Amendment rights.''

Abrams also conceded that Bork had recanted some of his more extreme views in the *Indiana Law Review* in a letter which he sent to the *American Bar Association Journal* in 1984. He made it clear that he no longer believed that First Amendment protections excluded ''moral and scientific debate'' as he had argued at Indiana. He had also made similar retractions earlier in 1987, and in interviews immediately before the hearings to *Newsweek* and *U.S. News & World Report.* In *U.S. News & World Report* he made it clear that he never intended his views on clear-and-present-danger to prohibit Dr. King's advocacy of civil disobedience.

The problem, Abrams explained, was that most of these retractions were recent, especially on the civil disobedience point, and had certainly not been obvious from his earlier statements. Abrams was simply not convinced by the retractions, especially as they related to domestic dissident activity.

Specter was not privy to the Abrams briefings, but he clearly shared the sentiment. He was not only upset with Bork's attack on the revered clear-and-present-danger test but also with Bork's views about John Stuart Mill. "Bork's writings about John Stuart Mill and permissiveness and [Bork's] notion that our society ought to be ruled by Madisonian Majoritarianism had tremendous implications. . . . It is important because he is saying that John Stuart Mill is the dominant philosophy which has come into our constitutional law, and he's saying it's permissive, and when the majority vote seems to establish a uniform approach on a variety of matters, that's what ought to dominate us—governmental authority."

He was also very dubious about the various recantations. After reviewing all of Bork's writings, he was convinced that his hostility to constitutional protection for domestic dissent was at the core of his philosophy. "It was in his bones. . . . It was in back of his mind. It was the lubricant of his cerebrum. It was all over his head."

In 1987 Patrick Leahy was the forty-seven-year-old junior Senator from Vermont and a member of the Senate Judiciary Committee—the first Democrat ever to be elected to the United States Senate from Vermont. Leahy is an unpretentious, garrulous man.

Like Specter he was a former prosecutor. He had begun his political career as the district attorney for Burlington, the largest city in Vermont and the home of the university.

Leahy proudly points to the fact that in the spring of 1970 when, as a result of the incident at Kent State, college campuses around the nation erupted in violent demonstrations, the University of Vermont saw no riots.

"For four days I got about two hours of sleep a night. I virtually lived on the campus. The students could march up and down freely wherever they wanted but we kept the peace."

Leahy was under pressure to do otherwise. Richard Nixon's Justice Department instructed local United States attorneys, and J. Edgar Hoover told local field offices of the FBI to take a tough line on campus unrest. Vermont's United States attorney disagreed fundamentally with Leahy's more conciliatory approach. The FBI agreed with the U.S. attorney.

Leahy is described by one political commentator as having the "kind of quiet, thoughtful temperament, combined with a certain zest for life and puckish sense of humor, that seems to be part of the Yankee heritage in

Vermont.'' It is reflected in how he dealt with the prospect of campus demonstrations.

Leahy reminisced with a twinkle in his eye, ''One afternoon during one of the large demonstrations on the campus green, I was wandering around seeing how things were going. Four identical Chevrolets, with Albany, New York, license plates pulled up. These guys get out. I figured they were either IBM salesmen (IBM is the largest employer in Vermont) or FBI agents. You know, they were wearing white shirts, almost identical dark suits.

''I asked to take the microphone, and I said, 'One thing we ought to do. You know, everybody has the right to express whatever views they like. I note that we now have a dozen FBI agents here. Why don't we welcome them?' The [agents] got all shook up and left.''

Later as a member of the Senate Intelligence Committee, he read his own FBI report and found that the incident had been dutifully reported to FBI headquarters. ''They were not pleased,'' according to Leahy.

The conservative Republican governor of Vermont also was concerned but was generally supportive of the way Leahy ran the D.A.'s office. He called Leahy and asked whether he should call out the National Guard.

Leahy had made it clear to all the authorities that he was not going to permit destruction of property. ''Calling in the National Guard would be the craziest thing in the world,'' he told the governor. ''If things get out of hand, we can mobilize the M.P. units just like that.'' He snapped his fingers. ''But even to announce that they're on standby would be crazy.'' The governor agreed.

By the middle of August Leahy was poring over the volumes of Bork speeches and opinions his staff had sent up to him. His diary entry for August 15 recalls the following: ''I am reading several hours of material a day. In Washington, it's difficult to put ten uninterrupted minutes together. Here [at his rural Vermont retreat], I can sit on the lawn, under the apple trees or by the pool, and the only interruption is an occasional car or truck kicking up dirt on the gravel road. I've got a view through the valley of Camel's Hump; hawks circle overhead. Today I didn't even notice two deer that had moved quietly by me to the edge of the woods. In these surroundings, I am getting to know Robert Bork.

''The serenity is in contrast to the sense of coldness I am getting from Bork's opinions. I am struck by the harshness of his criticism of the Supreme Court. When will I discover a sense of humanity, a sense of person in his writing? What I read is a sense of righteousness that is chilling, so different from the man I spoke to briefly outside the Senate.''

Leahy had had a brief encounter with Bork on the Senate steps in Washington in July. Bork was with their mutual friend Tom Korologos. Leahy made it clear then and in a later meeting that he wanted to talk about Bork's First Amendment views.

Like Specter, Leahy was not happy with what he was learning that August about Robert Bork and especially about the judge's views on domestic dissent. Bork's hostility to dissent, his fear that our society could not tolerate it, simply did not square with their own practical experience as former law enforcement officers. It was a subject on which both former trial lawyers were anxious to cross-examine the judge.

CHAPTER 10

TRIVIALIZING THE CONSTITUTION

TWO OTHER MEMBERS of the Senate Judiciary Committee, New Right Republican Orrin Hatch and conservative Democrat Dennis DeConcini, also spent August reading the Bork record. DeConcini and Hatch were close personal friends, who agreed on many questions, especially the conservative social agenda that had brought Robert Bork to the attention of the Reagan Administration.

Hatch was elected to the United States Senate in 1976, as a last-minute entrant to the race. A newcomer to Utah, he decided to enter the race because he felt that the Republican challengers were too moderate. He ran a negative campaign against the incumbent, Democrat Frank Moss, and with the help of the New Right's wizards of direct mail, scored an upset victory.

Hatch soon developed a reputation as a workhorse who took his job and his beliefs seriously. When the Republicans took control of the Senate in 1981, he gained the chairmanship of the Senate Subcommittee on Constitutional Rights from the defeated Birch Bayh. Under Bayh's stewardship the subcommittee had become a safe haven for civil rights advocates and civil libertarians. Orrin Hatch had dramatically different views from Bayh on the question of gender discrimination under the Constitution. As a bishop in the Mormon Church, Hatch was an opponent of the ERA. He did his homework, and as liberals were to learn to their dismay, he could be a very effective lawyer and a politically smart one at that.

Dennis DeConcini was elected to the Senate from Arizona in the same year as Hatch. They had served together as chairman and ranking member on many different subcommittees of the Judiciary Committee over the years. They clearly enjoyed working together, and their staffs were close. Two members of their staffs had opened a lobbying office together, and over the years Hatch and DeConcini Judiciary Committee staffs cooperated on many projects.

As Ed Baxter, DeConcini's counsel at the Judiciary Committee in 1987, pointed out, they were about the same age, were from contiguous states, and

DeConcini not only endorsed but sought enactment of much of Hatch's conservative social agenda for the subcommittee—constitutional amendments on a balanced budget, reversing the *Roe* v. *Wade* decisions, and in favor of school prayer. However, they had divided over important Reagan Justice Department and judicial nominations.

On the contentious nomination of Brad Reynolds to be associate attorney general in 1985, an important harbinger of the Bork fight, DeConcini had been a pivotal vote to kill the nomination. Confirmation of Reynolds was a high priority for Hatch and the Administration.

The real issue in the Reynolds fight was not simply his position on various issues but embarrassing inconsistencies in his testimony on how he handled several sensitive civil rights cases. DeConcini decided he would vote "no" on the basis of Reynolds' testimony. He asked Baxter to prepare a memorandum reflecting his review of the transcripts of the hearings, summarizing the reasons Baxter and he had discussed for opposing the nomination. DeConcini's press office released the memorandum. The Justice Department prepared a detailed response to Baxter's memorandum and released it to the press.

Hatch, as a close personal friend of DeConcini, felt he could persuade him to change his mind. Privately he took the Justice Department memorandum to DeConcini and tried to talk him into changing his vote. DeConcini refused.

The Reynolds fight generated a significant amount of attention for Hatch and DeConcini. Baxter explained that "Hatch and DeConcini went on a lot of talk shows together [on opposite sides of the Reynolds fight]. They went on McNeil–Lehrer, C-Span . . . and had a debate. . . . That was not the most pleasant thing in the world for them. They were friends and liked each other. Here they were debating this thing on national television, and Reynolds was very important to Hatch."

In the case of the Bork nomination, Hatch hoped that he would not see a repeat of the Reynolds vote from his friend Dennis DeConcini. The initial signals were encouraging.

DeConcini had been quite upset about Kennedy's initial speech. As someone close to DeConcini explained, "He thought that the speech was premature. He thought that it was as wrong to do what Kennedy had done as it was to say before the hearings started that Bork was the greatest thing since sliced bread. His speech made it much more difficult for people like DeConcini to vote against Bork. . . . Rather than 'How can you vote against Bork?' it became [for us] 'How can you be on the same side as Ted Kennedy?'. . . . It would have been impossible for DeConcini or Heflin or any of the moderates outside the committee to take a position against Bork until after the hearings because of the speech. They had to wait for an intervening reason to vote no."

Soon after Kennedy's speech, DeConcini sent a letter to many of his colleagues, urging caution in taking an early position. The letter was considered a bad sign by many of us organizing the opposition to the nomination. It seemed like a clear signal from DeConcini that he was leaning in favor of Bork.

However, there were some reasons for hope. One of the few issues on which Hatch and DeConcini disagreed was the Equal Rights Amendment, and Bork had expressed doubts about the wisdom of it too.

DeConcini was deeply committed to women's rights. As his chief of staff Gene Carp pointed out, his wife, Susan, and his daughters, both professionals, were keenly interested in these issues and in Bork's position on them. During the summer of 1987, not only did Dennis DeConcini pore over Bork's speeches and opinions but so did Susan DeConcini.

In 1977 soon after his first election, DeConcini had weighed in in Arizona on behalf of the ratification of the ERA, which was struggling unsuccessfully through the state legislature. He came back to Arizona to testify in favor of the ERA before the legislature.

Despite a consistently Pro-Life position on abortion, Dennis DeConcini had been reared in an environment in which women were encouraged to pursue their ambitions. "My mother was very active in the community. . . . She was a founding member of the League of Women Voters. I remember going to meetings with her. I grew up where women should be part of everything."

Equal rights easily became a part of his political creed. "When I ran for public office my first time as county attorney [in 1972], I made a commitment to hire women prosecutors because they had none. . . . Sure enough, we hired the first woman prosecutors. There were six of them out of thirty-six. I used that as my political commitment to equal rights. . . ."

"One of them turned out not to be so good, but the other five turned out to be crackerjack lawyers. [I did this against the advice of] my own staff when I came in. All the prosecutors said, 'You can't put women in here—dirty language, dirty cases—they can't hack it'."

Thus, when he first ran for the Senate in 1976, "I was very easily comfortable with [my] public position [in favor of] the Equal Rights Amendment."

Defeat of the ERA was one of the highest priorities for Orrin Hatch and his allies on the Right. On July 1, 1982, time expired for ratification of the ERA. It was a major victory for conservative forces, especially Phyllis Schlafly, an Illinois housewife, and spokesperson for the conservative effort to defeat the ERA, through an organization she created, the Eagle Forum. The day before the ratification period expired, she appeared at a 1,000-person celebration at the Shoreham Hotel in Washington. Leading lights of the New Right joined her. According to the *New York Times,* Paul Weyrich "pumped hands and the Reverend Dr. Jerry Falwell, the television evangelist, signed autographs."

Falwell, who received a "special service award" for his opposition to the amendment, explained Schlafly's role: "Phyllis has succeeded in doing something nobody has ever done. She's mobilized the conservative women of this country into a powerful political unit. This is just the beginning."

The questions of whether women were "already protected by the Fourteenth Amendment" and whether the ERA sanctioned "homosexual marriages" or required "unisex toilets"—favorite anti-ERA arguments—were matters on which Robert Bork had expressed firm opinions, opinions that troubled Dennis DeConcini. Robert Bork's concerns about the Equal Rights Amendment—and especially the question of whether gender discrimination was or should be covered by the Constitution—was no simple-minded antifeminist position. It represented a more fundamental concern on his part on how the equal protection clause of the Fourteenth Amendment ought to be interpreted.

In 1868 the Fourteenth Amendment to the Constitution was ratified. Section 1 reads as follows:

> All persons born or naturalized in the United States, and subject to the jurisdiction thereof, are citizens of the United States and of the State wherein they reside. No State shall make or enforce any law which shall abridge the privileges or immunities of citizens of the United States; nor shall any State deprive any person of life, liberty, or property, without due process of law; nor deny to any person within its jurisdiction the equal protection of the laws.

"Privileges or immunities" of citizenship, "due process," and "equal protection" of the law—these were vague concepts which would ultimately command thousands of pages of interpretation in Supreme Court opinions in the century which followed. Original intent was essentially useless in interpreting these provisions, as the legislative history is cursory at best. As one commentator has pointed out, "The framers of the Fourteenth Amendment had great difficulty in articulating any specific content for its broad phrases. . . ."

Within five years of its ratification, the Supreme Court had the opportunity to interpret the provision in the so-called *Slaughter-House* cases. Butchers in New Orleans challenged a state-chartered monopoly from which they had been excluded, arguing that they had been deprived of the right "to exercise their trade," violating all three clauses of Section 1. The Court split 5–4 against the butchers, and Justice Miller wrote an opinion that would forever make the privileges-or-immunities clause a nullity, and so narrowly construed the other two that it would take generations to undo the mischief.

To Miller the purpose of Section 1 was to overturn Justice Taney's infamous *Dred Scott* decision, a major precipitating factor of the Civil War. In that decision, Taney declared that slaves were not citizens. For Miller Section 1 simply said that they were citizens and then went on to elaborate the definition of citizenship.

In a very clever parsing of the language of Section 1, Miller concluded that the Constitution only protected the privileges and immunity of United States citizenship. The privileges and immunity of state citizenship, "whatever they might be," are not protected by the Constitution. Therefore the provision did not protect a citizen against the "legislative power of his own state." The Court would not put itself in the position of a "perpetual censor upon all legislation of the States."

The Court summarily dismissed the due process claim, and as for equal protection, it concluded, "We doubt very much whether any action of a State not directed by way of discrimination against negroes as a class, or on account of their race, will ever be held to come within the purview of this provision." In short, the Fourteenth Amendment was intended to apply to former slaves or racial discrimination, and that is all.

Two dissents were filed. Justice Field makes the obvious point that the majority appears to interpret the privileges or immunities clause as simply being redundant with the existing language of Article IV of the Constitution. Justice Joseph P. Bradley angrily complains, "[It] is futile to argue that none but persons of the African race are intended to be benefited by this amendment. They may have been the primary cause of the amendment, but its language is general, embracing all citizens, and I think it was purposely so expressed."

Justice Miller and the majority seemed particularly concerned about the impact of the Bradley interpretation on the relation between the state and federal governments and in particular on the federal court system. Bradley rejected that out of hand: "The argument from inconvenience ought not to have a very controlling influence in questions of this sort. The National Will and National Interest are of far greater importance."

Much of the next century of Fourteenth Amendment jurisprudence was spent reversing the narrow interpretation adopted by the Court in the *Slaughter-House* cases. The Court would do so, not by reinterpreting the privileges or immunities language, which had been frozen by Justice Miller's opinion, but through generous interpretations of the due process and equal protection clauses. As that jurisprudence has developed, it has raised many of the issues that concerned the majority in 1873, and it was at the heart of Judge Bork's critique of Fourteenth Amendment jurisprudence in the summer of 1987.

Judge Bork was profoundly concerned about the scope of protection of the Fourteenth Amendment. For example, should the Fourteenth Amendment protections be expanded beyond the "slave race" to women? Justice Miller and his colleagues faced that issue the same year they decided the *Slaughter-House* cases. Their answer was an unequivocal no.

The Court first directly addressed the issue of the status of women under the Fourteenth Amendment in 1873, when Mrs. Myra Bradwell applied to become a member of the Illinois Bar. The Illinois Supreme Court rejected her Fourteenth Amendment claim, reminding Bradwell that Illinois had adopted the common law of England and that under common law, "female attorneys at law were unknown in England and a proposition that a woman should enter the courts of Westminster Hall in that capacity, or as a barrister, would have created hardly less astonishment than one that she should ascend the bench of bishops, or be elected to a seat in the House of Commons."

Bradwell appealed to the Supreme Court of the United States, arguing that the denial violated the Fourteenth Amendment. She argued that admission to the bar is one of the "classes of privileges which a State may not abridge" under the privileges-or-immunities clause of Section 1.

Justice Miller, writing for the Court, relied specifically upon his opinion in the *Slaughter-House* cases, "the right to control and regulate the granting of licenses to practice law in the courts of a State is one of those powers which are not transferred for its protection to the Federal Government. . . ."

Even Justice Bradley, who wrote the dissent in the *Slaughter-House* cases, would not side with Bradwell. Indeed his concurring opinion is more explicitly sexist than is Miller's. Bradwell's argument, Bradley noted, "assumes that it is one of the privileges and immunities of women as citizens to engage in any and every profession, occupation, or employment in civil life." Nothing could be further from the truth: "Man is, or should be women's protector and defender. The natural and proper timidity and delicacy which belongs to the female sex evidently unfits it for many of the occupations of civil life. . . . The paramount destiny and mission of women are to fulfill the noble and benign offices of wife and mother. This is the law of the Creator."

Bradwell v. *Illinois* was in some respects a *Dred Scott* case for women. After it, women were simply not full citizens, and men were simply not bound to respect many of their rights. As Bradwell learned in 1873, one of those rights that men need not respect was the right to practice law. Two years later, in *Minor* v. *Happersett,* the Court denied Virginia Minor's claim, under the Fourteenth Amendment, to be allowed to vote.

For the next century the Court followed a very simple-minded rule. In the case of race or ethnic discrimination, the Court would place a heavy burden upon the state legislature. It must demonstrate a "compelling state interest" in the discrimination because classifications based on race or ethnicity were "suspect." However, with respect to other discrimination—based on gender, for example—great deference was shown to the legislature.

In many cases the discrimination was in the name of "protecting women." For example in 1912 Montana exempted women from a tax on laundries. Justice Holmes noted, "If Montana deems it advisable to put a lighter burden upon women than upon men with due regard to an employment that our people commonly regard as more appropriate for the former, the Fourteenth

Amendment does not interfere.'' In the same vein the Court in 1924 upheld a New York statute that prohibited women from working in restaurants between 10 P.M. and 6 A.M. In 1948, the Court upheld a Michigan statute that forbade any woman to act as a bartender unless she was the wife or daughter of the male owner of the bar. As Justice Frankfurter explained in upholding the Michigan statute, ''Since the line they [the legislators] have drawn is not without a basis in reason, we cannot give ear to the suggestion that the real impulse behind this legislation was an unchivalrous desire of male bartenders to try to monopolize the calling.''

The ''rational'' or ''reasonable basis'' standard described by Frankfurter was impossible for a female plaintiff to overcome. Ruth Bader Ginsburg, who in 1987 was a colleague of Judge Bork's on the United States Court of Appeals, had been a professor and one of the primary women's rights litigators in the 1960s and 70s. She explained that except for the Nineteenth Amendment, which explicitly gave women the right to vote, until the 1970s ''the Constitution remained an empty cupboard for people seeking to promote the equal status and stature of men and women under the law.'' Even the Warren Court preserved the century-old view of the equal protection clause, deciding in 1961 that women could be excluded from juries.

As Ginsburg explains, it took the conservative Burger Court to recognize that ''legislation apparently designed to benefit or protect women could often, perversely, have the opposite effect. Laws prescribing the minimum wages they could receive; laws barring females from 'hazardous' or 'inappropriate' occupations (practicing law in the nineteenth century, bartending in the twentieth); remnants of the common-law regime which denied to married women rights to hold and manage property, to sue or be sued in their own names, or to get credit from financial institutions (thus protecting them from their own folly or misjudgment)—all these prescriptions and proscriptions were premised on the base line assumption or belief that women could not fend for themselves; they needed big brother's assistance.''

This began to change dramatically with the case of *Reed* v. *Reed,* decided by the Supreme Court in 1971. In 1967 Richard Lynn Reed died without a will in Ada County, Idaho. His adoptive parents, who had since separated, vied for the right to be executor of the estate. The probate judge felt bound by a presumption in favor of males in Idaho probate law and appointed the father. Sally Reed appealed the decision through the Idaho court to the Supreme Court, arguing that the presumption in Idaho probate law violated the equal protection clause of the Fourteenth Amendment.

Professor Ginsburg joined Sally Reed's attorney in preparing the brief for the Supreme Court. Ginsburg and her colleagues argued that there were two basic standards under which the Supreme Court examined equal protection claims: the ''rational basis'' standard and the ''suspect'' classification standard. Under the latter standard, when a statute distinguished on the ''basis of race or ancestry,'' it ''embodies a 'suspect' or 'invidious' classification and, unless supported by the most compelling affirmative justification, will not pass constitutional muster.''

Ginsburg argued that the gender-based discrimination reflected in the Idaho statute was a '' 'suspect classification' for which no compelling justification can be shown.'' It was a revolutionary argument for that era. Professor Ginsburg was asking the Court to throw out over a century of jurisprudence under the Fourteenth Amendment and treat gender discrimination the same as race discrimination. Alternatively, she argued that the statute in this case violated the traditional ''reasonable'' or ''rational basis'' test.

Chief Justice Burger wrote for the Court. Although the opinion is not explicit, it appears that the Chief bought Ginsburg's argument that the Idaho statute was unreasonable and arbitrary. The primary defense of the statute was that the presumption was designed to cut down on intrafamily contests and reduce the workload of the probate courts. The Supreme Court decided that was an inadequate justification, the ''very kind of arbitrary legislative choice forbidden by the Equal Protection Clause of the Fourteenth Amendment.''

That same year, the California Supreme Court chose the higher of the two standards that Professor Ginsburg advocated in the *Reed* case. In the case of *Sail'er Inn, Inc.* v. *Kirby* the Sail'er Inn sought to prevent the California Department of Alcohol Beverage Control from revoking its liquor license because it hired women bartenders in direct violation of California law.

Justice Peters, writing for the California court, found that sex should be treated as a suspect classification under the equal protection clause of the Fourteenth Amendment and that the state should demonstrate that it had a compelling state interest in prohibiting women from becoming bartenders. Justice Peters acknowledged U.S. Supreme Court decisions to the contrary, but reviewed the history of other circumstances in which the Court had applied the ''stricter scrutiny'' test—race and lineage—and determined that sex should receive the same treatment. ''Sex, like race and lineage, is an immutable trait, a status into which the class members are locked by the accident of birth. . . . Women, like Negroes, aliens . . . have historically labored under severe legal and social disabilities.''

Ginsburg cited the *Sail'er Inn* opinion in her brief in *Reed* for the proposition that sex should be treated as a suspect class. The Burger Court was simply not prepared to go as far as the California Supreme Court.

Marcia Greenberger is the director of the National Women's Law Center, a public interest law firm that specializes in women's litigation. She is a feminist lawyer, who speaks earnestly about the Supreme Court's decisions under the equal protection clause and has been deeply involved with many of the recent cases, often as a friend of court. She has also worked for legislative initiatives that advance the feminist cause, from the ERA to legislation designed to reverse adverse Supreme Court decisions.

The composition of the Supreme Court, and in particular the nomination of Robert Bork, was a matter of the utmost concern to her in the summer of 1987. When she speaks of the Supreme Court and its impact on the rights of women, her voice unconsciously drops. Serious, without being self-righteous, her tone is one of concern: ''[Until the *Reed* case in 1971] the courts were simply not a place to go to challenge the state's distinctions that often worked a real injustice to women. The courts were not an available place for a remedy. That changed only in 1971 with *Reed* v. *Reed*. . . . [But] it was very unclear in 1971 on what basis [the Court was striking down the Idaho statute]: Whether they were applying the same old 'rational basis test' but looking at 'rational' in a different way than they had in the past when gender discrimination was an issue; whether they were really moving to a different test [some middle-tier test] that was different from the rational basis test; [or] whether they were in the end moving so far as to apply what's called a strict scrutiny test [which applies to blacks and aliens]. . . .''

As Greenberger explains, the next time the Supreme Court addressed gender discrimination under the equal protection clause, in 1973, it was aware of the confusion that it had caused by the *Reed* decision. Lower courts simply did not know what standard to use in gender discrimination cases.

In the case of *Frontiero* v. *Richardson,* Sharon Frontiero, a lieutenant in the Air Force, sought increased medical and housing benefits for her husband Joseph. Joseph was a full-time student at Huntington College in Montgomery, Alabama, where the Frontieros were stationed and was ''dependent'' upon Sharon for a significant share of his living expenses. If the circumstances had been reversed, under federal law Sharon would have been entitled to support as a wife of a serviceman. However, the statute placed greater burdens on Sharon, as a female member of the Air Force, and the benefits were denied.

The district court presumed that Congress's purpose in the statute is that the husband is generally the breadwinner and the wife the dependent and ''it would be more economical to require married female members claiming husbands to prove actual dependency than to extend the presumption of dependency to such members.''

Unfortunately, the Supreme Court, even in deciding the case in favor of Sharon Frontiero, did not definitely answer Marcia Greenberger's question or Ruth Ginsburg's plea. After *Frontiero,* it was still not clear which standard of review applied to gender claims under the equal protection clause. For sure, four of the Justices—Brennan, Douglas, White, and Marshall—decided that sex was a suspect classification and that, as for race, the higher strict scrutiny test applied. Professor Ginsburg, who had argued Frontiero as a friend of the court on behalf of the American Civil Liberties Union, repeated the contention she had made in *Reed* that sex should be a suspect classification. Brennan, writing for the four, agreed with Ginsburg and found that the Air Force's argument that the presumption against husband dependency for "administrative convenience" simply did not meet the compelling state interest requirement that applied to a suspect classification.

Three other justices—Powell, Burger, and Blackmun—agreed with the result but rejected the Brennan conclusion that sex was a suspect qualification. They were satisfied that the case could be decided under the *Reed* analysis, whatever that was; furthermore Justice Powell, who wrote for the three, argued that Congress had just sent the Equal Rights Amendment to the states, which in his mind, "would resolve the substance of the precise question" and that it was inappropriate and unnecessary for the Court to reach the question. Powell obviously assumed that, if adopted, the ERA which read "Equality of rights under the law shall not be denied or abridged by the United States or by any State on account of sex" would mean that the "strict scrutiny" test would then apply to gender.

Justice Rehnquist dissented. Justice Stewart concurred with the majority, but in a one-sentence opinion simply cited *Reed* v. *Reed*. Where Justice Stewart and a majority of the court stood on strict scrutiny for gender discrimination was unclear. As Greenberger explained, the fact that Stewart had not sided with either the Brennan camp or the Powell camp "left one wondering whether he might be the fifth vote at some point."

Ginsburg was harsher in her assessment. In interviews years later, she felt that Brennan had moved too quickly in *Frontiero* toward a strict scrutiny standard, before Stewart was ready. According to one analyst, Ginsburg thereafter "adjusted her objective in response to the outcome in *Frontiero* and attempted to get the Court to enunciate an intermediate level of scrutiny for sex classifications."

Greenberger and her feminist colleagues were to be disappointed with the Supreme Court in the years that followed. The majority for a strict scrutiny standard never materialized. As Greenberger explained, in a series of cases in the mid-1970s, the Supreme Court began to develop the middle standard that Ginsburg first suggested in her brief in *Frontiero,* "and the key case that really set that standard out in very concrete terms was *Craig* v. *Boren*"

In this 1976 case the Court was considering the constitutionality of an Oklahoma statute, which had a lower drinking age for women (eighteen) than it did for men (twenty one). Here again Professor Ginsburg filed a friend-of-court brief for the American Civil Liberties Union.

The feminist cause again failed to muster a majority for the strict scrutiny standard, but Ginsburg, Greenberger, and the feminists clearly had a victory in the *Craig* v. *Boren* case. Justice Brennan wrote the opinion of the Court and after reviewing all the gender cases articulated what came to be known as the third or middle-tier standard for gender discrimination: "To withstand constitutional challenge, previous cases establish that classifications by gender must serve important governmental objectives and must be substantially related to achievement of those objectives.'' Clearly Brennan was groping for some stricter standard of review for gender cases, but lay readers could be no more confused by this opinion than were most constitutional scholars.

Six justices clearly approved of that standard or at least some middle standard for gender discrimination—Brennan, White, Marshall, Stewart, Powell, and Blackmun. The feminists had finally persuaded the Court to move away from the elusive and unsatisfactory rational basis test. It was not the strict scrutiny test that blacks and ethnics enjoyed, but women had come a long way from the cases in the 1870s when the Court thought that denying entry to the bar or voting—or even in 1961 protecting them from jury service—was ''rational.''

For Greenberger, *Craig* v. *Boren* ''was the case where the Court basically said, 'We're going to treat gender discrimination cases in a somewhat distinct way.' We think that, given the history of sex discrimination and the fact that the government has disadvantaged women, it isn't appropriate for the Court to give the kind of deference to the government that a rational basis test would allow, thereby giving the states almost a carte blanche to draw any distinctions [they want] on the basis of gender.''

On the other hand, Greenberger conceded that the Court had not gone for the feminists' strict scrutiny argument. It was the decision cited by lower courts for the middle-tier test.

Furthermore, Justice Stevens, President Ford's new appointee to the court, until then an enigma on these issues, clearly agreed with the middle standard result and seemed to see the need, in gender cases, for some test stricter than rational basis. However, he filed a concurring opinion in the case, which opinion was to play an important role in the hearings on Robert Bork. Stevens agreed with the result but expressed dismay with the so-called third standard.

''There is only one Equal Protection Clause,'' he wrote. ''It requires every state to govern impartially. It does not direct the Court to apply one standard of review in some cases and a different standard in other cases.''

Stevens argued that even the two-tiered analysis was not ''completely logical.'' All the equal protection cases actually employ a ''single standard,'' he said, but he declined to ''articulate it in all-encompassing terms.'' In effect, Stevens was arguing for a case-by-case analysis. Stating that the statute is not ''irrational,'' he explained that the statistical evidence advanced in its behalf—that young men are more likely than young women to abuse alcohol—was not persuasive.

The period after *Craig* v. *Boren* presented three challenges for feminists. For one thing, the Democrats lost the White House in 1980, and Ronald Reagan appointed Sandra Day O'Connor to the Court to fill the vacancy caused by Justice Stewart's retirement. Justice O'Connor's position on gender discrimination under the equal protection clause was a mystery. Second, the ERA, which had been submitted to the states in 1972, appeared to be in increasing trouble especially with the growing power of the conservative cause, which opposed it. Third, the record under *Craig* v. *Boren* in the lower courts was mixed at best.

The last great gender discrimination case under the equal protection clause pertains to all of these issues. *Mississippi University for Women* v. *Hogan* involved the application of Joe Hogan, a registered nurse, to an all-female nursing school at the Mississippi University for Women (MUW). The application was rejected.

The state argued that the MUW program was in effect an affirmative action program for women. It was precisely the kind of argument that had been succeeding under the *Craig* v. *Boren* standard. The "important interest" that the state had for the all-female program was to compensate for past discrimination against women, and the women-only admission policy bore "a substantial relation" to that interest. At stake was the continued existence of women-only institutions nationwide.

Ironically the opinion came down on July 1, 1982, the date for expiration of the ERA. Justice O'Connor wrote for a slim 5–4 majority but with a resounding reaffirmation of the *Craig* v. *Boren* standard. O'Connor cut through the affirmative action argument, pointing out that MUW's women-only programs were not established to compensate for past discrimination. Indeed the nursing program was established in 1971, when similar programs existed in other institutions in Mississippi. Besides, nursing was a predominantly women's profession. She concluded that the women-only policy perpetuated "the stereotyped view of nursing as an exclusively woman's job."

Most gratifying to the feminists, O'Connor seized upon the Court's language in one of its earlier cases interpreting *Craig* v. *Boren* and required the state to establish an "exceedingly persuasive justification" for gender-based discrimination. Indeed in one footnote in the opinion, O'Connor seemed to be leaving open the door to a strict scrutiny standard for gender discrimination.

It was a stunning victory for the feminists in the midst of the Reagan revolution, handed to them by Reagan's own appointee to the Court. O'Connor was definitely an improvement upon her predecessor, Justice Stewart, when it came to the issue of gender discrimination. However, as Greenberger points out, feminists recognized that it was a fragile victory—the majority was a thin 5–4, and the standard was still subject to interpretation. By the summer of 1987, the feminists were watching the Supreme Court with great anxiety. Ronald Reagan had appointed Antonin Scalia to replace Burger, who had been an occasional supporter of their cause, and promoted the most consistent opponent of their cause, William Rehnquist, to the position of

Chief Justice. Now, Lewis Powell, who had joined their coalition in *Craig* v. *Boren*, was to be replaced with Robert Bork.

As feminists reviewed Judge Bork's writings on this subject in the summer of 1987, they realized that they had much to be concerned about. His views on gender discrimination under the equal protection clause were simple and direct. The court had erred in ever applying the equal protection clause to women.

For example in his *Indiana Law Review* article Bork noted that "The Supreme Court has no principled way of saying which non-racial inequalities are impermissible [under the equal protection clause]."

In April 1982, just three months before Justice O'Connor's opinion in *Mississippi University for Women,* Bork spoke to his friends in the conservative Federalist Society. Employing language familiar to those who had read his writings about liberal judges interpreting the First Amendment, he warned, "When they [federal judges] begin to protect groups that were historically not intended to be protected by that clause, what they are doing is picking out groups which current morality of a particular social class regards as groups that should not have any disabilities laid upon them. . . . All of these are nationalizations of morality, not justified by anything in the Constitution, justified only by the sentimentalities or the morals of the class to which these judges and their defenders belong."

Bork saw what the courts were doing as "nothing more than the imposition of upper class values on society." These views, he argued, as he had in the First Amendment area, are coming from the two institutions which the Court responds to—the press and the law school faculties. "They want sexual freedoms; they want freedom for abortion. . . . They want every kind of expressive behavior, or any kind of behavior that can remotely be called expressive, protected by the First Amendment."

In the question-and-answer period following the speech, Bork continued the theme: "With the extension of the equal protection clause to groups that were never previously protected . . . what they are doing is picking out groups which current morality of a particular moral class regards as groups that should not have any disabilities laid upon them."

Bork held to these views as recently as a month before his nomination. On June 10, 1987, in an interview Bork said bluntly that he thought "the equal protection clause probably should have been kept to things like race and ethnicity." Referring to *Craig* v. *Boren,* Bork continued, "When the Supreme Court decided that having different drinking ages for young men and young women violated the equal protection clause . . . that was to trivialize the Constitution and to spread it to areas it did not address."

Feminist lawyers, who viewed *Craig* v. *Boren* as the key case establishing the middle-tier standard for gender discrimination under the equal protection clause, were obviously offended by and distressed with the notion that the

Court had ''trivialized'' the Constitution in that case. Not surprisingly Bork's doubts about the wisdom of an Equal Rights Amendment only heightened their concern.

The concerns Bork expressed about the ERA and whether a strict scrutiny standard should be applied to gender discrimination were not unique. Indeed, they had been expressed by respected moderate scholars as early as 1971.

In the summer of 1982 the Democrats reintroduced the ERA soon after it died, and ironically the first hearings would be before Orrin Hatch and his Constitution subcommittee. Hatch's carefully crafted hearings were designed to kill the ERA. He had focused exactly on the argument that had concerned Bork and killed the amendment in the states—that a strict scrutiny test would have untoward effects, sanctioning homosexual marriages, mandating unisex toilets, invalidating veterans' preferences, requiring combat roles for women in the military.

As ranking member, DeConcini was responsible for overseeing the hearings for Democrats, and they should have been more visible, but then again even ardent liberals like Ted Kennedy only showed up for a fraction of the sessions. However, when Hatch set up a hearing on the most explosive argument against the ERA—that it would make unconstitutional the Hyde amendment, a statute that prohibited Medicaid funding of abortions—DeConcini came to the subcommittee to take on his friend Orrin Hatch.

DeConcini had an anomalous position on these issues, which made him particularly vulnerable to Hatch's new line of attack: ''The obvious conflict to many is 'How can you be for equal rights and be Pro-Life?' To me it's very easy . . . Every time I ran for the Senate [the Pro-Lifers] would accept my strong commitment to women's issues, including family planning, funding for family planning but not for the right to fund abortions.''

As for the fate of the ERA, it was essential that the ERA not be perceived as affecting the abortion matter. There were close to a dozen pro-ERA, Pro-Life members of the Senate, and the vote was close enough in the Senate that it was crucial that these members not be forced to choose. Besides, it was clear that, if the issue were not resolved, the powerful Catholic Conference was likely to oppose the new amendment.

DeConcini did an excellent job defending the pro-ERA witnesses and taking on his friend Orrin Hatch. However, by the time the hearings were over, the ERA seemed to flounder in the Republican-controlled Senate and indeed has not been revived since then.

So by the summer of 1987, the ERA was stalled. The 1972 effort was dead, and any new effort seemed unlikely in the foreseeable future. The only hope was the Supreme Court of the United States, and all eyes were on Bork, who not only opposed the ERA but had serious doubts that gender discrimination should be covered by the equal protection clause of the Fourteenth Amendment.

Orrin Hatch began the August recess in 1987 hoping that his relationship with DeConcini and DeConcini's conservative, even Pro-Life, political values gave him and the Administration a strong shot at his vote for Bork. Dennis DeConcini began the August recess with a strong presumption in favor of the President for any nominee. Indeed he wanted to "find a way to support the nomination." However he also felt deeply about the protection of women's rights under the Constitution and the right to personal privacy and the importance of family planning short of abortion. What he read of Robert Bork's views on these issues concerned him that summer. And what DeConcini, perhaps the most important pivotal vote on the Bork nomination, thought about these issues should have distressed not only his friend, Orrin Hatch, but the rest of Bork's allies.

If what Dennis DeConcini learned about Robert Bork during August was indeed the "real Robert Bork," the nomination was in serious trouble. DeConcini, like Specter and Leahy, was a former prosecutor, adept at cross-examination. He now began to look to September when he too could question the judge.

CHAPTER 11

TOXIC DETRITUS

AT THE SAME TIME that members of the Senate Judiciary Committee were immersing themselves in his writings, in an effort to find the real Robert Bork, there were others who needed no introduction to Bork. In the law schools, in the bureaucracies of the civil rights and fundamentalist movements, experts combed the record for further evidence that Bork was either the worst or the best nomination to the Supreme Court in recent memory.

The ammunition that they gathered was to be given not just to the members of the Judiciary Committee, to help them analyze the nominee, but to editorial boards, television news producers, and ultimately to the public in the upcoming hearings. Increasingly, the hearings and Bork's appearance before the committee were viewed as climactic events, and academics and denizens of the Right and Left clamored to have last-minute input to the two leading protagonists in the hearings—Biden and Bork—as they prepared for September 15.

Perhaps Robert Bork had legitimate reasons, as expressed in his recent book, to be surprised about the reaction of the editorial boards or even the breadth of opposition in the civil rights movement. One group's opinion of the nomination should have come as no surprise—law professors. One of Bork's favorite targets was liberal domination of law school faculties.

On April 3, 1987, less than three months before he was nominated by President Reagan to be an Associate Justice on the Supreme Court, Judge Robert Bork delivered a speech to the conservative Philadelphia Society in Philadelphia. In the speech, Bork described his ''wave theory'' of law reform. It was a scathing attack on the judiciary and the academic establishment.

Many judges, he charged, no longer feel bound by the original intent of the framers of the Constitution. Most law professors share that view and inculcate it in the minds of new lawyers, ''You will have difficulty, I think, naming even one full-time professor at a major law school who writes in favor of original intent. The five professors who once did have all been appointed to the federal bench by the present Administration. That is why I often say that, while my colleagues at Yale do not like much else about Ronald Reagan, they regard him as a great reformer of legal education.

"What is the point of all of this scholarship—I use the word generously . . . ?" Bork asked. It is to create "a society far more egalitarian, socially permissive, and morally relativistic than the one we have or any that the American electorate wants. . . ."

Bork had a solution. It inhered in his "wave theory." The courts in the "urgency of litigation" arrive at decisions but rather than base their judgment on theory, they "reason by analogy." Thus after World War II, courts addressed "what they regarded as social problems . . . without regard to any recognizable theory of constitutional interpretation."

The first wave of scholarship in the law schools "start[s] from the deformed notions judges have created and extrapolate[s] them. A rich, erudite, and mindless literature grows up. The courts then begin to adopt the extrapolations. The future of the law begins to look extremely bleak." The "intellectual and moral excesses of the second wave are breathtaking. . . . Theorists exhort the courts to unprecedented imperialistic adventures."

The second wave of theorists point out that the first-wave theorists make little sense. "The second-wave theorists return to first principles. They ask what the purpose of the law is, what legitimates the courts' behavior, and they begin to construct better theories of how courts should decide cases. Since the second-wave arguments are much better, they slowly come to dominate the intellectual world, the new ideas slowly percolate through to the courts, and the law is on the road to respectability.

"It will take ten years, it may take twenty years, for the second wave to crest, but crest it will, and it will sweep the elegant, erudite, pretentious, and toxic detritus of nonoriginalism out to sea."

This expression of Bork's disdain for most of his academic colleagues worried some Senators. How would it affect his decisions once he was named to the Court? How many civil-rights advances were included in "toxic detritus"?

Bork was right about one thing. By the late 1980s some prestigious academic campuses, Harvard in particular, were riven with ideological factions. In a conference before Harvard alumni in New York City, the future dean of their alma mater, Robert Clark, described the contending forces on the law school campuses: "There are three major intellectual movements in the law school world: the Law and Economics movement; the Law and Society movement; and the Critical Legal Studies movement.

The Law and Economics or Chicago School, represented by Bork and others, use economic analysis to explain the impact of the law. Although the school is predominantly conservative, there are some liberals who consider themselves in the Law and Economics School.

The other two schools, to Clark, represent the liberal and the radical left in the law schools. The more traditional liberal scholarship is represented by what Clark calls the Law and Society movement, centered primarily at the University of Wisconsin law school. It applies sociological concepts to explain legal rules.

At the extreme left is the Critical Legal Studies movement or the "crits," as they had come to be known on campuses around the nation. Clark, an avowed opponent of the crits, described them as follows: "They avoid or even condemn empirical research, as well as ties with the conventional legal profession. Politically, they are radically left-wing, and they save their hardest-hitting criticisms for the thought patterns of liberal Democrats, not conservatives."

Nowhere had the ideological battle lines been more dramatically drawn in the mid-1980s than on the campus of Clark's own Harvard. However, it was not the Law and Economics group who were the alleged culprits but the crits.

The outside world first learned of this pitched battle in the upper reaches of legal academia in an article in the *New Yorker* in March of 1984. Calvin Trillin described a battle that "has taken on some aspects of a generational dispute and an intellectual debate and a way to settle old grudges. . . ."

In the 1960s and early 1970s, the notion of law as neutral principles—a school of thought called "legal process"—dominated law teaching, especially at Harvard. Traditional teachers, many of whom considered themselves political liberals, were strongly attached to this approach and "retained a kind of detached, conservative style."

In the 1970s three young professors arrived at Harvard—Morton Horwitz, Duncan Kennedy, and Roberto Unger. "They would maintain, for instance," said Trillin, "that the effect of a Legal Process approach in the fifties and sixties was to argue for judicial restraint during a period when the courts were trying to extend individual rights and racial equality." Thus was born the Critical Legal Studies movement.

Even conservative opponents of the crits, like Paul Bator, describe the three founders as "brilliant." The problems came with the extremism that began to characterize the writings of some crits, in particular Duncan Kennedy. As Trillin points out, Kennedy often makes proposals "that seem astonishing." Like Bork, Kennedy seemed to overstate his point for effect.

Kennedy felt that the law school simply perpetuates another "illegitimate hierarchy." Therefore Harvard students ought to be selected for admission by lot; members of law firms should be selected in much the same manner; legal services should be free and equal for everyone; all law students who pass the bar should be guaranteed a job, and finally there should be equal pay for professors and janitors at the law schools.

The real battle was joined at Harvard when the crits moved their theories from the journals to the faculty meetings. As Trillin pointed out, "One way [the crits faction] differed from the rest of the faculty was in its willingness to lobby, trade votes, and proselytize.'' With the influx of more junior professors, they gained the one third votes necessary to block the appointments of new faculty. And in the words of one conservative member of the faculty, ''They goaded us into being uncivil.''

By 1987, ten of fifty-nine tenured positions at Harvard were crits. That was enough to block positions, but it was not enough to protect one of their own.

In 1987, in a nasty tenure fight over Clair Dalton, a crit, the faculty split: twenty-nine of forty-nine in favor but not the necessary two thirds to gain tenure. Many noncrits had praised Dalton's writings but another noncrit, David Rosenberg, had unleashed an eighty-nine page memorandum impugning her scholarship. Yale denied tenure to several crit professors, and in December 1986 the board of trustees at the New England School of Law fired four crits.

Robert Clark, then a professor at Harvard, remarked that the Law and Economics School factions in other law schools played the same kind of favorites in tenure decisions as had the crits at Harvard. He pointed out, in the meeting with Harvard alumni in 1985, that the Chicago School adherents tend to give high ratings to professors who people on the outside would think are ''not all that bright or great or careful.''

However, at no other school was the battle so divisive and so clearly ideological. *Time* magazine pointed out in 1985 that Harvard had not hired a professor for a tenured position in four years. A dean at a rival law school remarked that Harvard is ''an extremely unpleasant and politicized environment.''

Into this highly politicized environment stepped a new organization, organized not by faculty but by students and not at Harvard initially but at Harvard's archrival, Yale Law School. Critics contend that the Federalist Society is not so much an academic school of thought—although it is roughly aligned with the Chicago School—as it is a conservative political organization.

The Federalist Society grew out of the friendship of three young lawyers when they were undergraduates at Yale in the late 1970s. Steven Calabresi was the nephew of Yale's distinguished Dean Guido Calabresi, Lee Lieberman, a conservative political activist on campus, and David McIntosh, another political activist but of a more moderate stance. All three were captivated by conservatism but in particular by libertarianism.

In 1980, Calabresi and Lieberman came to Washington and worked in the U.S. Senate, and ultimately became Reagan delegates to the Republican convention. After the election, all three went on to law school: Calabresi to Yale, Lieberman and McIntosh to the University of Chicago.

Calabresi and four other first-year students decided to create the Federalist

Society as a counterpoint to the liberal bias of the Yale faculty. One of the founding students claimed that liberal Yale professor Owin Fiss "laughed in [the student's] face" when he suggested a libertarian topic for a paper.

Similar complaints were heard by students at Harvard. Paul Capuccio, who ultimately became a Federalist, arrived at Harvard as a liberal but told Robert Bork's son Charles, "I can't emphasize enough how left-wing Harvard is, you are branded a fascist for talking about the Framers' intent. . . ."

"I definitely got pushed to the right after three years at Harvard Law. And I ran into a number of people who seemed to leave Harvard a good deal more conservative than when they came in."

In 1981 Calabresi went to Ralph Winter, then a conservative law professor at Yale, with his ideas for organizing the Federalist Society. Winter, who would ultimately be named by Reagan to the Second Circuit Court of Appeals, suggested that Calabresi organize a national conference on conservative legal scholarship. Winter also suggested that Calabresi contact the Institute for Educational Affairs, a conservative foundation, for funding. As Jill Abramson explained in her profile of the Federalist Society in *American Lawyer*, the vice chair of the Institute is Irving Kristol, "the intellectual godfather of the neoconservative movement." The institute came forward with $25,000, providing the critical seed money for the first annual conference of the Federalist Society for law and public policy studies held at Yale.

The 1982 symposium was a big success. All of the leading lights of conservative jurisprudence and scholarship were present—Antonin Scalia, Richard Posner, Grover Rees, Paul Bator, Charles Fried, and Robert Bork. Soon thereafter, the Olin Foundation, chaired by former Treasury Secretary William Simon, funded a speaker's bureau, and the Federalist Society was off and running.

It became the most important conservative organization in legal academia. Lieberman and McIntosh opened a chapter at the University of Chicago soon after the conference, built around stalwarts of the Law and Economics movement—Posner, Easterbrook, and Richard Epstein. The Law and Economics adherents were also the core of the Stanford chapter. At Harvard, the Federalists organized around a fledgling student publication, *The Harvard Journal of Law and Public Policy*, which had been denied law school funding because it was "too political."

With funding from the same conservative foundations as the society, the Federalists had their own journal, and by 1986 it had spread to seventy-five campuses and was conducting a national conference every year with attendance in the hundreds. It had an annual budget of $400,000, coming predominantly from conservative foundations like the Sarah Scaife Mellon Foundation, Olin, and even the Reagan Administration's National Endowment for the Humanities.

The real source of the Federalist Society's power, however, was its relationship to the Reagan Administration. According to Abramson, within the Reagan Administration, Ken Cribb, Meese's principal deputy, saw the primary role of the Federalist Society "to scout and recruit young conservative lawyers. Not surprisingly, the Federalist Society has been Cribb's key talent bank."

By 1986, over half of the 153 Reagan-appointed positions in the Department of Justice and all twelve assistant attorneys general had either spoken at Federalist Society meetings or were members. Calabresi was appointed to Meese's personal staff, and Lee Lieberman was clerking for Federalist sponsor Antonin Scalia, who was by then an Associate Justice of the Supreme Court. As a clerk on the U.S. Court of Appeals for the District of Columbia told Abramson anonymously, "[conservatism] is where the jobs are." And the Federalist Society was the pipeline.

To assume that the Federalist Society was simply a job bank is to understate its importance. Charles Bork proudly points to a quote in the *Washington Post* from 1985 describing the Federalist Society as the greatest outside influence on the Reagan Administration's selection of federal judges. By then the Reagan Administration had appointed four of the five leading "originalist" scholars to the U.S. Court of Appeals, one of which was his father, all of whom were aligned with the Federalist Society.

The Federalists had also eclipsed the Critical Legal Studies movement. Although the crits claimed 400 members nationwide, the Federalists exceeded that number and, more importantly, could exercise real political power through its relationship with the Reagan Justice Department. However, the crits continued to be an important foil for the Federalists. Indeed, one of its national conferences in 1984 had been specifically on the crits and legal education—the conference in New York City with Harvard alumni, at which Robert Clark had spoken.

Charles Bork certainly spoke for many Federalists and perhaps his father when he wrote in 1986, "As an intellectual movement CLS [Critical Legal Studies] represents the logical extension of the principles that had dominated legal scholarship for three decades. Liberal jurisprudence rejected the possibility of a 'strict construction' of law, . . . Critical Legal Studies pushed this liberal position to its radical conclusion. . . . [The crits] ripped away that thin veneer of constitutionalism. They believe that . . . legal interpretation . . . is merely the selection among political preferences."

He was echoing the traditional appraisal of the crits that they believe "law is simply politics by other means." Charles Bork boasts that the Federalist Society has jumped into the breach.

His father, in his famous "wave theory" speech, explicitly credited the Federalist Society with taking the lead in the necessary law reform. "There are many more younger people, often associated with the Federalist Society, who are of that philosophy [that is, his philosophy] and who plan to go into law teaching.'' And it would be their job to ''sweep the elegant, erudite, pretentious, and toxic detritus of nonoriginalism out to sea.''

On July 6, 1987, at the first broad organizational meeting between the White House and the Department of Justice staffs, it was decided that the Administration would reach out to the establishment bar and academia. In addition to Lloyd Cutler, approaches would be made to Phil Lacovora, president-elect of the D.C. bar, and Harry Wellington, a liberal former dean of Yale Law School.

The initial efforts were quite successful. One week later, Will Ball convened a meeting with Cutler, Lacovora, and Bork. Bork had also asked Ray Randolph. Randolph, a bright, intense appellate litigator, had worked for Bork when he was Solicitor General and had become a close personal friend.

At the meeting, it was decided that Ray Randolph would coordinate the effort to reach out to the establishment bar in many states. As Randolph explained it, the idea was to ''contact prominent members of the bar in various states and ask them to state their views regarding their perception to various members of the Senate.'' The dean of the University of Chicago Law School, Gerhard Casper, was supposed to be in charge of contacting academics in a similar effort. However, as Randolph explained, ''Casper went to Australia during the period, [and] sort of slowed that down.''

Brad Reynolds suggested that someone else be brought in to help staff the effort to reach out to academics. Lee Lieberman was finishing her clerkship with Justice Scalia and was an obvious choice. She could rely on the Federalist Society network, which she had helped to create, and she was very well acquainted with the Meese Justice Department. Indeed, Lieberman had helped to staff the department's process for reviewing prospective Supreme Court nominees and had helped Scalia prepare for his nomination hearings.

Lieberman would work out of Randolph's law office. As far as Reynolds was concerned, Lieberman was in charge of ''outreach to the academic community.'' White House counsel A. B. Culvahouse agreed. In effect, Lieberman would coordinate the activities of a group of distinguished members of the bar—Cutler, Lacovora, Randolph, and former Republican Justice Department and White House officials like Fred Fielding, Jonathan Rose, and Michael Ullman.

Lieberman's initial plans were ambitious. On July 21 and 22 she prepared extensive lists of potential supporters. Her group was attempting to elicit the support of well over 200 legal academics, another eighty academics outside the law, forty former Justice Department officials, eighty members of the bar, almost half of whom were characterized as the ''[Lloyd] Cutler List.''

In a memorandum to Cutler and the others, Lieberman passed on a list that identified thirty Senators who were ''swing'' votes on the Bork nomination. She assigned states in which the recipients were to recruit Bork supporters in the law schools and the local bar. The idea, according to Randolph, was that the professors and lawyers would lobby the "swing Senators." By July 24, she could identify forty-four academics in favor of Bork, seven "leaning toward/rumored to support," another fifteen either taking no position or opposing, and thirty-four prominent members of the bar supporting the nomination.

It is easy to overstate the impact—and perhaps even the intent—of this effort. It is not clear that the effort was well coordinated with the White House. It also seems somewhat unsophisticated. Some of the lists appear overly optimistic, and the early legal academic lists contained names of professors whose "endorsement [was] likely" who actually ended up testifying against Bork. Even the honed-down list of the prominent members of the bar contained the name of former Attorney General Nicholas Katzenbach, who testified against the nomination. In the end only 100 academics endorsed Bork.

On the other hand, the effort among the anti-Bork forces to recruit academics began much more tentatively and with much less optimism. Ricki Seidman, legal director of People for the American Way, and William Taylor, a stalwart of the LCCR, led the project. Both had undertaken a similar effort with the 1986 Daniel Manion nomination to the Seventh Circuit Court of Appeals. That nomination struggle revolved around the question of whether Manion had the necessary professional credentials to serve on the court. Although the nomination was ultimately approved on a one-vote margin, Seidman and Taylor had little trouble drumming up opposition in the academic community.

Taylor and Seidman decided to attempt two initial forays into the academic community on the Bork nomination. First, they would approach law deans as they had in the case of Manion, and simultaneously they would approach constitutional law professors. One of the greatest assets they had was the opposition of three of the most prominent constitutional law professors in the country, all Biden advisers: conservative Philip Kurland at the University of Chicago, and liberals Laurence Tribe at Harvard and Walter Dellinger at Duke.

Taylor's initial contacts with law deans were not encouraging. One dean who had helped on Manion told Taylor, "Manion is one thing, because Manion was a basic question of competence and standards, and Bork is something else and . . . I don't think you ought to make this effort, because you'll have a showing that is much less impressive than the showing you had on Manion."

Taylor responded: "Well, we're going to go after con law professors simultaneously, and see where we come out."

It took a lot of work, but by the second week in September, thirty-two deans had signed a letter in opposition to Bork—not as many as had opposed Manion, but an impressive turnout.

By late August, Seidman had negotiated the text of a letter acceptable to Kurland, Tribe, and Dellinger, and began to circulate it. Seidman and Taylor were surprised by the result. They had identified scholars who were likely to be sympathetic, but, as Taylor pointed out, "once it got rolling, the names started rolling in by themselves."

When they realized how positive the reaction was to the constitutional law letter, they decided to expand beyond constitutional law professors. As the usually staid Taylor pointed out with a twinkle in his eye, "What we discovered is that by late August the Bork nomination was a live issue on law school campuses." By the time the hearings were underway "the outpouring was incredible."

Upon reflection Taylor believes the anti-Bork reaction was motivated by the reverence these law professors felt for the Supreme Court and the direction they feared Bork would take it. "In one way or another these professors felt that their lives had been touched by the work of the Supreme Court on civil rights and civil liberties in the last three decades. And they could see that could eventually unravel, and they could see Bork as the symbol for that."

Chris Schroeder, at Biden's direction, spent much of the late summer and early fall of 1987 on the phone with scores of law professors. Schroeder's view was that the strong opposition to Bork was also a reflection of the highly politicized environment in the law schools and the role which Bork and the Federalists had played in fomenting that unrest.

Although Schroeder agreed with Taylor that the professors who opposed Bork strongly disagreed with where he would take the Court, Schroeder and Taylor also felt a strong negative reaction to Bork that had to be explained by something even more subtle: "One thread of the complicated reaction that people have to Bork in the law schools is that clearly he wants his ideas to make a difference there. He never says this right out but you can't read his 'wave theory' speech or a number of other speeches and believe that he doesn't expect that academic professionals ought to have his view of constitutional theory. And that's going to happen in one or two ways: through attrition and death of the liberals and replacement with people who think like him; or through tenure, promotion and hiring decisions that faculties make."

Schroeder is quick to acknowledge that some members of the Critical Legal Studies movement comprise a radical fringe in law schools today. Indeed, he points out that what was significant about the reaction to Bork in academia was that it went so far beyond the crits—well into the mainstream and middle-of-the-road ranks of the law schools. However, he felt the reaction to Bork might also have been a reaction to the Federalists and the role they were playing in the law schools. "People see the Federalist Society and all that it stands for and Bork as the head of it as having real life practical consequences for their friends in the law schools and now for the Supreme Court. Bork gets on the Court, and arguments that Tom Grey [whom some would label a crit or at least a strong nonoriginalist] might make in an amicus brief aren't going to mean a 'tinker's damn.' They aren't going to be listened to. Or worse yet that any argument that wasn't strictly 'originalist' would be ignored.''

However, most of the professors whom Schroeder recruited to testify against Bork or who signed the letters in opposition did not do so because they felt personally attacked or threatened by Bork. As Schroeder points out, ''It was clear that Bork's sharpest words were leveled at so-called crits and two or three other people who are not associated with the Critical Legal Studies movement, but who have written, to my mind, fairly wild theories of constitutional interpretation. Dworkin is the principal one. Dworkin and Bork have slugged it out verbally a number of times. I don't think that Bork has ever named Dworkin in print but many people are convinced that some of his 'toxic detritus' was aimed at Dworkin and others like [him].''

Taylor wonders, ''How could a guy who engaged in such verbal violence in his writings, like in *Indiana Law Review*, [how could he] think that would not have consequences?'' Schroeder agreed, but he felt the issue was not simply that people in and out of academia were concerned about what Bork would do to the Court but the consequences that those words were intended to have for academia itself. More important, Bork was playing into the political struggles that were going on in many of the law schools. As Schroeder explained, ''So many of his speeches were delivered to Federalist Society groups, and those two groups, Federalist Society and Critical Legal Studies, were the yin and yang of academic politics today, especially at the student level as well as the faculty level. There are active philosophical or ideological groups in law school student bodies today. They are the Federalist Society for the neoconservatives and the crits for the follow-on to the student movement activists of the 60s.''

The fear—paranoia in some cases—and the deep personal hurt on both sides of these battles played a role in this struggle. For example, one prominent professor was extremely reluctant to testify against Bork, because she was up for tenure at one of the best law schools and feared that her position would be used against her when the faculty vote occurred. One prominent anti-Bork scholar was under so much pressure from his colleagues not to testify that he contacted the chairman and asked that his name be stricken from the list. He changed his mind after a personal visit with Biden. Taylor claimed that Walter Berns, a constitutional scholar at a conservative think tank, ''practically physically attacked me'' when he expressed his opposition to Bork at a forum.

Clearly however, the deepest hurt was to Bork and his allies, since the opposition came from their colleagues. Although Bork's language in speeches like the ''wave theory'' speech was strong—and apparently taken personally by some—Bork himself was ecumenical in his private life and had many friends who disagreed fundamentally with his jurisprudence.

Barbara Black, dean of Columbia Law School, had been a close friend of Bork's first wife, Claire. After Claire died, Black had been like a mother to Bork's daughter Ellen. Black did not sympathize with Bork's jurisprudence and did not want to see him on the Court. She was under considerable pressure from her colleagues to oppose the nomination but never took a position. Ellen was furious that Black did not publicly support her father, and she did not speak to the dean for a year.

Harry Wellington, the former dean at Yale, had a similar experience. He had been suggested at an early White House meeting as possibly being in favor. Despite urging from both sides, Wellington basically stayed out of the fight. Later he asked Bork for his forgiveness but Bork was in a "blind fury," and he promised never to speak to him again.

Eventually 2,000 law professors, 40 percent of legal academics, publicly opposed the nomination. The feelings ran deep, and they related to matters of great principle. However, there is little doubt that legal academia itself is far from a reflection of where ordinary Americans are on issues related to the Supreme Court. Bork's supporters are correct. Law professors are probably well to the left of most Americans on the great constitutional issues of the day.

As Taylor points out, "If this had simply been a battle of law professors, with us having 2,000 against him and [their having] a couple of hundred for him, Bork would have won."

CHAPTER 12

MORAL FERVOR

OF COURSE, the Bork battle was not to be just a battle of lawyers and law professors. Bork's and Ronald Reagan's views about the social agenda, and the role of the Supreme Court in shaping that agenda, engaged the moral passions of the Left and the Right. Like the lawyers and law professors, the religious fundamentalists on the Right and the civil rights/civil liberties community on the Left were not representative of average Americans. However, unlike the legal profession, the organized Right and Left were not bashful about attempting to influence public opinion. Indeed, it was their reason for being.

Presidential candidate Jimmy Carter introduced the fundamentalist Right to national politics in the 1976 election when he announced he was a "born again Christian." It had its political benefits to Carter, activating a powerful new constituency, but Carter also tried to defuse its impact with an interview in *Playboy* magazine.

The controversy introduced an important fundamentalist to the national stage. The Rev. Jerry Falwell, who in 1976 was only known to his radio listeners on "The Oldtime Gospel Hour," condemned the fact that Carter agreed to be interviewed by *Playboy*. Falwell's condemnation of Carter was immediately picked up by the national media, including the *Washington Post* and the *Los Angeles Times*.

Falwell was also noticed by conservatives in Washington. One was Eddie McAteer of the Christian Freedom Foundation. McAteer shared with Howard Phillips of the Conservative Caucus an interest in marrying the evangelical movement and the New Right political agenda.

McAteer had talked with Falwell about the importance of his "speaking out on the issues" and arranged meetings with Phillips, Paul Weyrich of the Committee for the Survival of a Free Congress, and Scott Stanley, editor of the John Birch Society's *American Opinion*. It is not clear whether it was Weyrich or Phillips who first mentioned it, but according to McAteer, when the notion of a Moral Majority with Falwell as the head was mentioned, "that was when Jerry's ears really perked up." The Moral Majority was chartered in 1979.

Paul Weyrich was twenty-four when he came to Washington to be press secretary for Republican Sen. Gordon Allott of Colorado in 1966. Weyrich was frustrated with the ineffectiveness of the Senate conservatives. In 1968, as he explained to David Broder in an interview, he found out what was needed. "Senator Allott had a reputation for being a liberal on civil-rights issues, and in 1968 he was invited to attend a strategy session on open-housing legislation. He couldn't go, and I asked him if I could attend in his place. . . . And there, before my very eyes, was the coordination mechanism of the opposition. . . . I wasn't entirely stupid, and I would see these battles come up [in the Senate] and I would see the orchestration of them, but until that meeting I never understood the mechanics. They had the aides to all the Senators there, and they had the authority to commit their bosses to specific strategies. They had the representatives of foundations, which could supply data on this or that. They had a legal group. They had the outside lobbying groups, and they could say, 'We need some pressure when we get down the line, and if they come up with this amendment, we want the whole country alerted.' And they had a couple of columnists who said, 'I can write something; just give me the timing on it.'

"It was one of the best meetings I ever attended, and it gave me a tremendous insight into how the opposition operated. I determined from that moment on that if I had any reason to be here at all it was to duplicate that effort on the Right."

That dream became possible once Weyrich came to know Adolph Coors of the Coors brewery, who was to become a financial darling of the New Right in the 1970s. Together they created the think tank of the New Right—the Heritage Foundation—and one of its most effective political arms—the Committee for the Survival of a Free Congress. The committee soon became one of the best-funded political action committees, credited with providing the wherewithal for Orrin Hatch's surprise victory in 1976.

Weyrich's effort to duplicate the machinery of the Left needed a consistent source of funds. It could not depend upon a few big givers like Coors. Richard Viguerie and the Viguerie company are the secret to that success. Viguerie is a direct mail expert, a master at drafting and mailing fund-raising solicitations to carefully screened lists of conservatives.

Viguerie, like Weyrich, recognized that what the Right needed was not more ideas but a better strategy for communicating those ideas to average Americans—in short, marketing:

"We had outstanding writers, debaters and public speakers like Bill Buckley, Bill Rusher, Russell Kirk. . . . I realized that what we didn't have was someone who could take ideas, the writings and the books, and market them to the people."

Viguerie learned the art of direct mail as executive director of Young Americans for Freedom (YAF) in the early 1960s. He honed his skills with the Goldwater presidential campaign in 1964, raising over $5 million through direct mail and doubling the take with the Wallace campaign in 1968.

In 1978, Viguerie raised over $5 million for the reelection campaign of a single U.S. Senator—Jesse Helms of North Carolina. However, Viguerie's greatest impact was in direct mail solicitations pertaining to single issue groups — Pro-Life groups, antigun control groups—and especially in concert with specific legislative struggles: against the Panama Canal treaty, labor law reform, and public financing of campaigns.

Weyrich, Phillips, Viguerie, and Terry Dolan of the National Conservative Political Action Committee (NCPAC) had by 1980 literally changed the face of the United States Senate. In 1978, they had replaced three more liberals in Colorado, Iowa, and New Hampshire with the election of William Armstrong, Roger Jepsen, and Gordon Humphrey. By 1980, they were credited with the defeat of a number of nationally known establishment liberals—George McGovern, Birch Bayh, John Culver, Frank Church, and Gaylord Nelson—and shifting control of the Senate to Republican hands for the first time in a generation.

By the late 1970s Weyrich, Phillips, and Viguerie had managed to "marry" fundamentalist electronic ministries with the profamily movement. At its heart, the three New Right strategists were well on their way to realizing Weyrich's goal of building a political apparatus that could deliver on the conservative agenda, which they had hoped that Barry Goldwater in 1964 and Ronald Reagan in 1968 and 1976 would bring to the White House. They were determined to build that structure, whether or not they took the White House. Indeed, by 1980 they had practically given up on Barry Goldwater and even harbored some doubts about Ronald Reagan. They had built a political apparatus that could not only elect members of Congress who would follow their rigid ideology but could defeat those who did not.

The Old Right, mainly the John Birch Society, with its "Impeach Earl Warren" road signs in the 1950s and 60s has always taken aim at the Supreme Court. From the *Brown* case up through the cases involving rights of criminal defendants, pornography, abortion, school prayer, and school busing, Supreme Court decisions have regularly raised the ire of traditional conservatives.

In the winter of 1980 Paul Weyrich was concerned that, despite the Reagan victory, the conservatives had not reduced those concerns to a specific agenda for action. He summoned to his office Paul McGuigan, a young medieval historian whom he had recruited to write newsletters for his foundation, and Randall Rader, a new counsel on Senator Hatch's Subcommittee on the Constitution of the Senate Judiciary Committee, which had just changed hands to Republican control.

"O.K., boys, we've had three elections in a row where we've gotten stronger in the Congress. Ronald Reagan won't be perfect, but he'll do a good job in the Executive branch. What does that leave?"

McGuigan, as a historian, quickly got the drift: "The Judiciary."

"Right. We need a bluebook for judicial reform, and I want you two to get to work on it right away."

McGuigan and Rader started out with a lengthy outline and eventually reduced it to one page. That outline became the table of contents of *A Blueprint for Judicial Reform*, which McGuigan and Rader edited. The premise of the report was that the general public wanted dramatic change in the legal system.

The assumptions about public opinion were based upon a poll conducted by the Heritage Foundation that summer. Weyrich announced in releasing the report that the public is "fed up with judicial oligarchy and undemocratic courts." Much of what the report recommended was supported by the poll results, and the reforms proposed were nothing less than radical:

- Stripping federal courts of jurisdiction to hear cases involving busing and abortion.
- A constitutional amendment that would permit the Congress, by two-thirds vote of each house, to overrule any Supreme Court decision that struck down a state statute.
- Congressional oversight hearings of the courts to determine if decisions "violate the spirit and letter of the Constitution" and calling before Congress judges who abuse their powers before Congressional committees to explain their actions.
- Retention elections for federal judges.

Nearly all of these got at least as far as congressional hearings; none has, to date, been passed by Congress.

Six years later, in the summer of 1987, Randall Rader was Orrin Hatch's chief counsel for Judiciary Committee matters, and Patrick McGuigan chaired a group called Coalitions for America, a group of conservative political organizations. Randy Rader would serve as Orrin Hatch's point man on the Bork nomination. McGuigan and his close friend, Dan Casey, of the old-line conservative American Conservative Union (ACU) would "pour their hearts into" coordinating the work of right-wing grass roots efforts to get Robert Bork confirmed.

Patrick McGuigan grew up in a conservative Catholic family in Oklahoma. McGuigan's idol, as a young man, was John Kennedy, and snide comments from a fellow student in June 1968 about Robert Kennedy, who had just been assassinated, provoked a fight. Although he generally supported the Vietnam War, he wore a black armband in high school in protest of the My Lai Massacre. Somewhere in the early 1970s he turned on the Democrats and liberalism generally over flag burning and the antiwar movement. By the middle 1970s he was a fully committed movement conservative, who met Weyrich through a Phyllis Schlafly-sponsored seminar at Oklahoma State University, where McGuigan taught.

After compiling the *Blueprint for Judicial Reform,* McGuigan became one of the New Right's most prominent spokesmen and scholars on legal and judicial reform issues. Even though he was not a lawyer, for each of the years of the 80s, he wrote or edited a book or book-length report on the subject.

In the fall of 1983, after a conference he had conducted on criminal justice issues, McGuigan was again summoned to Weyrich's office for a new mission—to build a lobbying organization for their judicial reforms.

The 721 Group and Coalitions for America are two names for the same group, which McGuigan and others eventually built to respond to Weyrich's proposal. By the summer of 1987, it was composed of some fifteen pro-law enforcement judicial-reform groups, including Concerned Women for America, a conservative women's organization, Phyllis Schlafly's Eagle Forum, the National Law Enforcement Council, and the National Right to Work Committee. The organization had been involved in many of the high profile nomination fights that had occupied the Senate Judiciary Committee in the previous four years—the Sessions, Manion, Reynolds, Meese, and Rehnquist struggles.

McGuigan knew from the moment Powell resigned that, if Bork was chosen, it would be "the biggest fight of my life." He, Dan Casey, and their coalition met at 8:30 A.M. the day after the nomination was announced. Casey described the strategy agreed upon that day: "First, we will try to alert and influence opinion makers, editorial boards, church leaders, and others with the ear of a Senator in order to urge them to weigh nominations on the merits, resist pressures from liberal special-interest groups, and exercise good judgment in confirming Judge Bork. The second track is helping funnel information to grass roots organizations, so that they in turn can feed it to their active members to energize . . . efforts."

Casey described a full-fledged political strategy for winning the Bork fight in two tracks. The first, in the jargon of political professionals, was a field operation, with local activists clamoring to influence their elected representatives in face-to-face meetings, and the second was direct mail.

The second track of the strategy was to get off immediately to an excellent start—an aggressive fund-raising effort centered on the Bork nomination:

- Casey immediately sent the top 1,000 contributors of the ACU a fund-raising solicitation and planned to send another 40,000 to 60,000 letters by the end of July. Casey told the *Washington Post*, "This is an issue that will fund itself because it's what they would say in the direct-mail world is a 'hot button' issue."
- Citizens for Decency Through Law borrowed $140,000 for a direct mail

campaign and pleaded with its constituents, "Your gift will block the efforts of the liberals who have had too much influence for too long."

- The Christian Voice, an evangelical organization, in a fund-raising solicitation on July 27, argued that Bork would give the "Supreme Court its first conservative majority since the 1930's. . . . Schoolchildren can't even say a silent prayer let alone study creationism. Bork could help correct this." Asking for a $10 or $20 gift the letter implored, "This is the most critical battle we've fought."
- Jerry Falwell announced in his Moral Majority solicitation, "I am issuing the most important 'call-to-arms' in the history of the Moral Majority. . . . Our efforts have always stalled at the door of the U.S. Supreme Court. . . . President Reagan has chosen Judge Robert Bork . . . a pivotal person in getting the Supreme Court back on course. . . . I need your gift of $50 or $25 immediately. Time is short."
- The American Life League, a Pro-Life group, warned that the battle for Bork was going to be the "most massive, most critical and most expensive effort you and I have ever undertaken. . . . I need your gift of $18 or $50—or whatever you can afford to help restore the paramount right to life."

Altogether hundreds of thousands of solicitations were mailed, potentially worth millions of dollars in contributions and thousands of letters to members of the Senate on behalf of Robert Bork. Within a few weeks senatorial offices were flooded with pro-Bork mail, and it seemed to be outnumbering anti-Bork letters.

Viguerie had boasted in the beginning that "whatever the liberals have, we're going to have—radio, television, newspaper ads." However, within a few weeks, McGuigan and Casey began to get a little nervous about Viguerie's promise that the Right would be able to match the Left. The problem was money. Several of the groups in their direct mail letters specifically asked for funds for an advertising budget. Concerned Women for America (CWA), for instance, promised that each $25 dollars contributed would buy 1 inch of newspaper ads; the Moral Majority and Citizens for Decency Through Law made specific pitches for funds for a "media campaign." CWA promised that some of the funds they raised would be used to establish "phone banks" to lobby members.

The most ambitious plan was announced by Bill Roberts, a long-time Reagan supporter from California. Roberts, who had managed Reagan's first gubernatorial campaign, would work with the Dolphin group, which had helped lead the effort to defeat Rose Bird, the liberal California Supreme Court Chief Justice, in her reelection campaign in 1986. Roberts and the Dolphin group would create a new organization for this effort called We the People, sponsored by former President Ford and other Republican luminaries, which promised to raise $2 million in sixty days. The money would be spent by the pro-Bork coalition in ten target states.

The political apparatus of the Right seemed formidable to those of us who opposed the Bork nomination. However, it turned out to be a poor match for its counterpart on the Left.

With his famous speech at the Dexter Avenue Baptist Church in 1956, Martin Luther King, Jr., launched the modern civil rights movement out of the black churches of the Deep South. In the 80s the New Right, based in the moral fervor of Southern churches, would emulate it, developing into a sophisticated legislative operation with a specific agenda for change. But the civil rights movement had not abandoned its original drive, and by 1987 that operation was the Leadership Conference on Civil Rights (LCCR).

The LCCR predated Martin Luther King and the modern civil rights movement. It had been created by A. Philip Randolph, Roy Wilkins, and Arnold Aronson in 1950 to implement President Truman's unprecedented report on civil rights, "To Secure These Rights."

It began with thirty civil rights organizations, but by 1987 it was composed of over 180 organizations representing "minorities, labor, women, the major religious groups, disabled persons and older Americans." The conference boasts an impressive list of accomplishments: "Beginning with the Civil Rights Act of 1957, the Leadership Conference coordinated the campaigns that resulted in the passage of all the civil rights laws of this century, including the landmark Civil Rights Acts of 1960 and 1964; the Voting Rights Act of 1965; the Fair Housing Act of 1968, and the 1982 amendments to the Voting Rights Act." The LCCR had also "coordinated the campaigns" that resulted in the rejection of the nominations of Clement Haynesworth and G. Harold Carswell to the Supreme Court."

The meeting on fair housing that Paul Weyrich was invited to attend in 1968 in the place of Senator Allott was a meeting of the Leadership Conference on Civil Rights. So Paul Weyrich's dream, as told to David Broder, was to emulate for the Right the LCCR.

In the summer of 1987, the LCCR, under the leadership of its irrepressible executive director, Ralph Neas, was alive and well. Pat McGuigan was supposed to be the New Right counterpart to Neas, and his Coalitions for America was the realization of Weyrich's dream. However, as McGuigan would be the first to admit, he and his group could not begin to match the sophistication and the three decades of experience that Neas and his organization could bring to the effort to block the Bork nomination.

Ralph Neas, a former Senate staffer himself, worked well with staff members in the Senate. He was personally friendly with many members of the Senate on both sides of the aisle, liberals and conservatives.

The LCCR was no stranger to McGuigan or nomination struggles in the Judiciary Committee. Biden, Kennedy, and others on the committee had worked closely with Neas in a number of earlier battles—the Manion, Sessions, and Rehnquist judicial nominations and the Reynolds and Meese Justice Department nominations, all of which they opposed. McGuigan and the Coalitions for America had worked closely with the Justice Department, the Reagan White House, and Republicans on the Judiciary Committee in favor of the nominations.

However, all was not well for Neas, the LCCR, or the liberal groups that summer. One issue that united the members of McGuigan's coalition in favor of Bork tended to divide Neas and his friends. That issue was abortion.

The Pro-Choice groups—the National Abortion Rights Action League (NARAL) and Planned Parenthood—were not formal members of the LCCR. In the summer of 1987, Planned Parenthood's application for membership had been pending for six years. As Neas explained, "The NAACP which helped to found the Leadership Conference has never taken a position on the issue [of abortion] and other mainstays of the coalition, like the Hispanic groups, tended to lean Pro-Life, or like the Catholic Conference, were avidly Pro-Life."

It was not a new problem. The division on the issue between the traditional civil rights organizations (which, being church-based, tended to have a membership that was Pro-Life) and the women's groups (which were almost all Pro-Choice) came to a head in the struggle to reverse by legislation the Supreme Court's 1984 decision in *Grove City College* v. *Bell*. In that decision the Court had finally bought an argument that Brad Reynolds and the Reagan conservative civil rights strategists had been making for a long time. The Court held that Title IX of the civil rights law, prohibiting sex discrimination in federally funded education facilities, only applied to specific programs that received federal funds, not to the whole educational institution.

Neas explained, "While the decision only applied to sex discrimination policy, Reynolds had made it clear that he intended to seek to expand the *Grove City* rule to apply to all civil rights statutes." Title IX and all the civil rights statutes needed to be amended to blunt that attack. The LCCR, working with other interested parties, including feminist organizations like NARAL and Planned Parenthood, had drafted the Civil Rights Restoration Act of 1984.

Yet by the summer of 1987, the civil rights community had still not succeeded in getting the legislation enacted. The reason was abortion. Orrin Hatch and other New Right opponents of the legislation had discovered a clever argument against the Restoration Act, an argument not unlike the one they had used effectively against the ERA in 1982—an argument that forced Pro-Life, procivil rights advocates to make a painful choice. Hatch argued that the Restoration Act language did more than simply reverse *Grove City*; it required, under the proposed new prohibition on sex discrimination, that university hospitals perform abortions.

By March of 1985, the Catholic Conference had been persuaded by Hatch's argument and began to insist upon language explicitly exempting institutions from such a requirement. The women's groups, some of which, like NARAL, were not in the LCCR, and others like NOW, which were, adamantly opposed any compromise on the question of abortion.

One feminist political operative explained the position of Pro-Choice groups on the controversy: "The Leadership Conference on Civil Rights has never occupied themselves extensively with women's rights. There are groups in it that wouldn't be in it if it were going to actively lobby on Choice. . . . There were incredible internal tensions between the various agendas on [the Restoration Act]. NARAL could not achieve its goals by being low profile. They stayed there and fought."

Despite the Catholic Conference's concerns, Neas had managed to keep the coalition united on "abortion-neutral" language and beat back Pro-Life attempts to exempt abortion from the Restoration Act. In May 1987, he got Kennedy's Labor Committee to defeat an exemption by a 12–4 vote.

However, Neas conceded that by June, 1987 mainline civil rights groups, especially the NAACP, were getting very impatient with the impasse that had developed over the issue. "It was the cause of a two-year delay." Althea Simmons, the quiet but strong-willed Washington director of the NAACP was becoming increasingly vocal on the subject in LCCR meetings. The women's groups were not going to budge. It was not a comfortable position for Neas. The NAACP's chair, the Rev. Benjamin Hooks, also chaired the Leadership Conference, but it was the women's groups who had been most directly affected by *Grove City*, because it was a sex discrimination case.

Although the NAACP may have been impatient with the women's groups' refusal to compromise on the abortion question, the feminists felt that they were owed a certain amount of consideration in this regard. In 1984, on the eve of Senate consideration of the *Grove City* legislation and before abortion had become an issue, Senator Packwood, the lead sponsor of the legislation, came to the women's groups with a compromise. It was impossible, he explained, to get through the Senate the broader changes in the legislation which the LCCR wanted—changes in the race discrimination provisions. However, the Republicans, who still controlled the Senate at the time, were prepared to accept a simple reversal of the *Grove City* decision. The *Grove City* decision only directly applied to the one sex discrimination provision in federal law—pertaining to federal aid to education. The net result of this compromise would be total accommodation for the feminists, whereas the civil rights groups would not be accommodated at all.

The women's groups met separately late into the night that evening and finally decided to refuse the offer. However, as abortion became an issue, some civil rights groups were reluctant to return the favor and weigh in on behalf of the women to defeat the Pro-Life language. So when the black civil rights groups grew impatient with the delay, it simply added to the resentment among feminists, who realized that they would have been much better off if they had accepted Packwood's offer.

There had been earlier tensions between blacks and women in the Leadership Conference over similar questions of priorities. In the late 1960s, the mainline civil rights groups had resented efforts to expand the mandate of the Civil Rights Commission to explore gender discrimination before there was even a women's movement. However, activists who have been in the middle of these struggles point out that the problem with some in the NAACP and other old-line organizations is not so much that they are troubled by the abortion issue as skeptical of any effort to broaden the mandate beyond vindication of the rights of blacks. For example, Clarence Mitchell, Ralph Neas's predecessor as executive director of the LCCR, fiercely resisted the expansion of the coverage of the Voting Rights Act to Hispanics in the 1970s. Mitchell lost that effort, but the feelings are still there today. In July 1987, the tensions between the civil rights and women's groups were very much alive as well.

This history was very much in the minds of five women who played critical roles in the summer of 1987, attempting to resolve those tensions—Kate Michelman, Althea Simmons, Judy Lichtman, Melanne Verveer, and Mimi Mager. Three of the four had been intimately involved in the struggle over *Grove City*, and all four were determined not to allow that experience to jeopardize their goal in defeating the Bork nomination.

In June 1987, Kate Michelman had been executive director of the National Abortion Rights Action League for only two years and was not yet wise in the ways of Washington. Only two years earlier, she had been executive director of Planned Parenthood in Harrisburg, Pennsylvania. Yet the Powell resignation thrust her into the national limelight, for, as far as NARAL was concerned, the choice of a replacement for Lewis Powell by Ronald Reagan was a dangerous thing. It placed in jeopardy the Supreme Court case that represented NARAL's very reason for being—*Roe* v. *Wade*.

Althea Simmons did not see the Bork fight that way at all. For Simmons, the fight was not over abortion but civil rights.

The contrast between the two women is stark. Michelman reflects the white upper-middle-class professional women who typify NARAL membership—glib, urbane, yet dedicated to their cause. Althea Simmons (who passed away in 1990) was a black lawyer from Shreveport, Louisiana, who had spent twenty-six years as a field organizer for the NAACP in the South. As you looked in her eyes, you saw an absolutely fearless daughter of the South who had placed her life on the line for her cause in the late 1950s and early 1960s, when being a civil rights organizer in that part of the country was not exactly the safest line of work.

By 1987, Simmons had been the NAACP's chief lobbyist in Washington for almost a decade. She was a Washington insider with a close personal relationship with Biden and the other Democrats on the committee. A friendly woman, she was eloquent before a crowd of volunteers. Yet at the same time she could be very careful and precise in a face-to-face meeting with a Senator who was on the fence on a civil rights issue, when she was attempting to communicate diplomatically a precise and yet unmistakable message.

Nan Aron is a feminist lawyer who comes from a long line of women activists. "Many of my female relatives were involved in social movements. They were very feisty women," she boasted to writers Pertschuk and Schaetzel. In 1979, she persuaded twenty public-interest legal organizations, from the Consumer's Union to the National Education Association, to create the Alliance for Justice. The alliance's mission is to alert these groups to matters of common concern—"legal services, regulatory reform, and restrictions on lobbying and advocacy."

In November 1984, after a discussion with Prof. Herman Schwartz at American University Law School, an activist professor and former Metzenbaum staffer, and Bill Taylor, an intimate of Neas, Nan Aron decided to expand the alliance's mission to include closer scrutiny of Reagan judicial nominees. What had provoked the luncheon was a decision by Congress to create eighty-five new judgeships, which when combined with forty existing vacancies meant that Ronald Reagan would be able to name almost half of the federal judiciary. Ironically, it had been a decision by Howard Metzenbaum, Schwartz's former boss, to give the Republicans the new judgeships in exchange for a change in the bankruptcy law, which the labor movement desperately wanted, that led to this new opportunity for Ronald Reagan to shape the federal judiciary in his own image.

With the cooperation of the NAACP and the LCCR and other members of the alliance, the Judicial Selection Project was created with Aron as chair. In 1985 and 1986, the project was moderately successful in bringing troublesome nominees to the attention of the Judiciary Committee. However, truly high-profile nomination fights like the Manion or Sessions nominations were primarily the work of the Senate staffs in conjunction with the LCCR or People for the American Way. The Rehnquist struggle, the only Supreme Court nomination fight, had been coordinated by the Leadership Conference.

In June 1987, there was some question as to which organization—Ralph Neas and the LCCR or Nan Aron and the Judicial Selection Project—would coordinate the effort outside the Senate. Perhaps it was natural for certain groups which had not been a part of the Leadership Conference, especially the Pro-Choice groups like NARAL and Planned Parenthood to gravitate toward Aron and the Judicial Selection project.

In the days following the Powell resignation, Estelle Rogers, an outspoken, indeed at times impulsive, feminist activist, Nan Aron, and Kate Michelman all convened meetings and attempted to play predominant coordinating roles. Intimates of Neas were very concerned that, if the campaign by outside groups was coordinated outside the LCCR, it would have the strident quality reflected in statements by Michelman (pledging "an all-out frontal assault" against

Bork), by Aron ("there will be a mass mobilization"), and by Estelle Rogers (calling on Biden to resign his chairmanship because he had "endorsed" Bork). As Melanne Verveer of People for the American Way remarked, "You can imagine the potential for divisiveness and the prospect of the campaign going off in myriad directions or directions that weren't helpful."

In the early meetings of the LCCR, all of the groups agreed on a public strategy of persuading Senators not to act precipitately in endorsing Bork. But behind the scenes Neas and his allies had another equally important agenda—gaining control of the anti-Bork campaign. From the perspective of those in the Senate who would lead the effort, it was essential that we be able to deal with one campaign, and, most important, that the campaign be responsive to the strategy we developed. Neas recognized this and also realized it was essential that the organizations with huge national networks—the NAACP, NARAL, Planned Parenthood, and organized labor—be intimately involved in the process.

Judith Lichtman is a feminist lawyer, who along with Marcia Greenberger, is probably best known as the premier litigation strategist in the women's movement. However, in the summer of 1987, Lichtman's greatest contribution to the Bork struggle was her role as a fence mender and consensus builder. That first week she came up with a clever device for bringing the anti-Bork coalition under one roof. The coalition should be divided into various task forces: a media task force, a lobbying task force, a research task force, and a grass roots task force. Lichtman suggested making Michelman and Simmons cochairs of the grass roots task force.

In the second coalition meeting on July 7, Neas formally asked Simmons and Michelman to cochair the task force. It was a great opportunity for Michelman, and she knew it. For the first time she and NARAL would be brought into the formal structure of an LCCR effort.

Simmons was not at the meeting, because she was still at the NAACP national convention. "When I came back, I learned that I was a cochair . . . and then when they told me one of the other cochairs was Kate Michelman, I said, 'Oh my God!' "

When Simmons went to the first task force meeting, she made it clear she was unhappy with being cochair as long as Kate Michelman was a cochair. Neas understood that she was "deathly afraid that the abortion issue would bring down" the campaign. Simmons was critically important to Neas and his allies at this point, because everybody knew that a major civil rights battle could not be fought without the NAACP. Simmons did not want NARAL or any other "upstart organization"—for example, Nan Aron's Judicial Selection project—to run the campaign. Yet she would not give an answer at the first meeting, she had to go "think about it." That sent a clear message to Michelman and Aron that they had to play ball with the LCCR or not be a part of the campaign.

Michelman understood the problem that she presented. ''They didn't know what kind of player I would be. They didn't know my philosophy. They'd never really seen me at work, and so they were worried. Is she going to be a loose cannon on deck? I had to prove to them that I wasn't going to make this effort to defeat Bork a referendum on abortion.''

Michelman was determined to demonstrate that she could be a team player. When Simmons eventually acquiesced to Neas's pleas that she work with Michelman, Michelman recalls, the ''tone of her voice was very clear, she just did not trust me.'' They spent hours discussing the grass roots campaign, and eventually they became close friends, ''an unlikely alliance and friendship'' as Pertschuk and Schaetzel describe it in their book.

Getting Simmons and Michelman to agree to cochair the grass roots effort was only the first step. Grass roots coordination—field operations, in the jargon of modern campaigns—is a science, and Judy Lichtman realized that the Leadership Conference needed a professional to handle the day-to-day operation. The large national organizations, she explains, ''need help. It isn't that they don't know how to organize their grass roots; they're very good at it. But not any one of them could pick up this effort. When we worked for, and *saved* the Voting Rights Act extension [in 1982], it was because of some very sophisticated grass roots organizing—both the NAACP and the League of Women Voters put resources into it. But here, we really had to get that kind of activity and the Leadership Conference didn't have that kind of capability.''

During the Voting Rights Act extension fight in 1982, the LCCR had performed exactly as Weyrich had observed in 1968 and so envied for the Right. When the Senate leadership in the civil rights battle wanted to demonstrate to a wavering member that people in his state cared deeply about the issue, they were able to produce not just cards and letters but a meeting between a Senator and local activists, who had the ability to deliver real live voters to the polls. The only difference was that the Bork nomination would require many more such meetings in a much shorter period of time. In the Voting Rights struggle, the civil rights forces controlled the pace. Here the whole fight would be over in a matter of months.

Melanne Verveer and Tony Podesta, one of the founders of People for the American Way and a Kennedy confidant, had just the person for the job—Mimi Mager. Mager is a petit bundle of energy with a reputation as being one of the best field organizers in progressive politics. It was a reputation she would clearly exceed in the coming months. Every election she is part of some progressive's campaign. Over the years she developed a national network of progressive activists, the ''hottest Rolodex in town.''

Mager met Neas on July 7, the day Neas announced the creation of the grass roots task force, with Simmons and Michelman as cochairs. Mager and Neas hit it off immediately. ''He asked me to come to a meeting the next day at NARAL.'' It was the first meeting of the grass roots task force. Neas introduced Mager as the new coordinator for the project. ''I'd assumed that Ralph [had] talked to the people in the task force. But you could just see the jaws drop. A lot of people knew me from other work, but some were not prepared for this.'' One who clearly was not ready for it was Kate Michelman, who had hoped to name one of her own people as field director for the anti-Bork coalition.

Michelman did not say anything in the meeting and ultimately came to accept it. Mager said to Neas after the meeting, ''I didn't get the impression that anyone knew this was happening.'' Neas smiled. As he explained years later, it was ''a consolidation move.''

Some of Neas's allies were pleasantly surprised that he would agree to hire someone like Mager. As one said, ''Ralph had the good sense to do it, which is not consistent with his nature, because he's a one-man operation. He operates from his pockets like a Fifth Street lawyer, and he's very good at it.'' ''Fifth street lawyers'' are lawyers who represent indigent defendants in the local criminal courts in Washington, do not have offices, and seem at times to live out of their briefcases. Often Neas would be seen in the crowded corner of some congressional office borrowing someone's phone, with a bundle of notes to himself and memoranda under his arm as if he were carrying his whole in-box around with him.

With Mager in place, the LCCR was in a position to activate networks in each of the critical states on behalf of the anti-Bork campaign. In the third week of July, soon after Mager was on board, the first of many weekly meetings were held in my office on what role the anti-Bork network would play outside the Senate. Tony Podesta, then on Kennedy's payroll, Neas, Verveer, Mager, and I began to plot out a field strategy for the coalition. Immediately we focused on the states of the four ''swing votes'' on the committee—Arlen Specter's Pennsylvania, Robert Byrd's West Virginia, Howell Heflin's Alabama, and Dennis DeConcini's Arizona. Any state with two Democrats who appeared genuinely undecided, especially Southern states, would get special attention.

Mager immediately contacted whatever network existed in those states and in the four swing states hired professional organizers. The expenditure was modest. For example, in Alabama the LCCR spent less than $7,000 for organizers. All told, it funded coalitions in seventeen states, each usually in the $2,500 range. The purpose of the organizing effort was not to generate enthusiasm or create the illusion of concern that really wasn't there. The problem was to channel the energy into something productive.

As Mager explained it, ''We just had to harness and direct [the energy]. There were coalitions together the next morning after the Bork nomination. Usually you go around, and you have to look through the bushes and find the troops. The troops were already there. The troops needed the message.''

For Althea Simmons and Kate Michelman, it became more important to defeat Bork than to argue over issues on which they were, as Simmons would say, "miles apart." This sense of unity, this unprecedented willingness to seek common ground in the progressive movement, was replicated throughout the country. The Rev. Tim McDonald of the Southern Christian Leadership Conference in Atlanta remarked, "[Our war cry] 'Beat Back Bork' galvanized the community more than anything I've ever seen. The closest we came was on South Africa. I've never seen such cooperation. We had ministers who were strongly antiabortion, ministers who would scream about gay rights, but they would say—right now we've got one agenda."

This unity was in large measure a result of the decision by Neas, the coalition, and Bork opponents on the Hill, that a unified campaign message was essential to victory. The troops needed a message, and the message had to strike exactly the right tone—Senators do not respond well to strident threats.

The need to develop a cohesive message became another point of friction between the Neas faction and the Aron faction. Around the time that Neas hired Mager, Aron decided to hire Carol Foreman and Nicki Heidepriem, two experienced political operatives, with the mission of developing a "message piece" for the campaign. Fortunately Heidepriem and Mager had worked together closely on women's issues during the Mondale/Ferraro campaign in 1984 and had become close friends. Heidepriem began to attend the weekly meetings in my office and eventually developed a memorandum that served as an outline of the kinds of materials that Mager and others in the anti-Bork campaign sent to the field.

Working with the results of the Kiley poll and the various focus groups that were conducted for the anti-Bork campaign, Heidepriem and Bill Taylor developed two different message memoranda that were sent by Neas to field operatives through Mager. Both were essentially the same. Bill Taylor's made five arguments:

1. Bork opposed most of the landmark decisions protecting civil rights and civil liberties, specifically on race discrimination, restrictions on the right to vote (poll taxes, literacy tests, and one-man-one-vote), restrictions on privacy, and restrictions on free speech.
2. Bork is a judicial activist.
3. Bork would seek to reverse landmark cases.
4. Bork is an advocate of executive power, mentioning his role in firing Watergate special prosecutor Archibald Cox.
5. Senators have every right to consider Bork's judicial philosophy.

Nowhere in the four-page memorandum is abortion or *Roe* v. *Wade* even mentioned.

On August 13, Nan Aron's group released a memorandum addressed to the "Grassroots Leadership" on the "Message." Although the memorandum was from Aron's group and the Leadership Conference, it was on Alliance for Justice stationery and had been prepared by Heidepriem and made many of the same points Taylor had but in a clearly more disparaging tone:

- Bork was labeled "A Rigid Ideologue," "With an Activist Bent."
- It implied that once on the Court, Bork would "implement the Reagan Agenda."

Roe v. *Wade* was one of two cases mentioned in the cover memorandum, which was relatively devoid of any legal analysis (a list of other cases Bork had criticized was attached). The memorandum did imply that Bork would, once on the Court, reverse *Roe* and the *Griswold* case. Clearly, however, even in Heidepriem's piece, abortion was not a central argument.

By late August, it was clear that the LCCR's pledge not to make the Bork fight a referendum on abortion was not simply a promise by Washington leaders. It had become well integrated into the national campaign in every part of the country.

By early September, as the hearings approached, Neas and the Leadership Conference had a disciplined national organization in place, prepared to respond to the strategy that was evolving among anti-Bork leaders in the Senate. Furthermore, in Senator Kennedy, with the help of Tony Podesta, the anti-Bork forces had a national figure willing and able to augment the strategy by picking up the telephone and calling the leader of any progressive organization anywhere in the country. By the time the hearings were to begin Kennedy had, among other things:

- written a letter to every one of 6,200 black elected officials in the nation asking them to get involved;
- telephoned prominent black Southern mayors in New Orleans, Birmingham, and Atlanta;
- persuaded the Rev. Joseph Lowery, the head of King's old organization, the Southern Christian Leadership Conference, to make defeating Bork a central focus of the group's summer meeting. As a result, in hundreds of churches that summer, black ministers interrupted their services so that congregants could write an anti-Bork letter to their Senators.
- called each of the thirty members of the executive committee of the AFL-CIO and forty state labor leaders.

Two huge political movements in America were engaged that summer by McGuigan and his friends on the Right and by Neas and his friends on the Left. Ironically, both were to some significant degree built around a constituency that was based in Southern churches and fixated on Supreme Court decisions. The mammoth black civil rights bureaucracy was forced by events in 1987 to reach an accommodation with Pro-Choice groups, which had not always been natural allies. It was a moment of maturation for the civil rights and the women's movement.

On the Right, the fundamentalists engaged their constituency in the churches and produced thousands of letters but little more. The pro-Bork direct mail efforts hardly paid for themselves and certainly were not making enough money to fund the first track of the strategy. By early August there appeared to be no money immediately forthcoming from the Dolphin group. Although McGuigan and his friends could flood Senators' offices with preprinted mail, without additional funds there would be no local field operations, no phone banks, and, most important to McGuigan, no newspaper or television ads.

As the hearings approached, it was becoming obvious that something more might be needed to make the Moral Majority a reality in the Bork fight. McGuigan and Dan Casey were assured by Republican and conservative leaders that money was still forthcoming from the Dolphin group. However, they became increasingly dubious and pressed for more direct presidential activity. ''We were promised an August offensive by the President.'' ''It was their term, 'an August offensive'.'' But the President was on vacation at his ranch in California—not to be interrupted.

By early August, Concerned Women of America had placed a few pro-Bork ads in Alabama and Pennsylvania to influence Heflin and Specter, critical swing votes on the committee. Howard Phillips had gone to Oregon to attempt to create pressure on Republican Senator Packwood, who had made it clear he was inclined to oppose Bork. By late August pro-Bork demonstrations had occurred on a relatively small scale in Oregon and Illinois. Pro-Life and other pro-Bork demonstrators were dogging Biden and Simon on the primary campaign trails in Iowa and New Hampshire.

August came and went, and the President's ''August offensive'' never materialized. The President mentioned the Bork fight in a speech on Iran–Contra just before he left Washington for California; he boldly announced that confirming Bork was his Number 1 domestic initiative, but then only made two appearances for Bork the rest of the month—one, a stopover in Nebraska on the way to his ranch in California and a brief meeting with pro-Bork law enforcement groups in California.

Neas and the leadership conference spent August doing what McGuigan and his coalition only dreamed of doing—building a formidable field operation. Furthermore, direct mail efforts at People for the American Way were a big success and the LCCR had plenty of money to pay for a poll, focus groups, and advertising, and a modest amount of money to nurture its field operation. The effort on the Right not only failed to raise money from direct mail, but received no assistance from the White House in fund-raising.

Kennedy was doing for the anti-Bork effort what the White House political operatives, out of fear of using scarce political capital during the Iran–Contra period, refused to do.

All of this was well and good, but Biden kept repeating to his confidants throughout August, ''Look, I'm happy we have the groups working with us and keeping the enthusiasm going in the right direction. But my job is to explain this man to average Americans. If we don't, we won't do much better than we did on Rehnquist, and that isn't good enough.''

To win the fight, Biden and his allies in the Senate had to do something for which Ronald Reagan was famous—communicate simply and directly with average Americans about what was at stake. Fortunately for Biden and unfortunately for Robert Bork, Ronald Reagan never even tried. Biden thought of little else in August and early September. He was determined to develop a message that would communicate those stakes to the American people, a message consistent with what Neas and Kennedy were saying to the groups but a message that would be very different.

The vehicle would be speeches, meetings with editorial boards, and, most important of all, the hearings themselves. The hearings would be the greatest challenge of all because, although he was chairman of the committee, he could hardly control the medium. In the cross-examination of Bork and the hostile cross-examination of carefully selected witnesses who would convey the message, Biden faced a daunting challenge. Kennedy, Neas, and the LCCR spent August carefully fostering and calibrating the intensity on the Left, while Biden, his staff, and advisers were immersing themselves in what one civil rights activist called Biden's ''intellectual piece,'' cultivating opinion leaders and recruiting witnesses.

CHAPTER 13

DR. JEKYLL AND MR. HYDE

JEFF PECK AND CHRIS SCHROEDER spent almost every waking hour between August 6 and August 21 writing the response to the Administration's Blue Book on Bork. Paul Bland, a lawyer from Biden's personal staff, and Phil Metzger, a writer whose hobby was jurisprudence, were brought in to help out Peck and Schroeder. Peck began with a series of memoranda he and Bland had prepared in late July and early August, analyzing Bork's opinions, writings, speeches, position on *stare decisis,* and his changes in position.

By the middle of August they had prepared a seventy-five-page single-spaced brief. It took each of the major assertions of the White House paper and responded:

- In response to the White House's assertion that only Bork's opinions and his qualifications were relevant to the Senate's consideration, Peck and Schroeder used Bork's own statements to prove that his academic writing and speeches were relevant.
- Bork is not the "principled proponent of judicial restraint" he was portrayed to be by the White House, but statements by his fellow jurists on the D.C. Circuit were used to show that he was a conservative judicial activist.
- They argued that Bork was not the "consistent and principled" protector of civil liberties and privacy that the White House described but had "repeatedly and consistently rejected the right to be free from governmental interference," referring to his position on *Griswold* and other cases.
- Bork was hardly a "powerful ally of the First Amendment" as the White House asserted, but had a narrow view of the First Amendment.
- Peck and Schroeder pointed out important differences among Bork, Harlan, and Powell, concluding that Bork would not, as the White House asserted, follow in their "mainstream tradition."
- Bork was not a strong supporter of civil rights but "opposed virtually every major civil rights advance on which he has taken a position, including . . . the public accommodations bill, open housing, restrictive covenants, literacy tests, poll taxes, and affirmative action."

▪ They attacked the White House's statistical analysis, pointing out, for example, that none of Bork's 400 opinions had actually been reviewed by the Supreme Court and also explained how the disingenuous use of a *Los Angeles Times* quotation suggested that the paper endorsed the nomination.

The basic approach of the report was to take any particular assertion by the White House and use it as a basis for a wide-ranging review of Bork's jurisprudence. It met Biden's direction on August 6 to be fair but to use the White House assertions to critique Bork's jurisprudence. As Peck understood Biden's mandate to them: "It's like what's permissible cross-examination. Anything that's opened up in direct is fair game. And [what] they opened up [in the Blue Book] you could drive a truck through."

For example, the assertion that Bork was in the mainstream tradition of Harlan, Frankfurter, and Powell presented Peck and Schroeder with a tremendous opportunity to range widely through Bork's jurisprudence. As Peck explained, in responding to that bald assertion, "we were able to put in our whole case against Bork."

Writing the piece was frustrating because it was being composed while scores of Bork speeches and articles were still dribbling into the committee's files. At some point Peck complained they would conclude, "We now have everything Bork's said on privacy, and [then] four more speeches would come in." Or they would decide, "We now have everything Bork's said on the First Amendment, and [then] five more speeches would come in."

However, for Peck the process was exhilarating. "When I came up here, I'd tell my friends what I was doing and they would say, 'Well, it'll be a great experience, but you don't *really* think you can beat him? Don't get me wrong, it'll be worthwhile.' I thought to myself at the time, 'I [don't] care.' "

By August 15, as the response piece and the case he and Schroeder were building against Bork was falling into place, he began to believe that his friends might have been wrong. "I left work that day. It was a beautiful warm summer night. I went home and said to [my wife], 'This is great. We're going to win,' and she said, 'What do you mean?' I said 'I have this gut feeling we're going to win.' "

By the third week in August, Joe Biden still did not yet share Peck's optimism. Peck and Schroeder's piece was still in their word processor. There was no strategy for its release, and no hearing strategy. Who were going to be the other witnesses? In what order? What was Biden going to ask Bork? Clearly the hearings were going to be the main vehicle for making the case against Bork, but what was the public message? He had begun to review what Peck and Schroeder had written, but it was too technical, too lawyerly to make the case on national TV to average Americans.

Biden had taken a few days off with his family at Bethany Beach, Delaware. He decided to interrupt his vacation to come to grips with these questions and to deal with similar strategic questions in his presidential campaign. The campaign at that point appeared to be in disarray. The leadership of the campaign had decided to move the whole staff from Washington to Wilmington, and a major power struggle was underway in regard to strategy. Pat Caddell was threatening to come out of self-imposed exile in California, and he wanted to take control of the campaign. He insisted on bringing the issue to a head that week.

On August 20, Biden asked to see Tom Donilon and Pat Caddell. He was still struggling with the message for the campaign. He had not talked with Caddell about it since the meeting in the hotel in Chicago in late June, immediately before Bork was named. Donilon and Caddell suggested that political commentator Bill Schneider of the American Enterprise Institute come along. He had given Donilon and me a videotape, which the opposition leader, Neal Kinnock, had used in the most recent British election. Biden had been taken with the tape and enjoyed talking about political communications issues with Schneider. They spent the day discussing the message for the campaign and the Bork effort. Schneider had just filed a column with *National Journal* on the Bork fight and how his positions threatened to open civil rights wounds in the South and that Southern Democrats should want to avoid that. Biden liked the argument. As the day wore on Biden found the discussion interesting but did not feel resolved that he had a definitive message for the presidential campaign or the Bork effort.

That afternoon he asked me to arrange a meeting with Prof. Laurence Tribe of Harvard for the next afternoon. He wanted Peck and Schroeder there. The meeting would follow a campaign meeting in the morning. He wanted Tom Donilon and Caddell to attend both meetings.

Laurence Tribe is the foremost liberal constitutional scholar in the country. He had been a strong advocate in recent years for a more thorough review of the jurisprudence of Supreme Court nominees. Tribe had begun working closely with Biden in 1986 along with Kurland, as it became clear that the Administration was engaged in a calculated effort to affect the ideological complexion of the federal courts.

Tribe is brilliant, self-confident, and seemed to relish the role of insider. He had not yet taken a public position on the Bork nomination, but he was working with the Kennedy staff and was likely to agree to Biden's request to join us the last minute. In his recent book, Tribe had attempted to cast the argument over Supreme Court nominations in a way that lay people would understand. I hoped having Tribe and Caddell with Biden might provide just the right catalyst for some original thinking on how to present the Bork case in a way that average Americans could understand.

Tribe immediately agreed to fly down to the meeting. He was brimming with ideas. Tribe, who was an expert on the right to privacy under the Constitution, was happy to hear that Biden and Caddell were enamored with the privacy/unenumerated rights argument. The meeting started in blistering heat on the open deck of the beach house that Biden had rented. Caddell had been supplied with all of the substantive briefing books that Biden had received. He and Biden were almost as conversant with Bork's record as Tribe. The three engaged in a dialogue about the case against Bork, which continued for several hours.

At times it seemed as if no one else was there. The three almost totally ignored other members of the campaign staff, as the deck slowly filled up. Schroeder and Peck looked on in amazement. There was no organized agenda, and it was clear, as the meeting progressed, that Biden was testing out his idea about privacy and unenumerated rights. He had discussed these same matters in his briefing with Chris Schroeder on August 6 and with Donilon and Caddell the next day in Wilmington. But with Tribe and Caddell agreeing with the basic points he was making, you could see Biden's self-confidence grow.

Hours later, Chris Schroeder would ask me in a puzzled tone of voice, "What did you think of the meeting?"

I responded, "Fantastic!"

It was one of Schroeder's first strategy meetings with Biden and certainly his first in Caddell's presence. "But there was nothing new in that meeting," he pressed gently. "Biden has discussed all of that with you and me before."

I smiled. "But you and I are not Larry Tribe and Pat Caddell."

Biden was trying out his ideas on one of the brightest constitutional scholars and one of the shrewdest political minds in the country. He was satisfied that he had a winning argument. Rasky remembers the meeting fondly: "We walked out of that meeting thinking we knew how to win the fight."

In the middle of the afternoon, Biden seemed satisfied, and he turned to Tribe to thank him. He remembered the response piece that Schroeder and Peck had been writing, and he asked Tribe to review it. Tribe readily agreed. Then after a brief discussion with Tom Donilon and me, Biden decided it was still not appropriate for him to be saying anything more publicly about the nomination until his opening statement in the hearings. He broached with Tribe the idea of releasing the Schroeder–Peck piece in the names of Tribe, Kurland, and several other scholars who were working with us. Tribe was initially reluctant, but he said he would give it serious consideration.

The campaign portion of the meeting began with the perennial discussion of scheduling more time for Biden in Iowa and New Hampshire. As usual it was inconclusive. Biden was not the least bit interested in spending more time on the campaign trail, and once he made it clear that he would not spend a single day less than planned on preparing for the Bork hearing, the subject changed.

Mike Donilon, Tom's brother and an employee of Caddell's polling firm, began to brief on the results of the most recent poll in Iowa, the first primary state. The numbers were better than anyone expected. Biden was moving into double digits.

John Martilla began to discuss a possible press strategy for dealing with the new polling information. "You know what this poll means? It means we're going to be the front runner in Iowa by the end of October, no matter what happens on Bork. And if you win Bork, you've got the nomination."

Stung by several recent stories debunking the Biden campaign, Biden asked, "Does the press know this?"

Martilla responded quickly, "No, and they shouldn't. We shouldn't say a thing. Let them figure this out for themselves so that we don't raise expectations."

Caddell immediately agreed. "They don't get it. The press still looks at our national numbers, and they are determined to prove that our message isn't working. This poll shows that it is."

He paused for a second and stroked his beard.

"Of course, the other campaigns probably have the same numbers. They must be going crazy knowing that we're going into the hearings and will get a ton of attention. I wonder what they'll do?"

Caddell seemed to relish the moment. Biden did not. As the meeting moved from the good news of the poll to bad news of the upcoming schedule the next day in Iowa, Biden's mood changed markedly.

"I'm not ready for the debate at the state fair. And I saw the closing statement you've prepared for me, and it needs a lot of work. I don't know what I want to say. I don't know why our numbers are so good. I disagree with Pat. I don't think we have a message in Iowa. I guess I'll just have to write something myself."

The meeting ended on that angry note.

What Biden, Caddell, and Tribe were struggling with on the deck of the Bethany Beach house and Tom Griscom earlier in the month as he crafted the Bork passages of the Iran–Contra speech are what is known to communications professionals as the public message. However, especially with a Supreme Court nomination, there is a battle to be waged among the elites and intelligentsia, who are influenced by the editorial pages of the major daily newspapers and the editors who shape the coverage to be given by the dailies and the weekly newsmagazines.

For Biden this battle for the opinion leaders had at least three elements. First, we had to choose good anti-Bork witnesses. Second, we had to cultivate important opinion leaders around the country, and, third, we had to engage in a deliberate campaign in the editorial boards themselves with face-to-face meetings.

The first issue in scheduling witnesses for the hearings was the American Bar Association. In late August the consensus was that the ABA would endorse Bork and that that testimony should be countered by former ABA presidents. Biden and Kennedy were ultimately able to persuade three former presidents to testify against Bork.

The most important witnesses would, however, be those who would carry the essential anti-Bork message. From the beginning an elaborate strategy was undertaken to recruit former Republican Secretary of Transportation William Coleman and former Congresswoman Barbara Jordan to testify. A black Republican, former Ford Administration Cabinet official who hailed from Arlen Specter's home town, Coleman was also the chair of the NAACP Legal Defense Fund. No political novice, he had campaigned in South Carolina for Strom Thurmond during the ranking member's last election.

Coleman was not only a leader of the civil rights movement, but as an experienced Supreme Court litigator who had clerked for Felix Frankfurter, he was looked upon by the Supreme Court as a respected advocate on the subject. When in 1983 the Supreme Court decided it wanted to ask for an outsider to defend the traditional Executive Branch position against tax exemptions for segregated institutions in the *Bob Jones* case, it turned to Coleman. He was asked to argue the case when the Reagan Administration declined to defend the antisegregation policy, because of right-wing pressure from Capitol Hill.

He was also among the most prominent members of the Washington corporate bar. He was every bit the darling of the establishment as was Lloyd Cutler, Bork's champion among liberal Democrats.

Jordan, as a member of the House Judiciary Committee, had distinguished herself during the Nixon impeachment hearings in the early 1970s. A black woman elected official from Texas, she was the living embodiment of what the civil rights movement could accomplish.

Both Coleman and Jordan were reluctant at first. Coleman was being heavily lobbied by the Administration and his close friend Howard Baker and A. B. Culvahouse, his former law partner, to endorse Bork. Biden spent considerable time on the phone with both to convince them that Bork should be defeated.

Coleman is not the only witness the White House and Biden and his allies struggled over. A similar battle took place with former Attorney General Katzenbach, whom Senator Kennedy finally persuaded to testify against Bork. The battle over Benjamin Civiletti, a Carter AG, was a tie. He never appeared. The White House also tried unsuccessfully to get Lewis Powell to speak out on behalf of Bork, as Justices White and Stevens had.

Biden used drafts of the Peck and Schroeder response piece as a briefing document to induce reluctant witnesses like Jordan to testify. It was also used by academics as a briefing device to prepare for the hearings.

Biden had a list of prominent Americans he was also constantly speaking to during August. Not just prospective witnesses like Coleman, Jordan, and

Young but Southern Democrats like Sam Nunn of Georgia and Bennett Johnston of Louisiana and Republican Robert Packwood and former Sen. Ed Brooke. He spoke with Hispanic leaders like Mayor Henry Cisneros of San Antonio, Gov. George Wallace, and former President Carter. In some cases he was attempting to recruit them as witnesses or asking them to approach a prospective witness, or simply requesting a statement. For example, he eventually persuaded Carter to issue a strong statement against the nomination to counter testimony by two prominent members of his Administration who had endorsed Bork, Lloyd Cutler and Griffin Bell.

Biden also was personally involved, with Schroeder's and Dellinger's assistance, in arranging six panels of academics who were expert on particular aspects of Bork's jurisprudence or who could address basic anti-Bork arguments.

The campaign for editorial opinion was also carefully orchestrated during August. The editorial pages have a subtle but important impact on how members of the Senate and their staffs and, more importantly, how managers of the electronic news media look at an issue. A *New York Times* or *Washington Post* editorial often becomes the conventional wisdom on any particular policy issue in Washington and can control how it is covered even on the television news. Editorials themselves are sometimes quoted on the evening news, and editorial columnists are frequent guests on television news and commentary programs.

Robert Bork entered his struggle for the nomination in 1987 with more than a few friends on the editorial pages of the major newspapers. George Will, who had a weekly column in the *Post,* had been in Bork's wedding, and William Safire with a weekly political column on the editorial page of the *Times* openly acknowledged his friendship with Bork. Will was also a close personal friend of Meg Greenfield, editorial page editor for the *Post.* Pat Shakow, the member of the *Washington Post*'s editorial board, who wrote most of the paper's editorials on Bork, knew Bork and some of his closest allies on a social basis.

The editorial page of a major paper, like the *Post* or the *Times,* is managed by an editorial page editor–Meg Greenfield for the *Post,* Jack Rosenthal for the *Times*–who control the process by which their paper arrives at a political position. They also have considerable influence over which signed editorials appear on the opposite page (left-hand page for editorials, right-hand for op-eds). Some columnists, for example George Will at the *Post* and William Safire at the *Times,* are practically guaranteed space in the paper on a weekly basis; other columns or signed editorials appear at the discretion of the editorial page editor.

According to Brad Reynolds, the Administration engaged in a sophisticated campaign to influence the nation's editorial pages. However, there was no evidence that the White House was any more successful in shaping editorial opinion than those who opposed the nomination.

Indeed, although the anti-Bork coalition was fearful of the influence that Will and Bork had on the *Post*'s editorial writers, the Administration had in fact no significant sway over the paper's opinions on the issues. Pat Shakow recalls running into Bork at a party soon after the nomination was announced and Kennedy had attacked Bork on the Senate floor. She told him things were going to get tough.

"We're already hearing from a lot of people," she said, referring to intense lobbying of the *Post* by the anti-Bork coalition.

Bork looked at her with a concerned expression on his face. "You're hearing from the other side, aren't you?"

"Not a word," she replied. Shakow claims she was never lobbied by the Administration on the nomination.

In fact, it was someone else on the *Post* who told her that the Administration had prepared their Blue Book. She called Terry Eastland, the Justice Department press spokesman, on a weekend to obtain a copy. Eastland was shocked to find out that the White House had not given her one. At the time they lived near each other, and he gave Shakow his copy.

Bork was clearly impatient with the Administration's reticence with the press on his nomination. After initial resistance, Korologos and Bork's other handlers relented and agreed to allow him to meet with the press. In late August and early September, Bork conducted extensive interviews with national newsmagazines and newspapers and even met surreptitiously with the editorial board of the *New York Times*.

Biden and the anti-Bork groups had no reticence whatsoever in approaching the editorial boards. Attempting to solicit editorials favorable to their positions was a strategy both Biden and the groups had used extensively in the past. The LCCR and especially the American Civil Liberties Union had an extensive network of editorial page contacts across the nation. Biden and the ACLU had worked together on a number of First Amendment struggles in the early 1980s and with the Leadership Conference on other nominations and civil rights legislation, and relied heavily on those contacts.

The hostility of the *Washington Post* editorial page to the anti-Bork effort in the first ten days of July came as a complete shock to the leadership of the anti-Bork effort. Editorials attacking the civil rights groups and later Biden, as well as similar signed editorials Greenfield printed, were the subject of extensive discussion between Neas and me. Our initial strategy of having civil rights stalwart Joseph Rauh write a letter to the editor complaining only prompted another negative editorial.

After several futile conversations with Pat Shakow, who we knew had written several of the editorials, Neas asked for a formal meeting with the *Post* editorial board.

Pat Shakow is a tough-minded lawyer and mother of three boys. She had spent many years on the staff of the late Republican Sen. Jacob Javits of New York. Shakow served with Javits when he was the Republican leader on civil rights efforts in the 1960s and 70s. Javits, in his day, was the most formidable procivil rights leader. As an intellectual, deeply committed to his cause, he demanded no less of his staff. Shakow filled the bill well and was personally close to Joseph Rauh and to Clarence Mitchell, the chief civil rights lobbyist of his day.

No one could question her civil rights credentials then or in the summer of 1987. Knowing that she was writing the editorials in the *Washington Post* was particularly galling to people in the anti-Bork coalition. It also made for a very difficult summer for Shakow.

"I had the worst summer in my life. . . . Friends of twenty-five years" were asking "how dare you not be a part of this" effort to defeat Bork. It got downright nasty at times. At one party that summer, the wife of a prominent liberal got so carried away in pressing the point "that she spit in my face."

It wasn't only her friends on the left Shakow was hearing from. That summer she was president of the alumni association of Yale Law School and in contact with prominent members of Bork's last academic home, including members of the faculty. She was astounded to hear severe criticism of Bork, even from those he thought were his friends.

The members of the editorial board of the *Washington Post* are a close-knit group. They are physically apart from the rest of the paper. The group often gets together socially and have come to look at issues in much the same way. Certainly on the Bork matter they did. The onslaught of criticism that Shakow took that summer undoubtedly drew her even closer to the other seven members of the board. Every morning around 10:00 they gather with Greenfield to discuss the events of the day. In those first weeks of July, there was no serious disagreement in the group about what the *Post* should be saying about the tactics of the anti-Bork effort.

The editorial board does welcome lobbying efforts, and therefore the request by Neas to meet with the board was not surprising. Greenfield agreed to meet in late July. When Neas arrived with John Buchanan of People For the American Way, Judy Lichtman, Bill Taylor, and Elaine Jones for the meeting, he was surprised to see not only the regulars from the editorial board but executive editor Ben Bradlee, publisher Katharine Graham, and her son and heir apparent, Donald.

The meeting was tense from the beginning. Neas began with a joke about overstatement. It didn't seem to help much, so he moved right into his presentation. The thrust of his argument was that if the LCCR truly believed in the values for which it had stood for almost forty years, it had to oppose Robert Bork. Neas reminded the room that Bork had questioned "dozens of cases" that were hard-won victories of the civil rights movement. Now Bork thought they ought to be reconsidered. "It was our obligation as citizens to get involved and to get as many citizens as possible involved."

Neas and his colleagues got the clear impression that Greenfield was angry and very skeptical about the presentation. The debate was tough and pointed. Greenfield, Shakow, and Peter Milius, who had written the first *Post* editorial, led the questioning. The issue was what Bork really stood for. Taylor and Lichtman fielded questions along with Neas and Rauh.

Neas recalls, "We hoped that we had scored some points with Kate and Donnie [the Grahams]. We did not think that we had scored any points with Meg." According to Shakow, the Grahams have never interfered in editorial policy, and Greenfield was clearly first among equals on the editorial board. The net result of the meeting was an impasse. The editorial position of the *Post* would have to await the hearings and the committee's questioning of Robert Bork and in particular his answers.

After hearing a report from Neas of the *Post* meeting, it was clear that the anti-Bork effort had much work to do with the editorial board of the *Post* and probably other editorial boards. Biden decided to visit eight editorial boards during August and early September.

Two of the editorial board meetings were viewed by Biden political operatives as necessary to his campaign effort, the *Boston Globe* because of its heavy New Hampshire circulation and the *Des Moines Register*. Six were directed at affecting major national media outlets and their coverage of the Bork struggle and especially the hearings—the *Los Angeles Times* on August 10, *Time* magazine on August 31, *Newsweek,* the *New York Times* on September 1, and *U.S. News and World Report* and the *Washington Post* on September 9.

Some of the meetings were full-dress dinners or luncheon meetings with the whole editorial board and key reporters—the *Los Angeles Times, Time, New York Times,* and *U.S. News and World Report*. The *Post* and *Newsweek* meetings were more informal, with some editorial writers and only reporters covering the Bork hearings.

The *Los Angeles Times* was already quite skeptical of the Bork nomination when Biden met with the full board on August 11. On the day after Bork was nominated, the newspaper questioned the nomination in an editorial labeled "Hard-Right Rudder," calling Bork a "rock-solid right-winger." Biden met with the paper the day before he was to deliver his speech to the ABA in San Francisco. He used many of the same themes and was well received.

By the time Biden did the next important editorial meeting, with *Time* on August 31, his argument had become even more sophisticated. The Peck and Schroeder response piece was almost finished and had become the primary resource document for Biden on the nomination. The *Time* meeting was a catered dinner at a restaurant near the magazine's headquarters. Rasky recalls, "Joe was cooking that night." Donilon agrees: "It was all on Bork. Everybody from the top guys down to the reporters were there. Joe took off his coat. He fielded all the questions well. I don't think anyone wanted to leave at the end of the evening."

At some of the meetings there was either an underlying skepticism about Biden or about his position on Bork, much as the *Post*'s Meg Greenfield had about Neas on Bork. The luncheon meeting the next day with the *New York Times* was one such meeting.

The *New York Times* is intimidating enough as it is. "The paper of record," as its managers liked to refer to it, was beginning to harbor some doubts about Biden by early September 1987. One editor commented, "Biden didn't know why he wanted to run for President." For example, Stuart Taylor, who had the Supreme Court beat and was covering the nomination for the *Times,* explained, "The boys in New York [the editors] saw everything Biden said as political, as part of his campaign. [To them] Biden was just trying to make a big deal out of something that wasn't so important." Taylor and his colleague Linda Greenhouse saw the Bork fight and what Biden and other opponents said about Bork as very important and were in a constant battle to get their stories in the paper.

According to Taylor, Greenhouse wanted to get more space on Biden's late July advice-and-consent speech on the Senate floor, not because she was trying to help Biden or the anti-Bork campaign but because she saw it as a critical argument—to convince wavering Senators that it was legitimate to consider ideology. New York disagreed. Taylor explained that the attitude seemed to be "to make it a big deal tended to credit Biden's argument and help his campaign. . . . Sometimes New York seemed more concerned about how [anything that the *Times* wrote] affected Biden and his campaign. That tended to be more important than what Biden or the opponents of Bork were saying."

Although no one close to Biden knew any of this at the time, experienced operatives like Rasky and Donilon could sense it. Biden, Rasky, and Donilon were elated after the *Time* meeting the night before. As they rode the elevator up to the ornate fourteenth floor meeting room of publisher Arthur Sulzberger in the *New York Times* building, they all began to tense up.

"You walk into this paneled anteroom that's about the size of the Oval Office. The paneling was probably put there when the building was built. On the wall were all these signed pictures to previous publishers—you know from Mussolini, Churchill, I don't know, probably Julius Caesar. Then out comes this little Jewish guy, sticks out his hand, smiles and says, 'Hi, Punch Sulzberger'." It should have relieved the tension but it did not.

The three joined the whole editorial board; the editorial page editor Jack Rosenthal and Pat Shakow's counterpart Jack Mackenzie were there, as were news editors—for example, Max Frankel, the new executive editor. Along with Punch Sulzberger was his son, Arthur Jr., "Pinch," the deputy publisher.

It was a good substantive discussion of the Bork nomination, with Mackenzie and Rosenthal asking thoughtful questions. The *Times* was already genuinely skeptical of the nomination and not the least bit upset about the anti-Bork campaign. After the meeting the editorial page continued to be very supportive of what Biden and the anti-Bork forces said about Bork. The feedback we got from the meeting hours after it occurred was that Biden had done well and was convincing on the nomination.

Mackenzie confirms that everybody in the meeting seemed a little "stiff" and that Biden was long-winded. "People were skeptical of Biden. Certainly there was no one there in a swoon."

As they left the building Donilon predicted to Biden that the *Times* would oppose the nomination. But Rasky, on the basis of some skepticism he sensed in the room about Biden, thought to himself, We've got problems at the *Times*.

The *Newsweek* dinner in the evening was even worse. Although Biden also made progress on the Bork matter itself, Rasky and Donilon both detected a certain cynicism about Biden himself. The questions were much more political than in any of the other meetings: "How can you possibly win this?" "Haven't you prejudged Bork?" "Aren't you going to be criticized for that?" There were questions about the campaign, about Jesse Jackson. Rasky recalled that the whole thing was "awkward," "unpleasant," even "nasty."

Robert Bork and his colleagues in the Administration had far from universal success with editorial boards that summer as well. One very important target of their attention was the *New York Times* editorial board with its obvious skepticism about the nomination.

Howard Baker had met with the editorial board in early July in an effort to allay the *Times*'s concerns. It was not unlike the Biden meeting, although the questions were even less pointed and substantive. Baker's main argument was Bork's credentials. He predicted that Bork would "charm the pants off the Senate."

The *Times* editorial process is quite similar to the *Post*'s. It is collegial, and just as Meg Greenfield and Pat Shakow worked closely on the Bork question, Jack Rosenthal and Jack Mackenzie worked together on Bork. Rosenthal and Mackenzie, like Greenfield and Shakow, have known each other for decades. Rosenthal was in Attorney General Robert Kennedy's press office when Mackenzie was covering the Justice Department for the *Washington Post*.

Mackenzie's office on the tenth floor of the *Times* is large, by *Times* standards, and has the feel of the cluttered refuge of an absent-minded professor. Mackenzie is a soft-spoken intellectual with strong views on jurisprudential issues. He is not one who had to be educated on the Court or constitutional law in the summer of 1987. Although not trained as a lawyer, he had covered the Court for three decades and had a good command of Robert Bork and his positions as soon as he was nominated.

Robert Bork insisted on having his late summer meeting with the *Times* outside its West 43rd Street offices. Sulzberger and his son, Rosenthal, Mackenzie, and columnist and former managing editor Abe Rosenthal met Bork in a nearby restaurant.

Sulzberger began the discussion. He was puzzled by why the Administration had nominated Bork when they could have nominated someone less controversial. Bork disagreed that he was all that controversial.

Mackenzie pressed, "Do you think your nomination is in trouble?"

Bork responded unequivocally, "No!"

The questioning became much more substantive. The day before, Jack Rosenthal and Mackenzie had discussed the implications of Bork's view that the *Griswold* decision was wrong, that there was no inherent right to privacy under the Constitution and that therefore there was no doctrinal underpinning for the *Roe* decision. They had decided to ask Bork the same question Justice Stevens had raised in a recent abortion case argument. If there is no right to privacy under the Constitution and abortion was basically a state issue, could a state mandate abortions as they do in China?

At first Bork tried to beg off the question, "That's just not realistic. No state would do that."

Mackenzie interrupted, "Wait a second, you just told us that doctrine and theory were important in constitutional law and that the problem is that the liberals don't have a theory. Shouldn't you be prepared to answer such a hypothetical question, whether or not it's realistic, in order to test your theory?"

Bork relented. "O.K., a state could do that, but don't be alarmed. No state is going to do that."

To Mackenzie, Bork had "laid an egg." He was not the "charming wit Baker had promised." Indeed, he seemed a bit "lethargic, perhaps even depressed."

Meanwhile back in Washington, Schroeder and Peck were putting the finishing touches on the response piece. It was becoming as long and as detailed as a court brief. It would be released as a report of two consultants to the chairman, Peck and Schroeder. However, we also wanted the imprimatur of our outside experts. Kurland refused. He felt that a lengthy and hard-hitting editorial he had written for the *Chicago Tribune* was all he wanted to do for a while. Walter Dellinger of Duke and Floyd Abrams were easy to accommodate. Clark Clifford and Tribe were more difficult.

Tribe would not consider going on the piece unless Clifford did. Clifford's problem was not the substance. He was satisfied that Peck and Schroeder knew what they were doing, and he was reassured by Abrams and Dellinger's willingness to sign the piece. Clifford was simply uncomfortable with having to defend it himself, since he had not been actively involved in its development.

Finally Biden called Clifford on September 1 from New York, after the *Times* lunch and before the *Newsweek* dinner. They came up with an excellent compromise. The report would be issued as a report of the "consultants" (Peck and Schroeder) that had been "reviewed" at Biden's request by Abrams, Clifford, Dellinger, and Tribe who "support wholeheartedly the substance of the views expressed."

As soon as Tribe found out about Clifford, he was willing to go on but only after extensive changes. I put him on the phone with Peck and Schroeder. It was essential that we oblige Tribe and do so quickly because we had been led to believe that, if we could finish it in the next day or so, it would get a big spread in the upcoming *Newsweek*.

I walked down to the room where Peck and Schroeder were on the phone with Tribe. Peck was clearly concerned. He placed his hand over the mouthpiece: Tribe was suggesting a complete reorganization. "We can't get this done by tomorrow, no way!"

I smiled, "There's got to be a way. Biden wants this out tomorrow."

In what was to become a weekly pattern for Peck and his colleagues, they stayed up all night and finished the draft in the morning. Tribe's changes were excellent. They did not affect the substance as much as they did the presentation. In the days before the Judiciary Committee had laser printers and agile word-processing systems it was a logistical nightmare.

Peck recalls trying to track Floyd Abrams down in Nevada, where he was in a trial, to clear some of Tribe's last-minute changes. Abrams returned his call at 1:30 A.M. on that Wednesday morning. He laughed when Peck answered the phone. "This is just like calling back Cahill, Gordon [his Wall Street firm] and finding an associate there at this hour. I can always count on it."

The response piece provoked a reaction that even Biden and his staff had not anticipated. Jane Berman, the committee press assistant, was deluged with calls. Since neither Biden nor Peck nor Schroeder were to do any on-the-record interviews, Berman had to deal with a swarm of angry television producers. The plan was to avoid complicating the fairness issue by having Biden, or anyone speaking for him to the press, put as much emphasis as possible on the document itself and to direct reporters to Tribe, Abrams, Dellinger, and Clifford. Tribe and Dellinger did a number of television and radio interviews.

Both ABC and NBC devoted three minutes, a sizable segment, to the nomination struggle, both leading with the release of the "Biden Report." Tribe appeared on the NBC segment.

Although it had little if any detectable impact on *Newsweek*'s coverage, it was a huge success with much of the rest of the print media. It produced more favorable press for Biden and the anti-Bork effort than anything done thus far. It was picked up immediately by the AP and UPI wires and was on the front page of hundreds of papers around the nation on Thursday morning September 3.

Despite a number of requests, the White House refused to make the original Blue Book available to the press, so we did. The White House's reticence just fed the story. I wrote the committee press release. It was explicitly designed to exploit conservative discomfort with the way Bork was being portrayed by the White House. It quoted conservative legal scholar and former Reagan Justice Department official Bruce Fein, "Judge Bork, even if he's portrayed as a moderate and is confirmed, is not going to alter his vote that way. . . . I think when you try to be a little too cute as the President is being, I believe, that no one is deceived. . . ."

The conservative *Washington Times* in covering the report conceded that Fein was not the only conservative concerned about what the White House was doing, and Terry Eastland, Justice Department spokesman and a genuine Bork loyalist, responded defensively to the *Washington Post:* "It's nonsense to say he's a judicial activist." Eastland argued that his career had been "spent in the service of defining and applying neutral principles." Eastland did not defend the White House Blue Book but instead made it clear to the *Post*'s Ruth Marcus, "It's not the briefing book that's been nominated, it's Judge Bork." That was exactly our point.

The *Post* devoted approximately fifty column inches to the story, including an extensive side-by-side comparison of the two portrayals of Robert Bork—the White House's and Peck's and Schroeder's. Marcus concluded, "The two documents offer a preview of the debate on Bork when the Senate Judiciary Committee begins two weeks of hearings on the nomination Sept. 15."

USA Today took a similar approach with a story which led off: "The battle over Supreme Court nominee Robert Bork is being waged with conflicting reports." In a separate box it compared "Biden" and the "White House" in "Disparate views of the same man." The story was not nearly as long as the *Post* but in the headline the anti-Bork forces got exactly the message they wanted to the hundreds of thousands of readers of the paper around the nation:

"BIDEN REPORT: WHITE HOUSE 'DISTORTS' BORK'S RECORD TO WIN OVER MODERATES."

By the last week in August, four major reports had been released by anti-Bork organizations outside the Senate—the American Civil Liberties Union, the National Women's Law Center, the AFL-CIO, and Public Citizen. When combined with the Peck and Schroeder piece, these reports represented a formidable case against the nomination. The Department of Justice Bork loyalists thought something more was needed. Mike Carvin and his team of young lawyers in the Office of Legal Counsel, who had done much of the spade work for the original Blue Book, prepared a lengthy response.

Unlike the original White House piece, Justice was permitted to prepare the response with little, if any, White House interference. Finally, Carvin was given the chance to make some of the substantive arguments in favor of

Bork's position that he had been forced to forgo in the original White House piece. He and his team took full advantage of this freedom in their "Response to the Critics." For example, the "Response" explicitly defends Bork's narrower view of the First Amendment and his critique of the one-man-one-vote decisions. The rhetoric of the "Response" was much more belligerent. The Peck and Schroeder document, which was labeled the Biden Report, was charged with "outlandish assertions" and all of the anti-Bork reports were characterized as "propaganda."

Stung by the Peck and Schroeder account, White House counsel A. B. Culvahouse felt that the Justice Department "Response" was "less intellectually honest" than the original White House Blue Book. "The Department of Justice wanted to do a diatribe so we relented. We said it's OK to get down on the same level but it's on your letterhead, not ours."

Although the Justice Department was trying to move away from the Administration "high road" strategy, the Response to the Critics piece still attempted on the whole to present Bork as part of the mainstream. Bork himself continued to pursue the strategy as well in his own press initiatives. For example, in an interview in the *Newsweek* that hit the stands on September 7, Bork portrayed himself as a moderate who had recanted some of his controversial views. The reason he no longer toed the narrow line on the First Amendment is that he had been looking for a "bright-line test . . . it turns out, as in many areas of life, bright-line tests don't make much sense." "I [once] said something rather harsh about [the abortion ruling in] *Roe* v. *Wade* but [what I said] really applied more to the line of reasoning that was followed."

In a long story in the *U.S. News & World Report* issue of the same date, Bork and his allies seemed to be making the same pitch: "In advance of the hearings, Bork has told senators that he would expect to hear arguments that a right to abortion *can* be found in the Constitution, that just because he hasn't found it doesn't mean it's not there."

The *Newsweek* and *U.S. News & World Report* issues on the Bork nomination, like much of the rest of the national press, described two portraits of Robert Bork—one by Bork's proponents and one by his opponents. However, for his opponents the articles were considered a disaster. For example, the lengthy essay in *U.S. News* by Michael Kramer was unabashedly pro-Bork. Kramer, who also interviewed Bork, concluded near the end of his seven-page essay, "At bottom, it appears that Bork has been principled rather than result-oriented, that he decides cases according to the facts presented by the litigants. This is not the mark of an ideologue."

The Biden effort to persuade *Newsweek* had failed, and on Wednesday, September 9, when Biden met for lunch with editors and reporters for the *Washington Post* and for dinner with *U.S. News*, he anticipated a hostile audience. The meeting at the *Post* was not an official editorial board meeting.

Executive editor Ben Bradlee was there with Greenfield and Shakow, national editor Robert Kaiser, and three reporters who were covering the Bork matter—Al Kamen, Ruth Marcus, and Ed Walsh.

Shakow recalls, "We were still mad at him because we thought that he had prejudged the whole outcome." She remembers a "very spirited discussion . . . he had obviously done his homework." Biden elaborated on his ABA argument, supplemented by the consultants' study, and especially the privacy and unenumerated rights arguments which he had discussed in various briefings and at the beach with Tribe and Caddell. Shakow and Biden argued in detail over the various cases. "We wanted him to know that we had read the cases, that we're not writing off the top of our heads or writing what someone tells us." Biden was trying to do the same. According to Shakow "he did" convince her that he knew what he was talking about. She was still not persuaded but was going into the hearing willing to listen to the case Biden would be making. "We [also] wanted to let him know what we were going to be looking for in the hearings—fairness. . . ."

Biden had been concerned about the "fairness" of his demeanor and the hearings for over a month, but the point was well taken. At the end of the lunch Biden walked up to Shakow: "You're one tough lady."

Shakow laughed. "That's what my three boys tell me."

In terms of directly influencing the paper's editorials, it was a draw, but considering the *Washington Post* and its attitude about the Bork opposition, it was a victory.

The *U.S. News* dinner that night at publisher Mort Zuckerman's house was even more of a success. Reporters like Gloria Borger and Michael Kramer, who had written the complimentary essay on Bork in the current issue, were there as was columnist and former Reagan White House communications director David Gergen. Rasky recalls it being "a very pleasant evening." Kramer and Biden did get into a long philosophical discussion, but it was very serious and even-tempered. "I walked out of that room thinking those people thought they were with potentially the next President." Gergen gave Rasky and Biden a ride back up to Capitol Hill, where Biden was staying that night, and they talked about the need for a bipartisan Administration.

That Friday, the notion that two radically different portraits of Bork were emerging, which was now dominating the media coverage, was further amplified through a series of exchanges between pro- and anti-Bork partisans. The anti-Bork forces fired the first salvos. Twenty-two national women's organizations announced their opposition to the nomination at a press conference at the National Press Club, and Senator Kennedy delivered another speech very critical of Bork at Georgetown Law School. To Kennedy, the White House was trying "to sell Robert Bork to the Senate by calling him a judicial 'moderate.' But the 'moderate' Bork is a far cry from the real Bork."

Kennedy went through Bork's statements on many of the same cases Biden had discussed at the ABA, analyzed his position on *stare decisis*, and labeled him a "judicial hyperactivist."

President Reagan responded off the cuff for the White House press corps at a rose garden ceremony. Bork's critics have been using "highly charged rhetoric . . . irrational and totally unjustified. . . . Don't let anyone tell you that those we nominate to high positions, especially to the Supreme Court, do not share in our commitment to the ideals of freedom and equality that all Americans hold dear."

Then he moved to the familiar theme, again right from the Blue Book: Bork "has a superior intellect, a high moral character and is a champion of individual freedom. Any suggestion to the contrary is pure politics—if politics can be pure."

At the end of the day, Brad Reynolds presented a defense of Bork to the Bureau of National Affairs in a downtown hotel. Except for an opening shot at Biden and Simon, similar to Reagan's "pure politics" remark, Reynolds delivered a dispassionate defense of Bork. Quoting the dean of the University of Chicago Law School, Reynolds described Bork as a "four star" appointment who has great respect for precedent, who has argued "forcefully and consistently" on behalf of women, who has never had an opinion reversed by the Supreme Court, who is "one of the leading legal scholars of our time" and who would be confirmed.

ABC nightly news carried excerpts from all four events that night, and NBC covered the President's remarks. All got extensive print media coverage the next day.

The two carefully cultivated images of Robert Bork were clearly in evidence as the final "curtain raisers" were written for the Sunday papers. Stuart Taylor of the *New York Times* was finally beginning to convince his editors that the anti-Bork effort was not simply a wholly owned subsidiary of Biden-for-President. Perhaps Biden's substantive presentation to the *Times* editorial board helped. On Sunday Taylor was given approximately fifty column inches in which to summarize the two portraits. Beginning on the front page the headline was, "JUDGE BORK: RESTRAINT VS. ACTIVISM." The lead was that two "sharply contrasting images of what he really stands for" was emerging. "Is he the exponent of politically neutral 'judicial restraint' that he claims to be—one who would respect even those precedents of which he disapproves? Or is he a right-wing activist who would uproot decades of settled precedent and write his own political views into the law for decades to come?"

The *Times* editorialized about the upcoming hearings. Pointing out the Administration's effort to portray Bork as a moderate conservative like Powell, the editorial set out an agenda for the hearings. The focus must be on Bork's writings, and Bork must show that "his views are not as stark as [his] writings suggest.'' Focusing in on many of the same issues that Biden had discussed in his meeting, the *Times* concluded, ''Whether Robert Bork deserves confirmation may depend on how plausibly he can explain that record.''

The Sunday news programs continued the two portraits framework. David Brinkley devoted his whole program to the nomination. Six guests appeared, Washington attorney Carla Hills and Sen. Orrin Hatch in favor of the nomination and ACLU executive director Ira Glasser and Professor Tribe against the nomination, and Senators Specter and DeConcini, who were both undecided. In introducing the topic, ABC correspondent Jack Smith used excerpts from what Kennedy and Reagan said on Friday to summarize the two portraits:

> SEN. KENNEDY: With his contempt for precedent and Congress, our most basic constitutional liberties would suddenly be vulnerable.
> PRES. REAGAN: He has a superior intellect, a high moral character, and is a champion of individual freedom.

Smith explained how the Administration had ''worked all summer to portray him as a moderate'' but followed it with a tape of Biden delivering the catch line from his ABA speech that, if Bork's views had prevailed on the Supreme Court for the last three decades, ''America would be a fundamentally different place than it is today.''

NBC's ''Meet the Press'' conducted a similar program with White House chief of staff Howard Baker on behalf of the nomination and Sen. Howard Metzenbaum against. Again the focus was on the two portraits. As moderator Chris Wallace concluded the program, he summarized the two competing portraits and quoted Professor Kurland on the importance of the hearings: ''The one thing we know is that the Senate should not be asked to consent to the appointment of both Dr. Jekyll and Mr. Hyde.''

Toward the end of the program Robert Kaiser, who was a guest commentator on the program, discussed with conservative columnist Robert Novak the political implications of the struggle. Novak saw nothing but trouble for the Democrats. Kaiser picked up on Biden's points at the *Post* meeting, which he had attended earlier in the week. ''One of the most interesting questions about Bork is his position on privacy. Bork argues that the Constitution does not contain a right to privacy. In the modern era, America has become a more tolerant country, and it has certainly come to believe in privacy. If the Democrats could cast this—and I'm not predicting they will because they are not the most competent of fellows—but if they could cast this as an argument about 'We are the party that wants to defend the privacy of people, for example, to do in their own bedroom what they will, and the Republicans are trying to impose an antiprivacy judge in the Supreme Court,' that's a different kind of an issue. And that could help the Democrats quite a lot.''

The next day *Time* magazine appeared on the newsstands. It was devastating for Robert Bork. The cover was a portrait of Bork in which he looked like a brooding medieval monk, and the stories themselves were even more negative. Certainly the most powerful was written by Richard Lacayo, in which he concluded, ''[O]ne thing is clear from his twenty-five years of unflinching and outspoken legal advocacy: he is not the mainstream legal thinker that the White House is now painting him to be.''

That article was accompanied by illustrations of Bork. The first showed Bork speaking. The second showed his head upside down. The clear implication was that Bork had reversed his positions on a number of issues. As Professor Kurland had asked, are we dealing with ''Dr. Jekyll or Mr. Hyde''?

In concluding its cover piece on the nomination, *Time* focused on how the fate of the nomination would be decided: ''In the television age, the way Bork comes across [in the hearings] could be critically important. . . . If Americans watching the hearings this week like what they see, if they are reassured by either Bork's mind or his manner, the advice and consent of the public will certainly be felt on the Senate floor. And if the public becomes convinced that Bork's views are, as opponents charge, so far from the mainstream that they seem to threaten the rights that Americans have come to cherish, such sentiments will likewise probably prevail when final votes are counted.''

As the curtain began to rise on the hearings on September 15, the challenge for Robert Bork was even greater than either he or his opponents recognized at the time. The only way he could succeed was if he engaged in a deliberate effort to reassure average Americans in his hearings, and if his Democratic opponents were as incompetent as Robert Kaiser had suggested they might be on ''Meet the Press.''

CHAPTER 14

IT'S STARTING TO COME APART. . . . I HOPE WE CAN STILL WIN.

TOM KOROLOGOS FIRST NOTICED the problem when he was taking Bork around to meet with members of the Senate, a practice known as "courtesy calls." Bork seemed stiff, even nervous. At the core he was a scholar and would lapse back into that role even in the private meetings, which were intended to be relaxed encounters where potential allies could get to know him. It tended to put off Senators. Korologos described his encounter with liberal Republican Lowell Weicker of Connecticut: "It was just the three of us. Weicker said, 'Hi'." Bork tried to steer the conversation toward some legal issue. Exasperated, Korologos told Bork afterward, "For Chrissake say, 'It's a nice day,' will ya? Relax!.' But he never did."

Bolton recalled a conversation he had with Bork in the first week of September. It took place in the cafeteria of the Senate Office Building, where they were having coffee during a break between appointments for courtesy calls. Bork relayed, with sarcasm, a conversation with Baker about the most recent Senate vote count. Bolton knew that the vote count in committee was "dicey," and he was appalled that Baker would share that with Bork immediately before the hearings. It was not the kind of thing that would help him relax. "It could shatter his confidence."

Bolton had a point. It probably was not the best thing to do immediately before a nationally televised confrontation that even the White House was arguing would determine the fate of the nomination. However, Terry Eastland was concerned that the leadership at the Justice Department was simply too insulated from the real world and was not aware of how much trouble Bork was in by late August and early September.

The Justice Department under Ed Meese and Brad Raynolds was the bastion for conservatives within the Administration. As Eastland wrote a year later, many conservatives during that era spent too much time burnishing their credentials with other conservatives, "in the process creating a sort of conservative ghetto. . . . These folks talked to each other—but not to the media or to others outside their world, whom they distrusted."

Eastland had no choice but to talk to outsiders, since it was his job to deal with the media for the department. Eastland realized that the Peck and Schroeder response piece had really "ginned up the press." For this and other reasons the media was becoming very "skeptical about the nomination by this period."

Meese and Reynolds had spent part of August on official business in China. At the department's first morning staff meeting after their return, on Tuesday, September 8, Eastland expressed his opinion that the Bork nomination "was dead," and that the Administration should begin to look for alternatives. Eastland was trying to jar the leadership of the department into recognizing the problems the nomination faced. As he explained the skepticism in the press and the failure of the Administration to take the offensive in August, he was met with stunned, awkward silence. Meese was the only one who spoke: "We'll have none of that negative talk today."

Although by September 8, the White House vote counters might have been concerned about the nomination, Bork himself uneasy, and the leadership of the Justice Department naively optimistic, everything would change the next day. On September 8, an American Bar Association committee, chaired by former Ford Justice Department deputy attorney general, Harold Tyler, finalized its recommendation on whether Robert Bork should be confirmed. On September 9 the results were leaked to the press.

It came as a rude shock to Bork's friends in the department. Although the fifteen-member committee did give Bork the highest rating, "well-qualified," there were five dissenting votes. One voted "not opposed," which means in ABA jargon that the nominee "while minimally qualified is not among the best available," and four voted "not qualified." It was the largest split on an ABA report on a Supreme Court nominee since the ill-fated Haynesworth nomination in the 1960s. Sheldon Goldman, an expert on judicial nominations, called it an outcome "unprecedented in modern times."

The problem with the vote is that it went directly to the heart of the Administration's case for Robert Bork—that he was qualified and from the legal mainstream. According to its own guidelines, the committee "does not investigate the prospective nominee's political or ideological philosophy except to the extent that extreme views might bear on judicial temperament or integrity." A significant number of these members of the legal establishment had doubts about the nominee on these grounds. As Tyler's September 21 letter to the Judiciary Committee explained, the minority was concerned about Bork's "judicial temperament, *e.g.*, his compassion, open mindedness, his sensitivity to the rights of women and minority persons or groups and comparatively extreme views respecting Constitutional principles or their application, particularly within the ambit of the Fourteenth Amendment."

Steve Markman, speaking for the Justice Department, put the best spin he could on the report: "I think it's quite a tribute to Judge Bork that he's received that overwhelming vote of highest approval from the American Bar Association." Biden emphasized the historical significance of the split vote in his meeting with the editorial board and writers at the *Washington Post.*

The next day Republican Orrin Hatch held a press conference and accused the ABA dissenters of being "willing to play politics" on the nomination. He added, "That is one of the problems we have had with the ABA in recent years, playing politics with the ratings." One of the members of the ABA committee, Jerome Shestack of Philadelphia, was an acquaintance of Biden's, a supporter of his presidential campaign, and one of the dissenters, but the Biden staff had not lobbied him on the vote. However, members of the ABA committee were deluged with written analyses of Bork's record by both sides in the struggle.

The day after the report was leaked, the *Washington Post* called it a "bombshell" and called upon the ABA to depart from its normal practice and explain the meaning of the dissent in testimony before the committee. "The specifics of the minority findings need to be made public, and the nominee should have a chance to reply."

Robert Bork was offended by what he saw as further evidence of the "politicization of our legal culture" in the episode. To Bork's "surprise," the ABA had become "a player in the game."

What Robert Bork did not realize, but Orrin Hatch and Bork's other friends at the Department of Justice surely did, is that the ABA had been "a player in the game" of judicial nominations for decades. Indeed, during the Reagan Administration, it had become a focal point of intense lobbying, especially by the Department of Justice.

The American Bar Association had been at the center of judicial selection politics for over half a century. The ABA's primary relationship is with the Administration, not the Judiciary Committee. Although the ABA committee does make its views known in correspondence with the committee and, if requested, in testimony before the committee, it is in almost constant informal consultation with the Department of Justice. In some Administrations, the ABA had a virtual veto over nominees, although its influence had decreased in recent Administrations.

The informal consultation process had been tested during the previous decade. Conservatives were angered by Carter Administration efforts to get more women and blacks through the ABA despite the availability of what the critics believed were more qualified white males. Liberals were angered by the Reagan Administration's effort to ignore moderates, women, and blacks generally to force less qualified whites through the ABA. One notorious case had involved the nomination of J. Harvie Wilkinson III to the Fourth Circuit Court of Appeals in 1983. The ABA initially opposed the nomination, because Wilkinson did not have the minimal legal practice experience, twelve years under the ABA committee's rules. The ABA committee reversed itself and endorsed Wilkinson after the committee was subjected to an aggressive lobbying effort orchestrated by the Justice Department and the nominee.

Obviously by the time of the Bork fight three years later, little had changed except that this time the Justice Department allies of Bork had conveniently forgotten what had happened in the Wilkinson case. Wilkinson's opponents in the civil rights movement were now Bork's opponents. They had not forgotten the events of 1984.

Activists like Estelle Rogers worked hard to be sure the national press found out how unprecedented were the dissenting votes in the ABA's report on the Bork nomination. Her counterparts on the Right were privately distraught about the report. Paul Weyrich sent McGuigan a note the afternoon the ABA report became known: "The Bork deal is not going well. . . . The ABA [rating] is a real problem—gives 'moderates' an out. . . . We need something dramatic—akin to the Burger endorsement, to change the atmosphere. This is slipping away."

Robert Bork also understood the significance: "The split vote . . . was extremely damaging to my nomination since the judgment was nominally about professionalism." As he recalls the period immediately before the hearings, the ABA report, and the campaign against him, his friends ". . . kept saying that matters would be rectified when the hearings began, and I had the chance to tell the facts as they were." In other words, they were saying to him that his fate was in his own hands through his testimony. It must have been a lonely feeling.

One of the decisions, at the very first large White House staff meeting on July 6, was that there would be "murder boards." As Korologos explains it, a murder board is a mock hearing, a practice session for the nominee, in which the participants play the role of hostile Senators interrogating him. They are intended to be worse than the actual hearing. "No one likes them . . . but [if you're the questioner] you've got to be as rotten as you can possibly be. . . ."

Korologos had made it clear to others from the beginning that Bork needed work as a witness. Bork, however, had discussed the process with Scalia and was skeptical that murder boards were a wise use of his time.

The first and only formal murder board was conducted in the Old Executive Office Building in August. It was a disaster. A gaggle of lawyers was present. As Culvahouse described it, "every smart lawyer had to be there. The White House couldn't be underrepresented. [Bork] wanted Randolph and Cutler."

Korologos chaired the session, and in addition to Culvahouse, Randolph, and Cutler, Kenneth Cribb and Ball from the White House, the Justice Department was represented by Charles Cooper, Bolton, and Reynolds.

The participants interrupted each other, and there was a lot of posturing.

As Reynolds put it, "They were more for the people to tell everybody afterwards that they had done a murder board with Bob Bork." Bolton recalls that the questions were "poorly prepared," "silly." "Bork was not intellectually challenged. Indeed he was not really pressed at all. He knocked them out of the park. Bork must have thought this was going to be easy." Culvahouse agrees: "He wasn't taking it seriously."

At times he was flip. Playing off Kennedy's July 1 statement, Ball asked Bork, "What is Bork's America *really* like?" Bork responded impatiently, "Is this where I give my Fourth of July speech? Okay, fine. Next question."

Howard Baker watched part of the session from the back of the room. According to Culvahouse, he wanted to "pump Bork up." He told Bork so and then went out and announced to the press, in an impromptu news conference, what a fine job Bork would do, then walked back across the street to his office in the White House. Culvahouse was worried after the meeting but thought Bork would "rise to the challenge."

Bork and his friends at Justice thought the three-hour session was a waste of time, and it was the last time that a formal murder board was held. Korologos complained to Doberstein and others at the White House, but from then on few meetings were held to discuss questioning at the hearing, and those were very private affairs at Bork's home on the two weekends preceding the hearing. According to Culvahouse, he and the White House thereafter lost touch with the hearing strategy to the extent that there was one.

Mike Carvin knew that more time needed to be spent in preparation for the hearings. He and Peter Keisler, a former Bork law clerk who was then working for Culvahouse in the White House, had both attended the White House murder boards as observers. They came up with the idea of having the private sessions at Bork's home. They would "secrete him away from the White House." Only those close to Bork would attend: Randolph, Reynolds, Carvin, and Keisler. Although Carvin didn't like the idea, Bork also wanted Cutler.

As Carvin recalls it, "It was not clear at the time which approach Biden was going to take—the approach he had taken in the ABA speech or the one he had pursued in the Rhenquist hearings." In the Rhenquist hearings the focus had been much more on integrity issues—whether the Chief Justice had intimidated black voters decades earlier in Arizona when he was in private practice. In the ABA speech Biden had, of course, focused directly on Bork's writings. The notebooks dealt extensively with Watergate, and the first private session, the weekend of September 4, was spent on the one integrity issue that threatened the nomination.

On Monday the meetings moved to jurisprudential questions. Carvin's briefing book proposed that for each issue Bork would use some homily and emphasize the constitutional value that his position stood for. They anticipated many of the questions that would arise in the hearings. Carvin was frustrated because Bork's attitude was not good. It was not clear whether the judge had even reviewed the notebooks, which he had taken with him on his vacation in Vermont in August. Bork grew restless after five hours, and the meeting was ended. He had a meeting later that week with academic colleagues in New York, including Henry Paul Monoghan of Columbia Law School. Carvin was beginning to get nervous about the hearings.

Reynolds recalls meetings that weekend and one the next Saturday. "The private meetings were very good. . . . The room crackled. There were a handful of us coming from different perspectives. Lloyd had his viewpoint, Bob had his, and I had mine, Ray was in there. They were great sessions. There were not specific questions and answers as much as going back and reminding Bob of what he had written and how he evolved from that and where he had evolved to and how one fit with the other and, where there were seeming inconsistencies, to find out whether there really were and had he changed and that kind of thing."

Things turned combative on Saturday, September 12. Cutler began on a very somber note, "Bob, you have managed to arouse the united opposition of all labor groups, all women's groups, and all civil rights groups. It's an extraordinary historical alliance, and it is going to be very tough to win this. You must separate yourself from the Meese–Reynolds school of jurisprudence."

Cutler told Bork to ignore Carvin's painfully constructed notebooks. To Cutler, Bork's real position on *Roe* was that the *reasoning* in the decision was bad, not the *holding* (decision). An absolute prohibition on abortion was unconstitutional, nothing more.

Carvin and others responded angrily. It would be perjury. It was inconsistent with years of scholarly writing. Robert Bork does not believe in the substantive due process represented in the *Roe* case.

Cutler argued that the original intent stuff was just something that Reynolds and Meese had made up. Bork responded that he had not gotten that from them. Cutler attempted to make the same case on affirmative action. Carvin produced quotes from Bork's writings to show that Bork held these positions before they had.

Finally, Randolph brought the argument back to the fundamental question of whether the historic coalition could be beaten. Randolph reminded Cutler that one man had beaten that coalition, and he had nominated Robert Bork.

That ended the discussion. Bolton recalled that the meeting and the interchange were discouraging. Perhaps at some level he and the others must have recognized that Ronald Reagan had a few communication skills that perhaps Robert Bork did not possess. Furthermore, Ronald Reagan did not seem inclined to use those skills on Bork's behalf.

As Robert Bork himself explained it, "I had prepared myself to answer questions matter-of-factly and to explain my view of judging fully." He would not pursue the "histrionics" of an Oliver North, which he felt was entirely inappropriate for a Supreme Court nominee. Histrionics or not, no one seemed to ask himself whether matter-of-fact answers would be enough, whether, after a summer of attacks on the wisdom of Robert Bork's jurisprudence, perhaps the judge ought to be more prepared to make the case in favor of his point of view rather than simply describe it.

In reflection, Korologos regrets that "there weren't enough guys like me around to smooze the political questions. They sat around and argued about the law. . . . I wasn't good enough to sit and argue with Bob Bork and Lloyd Cutler [on jurisprudence], [they were] legal geniuses. . . . [I should have spent time arguing] whether some answer was a good political answer and that was part of our downfall." Instead, what Korologos did, according to Carvin, was talk to Bork about perfunctory things like, before the hearings began, you walk up to Biden and shake his hand.

Joe Biden's problem in preparing for the hearings was altogether different. As Biden freely admitted, he had not exactly burned the midnight oil in law school. With one very notable exception, Biden would make fun in public of his law school education. For example, in the midst of the Wilkinson nomination hearings in 1984, he had remarked about the nominee's outstanding academic record: "He probably would not have spoken to me in law school; he would have had to go through too many people to get down to where I was." A favorite introduction to Biden's speeches before lawyers was for him to summarize a letter written by a professor on his behalf to a prospective employer: "You'll be lucky if you can get Biden to work for you," a not so subtle comment on his law school work habits.

Now he was facing the most brilliant legal scholar of the Right. George Will and Bork's other friends on the Right were gleefully framing the hearings as "Biden v. Bork," and it seemed as if Biden's whole political career, certainly his campaign, was hanging in the balance. To say that Biden took the process of preparing for hearings seriously is an understatement. Unlike Bork, though, Biden understood that the hearings were not going to be some dry matter-of-fact review of Bork's writings but the center of a national debate on the direction of the Supreme Court and the Constitution on its bicentennial.

So by the weekend of September 4, preparing for the hearings meant moving beyond mastery of the substance to crafting and polishing the central public message of the hearings. Biden was determined to communicate, not only to those who would be present in the hearing room but to average Americans who needed to know, what was at stake. Most of America had not had the benefit of a Yale Law School education or even a college education. Learning how to communicate with them about Robert Bork's jurisprudence without distorting it was Joe Biden's challenge for the two weekends leading up to the hearings.

The team that was to meet with Biden on those two weekends was much more diverse than Bork's. It had its share of substantive experts: Schroeder, Peck, Tribe, Walter Dellinger, and Ken Bass but also Caddell and Rasky who were much more interested in the communications side of the problem, and Donilon and me, who hoped to bridge the two camps.

I had been working with Tribe, Caddell, and Donilon in drafting an opening statement for the hearings. Bass, Schroeder, and Peck had prepared opening lines of questions, which carefully projected possible Bork responses and proposed follow-ups. The plan for the first day was for Biden to approve the opening statement and then to move the lines of questions in a sort of reverse murder board, with two people playing Bork. First, Ken Bass would play Bork as he was portrayed in the White House briefing book. Then Dellinger was to play Bork as he really was without any pretense at moderation or recantation, being much more combative.

Biden did not like the plan. To begin with he was very unhappy with the opening statement, which was basically a consensus draft by Tribe, Caddell, and me. We attempted to cover too much in the statement and in the opening line of questions. "Mark, I am not going to make the same mistake you guys led me into with Rehnquist. I was too abstract. No one knew what I was talking about. But, more important, I want my statement and my first few lines of questions to focus on one, maybe two, basic points. That's all people can absorb. And remember keep it simple. This is not a Yale faculty meeting."

In the Rehnquist hearings, in addition to the voter intimidation questions, Biden had attempted to focus in on more substantive questions, but they were abstract. Furthermore, Biden felt that Caddell and I often tried to make too many points in a speech. It was a problem that had plagued some of the campaign speeches.

He dictated a new outline for the statement. He placed much more emphasis on the importance of fairness in the hearings, the fact that his role was to assure that both sides had their say and that the difference between him and Bork was not personal but over principle and that the difference in principle was over his critique of the Supreme Court cases listed at the end of the ABA speech. We would struggle over how to express that difference in principle for most of the next two weeks. Indeed, Biden would not be satisfied that he had found a way to express the notion fairly and in a way lay people could understand until the evening before the hearings. By then Caddell and I had written and Biden had rejected five drafts.

There was a rich irony in Ken Bass and Walter Dellinger playing the Robert Bork role in the mock hearings. Both had clerked for Hugo Black, the Supreme Court Justice who best expressed the jurisprudence that Robert Bork espoused, a jurisprudence premised on the notion that substantive due process in whatever form was dangerous.

Both had attended Yale Law School. Bass had taken constitutional law from Bork in his freshman year. There were only eleven other students with Bass in Bork's class.

It was in the period before the *Indiana Law Review* article, when Bork was in his libertarian phase and was an enthusiastic supporter of the *Griswold* decision. Bass thoroughly enjoyed the course. "Bork was a delightful, engaging man, a true conservative, the first conservative I had ever met whom I could respect. I came away from [college] with the assumption that all the intellectuals were liberals, and Bork proved that to be the first of many fallacies I developed as a youth. He was . . . an engaging personality, a warm man."

Bass had written a long paper analyzing the pending fair-housing legislation (legislation prohibiting racial discrimination in the purchase, sale, or rental of housing), in light of the *Griswold* opinion and concluded that it went too far. The legislation should not cover rooming houses or rentals in single family homes, because it violated commonly accepted notions of privacy as reflected in the statutes of forty-eight states, which Bass had analyzed. Landlord-tenant law generally did not purport to regulate "personal" relationships of that kind, and neither should civil rights law. Most important, by analyzing the state laws, Bass had found extrinsic sources for what the unenumerated right to privacy might mean. Therefore judges would not be on their own to define the right. Bork liked the argument.

Bass had tried the argument out on Black when he clerked for him. Black was skeptical. Around the same time, Bork wrote the *Indiana Law Review* article and completely reversed himself on the *Griswold* decision.

Dellinger also was unconvinced by Black and Bork arguments about the dangers of the unenumerated rights argument. Indeed, as a Southerner, he was steeped in the natural rights arguments that Martin Luther King, and Abraham Lincoln before him, had made on behalf of civil rights and abolition. He spoke often of that tradition with Biden during those hours of preparation before the hearings. Likewise Bass pushed the Ninth Amendment argument on behalf of unenumerated rights, which Goldberg had used in his concurring opinion in *Griswold*.

Neither Dellinger nor Bass had been at the meeting at the Delaware beach house in August but Tribe, Caddell, and, most important, Biden were clearly in agreement as a result of that meeting. Unenumerated rights would be the message as the meetings moved into Monday with Tribe present. Biden was very engaged but still dissatisfied. We were not presenting the message in a way lay people would understand.

He asked his sons and Larry Rasky's wife to listen to the discussion and would often stop the proceedings to see if they understood. By the end of Monday he was very frustrated.

He stopped working on the statement and began to focus entirely on the questions and answers. "I'm still not satisfied with the statement, but we're wasting our time now. We'll come back to it next weekend. One thing I'm sure of is that the statement must have one message, and my first questions and answers must have the same message."

The staff-prepared questions began with a long series on civil rights and then moved into *Griswold* and unenumerated rights. Caddell was fixated on the poll numbers. Privacy and unenumerated rights were salient but so were civil rights. As usual Caddell wanted to do it all. After hours of argument Caddell relented. Biden insisted that the questions only focus on privacy and unenumerated rights. We stopped in exhaustion late on Monday evening.

Bass was upset about the approach the group seemed to be taking. In an effort to make the questions and answers understandable, each question dwelt on the facts of the case and the actual holding—the results. In a confidential memorandum to Biden a few days later, he argued, "Opposition based on specific cases is too much of a 'litmus test' and should be avoided. The more responsible grounds for opposing the nomination rest on Judge Bork's general judicial philosophy and constitutional doctrine, not the results of the application of that doctrine on specific cases."

Bass suggested that Biden spend five minutes of his first thirty-minute questioning of Bork explaining how Bork's critique of the *Griswold* decision illustrated the danger of his jurisprudence. When we met with Biden again on Sunday, we spent hours arguing about it. Caddell and I were very dubious. It was exactly that sort of abstract philosophical discussion that had not worked in the Rehnquist fight. Even more important, what if it took the whole thirty minutes to establish where Bork really stood on *Griswold?* It was essential not to cut short the effort to establish where he stood on *Griswold* just to make Bass's point.

Finally Biden suggested a novel idea. Instead of doing his opening statement first, as was the custom for the chairman, then waiting hours as other members delivered their ten-minute statements, why not save his statement until the very end? Then Biden would question immediately after the statement, and Bass's point about why the *Griswold* case was important could be made in the statement and the questioning could follow it. In effect then Biden would have forty minutes to make his point—ten minutes for the statement and thirty minutes for the cross-examination.

Donilon and Rasky were immediately taken with the idea, because it meant that Biden's statement and cross-examination of Bork would take place after the lunch recess. The national networks were only willing to do gavel-to-gavel coverage of the initial questioning of Bork. Biden's opening statement and Bork's opening statement, in a sort of point-counterpoint, and then Biden's questioning of Bork would lead off the national coverage.

That left unresolved precisely what questions would be asked of Bork on the *Griswold* case and more important what cases beyond *Griswold* to use in the first round if Biden could quickly establish Bork's position. Caddell and Bass immediately went at it again. Caddell was taken with the polling numbers on sterilization. The more they heard about Bork's criticism of cases involving sterilization, the more opposed respondents were to the nomination. It was a powerful argument against the nomination.

Kiley's questions were based on Bork's criticism of the *Skinner* case, the 1942 case involving involuntary sterilization of criminals in which the Supreme Court had used substantive due process to strike down an Oklahoma statute that allowed involuntary sterilization of repeat offenders. It was also based on a case called *Oil and Chemical Workers* v. *American Cyanamid,* a 1984 decision in which Bork had participated on the Court of Appeals.

The net result of the *American Cyanamid* opinion was that women working in a chemical plant in West Virginia were presented with a wrenching decision by their employer. The plant in which they worked produced a chemical that was dangerous to pregnant women and women of childbearing age. There was no technology that could correct the problem, so the company presented the women with a choice: They could either be sterilized or lose their jobs. For poor women in rural West Virginia, the jobs were more important, and many were sterilized.

Bork, as a judge, was faced with a very narrow legal question: According to Bork, "the only question before us was . . . whether offering the women the information to enable them to make a choice constituted an 'unsafe condition of the workplace' as defined by the Occupational Safety and Health Act." No constitutional issue was presented by the case, and it certainly had nothing to do with Robert Bork's view on unenumerated rights.

The case did provide the basis for ads raising the issue of "steril[ization] of workers" by Bork opponents. The full-page newspaper ads appeared on the day hearings opened. Caddell wanted to move directly from *Griswold* to *American Cyanamid.* Bass argued that the case had nothing to do with constitutional jurisprudence, and besides Bork was "getting a bum rap for the case." Biden agreed with Bass.

Many tactical decisions of this kind, on how to phrase the questions and which cases to do after *Griswold,* were decided Sunday afternoon as Biden sat down across from Tribe, who was playing Bork. Scott Miller, a talented campaign media consultant, was brought in to videotape the exchange and then to sit down with Biden and analyze each effort.

Biden tried the *Griswold* exchange, including questions on *American Cyanamid,* just to demonstrate to Caddell that it wouldn't work. Tribe was intimidating, much better than Bork would ever be in the hearings. As Jeff Peck noted later, "Larry Tribe was a much better Robert Bork than Robert Bork." To Bass, "Larry played Bork the way Bork was at the card table, not the way Bork was before the green velvet tables at the hearings in front of the cameras."

Tribe was devastating on the *American Cyanamid* case: "Senator, this case has absolutely nothing to do with the *Griswold* case. I don't understand why you are raising it here."

Biden: "I'll ask the questions here. The fact is you presented these women with a terrible moral dilemma."

Tribe: "Senator, it was a terrible dilemma. I did not present this dilemma, and I was powerless to do anything about it. I think it was unfortunate that you in the Congress did not give me the authority to decide that question and protect these women. Senator, why don't you propose such a statute?"

Biden interrupted the taping: "That's it, Pat. I am not going to ask that question. I don't care what that damn poll says. This case is irrelevant."

As Bass pointed out, it was clear that Biden was ready substantively for the hearings, maybe too well prepared. "In the first taping, he started behaving like a trial lawyer. He became combative and argumentative and windy. . . . The arguments became not principle, or politics or policy but legalistic, the verbiage became the classroom not the living room. Joe became engaged, agitated, angry. He wasn't the warm, mature, relaxed, confident person he became at the hearings."

Miller played the tapes back for Biden alone after each round and critiqued the performance. Biden brought in his wife Jill and his boys, and asked them to watch the later tapes to see if they understood the points he was trying to make. By late evening he was satisfied. He had assembled his own script, a bewildering set of cut-and-paste pages and hand-scribbled notes. He sent Peck and Schroeder back on the 11:00 P.M. train to Washington to have it typed up.

Caddell and I worked all day on Monday attempting to redraft the opening statement. Biden was busy with other responsibilities. As was usually the case with speeches we worked on together, Biden did not sit down with us until after dinner. He was going to make the most important speech of his political career, and it was still far from finished twelve hours before its delivery.

For hours we struggled with the notion he wanted to convey. At 11:00 P.M., he hit on the formulation he liked: "I want to make the unenumerated rights point as broadly and simply as I can, but I also want people to understand how it defines us as Americans. And, most important, they must understand that the secret of American greatness is this notion that rights in America have always expanded, not contracted—that happens in large measure because rights are not enumerated under the Constitution."

As he went to bed, he was happy with the language he would deliver the next morning. He insisted, however, that Caddell and I not "improve upon it." As he went up the stairs, he turned to us and said, "You know we might just pull this off." I thought to myself he was no longer thinking of himself as a C student from Syracuse Law School taking on the Einstein of the Right.

That same day Ball, Culvahouse, and Bolton concluded a meeting at the White House, going over final plans for the hearings. Everybody put on a good face in the large group but, as the meeting broke up the three gathered off to the side.

Culvahouse asked Bolton, "So, John, how are you feeling about the hearings?"

"Not good."

Ball and Culvahouse agreed.

The next day, the morning of the hearings, a full-page profile of Ralph Neas appeared in the *Washington Post.* In it Korologos was quoted as complaining about the work of organized groups on Bork's behalf.

Pat McGuigan was outraged. He immediately called Culvahouse. Culvahouse was busy, and his secretary tried to put McGuigan off. McGuigan in his frustration unburdened on the secretary: "Who the hell is this guy Korologos, and what planet has he been living on? I want to know if he's been working sixteen-hour days lately. How many weeks has it been since he spent time with his family? The man is an idiot if he believes what he said in the story is true. . . ."

He was kicked up to another secretary, and finally Culvahouse got on the line, "Pat, my people told me you were very upset after you read that article. I went back and looked myself, and immediately understood that you misunderstood what Tom was getting at. I can't speak for him, but I am certain he was not referring to the outside conservative groups."

"Then who in the hell was he talking about?"

Culvahouse was candid: "Well, I believe he was talking about what you call the corporate establishment—all the CEOs and public affairs officers who promised they would be there when we needed them, but who are not coming through now. The legal scholars, the Ivy Leaguers who promised to deliver for Bob Bork but who are now abandoning him. There are many others. It's starting to come apart, I'm afraid. I hope we can still win."

All was not well in the Biden camp on the eve of the hearings either. Indeed, at times it appeared as though things were "starting to come apart" for us as well. The problem was not with the Bork nomination struggle but with his own campaign for the presidential nomination. The threat for Biden that weekend before the hearings was not with the Reagan White House and Republican political operatives but with the national political press and his "friends" in the Democratic Party.

At the Bethany Beach, Delaware, meeting in August, Marttila and Caddell both predicted that, with the new polling information, it was clear that despite Biden's absences from Iowa, he was going to continue to climb. Even without success on Bork, as long as he handled it well, Biden had a good chance of winning in Iowa. They both wondered aloud whether the other campaigns realized that.

Two campaigns did—Gephardt and Dukakis. Both campaigns were alarmed by the poll numbers. Indeed, even before the poll numbers were available, Gephardt himself sensed movement in the Biden campaign in Iowa. "Forget about Dukakis. The challenge for me in this race is Joe Biden," he told his staff. His pollster saw the movement in the numbers within a few weeks. Gephardt voters were moving toward Biden.

As Tom Oliphant, a political reporter for *Boston Globe,* wrote in a book about the campaign he coauthored with Christine Black, "Most analysts failed to notice the definite, possibly explosive potential of Joe Biden." But as Oliphant goes on to point out, one who did not fail to notice it was Dukakis pollster Irwin "Tubby" Harrison. Harrison pointed out in a memo to the campaign that Biden's positions on issues—"on jobs, pocketbook, protectionism, fear of war, defense" were ones that moved Iowa voters.

Most dangerous from Harrison's perspective, Biden's strengths were Dukakis's weaknesses—"toughness," "leadership." "With his tough-liberal image, his perceived foreign-policy expertise, and his opportunity to demonstrate social issue liberalism with the Bork appointment, Biden may be well positioned."

Each campaign began to develop strategies to blunt the potential of explosive Biden movement in the fall. But in the end it was the Biden campaign that gave the Gephardt and Dukakis campaigns the silver bullet.

The press was suspicious of Biden. As *Newsweek* described him, "Biden was an impulsive crowd pleaser, given to hyperbole and carelessness." It was an unfair criticism, but Biden was the kind of speaker who was successful primarily because his goal in every campaign speech was to make a direct personal appeal to listeners. Not unlike Ronald Reagan, as one political reporter remarked, "he wanted above all else 'the connect' " with the audience. Biden felt that a major failure of Democratic candidates was that they failed to communicate directly, emotively, with middle-class voters. Biden could clearly do that because he was one of them.

When Biden saw a good line in another speech or from a speechwriter, if he thought it could awaken what he saw as a somnambulent Democratic electorate, he would use it. Usually he would remold it to his own use. The line would inspire him just as powerful lines in Ronald Reagan's inaugural address had been inspired by Franklin Roosevelt, in Kennedy's by none other than Warren Harding, and in Roosevelt's by Henry David Thoreau. Unlike Reagan, Kennedy, or Roosevelt, Biden would usually attribute the line, but in the heat of the campaign, on the stump, sometimes he didn't, especially when he was speaking from his handwritten notes.

Although Biden's speechmaking was the central attraction of his candidacy, this technique, and especially the focus of a skeptical press on Biden, was very dangerous. The skepticism ran deep among important political reporters, who had never covered Biden at the Judiciary Committee or the

Foreign Relations Committee, where he had most of his substantive accomplishments.

The skepticism ran deepest with two people in the media, who would play pivotal roles in the beginning of Biden's demise, on the weekend before the Bork hearings began. Adam Clymer was a top political editor of the *New York Times*. "I had a sense he didn't know why he wanted to be president. . . . He was running for president because he had been a senator for a while, and he looked at other people running for president and said I'm as good as they are, if not better and had people telling him how he could be president so he ran." It was a cynical comment by someone who had never talked to Biden about the subject, but it was clearly representative of what important people in the media thought of Biden in 1987.

Ken Bode, political reporter for NBC: "What has this man accomplished in the Senate? I didn't think there's much there." Bode recalls examining Biden's first term and concluding he had not accomplished much in the Senate. The fact is Biden had not accomplished much in his first term as he slowly recovered from the loss of his wife and child in an automobile accident before he was even sworn in. However, Bode did not cover Biden at the Judiciary Committee or the Foreign Relations committee and was not familiar with Biden's work on civil liberties, civil rights, crime control, and arms control—all of which took place in his second and third terms.

In the end the responsibility for this hostility in the press was largely the fault of Biden's campaign and Senate staff. As Ted Kaufman, his chief of staff, points out, "We recognized it as a problem as early as 1986, and we simply did not do enough to correct the record, to get those accomplishments out there to the right press people."

As Biden left Bethany Beach, Delaware, on August 21, he realized that he had formulated the basic strategy for the hearings that would defeat Robert Bork. What he didn't realize is that he also began that day on a journey that would lead to the end of his presidential campaign. He spent the next day prepping for a critical candidates' debate at the Iowa State Fair. He spent most of the day boning up on agriculture issues, but as he read the drafts of his closing remarks that Saturday afternoon, he realized that they would not "connect" with the crowd. He would have to write something himself. He was angry that, while he was totally preoccupied with Bork, his campaign staff could not even draft two minutes' worth of closing comments.

The next day, as he landed in Des Moines, he was met by his Iowa campaign director, David Wilhelm. As they shook hands on the tarmac Wilhelm asked Biden, "How's it going, boss?"

"Fine, David, except I don't have a close for this afternoon!"

Wilhelm could hear the frustration in his voice and walked silently with him to the van that would take him to a hotel in Des Moines to freshen up for the debate. As they settled into the van, Wilhelm turned back to Biden: "Why don't you use the platform stuff? It's working great out here."

"That's a great idea. That's what I'll do."

Biden pulled out a yellow pad and began scribbling out his speech text. The "platform stuff" Wilhelm was referring to was an ending Biden had used a number of times in Iowa and New Hampshire with great success. Biden was taken with a video clip given to him by William Schneider of an advertisement which Labour Opposition leader Neil Kinnock used in the last British elections. The ad had been responsible for moving Kinnock up nineteen points in the polls.

Kinnock made the point in the advertisement that Biden had been seeking all summer: that government should be concerned with the well-being of the middle class, as well as upper and lower classes. It was for Biden and his middle-class roots the precise message he wanted to use. To answer the question that Clymer never asked Biden, it was what he wanted to do as President. Biden had given a series of sober policy speeches in the month leading up to his announcement, where he had spelled out in detail how he would do that but he was frustrated that there was no pithy message in the speeches that captured the notion. Kinnock's ad did.

Kinnock led into the platform point with a brief family history, explaining how if it had not been for government providing that platform, he could not have gone to college and to fulfill his other ambitions. When Biden used the Kinnock idea, he would attribute the idea to Kinnock and then summarize his own similar family history.

As Oliphant points out, Biden "nearly stole the show" with his close that Sunday afternoon in Iowa. Women were crying in the front row as they listened.

There was one problem. Biden had forgotten to attribute the idea to Kinnock, and he had in effect used almost the identical lead in on his family history that Kinnock had. Biden aides immediately recognized the problem. There was disagreement. Some felt that all the national press knew that it was from Kinnock. Indeed the *Boston Globe,* whose reporters had heard him give the speech many times and attribute it, had mistakenly reported that Biden had attributed Kinnock in this instance. Others thought the safe thing to do was to acknowledge the gaffe, but as Ridley points out "typical of the Biden campaign, we never came to a resolution on what to do, so in this instance, as in many others, we did nothing."

John Sasso, Dukakis's campaign manager, saw it as an excellent opportunity to take a shot at Biden. Sasso obtained videotapes of Biden at the debate and the Kinnock commercial. The similarities were uncanny. At first he attempted to interest other Democratic politicians and then some reporters at the *Boston Globe* and elsewhere. No one was interested. They had heard Biden attribute Kinnock before. One *Globe* reporter had heard him do so on several occasions.

Finally, in the first week of September he found a reporter who was interested in pursuing the story. Maureen Dowd of the *New York Times* wanted to see a copy of the tapes. Sasso insisted that Dowd not identify its source. Sasso also arranged for the tapes to be sent to David Yepson, a leading political reporter for the *Des Moines Register,* and to John Ellis who developed political stories for NBC. In these cases as well, the source was to be protected.*

Ellis took it to producers of the "Nightly News." They were not interested because, like Oliphant, they recalled that Biden had attributed Kinnock before and therefore it was not really a story.

Yepson did write a story about it on Saturday, September 12. The story was on the second page of the *Register,* and although it did not identify the source, it made the point that an unnamed campaign was circulating an "attack video" to embarrass Biden.

The timing was obviously set for the eve of the Bork hearings, where, hopefully, it would undermine any advantage he would gain in Iowa. As Sasso later explained to Ellis, "I knew Joe Biden was coming on strong, and we had to blow him away."

Whereas the *Des Moines Register* played the story for what it was, a campaign tactic, the *New York Times* took a totally different tack. As Oliphant points out in his book, Dowd wrote a story that "screamed scandal."

Donilon and Rasky both spoke to Dowd during that first week in September, so the campaign knew the story was coming. They made the point that Biden had attributed Kinnock on a number of occasions, including in the *New York Times* in August. Indeed he had attributed it in an interview with David Frost taped on September 3. Dowd would not be dissuaded that she had a great story.

The campaign braced itself for the story on Saturday morning. Ridley went to Union Station to get an early edition of the *Times*. He rushed through the paper. He was relieved. He couldn't find it. He had looked at everything but the front page. It was the last place he expected to find it.

Paul Browne, Sen. Pat Moynihan's press secretary and someone wise in the ways of the national press, remarked, "I knew Joe was in big trouble when that story appeared on the front page." What he meant was that by placing a story on the front page, the leading newspaper in the country was telling the rest of the media that this was an important story.

Deciding what gets on the front page of the *Times* is a ritual. Every day at 5:00 P.M. Max Frankel, the managing editor of the *Times,* meets with the leadership of the most influential paper in the country to determine what the paper will say the next day. The most important decision is what the front page will look like. Although the final decision is Frankel's, it is a relatively collegial process.

* Eventually Dukakis fired Sasso for his involvement in the episode, and both Dukakis and Sasso apologized to Biden.

On Friday, September 11, Clymer recalls making the case to put Dowd's piece on the front page for the next edition. Clymer thought he had an exclusive story but regardless, "There was no real resistance to it for the front page because it was a good yarn." Never mind that Biden had finally settled on the pithy message as to why he wanted to be President—to build a platform for the middle class. Never mind that most reporters on the campaign trail had heard Biden attribute Kinnock numerous times. The leadership of the *New York Times* didn't hear the message. Dowd was mesmerized by a glitzy story that would get her on the front page. Clymer also thought the *Times* had the story exclusively. He did not know that the Dukakis campaign had given it to the *Des Moines Register* and NBC.

The story had a powerful impact. Pictures of Biden and Kinnock were side by side with the words each had used printed in parallel columns.

At NBC Ellis never told Ken Bode that he had a copy of the tape. So when Bode's producer called him first thing Saturday morning and asked him about whether he could do a story, he paused but recalled that NBC had a tape of the whole Iowa debate. That, plus a copy of the Kinnock commercial obtained from NBC's London office, was all Bode needed. Watching the tapes side by side on television that evening was devastating.

Biden's staff saw it as a one-day, at most a four-day, story, that would eventually go away.

CHAPTER 15

HE NEEDED A TEN STRIKE EVERY DAY

ON FRIDAY, September 11, Duke Short of Thurmond's office rushed into my office. Short was agitated. "We want President Ford to be our first witness." I did not think anyone on the Democratic side would object to this last-minute addition to the witness list. Well, there was one problem, Short said. "Are you guys going to ask him any questions?"

The Administration wanted to have Ford speak for Bork. However, they were not confident that Ford, who knew little about Bork and his writings, could handle cross-examination. Before the hearings opened at 10:00 A.M. Tuesday morning, the problem of questioning Ford was the subject of extensive discussions among Biden, Korologos, and others in the White House.

After having discussed it with his Democratic colleagues, Biden finally agreed to have Ford as the first "introducer," not as a witness. Biden was not interested in questioning Ford, but he couldn't be sure that his colleagues on the committee would feel the same way.

Clearly the selection of Ford was to demonstrate that Bork was from the mainstream, since Gerald Ford was considered a moderate. There was a certain irony in having Gerald Ford introduce Bork. Ford had apparently considered Bork at one point when Justice Douglas's seat became vacant in 1975. However, Ford's judicial selection policies were considered a great disappointment by Bork's friends on the Right, and the appointment went to moderate John Paul Stevens.

Steve Markman of the Meese Justice Department spoke for most conservatives when he criticized the Nixon Administration's failure to affect the "overall philosophy of the federal bench," a failure that Ford compounded. Markman pointed out, "The weakness of the Ford Administration may be seen in the statistic that a record 21 percent of its district court appointments went to members of the opposing party." Stevens, Ford's only Court nominee, had become a reliable member of the Pro-Choice bloc. The solution for Markman and others was a much more deliberate screening of nominees' judicial philosophies.

Biden was relaxed as he walked into the crowded formal Senate Caucus Room on the third floor of the Russell Senate Office Building on Tuesday morning. As he made his way toward Judge Bork, photographers swarmed around the two men like flies. The din of shutter clicks and flashes did not distract the two men as they looked each other in the eyes. Biden was wearing the stylized, almost steely, toothy grin that appears when he knows he's being photographed. Bork looked uncustomarily tentative. They shook hands.

After a brief statement explaining how the morning would proceed, Biden turned to Ford, who—along with Senator Dole, Sen. John Danforth of Missouri, a former student of Bork's, and Congressman Hamilton Fish, the moderate ranking Republican on the House Judiciary Committee—would introduce Bork to the committee.

Ford made a perfunctory statement praising Bork. As planned, Biden thanked the former President. ''I understand you have a very tight schedule, Mr. President. Do not feel required to stay. You are excused.''

Sen. Dennis DeConcini leaned forward, grabbed his microphone, and looked toward Biden. ''Mr. Chairman, I wonder if the chairman would indulge me to ask the President a question, seeing that he is going to leave. It will only take thirty seconds.''

Already the hearing was departing from the script. Korologos looked anxiously at the committee dais. Ford immediately agreed to answer questions. He had a schedule to keep but ''nothing today is more important than my presence before this committee on this vital matter.''

Biden made it clear that, as far as he knew, no other member had questions. DeConcini acknowledged that he had told Biden several days earlier that he was not interested in questioning Ford, but that morning had changed his mind.

''Mr. President, I wanted to ask you if you have read any of the opinions of Judge Bork since he has sat on the circuit court in the district.''

The former President had read a few, but mostly summaries or analyses of opinions.

''Mr. President, have you had a chance to read any of his *Law Review* articles, in particular the *Indiana Law Review* article of 1971. . . ?

''I have not read individual *Law Review* articles. I have read synopses. . . .''

DeConcini smiled. ''Thank you, Mr. President. Thank you, Mr. Chairman.''

It was a classic piece of cross-examination by an experienced prosecutor. Without comment he had established that President Ford was a prop who knew little if anything about the central issue of the hearing—the jurisprudence of Robert Bork.

Dole was next. The media had made much of the fact that both Biden and he, as presidential candidates, had a great deal at stake in the outcome of the

Bork fight. Dole made light of it with his customary sarcasm. He also departed from the text and made clear that Biden was right to have delayed the hearings in order for both sides to prepare. Korologos later agreed. Dole's message was clear: Let bygones be bygones; the political controversy over delay was just that, politics. It was time to move to a higher plane.

Fish and Danforth delivered similar statements. Biden excused the "introducers." Bork sat alone in the middle of the long table facing the committee. Now it was time to move to the Senators. For most of the next few hours, each of thirteen Senators, all but Biden, attempted to put their own special spin on what the hearings would be about.

Thurmond, as ranking Republican, spoke first, since Biden had waived his right to deliver an opening statement until the very end. For Thurmond, no doubt, the most important part of his statement was the very last paragraph. He was "pleased that both Chairman Biden and the distinguished minority leader have indicated that they agreed that" the nomination should not be bottled up in committee and should be reported to the Senate floor. Thurmond was not the only member on the Republican side who assumed that what happened in committee was not terribly important because the real fight would come on the Senate floor. It would turn out to be a serious miscalculation.

Kennedy was next. He basically gave a repeat of his speech on the Senate floor the day Bork was nominated: "In Robert Bork's America, there is not room at the inn for blacks and no place in the Constitution for women, and in our America there should be no seat on the Supreme Court for Robert Bork." It was a line carefully crafted for the evening news where it was carried that night.

The Senators alternated back and forth, Republican, then Democrat, for the rest of the morning. Republicans, except for Arlen Specter, praised Bork. The rest of the members raised "concerns" about the nomination, telegraphing what questions they would ask. Clearly undecided members like Specter, DeConcini, and Democrat Howell Heflin from Alabama delivered carefully balanced statements, which summarized arguments for and against the nomination.

When it came to Alan Simpson, Republican from Wyoming and deputy minority leader of the Senate, he delivered what had become for him a traditional statement at any controversial nomination hearing in the Reagan Administration: "Here we go again. We shall all be witness to one of the peculiar things we see often in this great city. What we now do is hereby targeted as 'high drama,' 'the most critical issue of the day,' a 'watershed,' the 'greatest test of the Presidency.' It is called the 4-H Club of hype, hurrah, hysteria, and hubris."

It was clearly designed to poke fun at the process. It always grated on Democrats and other critics of the nominee in question—he had done it in every controversial nomination fight in the previous seven years—but there was always an element of truth in what he would say. Then Simpson, the most popular and humorous member of the Senate, turned serious and leaned his full 6 foot 7 inch frame across the table and looked toward the Democrats: "Who among us here on the panel—we in the U.S. Senate—are designated the 'official score keepers' of our fellow humans? Who does or does not judge, when we put aside the mistakes, the utterances, the errors of our earlier lives, and who in this room has not felt the rush of embarrassment or pain or a feeling of plain stupidity about a phrase previously uttered or an act long ago committed? Who of us can pass that test. . . ?"

Throughout the hearing, Simpson would provide a running commentary on the process, a Greek chorus telling the members of the committee and the American people what was really going on. At this point Simpson wanted to send a warning to the opponents and those who were watching: "It seems to be an unpleasant reality that a Supreme Court nominee has every single constitutional protection until he or she walks into this room. And once in this room, unlike a defendant in a court of law, the nominee is not guaranteed any single right. . . ."

The comment caught Biden's attention. As soon as Simpson finished, Biden seized the committee gavel. Holding it aloft he looked at Bork and then Simpson. "Judge Bork, I guarantee you this little mallet is going to assure you every single right to make your views known, as long as it takes, on any grounds you wish to make them. That is a guarantee, so you do have rights in this room, and I will assure you they will be protected."

It was unplanned but a dramatic gesture, which communicated the most important message from Biden's perspective: Bork would be treated fairly by the committee. Like the carefully crafted Kennedy line, it also made the network news that night.

The committee broke at 1:00 P.M. after hearing three hours of opening statements.

It was Tom Donilon's idea that no staff should sit behind Biden while he delivered his opening statement, when the hearings recommenced at 2:30. The hearings were taking place in the most ornate and historic meeting room of the Senate where the Army–McCarthy, Watergate, and Iran–Contra hearings had been conducted. Immediately behind the chairman's seat was a large richly polished wood-paneled backdrop. In the television camera's eye it framed Biden's face and added to the sense of gravity as he began to speak. Donilon watched on a TV monitor upstairs in Biden's private office. Donilon, not one for public displays of emotion, exclaimed, "Wow! He looks fantastic and the nets are carrying it."

Biden noted, as his predecessors had in the morning, that September 17 was the Bicentennial of the Constitution. On that day in 1787, the convention in Philadelphia had finished its work.

''From that day in Philadelphia to this hour, the heart of the controversy over the Constitution had been over the basic question that is certain to animate the debate that may commence in the committee, . . . the tension between the rights of an individual and the will of the majority. . . .

''Each generation of Americans [has] been called to nurture, defend [the Constitution], define it and apply it.''

The founding generation not only crafted the Constitution but ''profoundly ennobled'' it by adding a bill of rights; within two generations, a civil war was fought over notions of equality, which were ultimately embraced in Thirteenth, Fourteenth, and Fifteenth constitutional Amendments, and 100 years later our generation waged the struggle for civil rights, which finally fulfilled the promise of equal protection of the laws.

''In each of these struggles . . . when the individual faced a recalcitrant government, the individual won his or her rights, always expanding; his or her rights always expanding.

''America is the promised land, because each generation bequeathed to [its] children a promise, a promise that they might not come to enjoy but which they fully expected their offspring to fulfill. So the words 'all men are created equal' took a life of [its] own, ultimately destined to end slavery and enfranchise women. And the words, 'equal protection' and 'due process' inevitably led to the end of the words 'separate but equal,' ensuring that the walls of segregation would crumble, whether at the lunch counter or in the voting booth.''

The ultimate question for Biden in the Bork nomination was: ''Will we retreat from our tradition of progress or will we move forward, continuing to expand . . . the rights of individuals in a changing world. . . ?

Biden summarized the same concerns he had expressed at the ABA about Bork's view on civil rights, privacy, and the First Amendment decisions of the Supreme Court. Biden celebrated the Supreme Court's defense of these rights, even where the Court, in doing so, resorted to the ''majestic'' but vague terms of the Constitution like ''equal protection'' and ''due process.'' In doing so, Biden suggested the Court was invoking a tradition older than the Constitution, a notion embedded in the Declaration of Independence:

''I believe all Americans are born with certain inalienable rights. As a child of God, I believe my rights are not derived from the Constitution. . . . They were given to me and each of my fellow citizens by our creator, and they represent the essence of human dignity.'' Quoting Justice Harlan: ''the Constitution is 'a living thing' . . . and . . . cannot be . . . 'reduced to any formula'.''

This notion of a living, growing Constitution, expanding to tip the balance constantly in favor of the individual against the state was diametrically opposed to Robert Bork's view. Biden turned to Bork for his opening statement. Bork dispassionately described the opposite point of view.

"As you have said, quite correctly, Mr. Chairman, . . . this is in large measure, a discussion of judicial philosophy. . . .

"The judge's authority derives entirely from the fact that he is to apply the law and not his personal views. . . .

"How should a judge go about finding the law? The only legitimate way, in my opinion, is by attempting to discern what those who made the law intended."

Without saying so directly, Bork was suggesting that, when a judge moves beyond the letter of the Constitution or the intention of the framers, especially in interpreting the Civil War amendments, he is walking on very dangerous ground. "If a judge abandons intentions as his guide, there is no law available to him, and he begins to legislate a social agenda for the American people. . . . When a judge . . . reads entirely new values into the Constitution, . . . he deprives the people of their liberty."

Although that basic principle underlay his critique of most, if not all, of the Supreme Court cases that Biden embraced, Bork went on to insist that, just because he criticized the reasoning in a particular case, it did not necessarily mean that he advocated reversal of that decision in the Supreme Court. It was a clever argument. Bork was addressing the most salient argument against his nomination. Those who supported many of the decisions that Bork questioned were concerned that, as soon as he got to the Court, he would vote to reverse them. Bork was trying to allay their fears—he was just criticizing the rationale, not necessarily the outcome.

It was a perfect place for Biden to begin his questioning.

BIDEN: I'm sure you know that one question to be raised in these hearings is whether or not you're going to vote to overturn Supreme Court decisions. . . .

He proceeded to quote back to Bork his prior statements that there were "dozens of cases" where the Supreme Court had erred; that as recently as January of 1987 he had made it clear to the Federalist Society that he had no problem in overruling decisions based on a constitutional rationale with which he disagreed.

BIDEN: Would you be willing to identify for this committee the dozens of cases that you think should be reconsidered?

BORK: I don't know how many should be reconsidered.

Bork proceeded to back off statements he had made in the Federalist Society speech. He now had a theory of precedent, which held that the Supreme Court should not reverse some cases that were wrongly decided because "it is simply too late to go back and tear that up." He named two lines of cases which were over fifty years old.

Biden began to press him on some more current cases. Bork was noncommittal. Then Biden turned to *Griswold.* He described what both he and

Bork agreed was a "nutty Connecticut law," which made it a crime to sell contraceptives to married couples.

Biden reminded Bork of his statement suggesting that the government has as much right to tell a married couple that they cannot use contraceptives as it does to tell a public utility that it cannot pollute.

BIDEN: Am I misstating your rationale?

BORK: With due respect, Mr. Chairman, I think you are. I was making the point that where the Constitution does not speak, there's no provision of the Constitution that applies in the case, then a judge may not say, I place a higher value upon a marital relationship than I do upon an economic freedom. . . . If there is nothing in the Constitution, the judge is enforcing his own moral values. . . .

BIDEN: Then I think I do understand it, that is, that the economic gratification of a utility company is as worthy of as much protection as the sexual gratification of a married couple, because neither is mentioned in the Constitution. . . . If the Constitution said anywhere in it . . . that a married couple's right to engage in the decision of having a child . . . was a constitutionally protected right of privacy, then . . . you would not leave it to a legislative body. . . .

BORK: That is right

BIDEN: But you argue, as I understand it, that no right exists.

BORK: No, Senator . . . I argued that the way this unstructured undefined right of privacy that Justice Douglas elaborated, that the way he did it did not prove its existence.

BIDEN: You have been a professor now for years and years. . . . You are one of the most well-read and scholarly people to come before this committee. In all your short life, have you come up with any other way to protect a married couple, under the Constitution, against an action by a government telling them what they can or cannot do about birth control in the bedroom? Is there any constitutional right anywhere in the Constitution?

BORK: I have never engaged in that exercise. . . .

Bork went on to argue that the *Griswold* case was a contrived case and that no one had ever been prosecuted under the statute. Several days later Biden received a letter from the attorneys in the case pointing out that, as a result of a 1940 Supreme Court of Connecticut decision, nine Planned Parenthood clinics in the state had been closed for twenty-five years until the *Griswold* decision in 1965.

Biden and Bork argued over Douglas's reasoning in the case and Goldberg's opinion that the right to privacy was encompassed in the language of the Ninth Amendment. Bork emphasized that he was in good company in his disdain for their reasoning, referring to Justice Black's dissent.

BIDEN: I am not suggesting whether you are alone or in the majority. I am just trying to find out where you are. As I hear you, you do not believe that there is a general right of privacy that is in the Constitution.

BORK: Not one derived in that fashion. There may be other arguments, and I do not want to pass upon those.

BIDEN: Have you ever thought of any? Have you ever written about any?

Bork reminisced about his libertarian days when he wrote the *Fortune* magazine article embracing the *Griswold* case but Bickel convinced him that he was wrong.

Biden then pressed Bork that, if he could not find a rationale to support *Griswold,* "then all the succeeding cases are up for grabs."

Bork again repeated that he could think of no rationale. Biden then moved to the earlier *Skinner* case involving the "right not to be sterilized."

BIDEN: Do you think that there is a basic right, under the Constitution, not to be forcibly sterilized. . . ?

BORK: There may be, but not on the grounds stated there [in *Skinner,* a decision in which Black incidentally joined]. . . .

Bork proceeded to make the point that perhaps there was an argument against the statute in the *Skinner* case, based on the equal protection clause of the Fourteenth Amendment. He would not, however, concede any right to have children or a right not to have children under the Constitution.

Biden summarized their differences: "It seems to me, Judge . . . that you say that a State can impact upon marital relations and can impact upon certain other relations, and it seems to me that there are certain basic rights that they cannot touch." Or, as he had said in his opening statement, there are certain God-given rights that even though they are not mentioned explicitly in the Constitution must be protected by the Supreme Court. That is precisely what the court was doing in *Griswold* and a myriad of cases before and after *Griswold*. Even though the Constitution never mentions it, as Biden had pointed out over a month earlier to the ABA, the Supreme Court has properly protected the right to educate your children in private schools, to teach them a foreign language, to live with your children if you like, to use contraceptives, to not be sterilized, and to have an abortion. These are rights that the government cannot completely take away from you.

The *New York Times* reprinted the whole exchange. It took up over seventy column inches in the paper. R. W. Appel, the *Times*'s premier political correspondent, explained:

> In a lengthy dialogue with . . . Biden . . . Judge Bork sounded at times like a dry technician, unwilling to get down to basics. Discussing *Griswold* . . . Biden kept talking about fundamental rights, Judge Bork about the rationale of the Court's holdings.
>
> For the lay audience—which includes many of the senators and most of the television viewers—Mr. Biden's sweeping invocations of human rights

> antedating the Constitution were far easier to grasp than Judge Bork's insistent examinations of the purported legal derivations of such rights.
>
> If that pattern persists, Judge Bork may find it hard to enlist the popular following that the White House has hoped he would be able to do.

That night, as the networks reviewed the day's events, the commentators focused immediately on how undecided Senators like Dennis DeConcini reacted. ABC's Britt Hume asked him what he thought of Bork's answers to Biden on the *Griswold* case: "I did not think it was very satisfactory as far as this Senator is concerned, and I have similar questions. He does not leave you with any satisfaction that there is a way in the Constitution to provide some privacy for married couples. I believe the Constitution includes that. The Supreme court so held. Judge Bork said no."

Bolton felt that Bork had a "shaky start" the first day. Senator Heflin had told him he thought Bork was "too professorial." Bolton reflected, years later, that "the privacy argument was a torpedo in the engine room." Duberstein and others who saw snippets of the coverage as the day went on had "a sinking feeling." Jack Mackenzie at the *New York Times* editorial board was surprised that Biden could intellectually "stay in the ring" with Bork.

It had not, however, been simply a matter of keeping up with Bork. Terry Eastland explained, years later, what had happened that first day, referring to Biden's frequent invocation of the notion of "inalienable" and "God-given" rights: "Bork wrapped himself in the Constitution, Biden in the Declaration of Independence. You're always going to win the thing if you're on the side of the Declaration. That's our most honored document."

It was not a bad day for Robert Bork, but it was not a good day either. As Reynolds pointed out, "the hearings were all important. They were the only way Bob could have won. . . . If Bork didn't do what Ollie North did, he would lose. The atmosphere and climate had been set. He had a task, he had to have a ten-strike every day of the hearings and he did not do that."

He had not established, in Professor Kurland's words, that he was Dr. Jekyll rather than Mr. Hyde. The first day was over, and Bork was already losing, and some of his advisers knew it.

That evening Bork tried to relax at home in his living room with a detective novel. Robert Bork, Jr., the judge's son, a reporter and dedicated supporter of his father's efforts, approached his father and told him he had done well. "But I have to tell you that you seemed a bit nervous. . . . You have to explain more. A lot of people won't know what you're talking about. You have to try to use more plain talk. . . . The people you want to convince out there are not just the Senators but the public, at large." Bork became defensive, and thereafter Robert, Jr., did not engage in postmortems with his father.

The committee had recessed at 6:30 on Tuesday evening, with only four Senators having questioned Bork: Biden, Thurmond, Kennedy, and Hatch, each using their full thirty minutes. Thurmond and Hatch had engaged in friendly cross-examination, designed to anticipate some of the attacks that would come from opponents. Kennedy did not really cross-examine Bork. He used his half hour very effectively to hurl charges at Bork to which the judge attempted to reply.

Wednesday began with Metzenbaum focusing almost exclusively on the Watergate affair. He made much of the fact that a federal district court had held that Bork's firing of special prosecutor Archibald Cox on behalf of Nixon was illegal. The judge found that Bork did not comply with a departmental regulation that created Cox's office. It was one of the few times during the hearings where Bork's professorial approach to the questions truly paid off. He explained that the court decision was eventually vacated, because by the time Bork set out to appeal it, a new independent prosecutor had been named, and the case was moot. Therefore, according to Bork, the case was not valid.

Biden interjected a few times in Metzenbaum's cross-examination, but for the most part he did not feel that the Watergate episodes impugned Bork's character in any way. As Milton Viorst, a liberal columnist, wrote at the time of the events, he had incorrectly assumed that Bork had acted "in conformity with Nixonite ideology of political expediency." Instead, he explained, Bork had been persuaded by Attorney General Elliot Richardson and deputy attorney general William Ruckelshaus to fire Cox. It seems that Richardson and Ruckleshaus had given their word to the Senate Judiciary Committee at their confirmation that they would not fire Cox under such circumstances. Bork had not made that commitment and believed as a matter of principle that the President could order the firing. Bork was reluctant, however, because he did not think that the President should have fired Cox. Richardson and Ruckleshaus prevailed upon Bork to execute the President's order, because if he had not, there would have been mass resignations at the Department of Justice.

Viorst concluded, "He's been holding the Justice Department together, and he believes in the correctness of what he's doing. Any suggestion I made to the contrary, I hereby take back."

From Biden's perspective there was an even more compelling reason not to lean too heavily on the Watergate issue. The committee in 1982 had confirmed Robert Bork for the U.S. Court of Appeals. Despite that confirmation, it was clearly proper to examine his jurisprudential views now, especially since he would no longer be bound by precedent set by the Supreme Court and would, in fact, be in the position of setting new Constitutional precedents, which he could not do as a Court of Appeals judge. However, allegations concerning his integrity should have been considered in 1982 and in fact had not been raised in any serious manner at that time.

Simpson followed Metzenbaum, belittling Metzenbaum's preoccupation with Watergate almost fifteen years after the fact. ''Fourteen years. This is a curious place. If you go out in the land and say, 'What were you doing on the night of the Saturday Night Massacre,' a guy will say, 'What are you talking about?' But in this town . . . they say, 'I was just finishing shaving. I was going out to dinner. I will never forget it my whole life. I went limp. My wife and I talked and huddled together and had a drink and just shuddered in shock.' '' The audience in the hearing room laughed.

Simpson went on to ask rehabilatory questions on Watergate, privacy, the *Griswold* and *Skinner* cases.

Next it was Sen. Dennis DeConcini's turn, the first of the truly uncommitted members to question. Bork's friends looked warily at DeConcini after his surprise questioning of Ford the day before. DeConcini began by picking up where Biden had left off on *Griswold* and unenumerated rights under the Constitution. DeConcini immediately focused in on the Ninth Amendment. Bork was reluctant to speculate as to what it meant. ''I do not think you can use the Ninth Amendment unless you know something of what it means. For example, if you had an amendment that says 'Congress shall make no' and then there is an ink blot, and you cannot read the rest of it and that is the only copy you have, I do not think the Court can make up what might be under the ink blot if you cannot read it.''

It was a facile argument. Of course, however, the Ninth Amendment was not like an inkblot. The language had a history, and it tended to favor the notion of natural or unenumerated rights which Biden and DeConcini were suggesting.

DeConcini then moved to civil rights questions and finally to the topic which was his major interest that day.

DeConcini: I cannot understand then why the precise words used in the Fourteenth Amendment, which are ''deny to any person within its jurisdiction the equal protection of the laws'' creates the confusion it does with you. It does not with me. . . .

Bork: A state can affirmatively protect racial groups and other groups. There is no problem with that.

DeConcini: But your position is that to deny any person within its jurisdiction equal protection of the law does not apply to other minorities.

Bork: No, no . . . I prefer the position that Justice Stevens enunciated.

DeConcini: I do not want Justice Stevens's position. I want your position.

Bork: Well, that is my position.

Bork summarized Stevens's position that there ought not to be several different standards for blacks, women, aliens, and others under the equal protection clause but that every class ought to operate under the ''reasonableness test.'' The more he explained it, the more it appeared to DeConcini that actually blacks would get more protection than women.

DeConcini quoted back to Bork a 1986 statement he had made to the effect that the "role that men and women should play in society is a highly complex business," and he questioned whether courts should be involved in sorting it out. Bork had been referring in that speech to the Equal Rights Amendment, but actually it probably reflected Bork's concern with a strict scrutiny standard for women under the equal protection clause.

DECONCINI: Now what troubles me, Judge, is why are the questions concerning sex discrimination any more difficult or any more complex and undeserving of constitutional, judicial resolution than other questions. . . ?

Bork again retreated to the reasonableness test of Stevens. DeConcini again pressed, and Bork admitted that under his test "it cannot apply just as it does to races. . . . It is possible to say, for example, that there shall be no segregated toilet facilities anywhere as to race. I do not think anybody wants to say that as to gender. Differences have to be accommodated. That is why the difference."

The response angered DeConcini. It was the same argument that had been used against the Equal Rights Amendment.

DECONCINI: But is not that a bogus argument? We are not talking about unisex toilets here. We are talking about—

JUDGE BORK: No.

DECONCINI (continuing):—fundamental rights that women for too, too long have not been provided.

BORK: That is right.

DECONCINI: And we are talking about your interpretation of whether or not, on the Supreme Court, you are going to look toward that equality for women, whether we have the Equal Rights Amendment or not.

Bork pressed his argument that a "reasonableness standard" was adequate protection for women. Bork was making the same mistake with DeConcini that he had made with Biden the day before. DeConcini was asking questions on a broader policy level—how can there be a double standard under the Constitution in which women do not get the same protection as blacks—while Bork was answering on a technical level. Just as his son had pointed out the evening before. Bork may have been correct in his answers, from his philosophical vantage point, but they were not the "plain talk" that lay people could understand.

So, DeConcini was not persuaded.

DECONCINI: You leave this Senator [himself] unsatisfied as to how this Senator can conclude that you are going to protect the citizens of this country in interpreting the Constitution on the court as it relates to sex. . . . It seems to me that there is a question as to how you treat the sexual segregation. And that is a trouble to me, but my time is up."

Bork was now alarmed. He pressed the argument that, in the Solicitor General's office, he had argued positions against gender discrimination that went well beyond what the Court would adopt. He was right, but DeConcini was unconvinced, since Bork had been advocating those positions on behalf of the Nixon and Ford Administrations, not necessarily upon his own behalf.

DeConcini would come back again to the same line of questions in his second round. The more he heard, the more disturbed he became. Having decided, in effect, to disown his past doubts about including women under the equal protection clause, especially under a strict scrutiny test, Bork and his friends gave up valuable ground to his opponents. Instead of arguing, as Hatch had so effectively in the Equal Rights Amendment hearings in 1982, that a strict scrutiny standard was not practical, Bork and his allies seemed to be ceding the argument. Hatch watched the whole interchange and remained silent. Neither he nor Bork made the arguments to his friend Dennis DeConcini that had practically killed the ERA years earlier—that if women were treated exactly the same as blacks and gender discrimination was subject to a strict scrutiny test, it would mean women in combat, the end of veterans' preference, and public funding of abortions.

When DeConcini finished his first round, Biden turned to Republican Charles Grassley. Though not a lawyer, Grassley could be a shrewd politician. In his round he played much the same role that Hatch had, attempting to give Bork the opportunity to rehabilitate himself.

Patrick Leahy was next. He was the first to undertake rigorous cross-examination of Bork on his most controversial piece of scholarly writing, the 1971 *Indiana Law Review* article. Leahy chose to focus on the First Amendment critique in the article.

Bork began by conceding that he had retracted some of the statements in the article on the narrow interpretation of the First Amendment. His first recantations had occurred two years after it was written, when he was before the Judiciary Committee for the Solicitor General's job. Leahy wanted to know where he was now on the subject.

LEAHY: How far would you say you have moved from the Indiana article in that 1973 period?

BORK: About to where the Supreme Court currently is.

Leahy was stunned by the answer. It sounded as if Bork was completely recanting his First Amendment views. He recalls writing the words down on the pad in front of him as Bork spoke them "where the Supreme Court currently is."

Bork described his odyssey from a very narrow view of the First Amendment to a broader view. He had originally sought a clearer or "brighter" line of demarcation between protected and unprotected speech, but "the more I thought about it, the sillier it became. I do not think a bright line test is available." Originally Bork had believed that only purely political speech was protected; now he believes that there are rights to be protected beyond this core notion.

Leahy continued to press.

LEAHY: What about something that advocated the violation of laws?

BORK: Well, you know, the Supreme Court has come to the *Brandenburg* position—which is okay; it is a good position. . . .

Bork had delivered another shocker. As recently as 1984, he had criticized *Brandenburg*.

Leahy showed no emotion and continued to press.

LEAHY: What about Martin Luther King suggesting civil disobedience?

Bork explained that, to the extent that King was advocating violation of laws that had been held unconstitutional—and segregation statutes, for example, had been held constitutional—"I do not see how the person who advocated breaking it could be held liable."

What about the situation, Leahy asked, where the statute they advocated violating turns out to be constitutional. Bork wasn't sure but in any case the *Brandenburg* case would apply.

LEAHY: Do you agree then with the Brandenburg case?

BORK: Yes, I do. . . .

There could be no doubt about it. This was diametrically opposed to what he had written before.

LEAHY: At one point, you felt the Brandenburg case . . . was a fundamentally wrong interpretation of the First Amendment. Today you feel it is right.

BORK: It is right.

Arlen Specter, along with DeConcini and Leahy the third former prosecutor on the panel, was to question next. His plan had been to focus on another area, but he was so surprised by Bork's answers on the First Amendment, that he couldn't resist picking up where Leahy had left off.

If he stuck by his answers to Leahy's questions and had moved to where the Supreme Court is now, Specter concluded, "I think these confirmation hearings may be very brief indeed."

As Neal Manne points out, Specter can quickly "get his back up" with a witness he feels is hedging on his answers. His plan was to press Bork to explain the obvious contradiction between what he was saying on September 16, 1987, and what he had said as recently as a month before his nomination.

He began to review carefully with Bork his previous statements on the First Amendment, focusing in particular on his view of the Holmes and Brandeis clear-and-present-danger test. As far as Specter was concerned, the *Brandenburg* rule—that only advocacy of "imminent lawless violence" was punishable—was the same as the clear-and-present-danger test.

SPECTER: You have said that you accept the *Brandenburg* v. *Ohio* and *Hess* v. *Indiana* decisions, which essentially state the Holmes clear-and-present-danger doctrine.

BORK: I do not think I necessarily accepted Hess, but what I was criticizing here is a statement by Holmes—his reasons, his reasoning in the case. I found his dissent in that case not to be a very coherent statement of a rationale. . . .

SPECTER: As to *Brandenburg,* you said *Hess* and *Brandenburg* are fundamentally wrong interpretations of the First Amendment. I do not want to belabor it any longer, Judge Bork, but it just seems surprising to me, that in the context where you characterize that doctrine as "fundamentally wrong" and attacked the rationale as "frivolous" that you can, at the same time, say that you now accept the current Supreme Court interpretation.

Spector had him. He knew it, and Bork had to know it. The contradiction was clear. Bork had simply changed his mind.

At the next break, as Leahy walked out of the hearing room, he was asked by a reporter to comment. He called it a "confirmation conversion." It was the press line of the day. Bork was clearly recanting some of his most controversial positions.

But it was in a succeeding line of questioning that Specter truly rattled Bork. Specter was looking for a way to dramatize the absurdity of Bork's very restrictive view of unenumerated rights and the fact that, unless a right is specifically spelled out in the Constitution, it did not exist and could not be recognized by the Supreme Court.

Neal Manne had been called by a federal judge during the summer as he prepared Specter for the hearing. The judge told Manne that he had attended a fascinating panel discussion on original intent. He had seen one of Bork's conservative allies on the panel defending the Borkian narrow view of original intent. The panelist had been speechless when confronted with the Supreme Court's decision in the case of *Bolling* v. *Sharpe.* That is the companion decision to *Brown* v. *the Board,* in which the Supreme Court struck down separate but equal for the federal government as well as the states.

The problem was that the equal protection clause of the Fourteenth Amendment did not apply to the federal government. However, the Court recognized that it would be ridiculous to prohibit segregated schools at the state level and permit them in the District of Columbia. The majority simply decided that the concept of equal protection was encompassed in the notion of due process contained in the Fifth Amendment. The Fifth Amendment did apply to the federal government. What the court was doing was none other than the substantive due process that Bork condemned. Manne suggested that Specter try out the question on Bork.

SPECTER: How can you justify *Bolling* v. *Sharpe* applying the due process clause to the stopping of segregation?

BORK: I do not know that anybody ever has. I think that has been a case that left people puzzled, and I have been told that some Justices on the Supreme Court felt very queasy afterward about *Bolling* v. *Sharpe*. . . .

Specter made him repeat it several times.

BORK: I think that constitutionally that is a troublesome case. . . .

Specter next made the obvious point.

SPECTER: If you can apply the due process clause as they did in *Bolling* v. *Sharpe,* why not in *Griswold* v. *Connecticut?*

BORK: Well, if they apply the due process clause that way, Senator, I quite agree with you. Why not in *Griswold* v. *Connecticut,* and why not in all kinds of cases? You are off and running with substantive due process, which I have long thought is a pernicious constitutional idea.

Specter came back a few minutes later and asked Bork a third time.

SPECTER: Final question: Do you accept *Bolling* v. *Sharpe* or not?

BORK: I have not thought of a rationale for it because I think you are quite right, Senator. . . .

SPECTER: Well, I know that you will not reverse *Bolling* v. *Sharpe* in any event, but it is a very uneasy conclusion, Judge Bork, when you talk about the needs of the nation.

It finally dawned on Bork that he had fallen into a terrible trap. If he had been on the Supreme Court in 1954, when it handed down the *Brown* and *Sharpe* decisions—because of his exceedingly narrow approach to constitutional interpretation—he would have had no principled way to protect "separate but equal" schools under the aegis of the federal government and in the District of Columbia. Bork asked Biden's permission to supplement his answer. The hearings broke for a few minutes. Bolton and Administration staff were terribly concerned about the implications of the answer and during the recess insisted that Bork clarify his answer.

Bork wanted to correct any misimpression he might have left: "My doubts about the substantive due process of *Bolling* v. *Sharpe* does not mean that I would ever dream of overruling *Bolling* v. *Sharpe,* as you suggested.

"And furthermore I should make it clear, as I have said repeatedly, segregation is not only unlawful but immoral. And I do not want my doubts about a constitutional mode of reasoning to be turned into anything other than that—not by you, Senator, I mean just by people who are listening to us."

It was still devastating. Bork was pleading with Specter and the listening audience to believe that he did not endorse segregation in the D.C. schools. Three talented trial lawyers, men who had made their living before they came to the Senate by cross-examining witnesses, had made Robert Bork look foolish.

Bork was particularly stung by Specter's cross-examination. In his book, Bork writes at length to debunk its effectiveness, but there is little doubt who had the better part of those exchanges.

Dennis DeConcini had raised doubts about whether Robert Bork believed women should have the same protections under the Constitution as blacks. Patrick Leahy and Arlen Specter had raised the question of whether Robert Bork was engaging in "confirmation conversions" on his First Amendment views, and Specter had him arguing that he wasn't a segregationist. In all three cases the Senators had pursued Bork on issues about which the three men felt deeply, issues about which they had committed themselves before they had even been elected to the Senate—gender discrimination for Dennis DeConcini and freedom of speech and dissent for Leahy and Specter.

The print media gave extensive coverage to DeConcini, Specter, and Leahy's questioning of Bork. That evening several networks focused on DeConcini, primarily because of his status as truly undecided. It was another bad day for Robert Bork. He certainly was not turning into another Oliver North.

Commenting editorially on the first day of hearings, the *Post* was pleased with the "appropriate" "informative" questioning. By the second day Shakow was clearly impressed with the committee and increasingly troubled by Bork's response. In an editorial commenting on Wednesday's questioning, she referred to the hearings as "remarkable" and having "accomplished their first purpose of clearly eliciting his views." She focused on three areas that required further elaboration by Bork. One was privacy. She asked, "Is there any level of intimate behavior not subject to majority will? He says, among other things, that he has never gone through the exercise of trying to figure that out. On so serious an issue, that is a strange and unsatisfying response."

She was also concerned about his views on the application of the equal protection clause to women and on political dissent.

By Thursday, Bork's friends on the committee were engaging in carefully orchestrated questioning designed to give him an opportunity to respond to the three main lines of attack that the opponents were using. Dennis Shedd, Thurmond's chief counsel, working with his friends at the Justice Department, concentrated on allowing Bork to respond to DeConcini's cross-examination on gender discrimination. Although Bork had never endorsed the Stevens approach publicly before the hearings, by Thursday he had totally embraced it. In response to Thurmond's questions, he eloquently defended the position that a reasonable-basis test would adequately defend the rights of women.

Thurmond also gave Bork an opportunity to respond further to Leahy and Specter's questioning on the *Brandenburg* case. Hatch engaged in a similar exercise. He focused on the fact that in both the race and gender areas Bork had an excellent record as Solicitor General. He entered into the record summaries of twelve cases where he had filed briefs on behalf of minorities and three cases where he had done so against gender discrimination.

Hatch also elicited from Bork a number of examples in which he had as Solicitor General argued to expand rights for women and blacks only to have them rejected by Justice Powell. Hatch pointed out, "In these five cases I have just named, [Powell's] actions were actually less sensitive to civil rights than yours, which I think flies in the face of the arguments against you: that you are out of the mainstream; that you are going to upset the balance; that you are going to hurt the Court. . . ."

Senator Kennedy responded by inserting in the record a nine-page single-spaced document listing controversial quotations by Bork. Later in the day Hatch inserted in the record a list of 100 law professors supporting the Bork nomination.

Finally, it came time for Specter to ask his second round of questions of Bork. It would turn out to be a pivotal moment in the hearings, although neither Specter, Bork nor anyone realized it at the time.

By Thursday afternoon Bork was quite defensive about Leahy's assertion that he was engaging in "confirmation conversions." The civil rights groups had made a deliberate effort to exploit contradictions in his testimony, circulating lengthy lists of contradictory quotes under the heading "Bork v. Bork." By Friday most of the major newspapers were making many of the same points.

In response Bork had been suggesting that his new position on *Brandenburg* was not "a great change of mind." Specter was blunt: "I raise a question with you, Judge Bork, about the candor of that representation. . . ."

SPECTER: You also said, in the University of Michigan speech, that "*Hess* and *Brandenburg* are fundamentally wrong interpretations of the First Amendment. . . ."

BORK: On *Brandenburg,* I did not say my mind had changed. I think it would have been legitimate for the Court to follow the line I took . . . what I said was, as a theorist, I doubted *Brandenburg*. I think that *Brandenburg* may have gone too—went too far, but I accept *Brandenburg* as a judge, and I have no desire to overturn it. I am not changing my criticism of the case. I just accept it as settled law.

Specter had doubts, but he was beginning to accept Bork's argument that he had no desire to overturn *Brandenburg* and no longer doubted the doctrine of clear and present danger, at least in its most recent incarnation. Specter's underlying concern was whether Bork could apply the doctrine to the next case, despite his past vehement criticism. So a few minutes later he returned to the subject just to reassure himself.

SPECTER: Assuming, and I accept your statement that you agree, or were willing to apply *Brandenburg* and *Hess* v. *Indiana,* but the next case—

BORK: Well, I didn't speak to *Hess* v. *Indiana,* Senator.

SPECTER: Okay, how about *Hess* v. *Indiana?*

BORK: All right. No, I am not so wild about *Hess* v. *Indiana.* That is a case of obscenity in the public streets, and sometimes the Supreme Court allows people to stop obscenities, sometimes it doesn't.

SPECTER: Well, the Supreme Court decided Hess on the *Brandenburg* doctrine flat out.

BORK: But I think there was a problem of obscenity in there and not just the problem of inciting to lawlessness. Now if the gentleman had said what he said without the obscenities, that's right, *Brandenburg* covers it.

SPECTER: Well, the Supreme Court said *Brandenburg* governed *Hess*. . . . I have got a copy that I can make available to you.

BORK: All right.

As Specter reflected on the exchange years later, he recalled, "[When] he said it was an obscenity case, I nearly fell off the chair. . . . First, because *Hess* was clearly a political speech case. Second, because Bork had written about it as a political speech case." Specter and every member of the Court at the time considered the fact that Hess had used an obscenity irrelevant. The issue was whether the speech would produce "imminent lawless action."

As far as Specter was concerned, it was the real Bork coming through. "It was the appearance of his own inner philosophy. He was going back to disagreeing with clear and present danger. He was trying to accommodate his own record and views to the continuum of constitutional jurisprudence. . . . It was an understandable attempt to accommodate [but] when it was pursued, his own differing approach came through, and it was drastically different from the continuum of constitutional jurisprudence. . . ."

Although Specter was surprised when he first heard Bork explain his position on *Hess,* it was not until several weeks later that he realized how much of an impact the interchange had had on his attitude toward the nomination. "I was leaning in favor of Bork when Bork finished testifying. That tells me that this didn't really gel until I'd had a chance to think about it."

When he really studied the interchange, he realized that "When he tried to wiggle out of *Hess* as a speech case, it was clear to me that he could never follow the Brandeis–Holmes line. . . . It was plain to me, it would not be realistic to expect him to follow *Brandenburg* when he had such deep-seated philosophical objections to it." Specter did not question Bork's integrity, but he became convinced that "when the next set of facts came up he would put them in a different category and decide the case without appropriate regard to precedents on freedom of speech. That's why I couldn't be for him."

Most of the media completely missed the interchange. That night the networks picked up a dramatic interchange between Kennedy and Bork over his views of executive power, the Thurmond interchange on gender discrimination, DeConcini's suggestion that the Thurmond interchange had "helped," and an interchange with Leahy, in which the Senator, expecting to castigate Bork for earning extraordinary amounts of outside income from private practice while at Yale, was mortified to learn that Bork had earned the income to pay for his dying wife's hospital bills.

Thursday had been a day when Bork's testimony had an impact that would not be obvious for several weeks. But Friday was a day for great theatrics, which made for excellent television. It could not have gone worse for Bork.

It began with Metzenbaum's cross-examination of Bork on the *American Cyanamid* case. Just as Biden and Tribe had anticipated, Metzenbaum made little progress on the substance of the case and its holding. Bork very effectively deflected the attack.

Bork was not, however, a match for Metzenbaum when he attempted to explain the real-life implications of the case.

METZENBAUM: Judge Bork, there were thirty women working for the Cyanamid company when the company adopted the be-sterilized-or-fired policy. This policy forced twenty-three of these women to be sterilized or be fired. Five were actually sterilized before the lawsuit was filed. Cyanamid forced 75 percent of their women employees to choose between their jobs and the possibility of ever having children.

Judge, I must tell you that it is such a shocking decision, and I cannot understand how you as a jurist could put women to the choice of work or be sterilized. . . .

BORK: My opinion is not an endorsement of a sterilization policy. . . . The basis of the decision was Congress's intent. . . . My opinion concluded that Congress had been concerned with physical conditions of the workplace, not with policies of offering women a choice. . . . I think that is not a prosterilization opinion. It is not an antiwoman opinion.

Bork explained that it was a unanimous opinion.

Metzenbaum exploded. He did not care who had joined Bork in the opinion. ''I cannot tell you strongly enough that the women of this country are terribly, terribly apprehensive about your appointment. . . . The women of America, in my opinion, have much to be worried about in connection with your appointment; the blacks as well. And it is only fair to say that you have made it quite clear in your appearance before this panel that you are not a frightening man, but you are a man with frightening views.''

It was a line that was perfect for a fifteen-second sound bite that night on the evening news. Bork tried to respond. Metzenbaum refused to be interrupted.

Finally Bork had his chance. He again defended his opinion in procedural terms and in conclusion he said, ''It was a matter of statutory construction, not a matter of constitutional law, and I suppose the five women who chose to stay on that job with higher pay and chose sterilization—I suppose that they were glad to have the choice. . . .''

In the basement of the Russell Office Building, Judy Lichtman watched the exchange and immediately picked up the phone to Joan Bertin, an ACLU attorney in New York City, who represented one of the women who had chosen to be sterilized. Bertin contacted Betty Riggs, her client. Riggs authorized Bertin to send a telegram to the committee, which Bertin had drafted for Riggs.

Metzenbaum chose a moment of great political importance to release the telegram. Sen. Robert Byrd, still very much undecided in the struggle, appeared in the hearing room late in the afternoon for his only round of questions of Bork. Metzenbaum chose to read the telegram from one of Byrd's West Virginia constituents into the record just as the majority leader took his seat:

''I cannot believe that Judge Bork thinks we were glad to have the choice of getting sterilized or getting fired. Only a judge who knows nothing about women who need to work could say that. I was only twenty-six years old, but I had to work, so I had no choice. . . . This was the most awful thing that happened to me. . . .

Betty Riggs
Harrisville, West Virginia''

It made for good television, and two out of three networks carried the story that evening. However, what Kennedy did that day was covered by all three networks.

On October 8, 1985, Bork had spoken at Canisius College in Buffalo, New York. After the speech, he engaged in a question-and-answer session with a student, and the exchange was taped. The subject of the exchange was the delicate question of under what circumstances the Supreme Court was bound by past precedents.

Copies of the audiotape had been made available anonymously to Biden's office and Specter's office. According to Neal Manne, as soon as he received a copy of the tape, a week before the hearing, Senator Specter instructed him to get it to the White House. For some strange reason, neither John Bolton at the Justice Department nor his counterparts at the White House ever came to get it. Manne speculated that they ''apparently thought it was some kind of trap.''

As soon as Biden found out about it on the evening of the first day of the hearings, he instructed me to have a transcript made of the tape and a copy of the tape itself. Copies were given to Bork the next day. On Thursday, Kennedy told Biden that he intended to confront Bork with the tape in the morning. Biden explained that Bork had a copy of the tape and the transcript.

That evening I had traveled with Biden to Wilmington. At about 11:30 P.M., I received a call in my motel room from a high-ranking member of the civil rights community. He was furious that a copy had been made available to Bork.

''Mark, we wanted to surprise him. You weren't part of this, were you?''

''I certainly was. Joe doesn't want to be part of any effort to 'surprise Bork'.''

''This was a terrible mistake, Mark!''

"No, it wasn't. I'll see you tomorrow."

I hung up.

The tape was extraordinary, not so much for what Bork said—he had said it on many occasions in the past—but because it was an audiotape. Kennedy could confront Bork on national television with his own voice. It would truly be a televised sound bite of "Bork v. Bork."

Kennedy introduced the segment by reminding Bork of some of his past statements that he had not changed his position on certain jurisprudential positions, and Kennedy quoted from a speech Bork had given in 1987. In the speech to the Federalist Society, Bork announced that "An originalist judge would have no problem whatever in overruling a nonoriginalist precedent. . . ."

Kennedy then asked for the staff to play the audiotape over the hearing room loudspeaker:

QUESTIONER: If I can follow up. Now, the relationship between the judge, the text and precedent, what do you think about precedent?

BORK: I don't think that in the field of constitutional law, precedent is all that important. . . . The Court has never thought constitutional precedent was all that important—the reason being that if you construe a statute incorrectly, the Congress can pass a law and correct you. If you construe the Constitution incorrectly, Congress is helpless. . . ."

The television camera zeroed in for a close-up on Bork as he listened to the tape. You could see the tension on his face. The muscles in his jaw rippled as he seemed to grind his teeth.

Bork defended it as a "quick aside after a speech."

BORK: Senator, you and I both know that it is possible, in a give-and-take question-and-answer period, not to give a full measured response. You and I both know that when I have given a full and measured response, I have repeatedly said there are some things that are too settled to be overturned. The Canisius College thing was not my speech. That was a bunch of students questioning me afterward.

It was one of the most tense moments in the hearings. Simpson was the next questioner. He again used his time to elaborate on the effort to "get Bork." As he spoke with his sometimes cutting humor, the tension in the room seemed to defuse somewhat.

Bork, however, remained tense and at times uncooperative even with friendly questioners. Grassley, who followed a few minutes later, attempted to draw Bork out on recent comments by Justice Thurgood Marshall criticizing President Reagan's civil rights policies and questioning whether we should celebrate the Bicentennial of the Constitution, because it had not always vindicated the rights of blacks.

GRASSLEY: I . . . found these remarks somewhat troubling, especially coming from one sworn to uphold the Constitution he finds defective.

He asked for Bork's comment. Bork would not cooperate.

BORK: I don't think one judge should be commenting upon the views of another judge. Justice Marshall has always been a very good Justice, and when I argued before him, I used to do fairly well. And I like him. . . .

GRASSLEY: Well, would you think that maybe the Justice was trying to be just a little provocative?

Bork still wouldn't bite.

BORK: I don't really want to characterize his motives or intentions or anything else.

GRASSLEY: Well, I thought maybe I might get you to say that people, even though they are on the Court, can be provocative. . . .

BORK: I don't want to characterize anything Justice Marshall did. . . .

Senator Humphrey had a similar experience. Pursuant to the strategy that the Administration had designed for the nomination, Republican Gordon Humphrey questioned Bork on criminal law. The Administration had specifically sought the endorsement of law enforcement groups in favor of Bork. Humphrey was attempting to get Bork to make some prolaw enforcement statements in his testimony.

HUMPHREY: Let's turn to criminal law. . . . This is an issue of importance to individual citizens because the statistics show that nearly every one of us, at some time in our life, will be a victim of crime, and that is if we are lucky, because lots of people are multiple victims of crime. . . .

Humphrey proceeded to describe several dramatic examples of crimes and turned to Bork with a leading question: "Let's talk about the rights of law-abiding citizens. What responsibility do judges have to protect society and individual citizens from criminals?"

Bork gave a few sentences on the importance of fairness and a passing reference to the danger of defendants getting off on "technicalities." But he hastened to add, "I am not an expert on criminal law, but I have participated in reversals on convictions."

He made the point of his lack of expertise twice more in the course of a few minutes. It was precisely the opposite of what the Administration and Humphrey were looking for.

According to Brad Reynolds, the effort by the White House to portray Bork as tough on crime was an area in which he and Bork both had "serious disagreement" with the White House. Apparently Will Ball and White House political director Frank Donatelli thought that the image would help politically. According to Reynolds, they thought "politicians would respond to [Bork's position in support of] the death penalty. Bob was pretty skinny in that area. . . . To portray him [that way] was . . . playing to Bob's weaknesses, not his strengths. I got a little miffed about it, and I think Bob got a little miffed about it. [He] felt quite uncomfortable. . . . [He was] not going to the court with that portfolio."

Earlier in the day Hatch had attempted to make the point that Bork was actually more procivil rights than Justice Powell. He sought to demonstrate that Bork had taken a more expansive view of the Voting Rights Act than had Powell. Bork also resisted.

HATCH: I am beginning to conclude that my critical colleagues might not have confirmed Justice Powell if he were sitting in your shoes today. . . . After all, he favored many narrower constructions of the civil rights laws than you have.

BORK: Yes, but I think, as we both agree, Justice Powell is a great justice and I think it should be said that these are matters about which reasonable men can differ.

HATCH: That is my point.

BORK: In interpreting these statutes, I do not want to contrast myself with Justice Powell in order to show that I am a greater defender of civil liberties. . . .

Although Friday had been the worst day for Bork, his defensiveness even with his proponents was a pattern that arose on practically every day of the hearings. The very first day, after Kennedy's opening line of questions, which had clearly been delivered to get his message on the evening news, Hatch attempted to help Bork out:

HATCH: Judge, Senator Kennedy said when it counted you were not there on some of these items, but I think what you have been able to show here today is that these major issues are not easily explained in thirty-second bites that we people in Congress are used to popping off about; is that correct?

BORK: Well, Senator, if you are suggesting that I have proved that I cannot explain them, I do not want to accept that. It is hard to discuss a complex issue in thirty seconds. That is correct.

Hatch was frustrated by these exchanges, He was deliberately giving Bork "some questions that were home run balls that he could hit out of the park and he did not."

At times Bork seemed quite oblivious to what was going on in the hearing room or perhaps had given up. For example, toward the end of the day on Friday, DeConcini laid out his concerns to Bork about his testimony throughout the week. DeConcini was "very concerned" about the privacy question, especially Bork's position on the *Griswold* case. He accepted Bork's explanation of the Saturday Night Massacre. His deepest concern continued to be whether women "would have really equal opportunity before the eyes of the nominee."

BORK: May I ask, Senator, why it is you think . . . that I might not protect women under the equal protection clause?

DeConcini again repeated his concern about Bork's past statements about the application of the Fourteenth Amendment to women and his new position on the Stevens standard. DeConcini was clearly concerned that Bork's position was completely unique and new, and seemed to reject altogether the current Supreme Court approach to the problem.

Bork simply reiterated his position rather than attempt to assuage DeConcini's obvious concern. Clearly puzzled by Bork's failure to respond to a clear invitation to defend his position, he said good-bye to the judge.

DECONCINI: Fine. I just had to share that with you as we proceed with these hearings and deliberate. . . .

To Bolton, Friday was the "worst day." In the words of one television commentator, the opponents had that day "rolled out the heavy artillery." Metzenbaum and Kennedy clearly scored major damage with the *American Cyanamid* case and the Canisius College tape. Both events dominated the television coverage that night and in the print media the next day. Dennis DeConcini sent a clear message with his final remarks to Bork late that afternoon that he was deeply troubled. The hearings were going into an unprecedented fifth day. Of the four undecideds, DeConcini was already slipping. Byrd and Heflin seemed truly hard to read, and Specter's cross-examination of Bork had been particularly tough. Heflin would send an important signal the next morning.

Heflin was the first to question Bork on Saturday morning. He picked up on a line of questioning he had begun the day before. He had expressed concern to Bork about his speech to the Philadelphia Society in April of that year, entitled "A Crisis in Constitutional Theory: Back to the Future." In it Bork described what he called "Bork's Wave Theory of Law Reform," in which he predicted that new intellectuals would take over the teaching of law. "There are many more younger people often associated with the Federalist Society and who are of that philosophy and who plan to go into law teaching. It may take ten years, it may take twenty years for the second wave to crest, but crest it will, and it will sweep the elegant, erudite, pretentious and toxic detritus of nonoriginalism out to sea."

After Heflin read the paragraph into the record, Bork responded.

BORK: That was an after-dinner speech, Senator. [Laughter]

LEAHY: It must have been one heck of a dinner.

HEFLIN: Of course, that causes me concern that you have got an agenda which would, in effect, be contrary to somewhat your previous statements on *stare decisis?*

BORK: I am not talking here at all about adhering to the law or to precedent. I am talking about the way constitutional theory is taught in the law schools. . . .

HEFLIN: Well, you mentioned some judges in it following this concept. I want to read it, and then I may ask some more questions about it later on, the full speech.

BORK: All right.

On Friday morning, Heflin simply asked that the full text of the speech be inserted in the record. Instead of asking any further questions, he simply stated, "You basically said that what you were speaking to there pertained to the movement, the waves, that would sweep out to sea the debris of the nonoriginalism philosophy that had prevailed in the Court, was directed to law schools.

"Well, of course, I think you can look at the speech and come up with different interpretations, and that is one."

Heflin would later remark that, although it was subject to a "milder interpretation," it was a "carefully prepared fifteen-page address that can leave a person with the impression that he is advocating a movement to sweep the debris of nonoriginalist decisions of the Supreme Court off the books and out to sea." It was one of several pieces of evidence for Heflin that suggested that Robert Bork had a "proclivity for extremism despite confirmation protestations."

Heflin did not ask Bork any questions as he suggested he might that Saturday morning, and Bork did not attempt to clarify the issue further with Heflin. Reynolds "sensed Heflin was slipping away." He speculated that Heflin might have been "intentionally misreading" the speech, but that Heflin saw it as evidence that "Bob was incapable of having an open mind."

With Heflin slipping away, the focus was increasingly on Specter. The evening before, Specter had asked for an extraordinary hour and a half block of time to finish his questioning of Bork. Reynolds, Randolph, and Bork had discussed how to handle Specter.

According to Hatch, Bork was privately critical of Specter, "but he was very deferential to Specter in the hearings. . . . He knew he had to have Specter. So he didn't want to particularly offend him."

Notwithstanding Hatch's comments and Bork's subsequent critique in his book of Specter's cross-examination, it was very effective. For Specter the central issue in the hearing was Bork's theory of original intent and whether a rigid adherence to that theory restricted the Court only to specifically enumerated rights under the Constitution.

SPECTER: I think there is some difference of opinion as to whether you can really find original intent, whether the tradition of U.S. constitutional interpretation looks to specific constitutional rights, as for example privacy, which we've talked about so often, or whether in a more generalized context, justices who advocate restraint like Frankfurter talk about values rooted in the conscience and tradition of the people. And that the history of U.S. constitutional jurisprudence, as I see it, has in many, many cases not been grounded in original intent. Sometimes yes, but frequently not.

BORK: We can't know the specific intentions . . . and indeed their specific intentions wouldn't help us a great deal because our task is to apply their general understanding, their public understanding of what they were protecting to modern circumstances as to which they could have no specific intentions.

But when I talk about the original understanding, what a judge needs from the Constitution is a major premise, what it is he's supposed to protect.

Bork next explained that, for example, with the First Amendment the framers intended protection of religion: no establishment of religion and the right to free exercise of religion, not "just a free-floating liberty." He made the same case with respect to the speech and press freedoms contained in the Amendment. When you flesh that out, you refer to the original debates, the ratification debates, Congressional history, and so on.

BORK: Now, judges who look for original understanding and look at the same evidence and think as hard as they can will, in the borderline cases, often come out differently. I don't mean to say that original understanding gives anybody a mechanical way to approach a problem. It doesn't, but it gives them a pretty firm starting point.

SPECTER: Judge Bork, as you define it, it doesn't seem to me that original intent provides any more specificity than the Frankfurter definition or the Cardozo definition of "rooted in the tradition and history of our society." . . . Why is the doctrine of original intent sacrosanct in terms of the great difficulty of applying it with specificity as you say, because you point out that their specific intent is not clear-cut? Does that definition [that is, original intent] really advance the definition of constitutional values more so than Cardozo. . . ?

Bork had practiced his answer with Randolph. Indeed Randolph claims he gave the line to Bork.

BORK: Well, Senator, you're making a very powerful argument from a very strong tradition. I think what I'm saying also comes from a very strong tradition in our constitutional law, going back to Joseph Story in the first Marshall Court. . . . Senator, reasonable men can differ. Strong arguments can be made on both sides. I adhere to my view that I want judges to be confined by the law, not make it up. There are others who disagree with that. . . .

Specter wrote on his pad Bork's phrase, "powerful argument from a very strong tradition." He looked pleased.

Specter continued with detailed give-and-take on antitrust law and the War Power Act and the national security authority of the President. Linda Greenhouse of the *New York Times* described the two as having engaged in a "spellbinding philosophical debate . . . an intellectual fencing match on an order rarely seen in a forum of this sort. Both men seemed to enjoy the experience."

Simpson followed Specter. Again he played the role of Greek chorus and commentator, speculating as to whether Bork should have answered all the questions but generally congratulating Bork on his performance. As his very last question, Simpson offered Bork one of those questions which, as Hatch complained, Bork had a tendency not to knock out of the stadium.

SIMPSON: Why do you want to be an Associate Justice of the United States Supreme Court?

BORK: Senator, I guess the answer is that I have spent my life in intellectual pursuits in the law. . . . I enjoy the give-and-take and the intellectual effort involved. . . . The Court that has the most interesting cases and issues, and I think it would be an intellectual feast just to be there and to read the briefs and discuss things with counsel and discuss things with my colleagues. . . ."

It was a revealing comment and one easily subject to ridicule. Elaine Jones, counsel to the NAACP Legal Defense Fund and a leading Bork opponent, encountered Senator Heflin on an airplane several days later. Jones had argued civil rights cases before Heflin when he was chief justice of the Alabama Supreme Court. She was afraid Heflin might have missed the exchange, so she repeated the "intellectual feast" line to him and then joked, "I wonder *who* the meal is going to be?"

Bork's friends saw it as a big mistake. Eastland saw it as a "terrible answer." Reynolds concedes that Bork knew Simpson was going to ask the question, "that was a bad one. We worked on that. . . . I don't know why he did it. It just came to him. He's not sure to this day why he did it."

Ed Walsh of the *Washington Post* best described the impact of the answer. It "deepened the impression of Bork as an oddly detached legal scholar, an intellectual without feeling."

On Saturday night, the networks picked up segments of the closing interchanges with Bork. CBS summarized the week's testimony and ran excerpts of decidedly noncommital statements from DeConcini, Heflin, and Specter. Bob Schieffer, who anchored the show that evening, introduced the segment by concluding that the "success" of the nomination was "very much in doubt."

Bork had testified for five days and thirty-two hours. The testimony was covered gavel-to-gavel on public television and C-SPAN. The networks devoted an extraordinary amount of time to the hearings. Although each night the average viewer saw only about a three-to-four minute segment on any one of the networks during the evening news, that often represented between 15 and 20 percent of the program for any single night.

According to national polls done after Bork's testimony, 61 percent of all Americans followed the hearings and 62 percent of Americans made up their minds on whether Bork should be confirmed on the basis either of watching Bork testify or of reading summaries in the newspapers or on network television of his testimony. If this information had been available to Bork and his friends, it would not have been good news. Bork had not done well before the television audience.

Tom Shales, television critic for the *Washington Post* who had thrown his share of barbs at the committee's performance, was even more critical of

Bork's. "Some viewers must have looked at Judge Bork and seen in him every haughty professor whose lectures they dreaded in college. The fact is, as America watched Bork, America learned to dislike Bork. He looked and talked like a man who would throw the book at you—maybe like a man who would throw the book at the whole country."

Two years later Ken Duberstein reflected on what went right for Biden and opponents of the nomination and wrong for Bork during that critical week. "I thought Biden would do well but not as well as he did. He did even better than I expected. His demeanor was great. He was trying to be fair. There was no sharp attack, and his basic approach was 'help us figure out what you're about,' 'explain yourself.' The approach put the burden back on Bork."

Duberstein believed that Bork's answers were too academic. "Bork's approach was to go for . . . the Yale faculty in terms of his answers. Whereas Biden's approach was to try and explain the complicated issue to average Americans and to the other Senators who were on the undecided list."

Conservative scholar Bruce Fein agrees that Bork lost it in his testimony. "Bork lost it on television, and that was because [the opponents] carried the intellectual argument on the television, and that's where the people [made up their minds]."

From Bork's perspective, he was trying to maintain the aura of a federal Court of Appeals judge. Korologos, Randy Rader, and Orrin Hatch all claim that during breaks they attempted to persuade Bork to respond to Metzenbaum and Kennedy when he felt they were distorting his record. Bork was reluctant to step out of a more cautious judicial posture. Hatch speculated that Bork was "offended" by all the coaching. But Hatch insisted that Bork could have engaged Biden, Specter, DeConcini, and Leahy on the critical issues which they had raised—privacy, unenumerated rights, subversive speech, and the application of the equal protection clause to women. Hatch believed that this could have been done in an "intellectual way."

Hatch is correct that there were powerful arguments on all of these issues, especially on the question of a strict scrutiny test for gender discrimination. Of course, Hatch himself did not engage that debate with DeConcini and the feminist bar, either, as he had done so effectively five years earlier when the ERA was before him.

Eastland made a similar point about the privacy argument. "Bork was hurt by the *Griswold* [line of questioning]. Privacy was particularly painful because it was an easy shot. He didn't respond in the political way he could have. When you have the specter of the state wanting to tell you what to do about birth control, that's enormously difficult politically, as opposed to the abortion question.

"That enabled Bork to be painted as an ogre, along with the sterilization stuff. The statist elements of those kinds of positions is quite ironic in light of Bork's libertarian past. . . .'' Eastland was referring to Bork's 1968 *Fortune* article embracing *Griswold.*

Eastland conceded that Bork was too academic, but what troubled him the most was that there were effective arguments to be made against Biden's ''natural rights'' jurisprudence, but they were not made. ''Biden was vulnerable on this. Do you believe in [constitutional protection for] every right under the sun? What are the limiting principles?''

Eastland sighed. ''It was a one-sided debate, which he lost. Some of it's his fault.'' Eastland paused. ''Much of it's his fault, or his handlers'.''

CHAPTER 16

WE BETTER WIN THIS BORK THING

DESPITE BORK'S STUMBLES before the committee, as the week wore on Biden became more the story than Bork. We were wrong about the Kinnock story. It was not just a two- or three-day phenomenon. The rival Democratic campaigns, jealous of all the attention Biden was getting in his successful hearings against Bork, fed the appetite of the national political press.

Two other sets of extremely damaging allegations began to surface in the press by the middle of the week. On Monday, the *San Jose Mercury* had run a story alleging that Biden had used quotes from Robert Kennedy and Hubert Humphrey without attribution. I had been involved in working with Biden and Pat Caddell on some of those speeches, and in each case Caddell, who is not a bad rhetorician himself, had supplied the paragraphs to us. Biden and I both thought it was original work.

Although we did not pay much attention to it at the time, it kept the Biden "scandal" story alive. But a much bigger story was in the works, which really added fuel to the fire. On Thursday, September 10, two days before the Dowd story broke, Jill Abramson, the editor of the *Legal Times,* a legal newspaper in Washington, received a call from an affiliate in Miami. It seems the dean of Syracuse Law School, Craig Christensen, had hosted a meeting of law school admissions officers in early September. On Friday, September 4, four professors, including one from Miami, went to dinner with Christensen.

When the discussion got to the subject of Bork and presidential politics, Christensen volunteered that he had received a letter in May from Biden, who was an alumnus of Syracuse Law. Biden had asked for a copy of his law school record.

Before sending Biden the file, Christensen had reviewed the sealed file, which contained material about an incident that had occurred in Biden's first semester in 1965. Biden was taking a legal writing course—a course in which students are taught how to research a brief and cite relevant legal materials. In those days the initial grading of the paper was by a fellow student. In this case the student noted to Biden's instructor that Biden had used material from a *Fordham Law Review* article and by mistake had not properly attributed it. The instructor was part-time and did not know how to handle the problem, so he took it to the dean. Biden was permitted to address the faculty, which ultimately decided that the matter did not reflect on Biden's character, that it was an academic, not an ethical mistake, and that Biden should be given an F in the course and required to take it again. Biden took the course again and got a B.

Christensen, in a letter to Biden in June enclosing a copy of the file, assured him that the record was confidential and would not be disclosed without Biden's consent. Apparently Christensen did not think that his own policy applied to him, for by the time the dinner in Miami was over, at least one person there believed that Biden had "plagiarized" in law school. He passed the allegation on to a reporter in Miami who in turn passed it on to Abramson.

Abramson had a hot story, but she was running up against a Thursday night deadline for *Legal Times,* and she needed quick confirmation. She had one of her reporters call me. I had never heard the allegation and told him so. She also called two other people. One was John Ellis at NBC. Ellis was a logical choice; because of his position, he was often at the center of the campaign rumor mill. Besides, Ellis and Abramson had worked together at the NBC elections unit. Ellis couldn't confirm it but set out to investigate it himself.

Abramson also tried Bob Shrum, a key strategist for Gephardt. Shrum had worked with Biden in the past, but more important was the fact that he, Caddell, and another Gephardt strategist, David Doak, had once been partners in a campaign media organization. The breakup of the firm had been messy. Doak and Shrum stayed together, but there was still considerable anger and paranoia about Caddell and vice versa. Abramson thought that, if anyone would be willing to confirm it, it would be Shrum. Shrum had not heard the story. Without confirmation Abramson did nothing.

A story as hot as this could not hold until the next Friday, and Abramson lost the opportunity to break it because by Wednesday, September 16, the second day of the hearings, four close journalist friends of Shrum had the story—Leslie Stahl of CBS, Larry Eichel of the *Philadelphia Inquirer,* E. J. Dionne of the *New York Times,* and Tom Oliphant of the *Boston Globe.* Abramson believes that Shrum passed on the tip.

The calls started pouring into Biden's press secretary, Larry Rasky, early Wednesday morning. As the day wore on, Rasky and Donilon felt they had to confront Biden. He left the hearing room in the midst of Bork's testimony. Biden, of course, recalled the incident. Rasky felt the campaign had to move quickly to answer the charges, but they needed a copy of the file. Biden immediately called Christensen and authorized him to release the file to a close friend of Biden's, who flew up to Syracuse to retrieve it.

Without consulting the staff, Biden decided to call a meeting of the Judiciary Committee to disclose the allegations, which were about to break. He offered to give up the chair of the committee if it was the consensus of the committee. All the members stood behind Biden. Thurmond and the Republicans were especially supportive.

Biden then called Rasky and told him what he had done. They both agreed that it would be in the news the next day, and it was essential that he call a press conference to answer the charges. Leslie Stahl broke the story that evening on CBS, but it was a balanced story. She pointed out that he was "cleared of the charges."

Biden and his staff were hopeful but anxious. Despite Biden's explanation, there were some who insisted that he admit that he "plagiarized." Many were adamant that he should not concede, that what had been a case of sloppiness was instead an ethical lapse that reflected on his character. The decision was made to release the whole file and let the press decide for itself. Biden would not concede that he had "plagiarized."

By the next morning it was obvious that it was an argument over semantics. The papers that had been tipped off in advance, the *Inquirer,* the *Globe,* and the *Times,* all used the term "plagiarism" in their headlines. The media stories on Thursday night and the press coverage the next day were only slightly better.

Members on both sides of the aisle jumped to Biden's defense—Alan Simpson, Howard Metzenbaum, Robert Byrd, Strom Thurmond. But the damage was done, and it was severe. Despite the fact that he had never conceded that he had plagiarized and none of the faculty memoranda on the subject used the term, it was irresistible to connect the Kinnock incident and the law school incident and talk about plagiarism. Indeed the *New York Times* headline said, "BIDEN ADMITS PLAGIARISM IN SCHOOL." Almost all the stories contained lengthy quotes by Biden's former professors and fellow students bolstering Biden's version of the events and the fact that the incident did not reflect on his character.

By Thursday evening the allegations were beginning to have a significant effect on the coverage of the Bork hearings themselves. On Wednesday and Thursday evening, the average viewer saw almost as much on the allegations against Biden as they did on Bork's performance in the hearings.

Ralph Neas had been meeting with Donilon, Rasky, and me at the end of each evening after the hearings were over. On Wednesday night, he came into Biden's conference room at about midnight to tell us that he had instructed members of the civil rights coalition to say things supportive of Biden or say nothing at all. As he later explained to Schaetzel and Pertschuk, "We wanted to make sure that no one said anything that was going to hurt Biden and hurt the Bork effort and hurt the coalition."

The next morning at a meeting of the key activists, Ann Lewis, an experienced Washington hand, told the group, ''What we say is this: 'Chairman Biden has run a great hearing; he's been fair—you can even ask Senator Thurmond.' . . .'' Indeed unlike difficult times for Biden at the beginning of the struggle, not one activist made anything but supportive comments.

Nevertheless, Biden's Republican colleagues, although they made nothing but supportive comments about the allegations in the hearing room, were not happy with the way the hearings were going. As Bork's testimony came to an end in the middle of Saturday afternoon, the Republicans and the Administration became increasingly angry over the fact that Biden had not yet published a witness list for the rest of the hearings. Committee staff director Diana Huffman recalls being ''exasperated'' herself with the process of putting together the witness list.

Bork and his allies assumed it was some elaborate strategy to deceive them when, in fact, preparing the witness list was simply a logistical nightmare. Schroeder and Huffman coordinated Biden's effort to canvass the academic community and develop panels in each of the issue areas covered by Bork's testimony. The other Democrats on the committee had their own ideas as to who should appear. Biden was committed to alternating witnesses on behalf of Bork with those in opposition. He had also promised Bork that he could have any witness he requested. However, at times Justice and Duke Short of Thurmond's office could not agree on which witness should appear in which slot.

By late Saturday afternoon, all Huffman could provide was a list for the first two days of the week. That list was enough to create considerable concern for some of Bork's allies. Biden would begin with three of the most articulate blacks in America: William Coleman, a former Frankfurter clerk, one of the most renowned Supreme Court litigators, and a former Republican Secretary of Transportation; Barbara Jordan, former member of the House Judiciary Committee, who had distinguished herself in the Nixon impeachment hearings; and Andrew Young, mayor of Atlanta, former ally of Dr. Martin Luther King, and former ambassador to the United Nations in the Carter Administration.

Hatch's chief Judiciary Committee staffer, Randy Rader, went to Hatch immediately when he saw the list: ''We must [persuade] Bork to come back after all their witnesses have testified.'' Hatch agreed, and he called Bolton.

As Hatch explained it, ''You know, I'm an old trial lawyer. The person who has been accused, even if he has done a wonderful direct examination, has got to come back and rebut the accusations made against him. In this case I thought it would be good for Bork to come back.''

Rader agreed. Bork was their best witness, and he was likely to be the most effective in rebutting the arguments.

On Sunday, Bork and his wife went to the Virginia country home of a friend to relax. When he returned to Washington on Tuesday, he decided that he would not reappear before the committee. But, in a lengthy letter to Biden, he agreed to respond to what he viewed as the legitimate outstanding questions from the committee.

The letter, while addressed to Biden, was clearly directed to two issues that Bork and his advisers thought were of concern to DeConcini—gender discrimination and privacy. In the letter Bork was more convincing and forceful on both matters than at any time in his live testimony.

On gender discrimination, he repeats his argument in behalf of the Stevens reasonable basis test under the equal protection clause. He makes a compelling case that the Supreme Court's current three-tier analysis is ill-conceived:

> Under this approach, the court adjusts the level of judicial review depending upon the court's perception of the relative political power of the group being disadvantaged. If the court determines that a particular group is a "discrete and insular minority" it provides the group with "special protection." . . . Suspect classifications such as race or ethnicity, are subject to "strict scrutiny" . . . other "groups"—aliens, illegitimate children, women and so on—are subject to . . . more lenient standards of review.

He attacked the "inherently subjective process" of determining which groups are "insular minorities." Besides, women are not technically even a minority in American society.

He explained that under his and Stevens's analysis, the Court would come to the same result it had in landmark profeminist results, for example the court's 1971 *Reed* v. *Reed* decision and its 1973 *Frontiero* result.

To those who argued that he had never, prior to the hearings, embraced such an analysis, he correctly pointed out that he had as early as the *Indiana Law Review* article in 1971 criticized the Court's holding in 1964 in *Goesaert* v. *Cleary,* in which the Court upheld discrimination against women bartenders.

His argument in favor of his privacy position also had more of a political bite to it than had his testimony. He made the familiar arguments that the Court's rationale in *Griswold* and later in *Roe* was nothing other than a reincarnation of the discredited substantive due process theory, through which the Supreme Court had struck down the New Deal legislation.

His primary point was that the right to privacy was an undefined right, that there was no principled way in which to draw the line between protecting the right to abortion and not protecting the right to homosexual sodomy. Indeed, in discussing whether the Ninth Amendment incorporated an unenumerated right to privacy, Bork noted with some glee that the Supreme Court had rejected Professor Tribe's argument, that the Ninth Amendment protected a "right to engage in homosexual sodomy." He continued sarcastically, "Equally plausible are claims that the Ninth Amendment protects drug use, mountain climbing, and consensual incest among adults."

It was an effective rebuttal to some of the most troubling arguments that Biden and others had made against Bork. There were, of course, answers. For example, on the question of gender discrimination, he still did not respond to the concern that his was a newfound solicitude for prohibiting gender discrimination under the equal protection clause. For as recently as June 10, 1987, he had declared that he thought "the Equal Protection Clause probably should have been kept to things like race and ethnicity." Also he was apparently not prepared to argue that, under his reasonable basis standard, he would necessarily have reached the same result as the Court had in *Craig* v. *Boren* or *Mississippi University for Women,* cases in which the Court had come closest to imposing a strict scrutiny standard on gender discrimination.

However, in the letter Bork was finally making the telling and more aggressive responses that Mike Carvin had been arguing for all along. Indeed Carvin helped Bork on the letter. It was probably a mistake on Bork's part not to have returned to the committee to make these very arguments in person—after the other witnesses had testified.

Hatch was convinced that Bork's decision was at least in part because "he didn't want to put Mary Ellen [his wife] through this again. His wife was being torn apart by this. . . . She had about as much as she could take." Hatch also believed that Bork was disgusted with the hearing process.

That was certainly not his public posture at the time. For example, Bork in his letter to Biden thanked him for the "courteous and insightful questions" by the committee. Perhaps a more honest answer was given by Bolton, who expressed concern that having Bork return might have exacerbated the confirmation conversion issue.

On Wednesday, the day after Bork and his wife returned to Washington, the first of three national polls was released on how the public reacted to his testimony before the Committee the week before. The news was not good for Robert Bork. The *New York Times* and CBS had surveyed over 800 Americans during Monday and Tuesday. Opposition to Bork had doubled during the week of his testimony. An earlier poll by CBS and the *Times* on September 9 found 12 percent unfavorable to Bork, 11 percent favorable, and 77 percent undecided. After his testimony, 26 percent were unfavorable, 16 percent favorable, and 57 percent undecided. Although the poll did not specifically ask the question, Phil Shenon of the *Times* concluded, "It seemed clear that [the growing opposition was a result of his testimony in which he] reaffirmed his opposition to Supreme Court decisions upholding abortion rights and personal privacy."

The next day two other national polls—one by the *Washington Post* and ABC, and another by the *Wall Street Journal* and NBC—reflected the same downward trend for Bork. The *Post* poll showed dramatic movement among undecided women and Southerners against Bork. Opposition among Southern whites moved from 25 percent to 41 percent. It was exactly what Caddell had predicted after reading the Kiley poll. Conservative Southern Democrat John Breaux of Louisiana was quoted in the story: "I better have a hell of a good reason" to vote for Bork.

William Coleman was the perfect choice to lead off the opposition to Robert Bork. Yet even Coleman's greatest admirers were surprised by his performance. He arrived that morning with a fifty-page brief, plus more than twenty-five pages of appendices, which supported his testimony. He had clearly prepared for the appearance as if he were arguing a major case before the Supreme Court.

As he closed his opening statement that morning, he spoke with self-confident eloquence of the essential case against Robert Bork:

"No principle is more fundamental to the preservation of a free society composed of diverse and sometimes fractious cultures, philosophies and individualists. We are held together as a nation by a body of constitutional law constructed on the premise that individual dignity and liberty are the first principles of our society. In this day and age can we really take the risk of nominating to the Supreme Court a man who fails to recognize the fundamental rights of privacy and substantive liberty, which means more than mere freedom from physical restraint, which are imbedded in the very fiber of our Constitution? . . .

"Having come this far toward a free and open society, we should not stop or turn back the constitutional development that slowly and steadily is removing the vestiges of slavery, of 350 years of legally enforced racial discrimination, and of centuries of irrational discrimination against women."

For the next several hours the proponents of the nomination tried every device at their disposal to unsettle Coleman. Thurmond tried a more direct attack, questioning how Coleman could challenge the Bork nomination to the Supreme Court when he had voted for Bork as "exceptionally well qualified" to serve on the Court of Appeals as a member of the ABA judicial screening panel. It was an easy question for Coleman. His position was the same as Biden's. The criteria for the Supreme Court are very different from those for the Court of Appeals.

Hatch aggressively cross-examined Coleman on the cases Bork argued as Solicitor General. After some preliminary fencing, Coleman ended his colloquy with Hatch by pointing out that, when Bork was nominated for the position, he said he would as Solicitor General merely take the position urged upon him by the assistant attorney general of the appropriate division of the department. Therefore, just because Bork argued a particular civil rights position as Solicitor General, one could not assume that Bork shared that enlightened view. This was especially true where the position was urged upon Bork by the assistant attorney general for civil rights, as it usually was.

Simpson tried charm. Coleman was every bit his match. Simpson called

Coleman by his first name and reminded the committee of their personal relationship and his deep respect for Coleman. Simpson expressed his oft-repeated concern that academics would be afraid to write as a result of the extensive criticism of Bork's 1971 *Indiana Law Review* article.

COLEMAN: I heard you make that point. That does give me concern, sir.
SIMPSON: Well, it should give every American concern.
COLEMAN: I would love to walk over sometime and have lunch with you. I think I can talk that one out with you. I do not think you are right.
SIMPSON: Good. I will be ready. I will buy.

Humphrey tried a similar approach, only to have Coleman suggest that the Senator go home and read certain portions of his prepared statement. By the end Humphrey was hoping to join Coleman and Simpson in their lunch.

It was indeed an ''intellectual feast'' for Coleman, and he was doing all the eating.

Biden was delighted with Coleman's performance. ''I must tell you, . . . I have been more impressed by you today than any witness I have ever sat and listened to in any hearing.''

By the time Professor Tribe had finished testifying on Tuesday morning, powerful advocates had presented each of the four central arguments against the nomination.

First, the heart of Coleman's testimony was the danger of placing a man on the court who did not believe in the notion of unenumerated rights, especially a right to privacy, under the Constitution.

Tribe placed the unenumerated rights argument in historical perspective: ''I am proud that we have a two-hundred-year-old tradition establishing that people retain certain unspecified fundamental rights that courts are supposed to discern and to defend. Chief Justice Marshall said it as early as 1810. It has been repeated by all of the great Justices in our history.

''Chief Justice Burger said it in 1980. Justice O'Connor said it in a unanimous decision upholding a prisoner's right to marry in June of 1987.

''Indeed, not one of the 105 past and present Justices of the Supreme Court has ever taken a view at odds with this basic axiom of our Constitution. If he is confirmed as the 106th Justice, Judge Bork would be the first to read 'liberty' as though it were exhausted by the rights that the majority expressly conceded to individuals in the Bill of Rights.''

Second, Coleman made the case against Bork's views on civil rights: ''With the exception of *Brown* v. *Board of Education*, . . . [Bork] has criticized and rejected every landmark civil rights case since that time.''

Barbara Jordan spoke with even greater passion—if it were possible—about civil rights issues. In the hearing, she did not have the charm and humor of a Coleman but the stern seriousness of the professor that she was.

But as she explained in her statement, her opposition more than anything else, "is really a result of living fifty-one years as a black American born in the South and determined to be heard by the majority community."

Turning to Bork's criticism of the one-man-one-vote principle, Jordan reminded the committee that Bork found "no theoretical basis" for the rule. Jordan's response was biting: "Maybe there is no theoretical basis for one-person-one-vote, but I will tell you this much. There is a commonsense, natural, rational basis for all votes counting equally."

Jordan could speak from personal experience. She ran three times for the Texas legislature before she was elected in the early 1960s—and then only because the courts had redrawn the election districts consistent with the one-man-one-vote principle.

Jordan pointed out that if Bork's view had prevailed, "I would right now be running for my eleventh unsuccessful race for the Texas House of Representatives. I cannot abide that."

Third, as for Bork's reasonable basis test in gender discrimination cases, Tribe responded to Kennedy: "I think, Senator, that the history of legal decision-making under the equal protection clause makes pretty clear that the reasonable-basis test is anything but a guarantee. It is much more likely to be a rubber stamp for laws that the judge thinks are basically okay and a kind of blank check for the judge to fill out a veto on laws that he thinks are not okay."

Coleman's concern about the new standard was not unlike Althea Simmons's concern about making abortion the central issue in the anti-Bork campaign or other efforts to protect women at the expense of blacks under the Constitution: "I do not mind opening [the Fourteenth Amendment] up to the women and other persons, but as a result of doing that, I do not want the Court to say that, because there is only one standard under the amendment, and the standard that applies to illegitimate children or women or anybody else is less than the standard that would govern [if] the Court applied the amendment only to blacks, that therefore I am going to apply that lesser standard also to blacks."

Biden had been taken with political columnist William Schneider's piece in the *National Journal* in August, arguing that one of the most effective arguments against Bork in the South was that he would "turn back the clock." Southern Democrats would understand that any effort to open up civil rights issues could reopen old wounds and destroy the fragile coalition that elects them.

Atlanta's black mayor, Andrew Young directly addressed the argument in his testimony: "Atlanta is a thriving city, but thirty to thirty-five years ago, when I left Washington as a college student, driving back to my home in Louisiana, Georgia was hardly a place where I felt comfortable, and Atlanta was not a city that I even wanted to stop in. And yet, in the period of three decades we have seen the city of Atlanta, the State of Georgia, and the Southern part of the United States move forward to the extent that I could not only be mayor, but could have served the Fifth Congressional District of Georgia. . . .

"All of these things, I think, were possible in large measure because of decisions that are now being questioned or challenged in the nomination of Judge Bork."

As mayor, Young could make the argument which really struck home with the Southern establishment—money: "In the last five years, we have seen the city of Atlanta attract some $41 billion worth of new investment and generate more than 400,000 new jobs. We have been able to do this because we have achieved a kind of level of cooperation between blacks and whites that has enabled us to get about the business of meeting the human needs of the region. . . ."

Biden's original plan had been to have a white Southern politician sit with Young and make much the same point. He spent hours in August speaking to sitting and former white Southern governors, Riley of South Carolina, Winter of Mississippi, Clinton of Arkansas. Governor Clinton had agreed to testify but had to cancel as the Bork testimony went on for a full week. He would have had to miss an important foreign trade mission for Arkansas. Clinton's prepared statement made many of the same points as Young:

"If Judge Bork were to follow his clearly enunciated views on the high Court, the stability and progress of my state and region could be threatened. The risk is not worth taking. The changes in the South have taken a lot of energy, but we have emerged as a vibrant, dynamic part of America. Once we stopped focusing on race, we began focusing on growth and jobs and education. We should not risk new conflicts over old issues, and that is the risk this appointment poses."

Dellinger served on a panel with black historian John Hope Franklin and New Deal historian William Leuchtenburg on Wednesday. The purpose of that panel was to bolster the argument that Young and Clinton were to make on the danger of turning back the clock. Professor Franklin gave powerful testimony on what it was like to be a young black academic in Washington prior to desegregation. All three explained the social impact of the dramatic changes in the South and throughout America wrought by the Warren Court decisions during the previous three decades.

September of 1987 should have been a moment of triumph for Biden. However, Linda Greenhouse in an October profile of the Senator in the *New York Times,* described the period with the words of Dickens, as the "best of times and the worst of times" for Joe Biden.

His hearing strategy was going just as planned. Bork had been a profound disappointment and our leadoff anti-Bork witnesses had been very effective. But Biden's campaign was hurtling toward disaster.

By the end of the first week of the hearings, Biden and his operatives knew that the campaign was tottering on the edge of collapse. It could not take another serious allegation. The civil rights community was supportive and did not seem concerned that the allegations were undermining Biden's performance and the credibility of the anti-Bork effort, but some of us were concerned that, if it continued, it had to hurt the effort.

As Ridley recalls it, "We made a decision . . . to wait out the coming weekend and see if Senator Biden got any credit for his steady stewardship at the Bork hearings. He didn't. Instead, the weekend talk shows and Sunday papers rehashed, in gruesome detail, the troubling events of the week—Kinnock, law school, etc."

Sunday afternoon Howard Fineman of *Newsweek* called Tom Donilon to tell him that the issue that would come out in the morning would relate an incident in New Hampshire at a campaign stop in early 1987, where Biden was badgered about his academic record by someone in the audience. Biden, tired and sick with a cold, lost his temper and exaggerated his academic standing (e.g., where he ranked in class). The incident had been videotaped by C-SPAN, and the exaggerations were documented by the complete law school transcripts, which Biden had released earlier in the week.

As Ridley explains it, "We were polling all through this period. The bottom fell out from under us in Iowa [and] New Hampshire Monday night," on the basis of the network coverage of the *Newsweek* story.

On Monday evening Ted Kaufman and Ridley convened a meeting with all of Biden's senior advisers. Kaufman went around the room asking each of us how we felt. I expressed concern that "If Bork was defeated, it would be in spite of us, and if he was confirmed, it would be because of us." Caddell was adamant that Biden could survive it if he would return to Iowa and New Hampshire to make his case. We repeated our assessment for Biden a few hours later.

Biden spent much of Tuesday and Wednesday coming in and out of the hearing room to attempt to recall specific facts that he had referred to in the C-SPAN tape or in other speeches. Reporters simply were double-checking everything Biden ever said. It was becoming patently ridiculous. Here he was attempting to manage the hearings on the most important Supreme Court nomination in our era, and some reporter wanted to know if he really had won the international Moot Court nomination while in law school. That was one of his claims on the C-SPAN tape. Biden had indeed won the competition.

Biden wanted to sleep on the decision and discuss it with his family on Wednesday night. Earlier that same day, I had induced Biden to join me in a meeting with Kennedy and his staff in his private office. Naturally, Biden was terribly distracted, but he agreed with the consensus in the room that we should end the hearings as soon as possible and press for an early vote. One problem was that all the civil rights groups wanted to testify. There was no disagreement in the room that it was very risky to ask them to testify, because they themselves would then become the issue. Kennedy agreed to meet with the groups to deliver the message.

At Biden's direction I had been meeting with the groups for several days, trying to persuade them to winnow their list or not to testify at all. Neas had been reluctant to make that decision and hoped that Biden and Kennedy would be the ones to ask the groups not to testify.

From early July, Mort Halperin, Washington director of the ACLU, had been telling me and the civil rights coalition that it was a mistake to testify. Halperin was considered an outcast because of his remarks, but he continued to press it all summer. However, the organizational interest of some of the groups in testifying was not totally altruistic.

As Pertschuk and Schaetzel explained it, "Testimony would provide a national platform for the display of individual organizations and their leaders, their hour in the sunlight. With one appearance, they could satisfy the claims of organizational identification for those grass-roots activists who had worked in relative anonymity for months; they could recruit new members, and they could reinforce fund-raising appeals."

In other words, the desire to testify might have little to do with defeating Robert Bork but a lot to do with building their organizations. And the risks were not necessarily immediately obvious to the leaders of the groups.

Halperin explained how he drove the point home to the president of the ACLU, Norman Dorsen. Dorsen had called Halperin to tell him that many people were urging him to testify, and he wanted to know where Halperin stood on the question:

HALPERIN: I have to tell you, I'm doing everything that I can to see to it that you and everybody else doesn't testify.

DORSEN: Why?

HALPERIN: Well, Norman, you think you're going to come down here and talk about the Bill of Rights and how important the Court's role is, but let me tell you what the first question is. The first question is going to be, "Mr. Dorsen, you say that Judge Bork doesn't understand the meaning of privacy in the Constitution. Is that right? Yes! You believe that privacy in the Constitution means that gays have to have the right to marry. Is that right? Yes! You're going to be talking about abortion on demand, and child pornography. . . ." Simpson has got all that stuff, he's ready to go: the groups say Bork doesn't have a mainstream view of the Constitution, and *they* are in favor of a dead fetus after eight months, child pornography flooding the country, gay marriage, and this is the coalition that wants him defeated.

DORSEN: I understand, I understand.

Not all the coalition was willing to have that kind of discussion with their presidents. Indeed in at least two cases, Molly Yard of the National Organization for Women and Ralph Nader, simply would have nothing of the argument. They were certain they could have handled the committee. It was patently obvious to those of us with responsibility for the process and many others in the civil rights coalitions that Nader and Yard were taking a tremendous risk. Especially with their prickly personalities, it was likely that they, not Bork, would become the issue.

Orrin Hatch later admitted that the strategy that Halperin outlined was exactly the one he and Bork's proponents would have pursued had the groups appeared: "If they'd have come in, some of us would have torn them apart. If People for the American Way had come in, they'd have had to give me an hour because I'd have just shredded them alive in front of everybody."

By Wednesday evening everybody but NOW and the Nader organization were on board. Late that afternoon, Biden's brother Jim told me that Biden wanted me to join him and a few other senior staff members for a meeting at his house to make a final decision. I could see the inevitable.

An hour before I was to get on the train with Biden, Neas called and asked me to come meet with the groups about where Biden stood on their testifying. By then I had spent scores of hours in meetings on the subject, and the right decision seemed painfully obvious to me. We met in the ACLU office across the street from the Senate office building. I was tired and impatient. I listened to another thirty minutes of Molly Yard and Nader's representatives talk about how they shouldn't be pushed around by right-wingers "calling us special interests" and "Democrats who are embarrassed to defend us." Yard looked at me when she said it.

I restrained myself and let another few members speak. Finally, with fifteen minutes left to make my train, I began to speak. You could hear a pin drop. "Joe Biden does not think your testimony is necessary, because we have carefully structured these hearings so that independent public figures are making all the points you would make in your testimony. I just don't think we can do better than Bill Coleman or Barbara Jordan or Andy Young or Larry Tribe. There's just too much of a downside."

I could see that Yard was still skeptical. She started to speak. I knew it was useless to debate her, so I interrupted:

"I'm sorry, Molly, but I've got to catch the train to Delaware. Joe's got to go home tonight and decide whether he has to make the ultimate political sacrifice in order to defeat the Bork nomination."

There was a stunned silence as I abruptly got up to leave the room. Kennedy's chief Judiciary Committee staffer, Carolyn Osolinik, got up and followed me out of the room.

As we reached the sidewalk, she said, "What do you mean, Mark?"

"I think Joe's going to pull out tonight because he thinks all these allegations are hurting the Bork effort."

She was shaken.

I smiled. "Besides, I couldn't think of any way of trying to get some of them in there to stop being so God-damned selfish. They seemed to care more about their own direct mail fund-raising programs than beating Bork.''

I doubt my comments made much difference but ultimately Yard did relent. Nader to this day insists that Biden barred him from testifying.

The ride to Wilmington was sad but relaxed. Biden spoke freely about what would happen after he withdrew. Would we stay with him? We all made it clear that not only would we see the Bork fight through, but that we all wanted to work with him to rebuild his image in the press.

Some of us had already begun a strategy to clear up the law-school plagiarism allegation. We asked the Delaware Supreme Court to review the allegations. If Biden was truly guilty of an ethical lapse and plagiarized, then he had lied when he filled in his Delaware bar application in 1968. It asked whether he had ever been disciplined for an ethical violation. Biden had answered no. In effect, we asked the Supreme Court to tell Biden whether he had answered correctly. Three months later, after a formal investigation, the court informed Biden through counsel that it found no evidence of an ethical lapse. They agreed with the Syracuse faculty that Biden's was an academic not an ethical violation and did not consider it plagiarism. In effect Biden was cleared of the allegation of law school plagiarism ninety days after it was made.

It was clear, however, as we talked about the problem on the train, that only through that kind of effort, taking weeks if not months, could all the allegations be sorted out. Caddell had been excluded from the meeting. He believed that the solution was to go to Iowa and make his case to the voters. There simply wasn't time for that kind of effort and to wage the Bork effort as well.

Biden went straight home to have dinner with his family while Tom Donilon, Larry Rasky, Ted Kaufman, Jim Biden, his sister Valerie, and I went out for a pizza. When we got to the house an hour later, the scene was like a wake. Biden's son Beau, a freshman at the University of Pennsylvania, was the most reluctant. It seemed so unfair: ''We're just conceding the argument if Dad withdraws.'' Biden's wife Jill said little. She had clearly made her views known privately and was not about to share her thoughts in the bigger group. His mother looked on anxiously as Biden paced the floor. Beau's concern clearly struck a responsive chord with Biden.

We each spoke for a few minutes.

I talked about the impact on the Bork fight.

Donilon spoke calmly and professionally: ''You've had tens of millions of dollars of negative TV thrown at you in the last week. It's time for a strategic withdrawal.''

Rasky was more emotional and spoke with a sense of resignation: ''The press is in a feeding frenzy. I don't know how to stop it now.''

Kaufman, the only one of us the family truly trusted, looked at Mrs. Biden and then Beau. "There's only one way to stop the sharks and that's to pull out. Then we can catch our breath, win the Bork fight, and come back into this thing sometime later."

Biden looked at Ted. Clearly he had already made up his mind, but as usual Ted had given him the argument that worked for him and his family. Beau nodded. Jill seemed to relax.

He turned to me and Rasky. "Why don't you guys draft up a withdrawal statement. I'll make my final decision in the morning."

We stayed up all night drafting with veteran Biden speechwriter Bob Cunningham. Ultimately Biden used a few of our lines but spent much of the car trip back to Washington the next day writing his own withdrawal statement.

When I brought him the typed draft of his notes in the hearing room, he stepped out to the phone to read it to Caddell. Caddell was still furious and wouldn't listen. As he got off, Biden looked at me and shrugged his shoulders. He had made up his mind. "Tell Rasky to set up the press conference."

I went out in the corridor and told Rasky. We were both exhausted. I put my arm on his shoulder as I saw the red in his eyes and a few tears. Donilon had said in the car coming down, "A dream is dying." I cried for myself and for Joe Biden. As I went upstairs and watched a videotape of Biden's performance earlier that morning, however, I could tell that he didn't need my tears or sympathy.

He was cross-examining former Chief Justice Warren Burger. There was a new crispness to his questioning. A few minutes into his questioning he politely pinned down the former jurist:

BIDEN: With your indulgence, I would like to read an extended passage from one of your opinions. . . . "The court has acknowledged that certain unarticulated rights are implicit in enumerated guarantees. For example, the rights of association and the right of privacy, as well as the right of travel, appear nowhere in the Constitution or Bill of Rights; yet these important unenumerated and unarticulated rights have nonetheless been found to share Constitutional protection with explicit guarantees. The concerns expressed by Madison and others have thus been resolved. Fundamental rights, even though not expressly guaranteed, have been recognized by the Court as indispensable to the enjoyment of rights specifically defined."

Mr. Justice, that is what this debate is all about, at least with Judge Bork and [me]. And I wonder if you could speak with us a little bit, educate us a little bit, about these unenumerated rights—the right of privacy?

BURGER: I see no problem about that statement, and I would be astonished if Judge Bork would not subscribe to it.

Biden was astonished. Obviously Burger had no idea where Bork stood on the central issue of the hearings. ''Let me ask you this, Mr. Chief Justice,'' he said. ''Does the Ninth Amendment mean anything?''

Burger fumbled around and tried to find the text of the Ninth Amendment in his copy of the Constitution, and as he looked he began to mumble something about the importance of the word ''persons'' and the *Dred Scott* case, in which the question of whether blacks were persons had been decided in the negative. He concluded, ''It is hard to say which amendment is more important than any other amendment, but surely the matter of 'persons' becomes terribly important.''

Biden ended his questioning by reading into the record the text of the Ninth Amendment, which does not employ the word ''persons.'' Biden had politely made it plain that one of the key witnesses on Bork's behalf, a former Chief Justice, had not grasped the central legal issue of the hearings.

Nothing became Senator Biden like his withdrawal. As E. J. Dionne of the *New York Times* described it, Biden ''betrayed little bitterness but some sadness. . . . In sharp contrast with former Sen. Gary Hart, who withdrew . . . in a blur of invective against the media, Mr. Biden chose to swallow most of his private anger and place the burden for the end of his candidacy on himself.'' He spoke in a packed Senate Judiciary meeting room:

''In my zeal to rekindle [America's] idealism, I have made mistakes. . . . Now the exaggerated shadow of those mistakes has begun to obscure the essence of my candidacy and the essence of Joe Biden.''

He had to choose between attempting to salvage that candidacy, by going to Iowa and New Hampshire, and defeating the Bork nomination. He could not do both. His first responsibility was ''to keep the Supreme Court from moving in a direction that I believe to be truly harmful. I intend to be deeply involved in that battle. I intend to attempt to bring it to victory. . . .

''I'm angry at myself for having been put in the position, for having put myself in the position, of having to make this choice.''

He took no questions and walked straight over to the hearing room to cross-examine Lloyd Cutler. Before the hearing reconvened, he approached Cutler at the witness table. Cutler was nervous, uncertain whether Biden would take out his frustrations on him. But Biden had made his decision and was moving on: ''Don't worry, Lloyd. You don't have anything to worry about. You'll do fine.''

No longer distracted by the campaign, Biden did something he had not done with other witnesses. Instead of just conducting his round and leaving the rest of the questioning to other Senators, with Cutler, Biden interrupted four times to cross-examine the witness when he felt further elaboration was warranted.

As the hearing ended that afternoon, I walked back to his office with Jill and Joe Biden. Biden was courteous and relaxed as he walked along, almost as if he were comforting some of the campaign staff and well-wishers he encountered in the halls. Jill was polite but clearly still distracted as she walked down the hall holding Biden's hand. When we started up the stairs and the three of us were alone, she turned to me. ''Now, Mark, we better win this Bork thing.''

I said, ''We will.'' To myself, I thought, We just might—but then again we don't have any choice.

CHAPTER 17

NINETY-SIX HOURS TO TURN THINGS AROUND

IN ADDITION TO COLEMAN, Jordan, Young, Tribe, and the Dellinger panel, there were other powerful witnesses against Bork. Two in particular stand out—former federal Judge Shirley Hufstedler and Prof. Phillip Kurland. Both hammered home the unenumerated rights theme.

The pro-Bork forces had a very impressive list of public figures and academics to make the case on Bork's behalf. Three former Attorneys General appeared on Monday. On Tuesday former Ford Administration Cabinet official Carla Hills headed a panel of distinguished academics. Later in the hearings impressive panels of scholars and law deans appeared for Bork as did former Attorney General Griffin Bell.

Behind the scenes on the podium, Republicans became increasingly angry as they saw their witnesses pushed later and later in the day and miss prime-time television coverage. On the first day, their effort to ''break'' Jordan and Coleman consumed hours of precious time, forcing their key witnesses that day—the former Attorneys General—to appear in the early evening, after the network cameras had shut down.

The next morning the argument boiled into the public record. Biden simply reminded the Republicans that the delay was their own fault. If they were going to insist on extensive cross-examination of witnesses, it was going to delay the appearance of their own witnesses, because Biden was going to pursue a strict rule of alternating pro and con witnesses. It was particularly ironic because not a single effort to embarrass the anti-Bork witnesses succeeded. Indeed in one case, Jordan so dominated the committee that she was in the end actually asking Senator Humphrey questions.

As the hearings wore on into the second and third week, it became increasingly obvious, especially with the release of the national polls, that it had been Bork's testimony, not pro and con witnesses, that was sealing the fate of the nomination. However, Biden and the committee were receiving plaudits for the quality of the witnesses and the fairness with which the hearings were being conducted.

Even Bork proponents on the committee—for example Simpson and Humphrey—had to acknowledge as much. Pro-Bork witnesses like former Chief Justice Burger and former Attorney General Griffin Bell congratulated Biden and the committee on the hearings.

By the time it was over, the hearings got rave reviews on the editorial pages of the nation's newspapers. The *Los Angeles Times* carried an op-ed that called the hearing process "an extraordinary civics lesson; it was a celebration of republican democracy at its best." In an editorial the paper specifically singled out Biden's performance. "None of the forecasts about Judiciary Chairman Joseph Biden's alleged shoot-to-kill hostility to Bork came true. Throughout, committee conservatives praised Biden for his fair-mindedness."

The day the hearings ended, Anthony Lewis in his weekly column in the *New York Times* called the hearings "remarkable." He summarized the value of the hearings in exactly the way Biden had hoped for as he designed them in August. "They have instructed all of us on the Court and the Constitution. They have confounded the cynical view that everyone in Washington has base political motives." The *Times,* in a subsequent editorial, called them "extraordinary hearings" and acknowledged that Biden was right when he later argued that "a debate of consequence and caliber" had taken place in the committee throughout the hearing process.

According to Bolton, by the end of the second week, the Administration's effort was in disarray. "Will Ball had disappeared. Culvahouse, who was never particularly political, was no longer playing a significant role" and the White House coordinating group was no longer meeting. Political operatives in the White House were stung with the findings of the national polls earlier in the week. Ellen Hume of the *Wall Street Journal* had remarked that "most surprisingly, one in four conservatives opposed the nomination." A few days later sources at the White House conceded that their own polls showed the same deterioration.

By then it was clear that a direct defense of Bork on the merits was not working. The White House changed the message and decided to attack the messengers. On Friday, September 25, Reagan spoke to the conservative Concerned Women for America. He began to focus his attack on the "interest groups." "Well, it's clear now that the charges that Robert Bork is too ideological are themselves ideologically inspired and that the criticism of him as outside the mainstream can only be held by those who are themselves so far outside the mainstream that they've long ago lost sight of the moderate center."

That same day White House spokesman Marlin Fitzwater lashed out at television and print ads the civil rights and civil liberties groups had been running. "The liberal special interest groups are producing slick, shrill advertising campaigns that not only purposely distort the judge's record, they play on people's emotions as only propaganda campaigns can. . . . To say that Americans will lose their freedoms, as these ads claim, is patently outrageous and deliberately untrue. Gregory Peck ought to be ashamed.''

Fitzwater was referring to a TV ad produced by People for the American Way and featuring actor Gregory Peck. Many Americans probably remember Gregory Peck as the courageous small-town Southern lawyer, Atticus Finch, in the movie *To Kill a Mockingbird*.

The sixty-second television ad begins with a shot of the Supreme Court. Peck's sober, but reassuring voice begins to narrate:

''This is Gregory Peck.

''There's a special feeling of awe people get when they visit the Supreme Court of the United States.

''They know our nation's highest court is the ultimate guardian of our rights as Americans.''

A family of four is walking up the steps of the Court, and the father points the building out to his children. David Kusnet of People for the American Way, who wrote the ad, lives on Capitol Hill. ''There's not a day that goes by that you don't see people with cameras and maps going to the Supreme Court building. It's not an overstatement to say you can detect a kind of awe when they go to these shrines of our democracy.''

Peck continues:

''That's why we set the highest standards for our Supreme Court Justices. And that's why we're so concerned. Robert Bork wants to be a Supreme Court Justice. But the record shows he has a strange idea of what justice is. He defended poll taxes and literacy tests which kept many Americans from voting. He opposed the civil rights law that ended 'whites only' signs in lunch counters. He doesn't believe the Constitution protects your right to privacy. And he thinks that freedom of speech does not apply to literature and art and music. Robert Bork could have the last word on your rights as a citizen. But, the Senate has the last word on him. Please urge your Senators to vote against the Bork nomination. Because, if Robert Bork wins a seat on the Supreme Court, it will be for life. His life . . . and yours.''

The ad ends with the camera focused on the face of the youngest child in the family standing on the court's steps.

In fairness, Bork had never defended poll taxes and literacy tests. He only criticized the Supreme Court for striking them down. In fact, Bork had opposed the Kennedy Administration's civil rights law pertaining to public accommodations in his *New Republic* article. As Biden demonstrated in the first day of Bork's testimony, Bork did not believe in a generalized inherent right to privacy. He did believe that specific privacy protections such as the prohibition on ''unreasonable searches and seizures'' were enumerated in the Bill of Rights.

The ad ran between September 15 and September 25 on the Cable News

Network and in Washington as well as in six important swing states—Alabama, Arizona, Pennsylvania, Georgia, Texas, and Florida. The "buy"—the amount spent to purchase air time—was small, only a little more than $160,000. As one media expert put it, that wasn't enough to "sell Kal Kan in Detroit."

All three networks covered Fitzwater's comments and all carried lengthy excerpts from the sixty-second ad. It was a terrible blunder by the White House. Only a handful of Americans had seen the ad before September 25, because so little had been spent to purchase air time for the ad. That evening tens of millions of Americans saw the ad, courtesy of the White House and the networks. Kiley's second poll found that literally one in five Americans said they saw the ad, and the only way they could have seen it was that evening on the network coverage.

Although Bork had been essentially oblivious to what was going on after he finished testifying, his wife Mary Ellen was not. She recognized that things were not going well. Finally, on Friday, after she had been pressing her husband for days to take matters into his own hands, he called Reynolds to express his concern. He also called Will Ball and asked for a meeting with Baker for the next day. Ball responded that Baker would be in Tennessee for the weekend but that Tom Griscom would convene a meeting.

As soon as Bork hung up, Reynolds called Bolton. "Bork just called. He's upset. Why's he upset?"

Bolton responded angrily, "Of course he's upset. He's losing."

The next morning in the White House, Bork came to the meeting with a plan. He wanted the President to address the nation the next week on prime-time television on his behalf; he also wanted Reagan and Baker to make calls to undecided Senators plus high-profile fund-raising by the White House to pay for pro-Bork television ads. He was to be disappointed on almost every count.

First, not only was Baker unavailable but so was his deputy, Ken Duberstein. Griscom would chair the meeting. As director of communications, it was his job to decide when and how the President would use his personal prestige on behalf of a policy objective. As Culvahouse explained it, "Everybody viewed Tommy as the guy who scheduled these kinds of things and unleashed these speeches."

Culvahouse was distracted with his responsibilities on Iran–Contra. He had just returned that morning from a meeting with the independent counsel's office, in which he had successfully negotiated an arrangement whereby the President could respond to written interrogatories instead of live testimony.

He recalls the meeting in the Roosevelt Room of the White House as tense. Mrs. Bork came with her husband. Reynolds, Korologos, Culvahouse, and Ball joined Griscom for the meeting.

Bork was blunt. "I've been trying to win this on my own. You guys aren't doing everything you can. I need the President. Unless there is a personal presidential effort, I am going to lose. I may lose anyway, but I can't win without the President."

Everyone looked to Griscom to respond. Ball explained that Griscom would be the one who would decide: "Do a speech, don't do a speech, do this kind of speech or that kind of speech." The Baker people were in agreement: "[The] strategy is to win the vote and not respond to the political trends of [each] twenty-four hours; in order to win the vote, the President fires his shot at the most propitious time."

And that's how Griscom responded to Bork: "Judge, you know, the President's got one shot. . . . In our estimation the time to take that shot is not at this juncture, because it would appear that there is nothing he can say or do that's going to reverse the way things are going right now. . . . We ought to wait and decide . . . once it comes out of the committee."

Bork was dubious. "Are you backing out? . . . I thought I had his commitment to make a speech?"

Griscom was firm. "It's just a matter of timing." But he then suggested another concern: "We also have to be worried about the President himself. If this thing doesn't go, he is going to take a pretty big hit on it."

Ball recalls that Bork and his wife continued to press for an early speech to "demonstrate the President's support." They also talked about press coverage. "Mary Ellen was very sensitive about press coverage. It bothered her a lot more than it bothered the judge."

Although Ball and the rest of the Baker people shared Bork's concern about the hearings coverage, especially on the privacy issue, they were united in their opposition to having the President do anything before the committee vote.

As the meeting came to a close, Griscom made it clear that, although he was not inclined to recommend that the President speak that next week, he would inform Baker of Bork's concerns. As Griscom recalls it, Ronald Reagan was at that very moment sitting in the Oval Office preparing to give his weekly Saturday morning radio address. "[The Borks] didn't know it, thank goodness, because I could have seen them getting up and trying to walk over there, and say let's talk to him directly."

All the Baker people recall Bork being angry throughout the meeting. However, they saw a bigger issue, and that was the restoration of Ronald Reagan's credibility. In Culvahouse's words, "I don't want to sound disloyal to Bob Bork, but we had a bunker mentality at the White House. [Presidential pollster Richard] Wirthlin's polls were devastating [on Reagan's approval rating when Baker was brought in]. We were about to see a fruiting of a long haul." In other words by September Reagan's approval rating seemed to be moving back up. It appeared that Reagan was recovering from Iran–Contra, and yet Bork's poll numbers were going down. "There was a very conservative notion that we had to put the President back to where he was, and we didn't want to risk that."

Although Culvahouse never said it directly, the consensus among several Baker people was that, not only would a Reagan statement at that point not help Bork, but it could clearly hurt Reagan. Reynolds agrees that there were some in the White House who thought, "If it was going to be a loser, that they didn't want the President to be the one who goes up in smoke." Reynolds felt that some of this is "after the fact rationalization," but he definitely felt that the caution with respect to using the President was typical and wrong. Reynolds liked and trusted Baker and did not associate that attitude with him but with the White House generally, no matter who was chief of staff. Reynolds commented with some disdain, "[It's a] mind-set that carried over after Baker left. . . . Whatever happens [we] can't have the President in a loss. So we have to move him offstage. It's a way of thinking, a way of life."

Although Griscom was reluctant to have the President speak that week, there was a clear consensus that Reagan should eventually address the nation on the nomination. Eastland worked with Carvin to produce drafts of a presidential address on the Bork nomination. Eastland himself produced three different drafts. "The drafts were consistent with the strategy—to portray Bork as a moderate. . . . But they disappeared into the White House."

Eastland and Bolton kept pressing Reynolds to get a commitment from the White House as to when the President would speak. At one point Eastland took matters in his own hands and called one Bork partisan in the White House to make the case for an early presidential speech, but the aide simply spouted the White House line: "We know when it's best to use the President."

On the weekend of September 25, when Bork had his meeting in the Roosevelt Room, Eastland already thought it was too late. He remarked to his wife that there was little time left. Bolton felt the pro-Bork forces had at most "ninety-six hours to turn things around."

The next week, as the hearings drew to a close, Hatch decided to take the "special interest" attack crafted at the White House into the hearing room. People for the American Way spent a little over $300,000 on full-page newspaper ads in the nation's largest papers. For example, during the first two days of the hearings an ad entitled, "Robert Bork v. The People" ran in the *Washington Post, The New York Times, The Chicago Tribune, The Los Angeles Times, USA Today, The Atlanta Constitution,* and *The Minneapolis Star and Tribune.*

On Tuesday September 29, Hatch spent ten minutes of his questioning round with a huge blowup of the ad and reading from a memorandum, which his staffer, Randy Rader, had prepared for him, entitled, "67 Flaws of the Bork Ad." Some of the criticisms were largely rhetorical. For example, Rader had written that the title " 'Bork vs. The People' grossly misleads and misconstrues his philosophy. More than any other jurist in modern history Bork would sustain the people's right to govern themselves."

The first charge in the ad pertained to the *American Cyanamid* case:

> **Sterilizing workers.** A major chemical company was pumping so much lead into the workplace that female employees who became pregnant were risking having babies with birth defects. Instead of cleaning up the air, the company ordered all women workers to be sterilized or lose their jobs. When the union took the company to court, Judge Bork ruled in favor of the company. Five women underwent surgical sterilization. Within months, the company closed the dangerous part of the plant. And the sterilized women lost their jobs. (*OCAE* [Oil, Chemical and Atomic Energy Workers] v. *American Cyanamid,* 1984)

Rader made many of the same points about *American Cyanamid* that Tribe had made that summer in Biden's living room, as they practiced questions and answers. Bork was limited by the federal statute protecting workers, which did not define this circumstance as a violation; an administrative law judge in the Department of Labor had found that there was no way the company could lower the lead levels; a review commission had approved the choice offered the workers by the company; the decision was a unanimous decision by the three-member Court of Appeals panel on which Bork served, and the full panel of the Court of Appeals, including such liberals as Abner Mikva and Pat Wald, refused to reconsider the case.

Rader made telling criticisms of some of the other allegations in the ad, but in the end his and Hatch's real problem seemed to be with the fact that there were ads. After all it is a little absurd to think that, in a sixty-second television spot or a full-page newspaper ad, the creators can be completely balanced and still communicate a message. The result would have been a law review article, which no one would listen to or read. The only way to create balance would have been for the pro-Bork forces to rebut the allegations with ads of their own. McGuigan and his friends on the Right tried desperately, but failed, to raise money to counter the anti-Bork ads.

The anti-Bork forces did attempt to document each of the charges against Bork included in their ads. Once the ads became controversial, they supplied this documentation to the Judiciary Committee. Other than this, the groups did not communicate with their friends on the Hill about their ad campaign. Indeed they rebuffed any discussion of the ads before they were made. Pat Caddell wanted to coordinate the negative ad campaign. Melanne Verveer steadfastly refused to give any ad copy to Caddell or anyone else in the Senate until the ads were cut.

Some of the allegations in ad copy did seem to go beyond the bounds or were clearly inaccurate. A Planned Parenthood full-page newspaper ad, which ran in eleven key states and in the national newspapers, alleged: ''Bork agreed with a local zoning board's power to prevent a grandmother from living with her grandchildren because she didn't belong to the 'nuclear family.' ''

The ad's authors were apparently referring to the Supreme Court's decision in the case of *Moore* v. *City of East Cleveland*. Since Bork did not believe in an inherent right to privacy, one might assume he disagreed with *Moore*. However, he neither participated in the case nor ever commented on the decision. He did once cite Justice White's dissent in the case.

An anti-Bork pamphlet in West Virginia suggested that Bork would return the nation to separate but equal while Bork had always steadfastly defended the Supreme Court's decision in *Brown* v. *Board*. Much to the chagrin of anti-Bork leaders in Washington like Mimi Mager, Alabama black leaders spread the word that Bork was an agnostic.

All in all, the anti-Bork forces spent less than $1 million for paid media. People for the American Way spent approximately $650,000 for TV, radio, and newspaper ads, Planned Parenthood around $200,000 for newspaper ads, and NARAL $115,000 for newspaper ads—well below the $10–15 million that Bork estimates in his book.

Most Americans never saw the ads when they were first played. A second poll, conducted by Kiley in early November, found that less than 20 percent of Americans had seen the negative print ads on Bork, where most of the money had been spent. Ninety-four percent said they based their decision on information from television news coverage, 76 percent from media news coverage, and 61 percent from following Bork's testimony in the hearings. In the end, then, it was Bork's own testimony in the hearings and media coverage of it that doomed his own nomination.

CHAPTER 18

STAMPEDE

DEMOCRATIC WHIP ALAN CRANSTON had contacted me at Biden's suggestion within a week of Bork's nomination on July 1. He wanted me to work directly with him in lobbying individual Senators against the nomination.

As Whip, Cranston's primary responsibility was to assure that the Democratic leadership had a majority of votes on party initiatives. Of course, opposition to the Bork nomination was hardly a consensus Democratic position in early July. Indeed in his meetings with Howard Baker and Attorney General Meese the week before, Majority Leader Robert Byrd expressed no interest in opposing Bork if he were nominated.

Cranston's position on the nomination was no surprise. For forty years he was the heart and soul of the liberal wing of the Democratic party in California. Cranston started public life in the 1930s as a World Federalist and a journalist who was the first to publish an unedited version of Hitler's *Mein Kampf*. However, as *The Almanac of American Politics* points out, ''Cranston is part dreamy idealist, part shrewd political operator.''

In the summer of 1987, he demonstrated both qualities, especially the latter. When I arrived at Cranston's office for my first meeting with him in July, Ralph Neas and Melanne Verveer of People for the American Way were there, along with Suzanne Martinez of Cranston's staff. We were to have six such meetings in the next three months, all on the same subject—a laborious, Senator-by-Senator discussion of the best intelligence of where each member of the Senate stood on the nomination.

Of course, the best intelligence came from Cranston himself. He carried around with him a long narrow vote-tally sheet, listing each member of the Senate, on which Cranston maintained his own personal vote count. By late September the folded-up scrap of paper was gnarled and ratty at the edges, but it was an absolutely accurate summary of Cranston's conversation with every Senator who might vote against the nomination.

Neas, Verveer, and I would work for hours before each meeting, summarizing all of the information we had gathered through discussion with staff, feedback from the civil rights field organizations, and from careful review of all public statements by Senators. However, it was Cranston's direct conversations with the members that were the most accurate reflection of where the vote stood at any point during the struggle.

At that first meeting, we counted forty-five Senators for or leaning for Bork, forty against, and the rest undecided. It was a surprisingly strong showing against the nomination, especially considering that there were only thirty members still in the Senate who had voted the year before against Rehnquist to be Chief Justice. However, by far the most interesting conclusion we reached was that the Bork opponents had a much better chance of defeating the nomination through a vote on the merits than through a filibuster. Many Democrats who were leaning against would not support a filibuster. Indeed many such Democrats felt that, the more the opponents spoke of a filibuster—which they believed would be perceived as an unfair delaying tactic on the nomination—the less likely they were to vote against the nomination.

When we reconvened two weeks later on July 27, Cranston was certain that his survey required that we abandon the filibuster strategy. Biden and Kennedy immediately agreed with that assessment, and Neas and Verveer spread the word in the next LCCR meeting: Stop talking about a filibuster.

However, the other clear conclusion that we reached after two meetings was that the fate of the Bork nomination rested with Southern Democrats, especially five freshmen Democrats elected the year before: Graham of Florida, Breaux of Louisiana, Shelby of Alabama, Fowler of Georgia, and Sanford of North Carolina. By the next meeting on August 7, the focus of all our efforts was to be on what it would take to get these new Southern freshman to consider opposition to the nomination.

Biden discussed the problem with Tom Donilon, Vince D'Anna, and me at his home in Wilmington on August 3, and it soon became obvious that our highest priority should be to get several of these freshmen to speak out on the nomination. "I've been talking to some of these new Southern freshmen. I'm sure they're going to try and find some way to vote against Bork with his civil rights record. These guys feel they owe it to their black constituencies." Cranston had been hearing the same thing in his discussions. When Cranston and he met with other Bork opponents, Kennedy and Inouye, the next day, they decided to approach two of the new Southerners, Sanford and Fowler, and invite them to join Biden on the Senate floor in a colloquy on the question of whether the Senate should consider Bork's ideology. Both gave strong speeches in agreement with Biden's July 23 speech to the effect that it was entirely appropriate to do so.

Although the Administration attached no real significance to the colloquy, it was gratifying to Biden. Neither Sanford nor Fowler took a position on the nomination, but they clearly indicated that Biden's approach to the nomination was correct. Sanford agreed soon thereafter to host a briefing by Duke Law professor Walter Dellinger for other Southern Democrats on the implications of Bork's jurisprudence.

In the 1950s and 1960s Richard Russell, the senior Democrat from Georgia and chairman of the Armed Services Committee, as well as president pro tem of the Senate, had the prime office in the Old Senate Office Building at the corner of Constitution Avenue and First Street. The second floor office had a panoramic view of the Capitol. In the most spacious room in the suite was a large custom-made oblong table, approximately the same size as the Cabinet table in the White House, large enough to accommodate almost two dozen Senators.

It was around this table that Russell regularly met with the Southern delegation, almost entirely Democratic in those days. Russell led the group in setting the strategy for defeating the civil rights initiatives of the Eisenhower, Kennedy, and Johnson Administrations. Joining him were the giants of the Senate in that era: John Stennis and James O. Eastland of Mississippi, Sam Ervin of North Carolina, John Sparkman and Lister Hill of Alabama, Russell Long and Allen Ellender of Louisiana, Strom Thurmond of South Carolina and Harry Byrd of Virginia, John McClellan and William Fulbright of Arkansas. They chaired most of the important committees. They were all adamant opponents of civil rights advances. They and their staffs worked closely together as a team, almost always voting together on issues, always together on civil rights.

V. O. Key, Jr., in his classic *Southern Politics in State and Nation* compared the Southern political regime of the late 1940s, when many of these men came to the Senate, to colonialism. Decades of political stability provided the seniority that was the source of these men's power, and stability was based on one very simple fact: most of their black constituents were prohibited from voting.

> The backbone of southern political unity—is made up of those counties and sections of those southern states in which Negroes constitute a substantial proportion of the population. In these areas a real problem of politics, broadly considered, is the maintenance of control by a white minority. The situation resembles fundamentally that of the Dutch in the East Indies or the former position of the British in India.

Key continued the parallel by explaining that, just as the colonial powers were able to maintain power as a white minority only with the "support, and by the tolerance of those outside," so the Southern political regime was able to maintain power primarily because of the acquiescence of the rest of America. That changed radically in the 1960s. Primarily because of Martin Luther King, in the middle 1960s the "tolerance of those outside" ended.

Poll taxes, literacy tests, gerrymandering of districts, and in some cases outright intimidation had kept blacks from the polls. In 1965 that changed radically with the adoption of the Voting Rights Act, which literally placed under federal supervision those districts that provided many of these Senators with their consistent margins of victory.

Overnight, the political dynamics of the South began to change. Within a decade moderates began to replace the old stalwarts. In 1978 Alabama Chief Justice Howell Heflin, an anti-George Wallace man, was elected to serve in the seat once occupied by Hill and Sparkman. Progressive former governors Dale Bumpers and David Pryor replaced Fulbright and McClellan. Senators like Lawton Chiles of Florida, Bennett Johnston of Louisiana, and Lloyd Bentsen of Texas openly sought black votes. The only members of the old guard who still survived in 1987—Thurmond and Stennis—were by 1987 supporters of the Voting Rights Act and other civil rights initiatives that benefited their new black constituents.

However, the real sea change in Southern politics came with the 1986 elections, when the five new Southern freshmen were elected with huge margins in the black community. Sanford, Shelby, Fowler, and Breaux were elected with white minorities but overwhelming majorities—in the 90 percent range—among black voters.

With the exception of Breaux, each of the new freshmen replaced a right-wing conservative, who had been elected in the Reagan landslide in 1980. Breaux replaced Russell Long, who had retired. And in each case Reagan had campaigned against them on the very issue of judicial nominations.

Late in 1986 conservative activist Dan Casey, then on the staff of the Republican National Committee, urged Reagan's political advisers to make the off-year elections a referendum on judicial nominations. From the conservative's perspective, it was a good strategy, but as Casey explained later, "It was too little and too late."

The basic speech that Reagan made in state after Southern state warned that, if the incumbent Republican was defeated, the Democrats would control the Senate, and either Kennedy or Biden would control judicial nominations. Reagan boasted, "We don't need a bunch of sociology majors on the bench. What we need are strong judges who will aggressively use their authority to protect our families, communities and our way of life. . . . And since coming to Washington we've been putting just such people on the bench."

For example, on October 28, 1986, in Columbus, Georgia, Reagan extolled incumbent Mack Mattingly and warned "Without him and the Republican majority in the Senate, we'll find liberals like Joe Biden and a certain fellow from Massachusetts deciding who our judges are."

In each case, the half-hearted effort late in the campaign failed, but worst of all for Ronald Reagan and especially Robert Bork, each of the victorious

Southern Democrats remembered vividly what the President said and that a majority of the voters in their state rejected Reagan's advice.

Southern Democrats no longer sit around the big table on the second floor of the Old Senate Office Building, now named for Richard Russell. Indeed, ironically, that table is still in the same suite in the Russell building, except that the suite is now occupied by Joe Biden. However, the staffs of Southern Democrats continue to be very close, especially their chiefs of staff or administrative assistants or the chief counsels or staff directors of the committees they chair. They meet regularly, and even after they leave the Hill, many stay in close contact and are usually intimately involved planning the reelection and the legislative strategies of the Southern delegation.

To a man they are a very savvy lot, all native sons: Howell Heflin's Mike House; Bennett Johnston's Charlie McBride, Darrell Owens, and Jim Oakes; Bob Graham's "Buddy" Shorenstein; Lloyd Bentsen's Mike Levy, to name a few. These men were in constant communication during that period about Bork and any other issues that were of particular interest to the delegation.

On August 7, Cranston wanted to talk about the Southern Democrats. I had lunch with Mike House that day. House, until 1986 Heflin's administrative assistant, was virtually Heflin's alter ego in Washington. Even more important, House was in close communication with the network of senior staff to Southern Democrats. As fellow Alabamians, House and I were close personal friends. House was also active in Biden's presidential campaign.

House was getting good feedback from Heflin's office about what was going on in Alabama. Mimi Mager at the LCCR had been working closely with the two major black coalitions in Alabama, which in turn had been in touch with Heflin. They clearly felt very strongly about the nomination and wanted Heflin to vote against Bork, but they made none of the mistakes that Hazel Dukes had made in New York or Molly Yard and NOW in Texas, West Virginia, and Florida. There were no public threats. Indeed no threats at all. Heflin was noncommittal but they understood that, as a former judge, that was his style.

I was most interested in what the other Southerners were saying. There had been no meeting on the subject and probably wouldn't be, but House had been in touch with all of the key offices, especially those of the new freshmen. The result was surprising and heartening. They were deeply troubled by the nomination, and they all remembered that one of the issues in their campaigns was Ronald Reagan's argument over judicial nominations. They wanted a more senior Democrat to take the lead. House was making it clear that Heflin was unlikely to be that Democrat, because he would not take a position until immediately before the committee vote. Furthermore, House was not even confident of how his former boss would vote. At lunch that day, we speculated as to which senior Southern Democrat would take the lead.

One Democrat who, House guessed, might be willing to take a more aggressive role against the nomination was Bennett Johnston of Louisiana. He had nothing objective to base it on, but he knew that Johnston was close to many of the new freshmen, and Johnston's staff thought that many Southerners would eventually vote against Bork.

A few hours later in the meeting with Cranston, I summarized the lunch with House. Neas's ears perked up when I got to Johnston.

"You know, that's funny. I ran into Johnston in the hall the other day. He's always friendly, and sometimes he's with us and sometimes not. He's very conservative. But he was very happy when I told him that we weren't going to fight the nomination on the abortion issue. He made it very clear that he wouldn't vote against Bork on that basis."

Neas also mentioned that he had run into Republican John Warner of Virginia on his way to the meeting, and Warner also seemed anxious to hear more about the case against Bork. Neas had promised to set up a meeting.

Perhaps they were straws in the wind, but Southern Senators were clearly undecided if not leaning in our direction. Cranston agreed with Biden; he thought we might have a chance of getting the whole Southern bloc. If that were the case, the nomination fight was over.

Bennett Johnston had represented Louisiana in the Senate since 1978. Earlier, Johnston had served in the Louisiana legislature for over a decade and had come out of nowhere to within a few thousand votes of being elected governor the year before. Although he had not been able to compete for black votes with Edwin Edwards, Johnston had been viewed as the reformer in the gubernatorial race. He campaigned on a platform to clean up corruption and favoritism in state government.

Johnston had practiced law in Shreveport with his father, whom one former staffer labeled an "Atticus Finch" kind of character. "Johnston would often ask himself what would Dad do in this situation." Johnston's father, during their years together in practice, instilled in him not only a deep sense of values but great skill as a trial lawyer. Johnston soon developed a reputation in the Senate as a smart lawyer and one of the body's best and most effective legislators. By 1987 he was chair of the powerful Energy Committee. He had also made an abortive attempt to wrest the Senate leadership away from Robert Byrd in late 1986.

Although the newly elected Southern Democrats did not side with Johnston in that leadership race, Johnston was well respected by the young southerners. "The younger Southern members in particular gravitated toward Bennett," says his close friend David Pryor. "He comes from northern Louisiana, which isn't known for its liberalism. His state has rough-and-tumble politics. He's been victorious, and he's been defeated. Bennett knows his politics."

The 1986 election in Louisiana had been a particularly brutal affair, especially on race issues. The Republicans, in the name of preventing fraud, had undertaken a "ballot security" program, which consisted primarily of "warning" black voters of the criminal statutes that applied to vote fraud. It angered black voters and turned them overwhelmingly to Breaux, who won the race with a record black turnout.

By late August Johnston was meeting with Louisianans for and against the nomination. His exchanges with representatives of Common Cause and with twenty Louisiana civil rights and labor organizations were encouraging, but Johnston remained noncommittal. A meeting with his staff and advisers in early September was dominated by the Bork issue, but he was still undecided. He was also "staffing himself" and not confiding to any staff as to where he might be headed. In his telephone conversations with Biden and other private conversations with the Southern freshmen in the first week of September, his opposition seemed more obvious. Although he was not prepared to announce anything until after the hearings, it was beginning to look like the Southern freshmen might have found a senior Southern Democrat who would take the lead.

Another important Southern Democrat was also becoming deeply troubled by the nomination. Lloyd Bentsen, the senior Democratic Senator from Texas, was in 1987 chairman of the Senate Finance Committee, the Senate's tax-writing committee. A sophisticated patrician Texan, Bentsen had been elected in 1970 by defeating George Bush, then a member of the Texas Congressional delegation. Bentsen is now "the bulwark of Texas Democrats," as the *Political Almanac* describes him, but he had to play some hardball to get there.

He got the Democratic nomination in 1970 in a bruising primary campaign against the incumbent Democratic senator, liberal Ralph Yarborough. He ran ads featuring the riots at the 1968 Democratic National Convention and criticized Yarborough for voting against southerner Clement Haynesworth for the Supreme Court.

However, once he got the nomination, he ran with strong labor and black support, which he has enjoyed ever since. He has built a strong political organization in all 254 Texas counties. Bentsen organized a voter registration drive among blacks and Hispanics in 1982, which helped to elect liberals statewide, like treasurer Ann Richards and attorney general Jim Mattox.

Bentsen had served seven years in the Congress in the late 1940s and early 50s. He was elected the youngest member of the House of Representatives in 1948. In the first year of his term, Bentsen would confront the divisive issue of race as a southerner.

As Earl and Merle Black point out in their classic on Southern politics, *Politics and Society in the South,* until 1944, "The most common and convenient device for preventing black participation in the selection of public officials was the white primary, the constitutionality of which rested on the doctrine that the Democratic party in the southern states was a purely private, voluntary association that performed no official functions.'' Of course, in that era the Democratic primary was, in effect, the general election, for there was no Republican Party to speak of in the South. In 1944 the Supreme Court in the case *Smith* v. *Allwright* struck down the practice as unconstitutionally excluding blacks from the vote.

It was the first major stimulus to black voter participation, and between 1944 and 1952 black registration increased almost tenfold to approximately a million voters. Many Deep South states had employed a variety of discriminatory voter registration devices to disenfranchise blacks, most popular being the literacy test and the poll tax. V. O. Key explained that the poll tax ''became obsolete with the invention of the white primary.'' However, with the *Allwright* decision in 1944, it again became a popular device for keeping blacks from the polls. By 1949 five states (Mississippi, Arkansas, Alabama, Virginia, and Texas) applied a poll tax to Democratic primaries and two (South Carolina and Tennessee) to the general election.

For most of the 1940s liberals in the Congress had been attempting to pass federal legislation to prohibit poll taxes. It had passed the House four times, only to be buried in committee or killed via a filibuster orchestrated by Richard Russell and his friends in the Senate. In 1948 President Truman had made such legislation a priority of his Administration.

On July 26, 1949, the legislation again passed the House after a particularly bitter debate with a number of parliamentary votes. The rhetoric was unusually bitter. Opponents argued that passage of the poll tax legislation would encourage the Ku Klux Klan. A South Carolina Congressman argued, ''The rise of the Ku Klux Klan in the South is a direct result of President Truman's endorsement [of the poll tax and other civil rights initiatives].'' A Mississippi Congressman argued that the legislation follows the ''communist line.''

In his campaign in 1948 Bentsen had made his position on racial discrimination very clear. As he said at a rally in Mission, Texas, on July 7, ''If we don't avoid discrimination, we may lose the America we know.'' He had made a similar point three days earlier and again in August.

Bentsen kept his promise and voted for the legislation. As he expressed it in a newsletter to his constituents a week after the vote, ''I regard the poll tax as an economic deterrent on a citizen exercising his inalienable right to vote.''

It was a very risky vote for a freshman Congressman from Texas. He explained twenty-five years later, ''I was one of two Texans that voted against the poll tax. Now that doesn't sound like much to you, but I promise you in 1949 there was blood on the moon when you did that. Like tarring and feathering you. I was from a rural district that was quite conservative and the only other one that voted for it was a fellow from Houston, from a liberal Houston.''

Throughout the summer of 1987, Bentsen, like Johnston, was deluged by mail and meetings with constituents for and against the nomination. There had been one raucous NOW rally in Texas, in which Molly Yard had made threatening comments about Bentsen. On the other hand, Bentsen had been very moved by a meeting with black ministers. The week before the hearings began, in a lunch with Mike Levy, he seemed inclined to vote for Bork.

However, the more Bentsen heard about Bork's position on the poll tax, the more uncomfortable he got. In 1964 in the case of *Harper* v. *Virginia Board of Elections* the Supreme Court struck down the poll tax, concluding that "Voter qualifications have no relation to wealth nor to paying this or any other tax."

In 1973 in his confirmation hearing as Solicitor General, Bork testified that he thought the decision was "wrongly decided." "It was a very small poll tax, it was not discriminatory and I doubt that it had much impact on the welfare of the nation one way or the other." He repeated the criticism in an essay in 1985.

He had not lived through the past few decades in the South, and possibly at Yale Law School it didn't seem to make much difference whether there was a poll tax, but to southerners like Lloyd Bentsen and Howell Heflin, it did. Just as Pat Leahy and Arlen Specter had real life experiences with Bork's views on civil disobedience, Howell Heflin—one week after Bentsen had his lunch with Levy—helped Bork and everyone who was listening understand what was at stake with the poll tax. Bork again made the argument that there was "no discrimination in" the *Harper* case. Heflin responded with a touch of incredulity:

> HEFLIN: There was no allegation [of discrimination]? Is that the distinction you made? Because there is no question to me that a poll tax . . . was designed to prevent the poor and blacks from voting.

He reminded Bork of history-of-payment, advanced payment, payment at the courthouse, and other requirements that worked against the underprivileged.

> HEFLIN: I do not think there is any question that that is it.

Bentsen was also upset with Bork's criticism in the 1963 *New Republic* of the Kennedy Administration's civil rights proposals to outlaw discrimination in public accommodations. Bentsen left the Congress after seven years, to go into business. One of his investments was a hotel in Houston, the first major hotel in the city to be integrated. This was in 1962, a year before Bork spoke out in the *New Republic* and two years before the passage of legislation that mandated such desegregation. Not surprisingly Bentsen found parts of Bork's article "repugnant."

All of the issues that motivated Southern Democrats to oppose Bork in 1987 were not related directly to racial discrimination. One of the biggest changes in the South in the past few decades has been increasing urbanization. Most of those urban areas, and especially the suburban areas around cities like Atlanta, Birmingham, Charlotte, and Richmond, are composed of young professional couples who have recently moved in from outside the South.

In 1920 less than 5 percent of the votes cast in the presidential election came from metropolitan areas. By 1980 that ratio had flipped, with approximately 5 percent of votes coming from those rural areas and over 54 percent of votes from large cities with the rest from medium-sized cities and towns.

This urbanization threatened rural control of state legislatures. By the early 1960s, states like Tennessee and Alabama, which were mandated by their state constitutions to reapportion the legislature, had refused for decades to increase representation in the urban areas. For example, the Tennessee constitution required reapportionment every ten years, but by 1962 the legislature had not undertaken such a reallocation of power in sixty years.

In the late 1950s and early 1960s, as the South began to elect progressive governors like Terry Sanford in North Carolina and Leroy Collins in Florida, they were continually frustrated with regressive state legislatures dominated by old rural counties. Indeed in 1963 Governor Collins was asked by Justice Hugo Black at a dinner party in Washington what his greatest disappointment was as governor of Florida. He told the justice it was his failure to persuade the Florida legislature to reapportion itself.

In 1962 in the case of *Baker* v. *Carr* and in 1964 in the case of *Reynolds* v. *Simms,* the Supreme Court held that the equal protection clause of the Fourteenth Amendment required that state legislatures be apportioned on the basis of one-man-one-vote. Justice Black told Governor Collins that Florida's experience had been discussed by the Court as it decided the *Reynolds* case.

In 1968, 1973, less than a month before he was nominated to the Supreme Court and again in the hearings, Bork had expressed strong disagreement with the one-man-one-vote principle. For example, in a June 10, 1987, interview, Bork concluded, "The Court stepped beyond its allowable boundaries when it imposed one-man-one-vote under the equal protection clause."

Bob Graham as a former governor of Florida understood the full implications of reapportionment. Florida had been one of the first states to be sued after *Baker* v. *Carr*. According to Ken Klein of Graham's staff, the 1970 census was a watershed in Florida politics, because it led to the 1972 reapportionment. What resulted was a "golden age" in Florida politics, where such progressives as Ruben Askew and Bob Graham could enact "government in the sunshine,'' education reform, and tough environmental protection legislation. It also meant an end to the North Florida rural ''Porkchop Gang's'' domination of Florida politics in favor of the south Florida urban areas around Miami. Bob Graham had grown up on a dairy farm outside Miami, which had been converted into a residential development known as Miami Lakes.

Without reapportionment Bob Graham and some of his fellow reformers in state government might never had been elected to the legislature. So Barbara Jordan's eloquent testimony in the hearings about the importance of reapportionment rang true to Graham.

Graham, like his other four Southern freshmen colleagues, was by the second week of October anxious to make his position clear. However, his senior colleague Lawton Chiles was up for reelection, and it would be a clear breach of protocol to go first and appear to force Chiles's hand. Fowler faced a similar problem in that Sam Nunn, his senior colleague, though not up for reelection, had not made up his mind either. Shelby of Alabama faced an even more acute problem in that his senior colleague, Howell Heflin, was a member of the committee, and Heflin had made it very clear he would not make up his mind until the eve of the committee vote.

Everybody in the Southern delegation, seniors and freshmen, wanted Heflin to take the lead. Heflin had done so in many of the fights in the past, because he had been forced to deal with nominations in the Judiciary Committee long before they became issues on the floor. However, in no case had Heflin declared his position until immediately before the committee vote, and he was not about to treat the Bork nomination any differently.

Indeed, it was because Heflin had been in the lead in the past that he had to be particularly careful in how he dealt with the Bork nomination. In a half dozen circumstances in the almost ten years he had been on the committee, he had voted in ways that pleased black Alabamians but angered some in Alabama's white establishment. He had shepherded two black federal judicial nominations for Alabama during his first two years on the committee, U. W. Clemon and Myron Thompson; he had voted against the promotion of Brad Reynolds to be associate attorney general because of his conservative civil rights positions, but by far the most controversial Heflin vote had been against Mobile's United States attorney Jefferson Sessions to be a federal district judge.

The *Mobile Press-Register,* one of the most conservative newspapers in Alabama, nearly dominated media coverage in that region of Alabama. It viewed Heflin, who had voted *for* Rehnquist, Manion, and Meese, as a Benedict Arnold because he had voted *against* Sessions. To the editors of the *Press-Register,* Heflin was ''simply another political hack who can be swayed by the liberal Eastern Establishment which is trying to block as many of President Ronald Reagan's judicial appointments as possible.''

Of course, the editorial forgot to mention the serious allegations against Sessions, who as a federal prosecutor had participated in what appeared to be a calculated effort to target newly elected black leaders for ''vote fraud,'' a program not unlike the ''ballot security'' program undertaken in Louisiana in 1986. Sessions's only conviction was overturned because the Court of Appeals concluded the prosecution was racially and politically motivated.

Sessions had called the NAACP ''Un-American'' and ''Communist inspired'' and said it was ''trying to force civil rights down the throats of the people.'' He described a Southern white lawyer who worked with civil rights organizers ''a disgrace to his race'' and once said that he thought the Ku Klux Klan was ''OK until I learned they smoked pot.'' Heflin concluded that Sessions's ''admissions, explanations, partial admissions [and] statements about [racial] jokes'' led to ''reasonable doubts about his ability to be fair and impartial.''

By the third week in September, the Mobile area, the second most populous area in the state, was a hotbed of pro-Bork activity, all directed at Howell Heflin. The chairman of the local Republican Party rounded up the representatives of the four Republican presidential campaigns active in Mobile to engage in a letter-writing campaign. He had a couple of thousand postcards ready to send to Heflin: ''It's time for him to fish or cut bait.''

Alabama in 1987 was no longer the Alabama of Bull Connor's dogs in Birmingham and Sheriff Jim Clark's brutality in Selma twenty-five years earlier. However, the situation in Mobile was suggestive of the rawness of the race issue in Alabama and elsewhere in the South—the wounds which could easily be reopened if the Bork matter was not handled with great adroitness by Heflin.

Heflin, better than any other Southern Democrat, understood the long-term and short-term political risks in the Bork vote. Bill Schneider in his column in *National Journal,* which had so caught Biden and Caddell's eye in August before the Bethany Beach meeting, said it best:

> It is a law of politics that when the race issue heats up. Democrats lose. And southern Democrats, elected by an extremely delicate biracial coalition are likely to go first. While a vote for Bork may mean trouble for them in the short run, in the long run it could mean ruination.

Clearly the short-run consequence for Heflin and his colleagues was the outrage of the *Mobile Press-Registers* of the South, and there were many. The long-run consequence, as Schneider explained, was that a conservative majority on the Supreme Court, with Bork on the Court, could reopen many of the race issues. Race issues on the front burner in relatively permanent status could mean the end of Southern Democrats.

Earl and Merle Black made the point in their 1987 book on Southern politics:

> The Democratic party is acutely vulnerable to racial, social and ideological cleavages that have no easy solutions; and it is not always possible to present a cohesive party in general elections. When Democrats divide, . . . Republicans are strategically positioned to construct winning ad hoc coalitions of real Republicans, independents and disaffected Democrats.

Despite their impatience, the freshmen Southerners simply would have to bide their time as the more experienced senior Democrats found a safe path through the minefield that the Bork fight presented. The senior Democrats seemed to Cranston, and to the rest of us who met with him on a regular basis, to be moving "with all deliberate speed" in the right direction. Our role was simply to keep feeding both substantive and political information to them that helped make the case against Bork.

Biden was constantly on the phone to me and other members of the Democratic staff to produce comprehensive briefing books for the senior Democrats off the committee, Nunn, Johnston, Chiles, Bentsen. They all focused on issues that they found most relevant to the South—privacy and civil rights in particular.

The week before the hearings, Cranston arranged for Caddell and Kiley to brief Johnston and other Southerners on the Kiley poll, making the case that Southerners, when presented with the case against Bork, tended to support a "no" vote. The Scripps-Howard organization released a poll the week before the hearings began, which brought heartening news for opponents of the nomination. In a poll of 1,000 voters in fourteen Southern and border states, 35 percent of Southern whites favored Bork, 30 percent opposed, and 35 percent were undecided. The poll circulated quickly among the Southern delegation along with memoranda prepared on the Kiley poll by Mike Donilon of the Caddell organization.

Mitch Daniels, until 1986 Reagan's top political aide, saw the danger signs. "Bork can't be confirmed without Southern Democratic votes," he said to a Scripps-Howard reporter on September 9, "and it will be necessary for public opinion to be more one-sided when the day (of the vote) arrives." By late September the polling data on Southern attitudes was overwhelmingly against Bork. A Roper poll, which had been circulated in the Southern delegation before its release on October 1, showed overall opposition in the South at 51 percent against and 31 percent for, and with Southern whites the number was a startling 46 percent to 42 percent against.

The most interesting thing about the Roper poll was that it indicated that Southern attitudes about Bork were really not that different from national attitudes. In none of the Southern states was Bork support over 40 percent in that poll. It was becoming increasingly clear that Southerners of all stripes, black and white, men and women, simply did not want Robert Bork on the Supreme Court.

To Merle Black the cause of opposition to Bork in the South was simple: ''Bork was a loaded cannon firing in lots of different directions.'' He threatened all kinds of Southern constituencies, not just blacks. His one-man-one-vote position threatened moderate and independent Southern suburbanites, as did his privacy position. ''Bork was seen as a right-wing ideologue who threatened lots of different interests in the South, enough to add up to a majority—blacks, white suburbanites, working class whites and the rest. The support for Bork reduced down to right-wing conservatives, and they're a minority in the South. If they set the agenda, they usually lose. That's the Republicans' Achilles heel. . . .''

By the end of the committee's hearings in the last week of September, the Southerners were clearly beginning to reach a consensus against Bork, but they were simply not prepared yet to speak out. Biden and Cranston knew their colleagues well, and to push them to move prematurely would be a mistake.

On Tuesday, September 29, Bill Bradley of New Jersey delivered an eloquent statement on the floor against the nomination, the first member of the Senate not on the committee to deliver a statement against the nomination. The statement focused on civil rights. Bradley's point was that most of the progress on race in this country was recent history and could be undone:

''We forget that fifty years after Emancipation, during the presidency of William Howard Taft, the Post Office, the Census Bureau, the Federal Treasury, and the Bureau of Engraving and Printing all practiced segregation.

''We forget that by the end of the Wilson Administration, over fifty years after ratification of the Fourteenth and Fifteenth Amendments, segregation had been extended to the galleries of the U.S. Senate and the lunchroom of the Library of Congress. Toilets in the federal buildings were marked 'whites only' and 'colored.'

''We forget that the United States Armed Forces was segregated until Pres. Harry Truman issued his executive order in 1948.''

Summarizing the 1960s and 70s, he moved to the present:

''We forget that during the 1980s in New Jersey, in Louisiana, and in Texas, there have been attempts to intimidate black voters from exercising their franchise [the so-called Ballot Security programs].''

Bradley's statement was news but not the kind of national news that would keep the momentum moving against Bork. Cranston felt the hearings were getting boring; they had moved off the front page and out of the national news. It was essential that the opposition do something else to maintain the initiative. Cranston decided to release a vote count on the nomination. According to his estimate, there were forty-nine likely to vote against Bork, forty likely to vote for him, and eleven undecided. Cranston concluded, ''I think he's licked.''

Neas and I spoke to each other on the phone that day, as soon as we heard the line. The numbers were close to our count, but Cranston was certainly taking some on faith. It was a master stroke, however. The line was carried on two networks, and it was all over the papers the next day.

The Administration reacted strongly. Bolton at the Justice Department labeled it "a transparent effort to show the appearance of momentum." Howard Baker in his courtly style said he had "genuine affection" for Cranston but said he was "the worst vote counter in the U.S. Senate today."

Cranston would be vindicated the very next day. Baker had spoken on Wednesday, September 30, the last day of the hearings. Unbeknownst to Baker, the Bork nomination died that day.

Arlen Specter was giving Bork one last chance to make the case on his own behalf. "[Bork] wanted to make his final argument."

Bork attempted to respond to what he perceived to be Specter's concern over free speech and gender discrimination. Then Bork turned to the *American Cyanamid* case. It had not been a matter about which Specter had expressed any particular concern.

Specter recalls the interchange vividly, even two years later. "Judge, I understand your decision on *American Cyanamid* on technical legal grounds, about the scope of review and the OSHA board."

Specter began to tell Bork a story about a case he had when he was district attorney for Philadelphia.

"One of my very experienced assistants was trying a very bad murder case. He had an expert witness who had falsified her credentials over the years. Somehow the defense attorney, John Patrick Walsh, had found it out and had her on cross-examination. And just crushed her. And the assistant DA withdrew her from the case on the commitment [that] he would use none of her testimony, and then it developed she was an indispensable witness on the chain of evidence. . . ."

In a criminal case, a prosecutor must show that physical evidence entered into the record in the case—for example, drugs seized from a defendant—was the same evidence that the defendant possessed, that there has been no break in the chain of custody.

"The judge, Spaeth, is one the best judges anywhere, and he would not let her testify as to chain of evidence. I went down [to the courtroom], and I said to him. 'Judge, you have an obligation in this case to do justice. . . . If you exclude this woman in chain of evidence . . . there will be gross injustice, and you have a duty not to let that happen.'

"Spaeth turned and twisted and finally let her testify, because he had a duty to see that justice was done in that case, to pierce through the procedural morass. . . ."

Specter then said to Bork: "There is a broader responsibility on a part of a judge, and . . . it was clear to me that in this trial Judge Spaeth had to do justice and that's what judges have a responsibility to do."

Bork didn't argue with Specter about it. He just said, "That's a very interesting concept."

As Specter recalled the conversation years later, he explained, "We were sitting around as a couple of lawyers." It was clear Bork either did not get what Specter was driving at or simply disagreed with him and decided to be "patient with him" as he now acknowledges he had done with Specter at other times in the hearings.

Specter had one last discussion with Lloyd Cutler that night. Bork thought he had done well in his last encounter with Specter and had addressed the Senator's concerns.

He had not.

The next morning Neas called me in a panic. "Specter's on the way to the floor to give his speech on Bork. Do you know what he's going to do?"

"No, I'll call Neal Manne."

"He won't tell you anything. I've already tried that."

"Do you think Joe would [be willing to] call Arlen?"

"I'll certainly try to get him to. I'll call you as soon as I know something."

"I'll say a few Hail Marys in the meantime."

The whole fight depended on what Specter did. I didn't have to explain it to Biden. He immediately picked up the phone.

He got Specter's inside line. "Is the boss in—it's Joe Biden."

At first Biden wouldn't look me in the eye as he listened to Specter. Finally, he looked up and smiled. "Thanks, Arlen, I owe you one."

Biden stood up, and we shook hands. "Arlen will take a lot of heat for this," he said soberly. Then he paused. "Now let's see what the Southerners do."

It wouldn't be long. Bennett Johnston was at that very moment on his way to the floor to deliver a statement against the nomination. He reviewed the hearings and concluded:

"What comes through is a brilliant professor, a fine lawyer. I think I would hire him as my Solicitor General, if given a chance. And I think he is honest, I have no quarrel with his honesty. But what it shows is a scholarship devoid of moral content. He misses the spirit of human rights in the Constitution.

"To Bork the law is a great game, an intellectual exercise, an intellectual smorgasbord; it's not as [Justice Oliver Wendell] Holmes once described it when he said 'the life of the law is not logic, it is experience.' What Judge Bork misses is the experience, the feeling, the spirit and the moral content of the law, as opposed to its logic. I have no quarrel with the ability of his logic. [My quarrel] is with the latter—that is, his inability to put into the law the life of experience and moral content."

It was the same point Specter had attempted to make to Bork in person the day before about the *American Cyanamid* case. According to Merle Black, it was a particularly important point for Southerners. Bork was a man of abstract principles, but he didn't appear to be a man of compassion and principle. Black explained, "Southerners don't think of rules. They think of individual justice. If they came before Bork in a court, they would be frightened to death of him. You wouldn't know where he's coming from today, but it would be a principle, applied inflexibly."

Two other important Southerners followed Johnston that day—freshman Terry Sanford and Johnston's good friend, David Pryor of Arkansas. The momentum was moving powerfully against Bork. The Republicans were focused primarily upon Specter.

"Specter hit the game-winning RBI," remarked Tom Korologos. But Ed Walsh, political reporter for the *Washington Post,* recognized the more significant development that day. "The Bork nomination collapsed on Thurs. Oct. 1. . . . It was clear then that the South had been lost."

Cranston sent Howard Baker the following telegram that afternoon which Cranston promptly released to the press.

> DEAR HOWARD:
> JOHNSTON, PRYOR, SANFORD—ALL DEMOCRATS FROM THE SOUTH AND ALL AGAINST BORK.
> THAT'S WHAT I EXPECTED.
> SPECTER, A REPUBLICAN FROM THE NORTH, ALSO AGAINST BORK. HE WAS "UNDECIDED" ON MY COUNT.
> I'M UP TO 50.
> WHAT ARE YOU DOWN TO?
> MORE TO KUM.
> YOURS FOR BETTER COUNTING—AND FOR A BETTER SUPREME COURT.
> ALAN CRANSTON.

It was Thursday, and the nomination was on the verge of collapse. The South seemed to be moving inexorably against Bork, and with Specter's opposition it began to look as though moderate Republicans would seal the fate of the nomination. But the White House was finally in full gear. Baker had met with Senate Republicans immediately after the Specter "defection" and announced that the President would engage in personal one-on-one meetings with undecided Senators.

The Administration had not given up on the committee, much less the rest of the Senate. Unwittingly the Democratic leader, Robert Byrd, almost grasped defeat from the jaws of victory.

With Specter's announcement, one of the four undecided members of the Judiciary Committee had committed against the nomination. DeConcini of Arizona, Heflin of Alabama, and Byrd himself were still undecided. The vote count was at this point six votes against Bork, five votes for, and three undecided.

Biden and Byrd had agreed earlier in the summer that the nomination would be voted out of committee, so the committee only had three options. The committee could vote the nomination out with a positive recommendation, a negative recommendation, or no recommendation at all.

On Monday September 28, as the hearings entered their last week, Byrd, without consulting with Biden, announced to the press that he thought the committee ought to send the nomination to the floor without any recommendation. As the *Post* explained it that day, it was a move "that would allow undecided Senators to delay a decision and give both sides more time to maneuver." DeConcini and Heflin both expressed approval for the tactic, although DeConcini made it clear that he would make his position known regardless.

The problem was that a noncommittal vote by the committee at this point, especially since members of the Senate off the committee were beginning to take public positions against Bork, could stem the tide that was moving against the nomination. Without the support of the three undecided Democrats, Biden could be at a distinct procedural disadvantage. Thurmond could hold his four pro-Bork Republicans plus the three undecided Democrats on a motion to report the nomination out without recommendation and against a Biden motion for a negative recommendation. Thurmond would win on both votes 8–6. Biden could see the headlines: JUDICIARY COMMITTEE REFUSES TO VOTE AGAINST BORK.

Orrin Hatch clearly saw the advantage. He told the *Washington Post* that he thought the "no-recommendation" approach "could be a good resolution." Biden was determined to blunt the effort.

After Byrd's announcement on Monday evening, the Senate Democrats met in their weekly luncheon caucus on Tuesday. Biden took on Byrd in the meeting. Many in the caucus agreed that it was time for his committee and the Senate to take a stand on Bork and get on with it. Much to Biden's surprise, Lloyd Bentsen jumped to his defense: "Let's get this over with." There seemed to be a general consensus that Biden was right, but Byrd was the leader, and there would be no open repudiation of him.

That same afternoon Byrd seemed even more adamant, telling the *Washington Post* that he would be against any effort by the committee to take a stand. Biden decided that he had to meet with Heflin, DeConcini, and Byrd privately. The meeting was scheduled for Friday afternoon.

On Friday, October 2, Lloyd Bentsen delivered his speech against the nomination. Bentsen eloquently voiced his concern about the privacy issue and civil rights. On civil rights and voting generally, he specifically mentioned his record on poll taxes, the desegregation of his hotel in Houston, and one-man-one-vote. He picked up on Bill Schneider's argument about opening old wounds in the South:

"I question whether very many Americans—black, white, Hispanic, or others—want to turn back the clock and revisit those questions. We don't need any more narrow legal debate on what is right and just for America when it comes to civil rights. We've already answered those questions. Now what we need to do is consolidate our progress and keep moving forward."

Bentsen concluded, "Judge Bork is a controversial, ideological nominee, who is staunchly opposed by so many ordinary citizens from so many walks of life." For this Southerner, Judge Bork was Merle Black's cannon shooting in all different directions.

That day, six more Democrats announced against: Baucus of Montana, Bingaman of New Mexico, Rockefeller of West Virginia, Mikulski of Maryland, Wirth of Colorado, and Riegle of Michigan. Two moderate Republicans, Chaffee of Rhode Island and Weicker of Connecticut, also joined the Democrats against Bork. So, as Biden went into his meetings with DeConcini, Heflin, and Byrd that Friday, almost a dozen Democrats had come out against the nomination, including two senior conservative Southern Democratic committee chairmen, Bentsen and Johnston, and Byrd's junior colleague from West Virginia, Jay Rockefeller.

The meetings went better than expected. By the time he met with Byrd, Biden had already secured a commitment from DeConcini and Heflin that they were prepared to take a position in committee the following Tuesday. Byrd resisted at first, concerned about his own reelection, but finally relented.

On Monday, October 5, DeConcini and Byrd both came out against the nomination. That afternoon Heflin informed Biden that he would oppose the nomination. As a courtesy, Biden called Howard Baker to tell him that Bork would be reported unfavorably from the committee on a 9–5 vote, in case the President wanted to withdraw the nomination. Baker said the President wanted a vote in committee regardless.

The vote the next day was anticlimactic, but the message was clear. The headline in the *Washington Post* was unambiguous: "SENATE PANEL VOTES 9–5 TO REJECT BORK."

On Monday the *New York Times* had editorialized against the nomination, labeling Bork a "flamboyant provocateur, with a lifetime of writings to prove it." The *Times* pointed out that Bork "is no racist, nor is he seriously so depicted." However, the editorial took issue with Bork's views on civil rights, free speech, gender discrimination, and privacy.

The next day the *Washington Post* also decided that Bork should not be confirmed. In an unusual Sunday meeting, the editorial board made the "agonizing decision" against him, and their discomfort was reflected in the editorial. It disapproved of the confirmation process itself in this case, but there was no disagreement on the conclusion. Their criticism of their friend was damning: "Judge Bork has retained from his academic days an almost frightening detachment from, not to say indifference toward, the real-world consequences of his views." Shakow and Greenfield were looking for evidence that "he had a feeling for justice, not just for the law."

The *Post* made much the same point Johnston had in his statement the week before when he said, "What Judge Bork misses is the experience, the feeling, the spirit and the moral content of the law, as opposed to its logic." It was the same point Specter had tried unsuccessfully to communicate to Bork with his story about Judge Spaeth in Philadelphia. So the *Post* concluded, "Many of the nation's clearest and ugliest inequities—racial discrimination and chronic malapportionment among them—have been mitigated only because judges used that elasticity to deal with issues that, for various reasons, the other branches would not."

USA Today announced that, with the committee vote, "President Reagan may be on the verge of the biggest political defeat of his administration." Yet the White House made it clear that the President would insist on a floor vote on the nomination.

Immediately before the committee voted, Biden responded to charges that the confirmation process had been unfair and to the White House's insistence upon a Senate floor vote no matter what the committee did. He said that, for the Administration to attack the anti-Bork lobbying campaign by outside groups "in a sense undersells and undercuts the wisdom of the American people." The public had, in watching the committee's hearings, witnessed a debate of "caliber and consequence."

Biden insisted the debate in the committee was "not about Judge Bork; it's about the Constitution. . . . Do I have certain inalienable rights because I exist, or do I have rights because my government confers them on me? Judge Bork's view is the latter; mine is the former. I never had any doubt where the public would come down." In response to the question as to why he thought the White House was persisting in seeking a Senate vote, Biden responded, "I said from the beginning the White House has . . . misunderstood where the American people are on these fundamental issues, and they seem not to have learned the lesson."

The day of the committee vote, five more Democrats and another moderate Republican, Stafford of Vermont, joined the opponents. And the day after the committee vote, the flood gates opened, and nine more Democrats joined the opponents, including five Southern Democrats. The proponents were also managing to get a few announcements in favor of the nomination each day. Usually there were twice as many opponents announcing each day as proponents.

Reagan, in his weekly radio address on Saturday, became even more strident than he had been with the Concerned Women for America: "Oldtime liberals here in Washington . . . viewed the courts as a place to put judges who would further their agenda—even if it meant being soft on crime. . . .'' With the Bork nomination, ''liberal special interest groups work to politicize the court system; to exercise a chilling effect on judges; to intimidate them into making decisions. . . . The nomination of Judge Bork, a distinguished jurist, has become a distorted, unseemly political campaign. . . . He has been subjected to a constant litany of character assassination and intentional misrepresentation. They are determined to thwart the desire of the American people for the judges who . . . will enforce the law and bring criminals to justice, not turn them loose and make our streets unsafe.''

''Well, don't let them do it. Tell your Senators to resist the politicization of our court system.''

That same week, the White House began to contact conservative grassroots organizations for help with the nomination. An aide to evangelist-presidential candidate Pat Robertson was approached to help rally the evangelical forces on Bork's behalf. Robertson commented, ''Now that the nomination is in trouble, the White House is talking about bringing all these coalition groups together. Regretfully, it may be too late. . . . Howard Baker felt he had the confirmation proceedings sewed up, and he deliberately did not call on either the conservatives or the evangelical Christians to assist him in the process.''

He told the *Washington Times* on September 29 that Bork had ''gone before the television cameras and said he is [in the judicial] mainstream and wouldn't do anything different from anybody else. . . . Some people are wondering why they should go to the mat for him.''

However, evangelicals did again jump to Bork's defense. Jerry Falwell sent out an urgent nationwide telegram on September 24:

> URGENT! THE BORK SUPREME COURT NOMINATION IS NOW IN TROUBLE. LIBERAL SENATORS KENNEDY AND BIDEN HAVE REPEATEDLY TRIED TO SMEAR AND DISCREDIT JUDGE BORK. N.O.W., P.A.W., A.C.L.U., N.A.R.A.L. PLANNED PARENTHOOD AND OTHER GROUPS HAVE BEEN EFFECTIVE IN THEIR ANTI-BORK CAMPAIGNS.''

Falwell asked the recipients to call their Senators and, of course, to send contributions.

On Sunday, October 4, John Bolton complained to the Associated Press that the opponents would like to leave the impression of a stampede. ''But it's a charade, not a fact.'' By Sunday, October 11, it was clearly no charade. Fifty-three Senators had announced against the nomination, and Justice Department and White House officials were telling the *Post* that victory for Bork was all but impossible.

The *New York Times* reported that "the cry that President Reagan is now incontrovertibly a lame-duck President grew louder" that week. For months the White House had labeled victory on the Bork nomination as its Number 1 domestic priority and, in the *Times'* words, a "pivotal test of strength."

Joe Biden and the other opponents of the Bork nomination were on the verge of winning that "test." However, the White House was not about to concede that loss without making the victors pay a price.

CHAPTER 19

I COULD NOT EXPLAIN IT

ON MONDAY AND TUESDAY, October 5 and 6, the day before and the day of the committee vote, Citizens for America and We the People ran full-page ads in the *Washington Post* and *USA TODAY*. Both of them followed the theme set by the President and Jerry Falwell. They attacked the anti-Bork advertising campaign:

The Citizens for America ad in the *Post*:

> They have called him a racist. They have accused him of wanting a return to back alley abortions. They have labeled him a major threat to the civil liberties of all Americans. They have poured money into a direct mail campaign and slick television ads. They have applied unprecedented pressure to the Senators who must confirm him. But Robert Bork bears no resemblance to their untruths.

We the People warned: ''You have been subjected to a stunning use of propaganda . . . extremists in groups such as the ACLU and NOW . . . spent millions of dollars to conjure images and perceptions of a one-man court turning back accomplishments of an entire nation. They lied. They threw ethics and integrity out the window.''

The ad then proceeded to suggest that some of the Senators on the committee have ''serious personal character flaws.'' Biden: ''admitted to lying and plagiarism''; Kennedy: ''You always wondered how he ever made it from the Chappaquiddick incident or getting expelled from Harvard for cheating''; Metzenbaum who had returned $250,000 ''when the public discovered and reacted badly to the way he realized great wealth by just making a few phone calls''; Leahy ''who cared so little about our national security that he personally leaked secret information to the point that he had to be replaced on the Senate Intelligence Committee.''

The pro-Bork forces were engaging in exactly the kind of behavior that Biden had cautioned his allies on the committee to avoid with respect to

Bork. Biden refused to challenge Bork's personal integrity and character. On a number of occasions he specifically made the point that he did not consider Bork a racist and discouraged the other members from raising personal issues.

The Right's personal attacks on the Senators backfired. Senator Hatch admitted that the We the People ad itself was responsible for the loss of at least three potential pro-Bork votes. Hatch lamented, "It was the wrong thing to do. It really turned people off."

That same week the Right also cut radio ads that basically took the guilt-by-association tack. The announcer warned, "You can tell a lot about a man by who his enemies are and who his friends are." As McGuigan described the spot, it "pointed out that the ACLU, who opposed Bork, believed that the Constitution protects child pornography and bans the death penalty for even 'heinous' murders."

Although the personal attacks might have been counterproductive, the attack on the process, particularly on the outside groups, was falling on receptive ears, especially at the *Washington Post*. The *Post* in its editorial on October 6 opposing the nomination took pains not only to disassociate itself from most of the campaign against Bork, but to condemn it: It "did not resemble an argument so much as a lynching."

The *Post*'s most stinging attack on the anti-Bork forces did not come from the pen of Meg Greenfield or Pat Shakow but from the usually even-tempered hand of David Broder, the chief political reporter for the *Post*. Picking up on the "lynching" line for their editorial that same day, Broder built a whole column under the title, "When Judges Are Lynched to Appease the Public."

Drawing a parallel to the successful 1986 effort by the Right to unseat California state Supreme Court Chief Justice Rose Bird because of her death penalty views, Broder admonished:

> The game of judge-bashing, which they learned from their opponents on the political right, ultimately profits no one. It inevitably damages and could destroy one of the major safeguards of freedom in this society: the independence of the judiciary. . . .
>
> It is one thing for responsible senators to conclude, on their own reading of his record, that Bork does not belong on the Supreme Court, or for reputable legal scholars to oppose Bird's continued service on the California Supreme Court, as some did. It is something else when judges are lynched to appease the public. . . .
>
> Both the left and right are ready to use all the tools of today's high-tech political communications industry on judges, as if it were a campaign for governor or senator or president. The radio-TV spots and the computer letters employ the same systematic exaggeration and repetition. Bird was beaten on the false allegation that she was "soft on crime" because she had voted "wrong" on case after case applying the death penalty. Bork is

> succumbing to the false charge that he is ''insensitive to personal rights'' because he has been ''wrong'' on cases of importance to women and minorities.

Unlike the *Post*, the *New York Times* was not the least bit squeamish about what had happened. The *Times* editorialized on October 7 ''Who started the politicizing if not Mr. Reagan? And who is keeping it political? Marlin Fitzwater, the White House spokesman, yesterday warned, 'We will not let anybody off the hook in either party' and will press for a vote so that 'we know exactly who voted for this nomination'.''

However, the lynch-mob motif, coming from such a well-respected columnist as Broder, lent tremendous credence to the new last-minute attack by the pro-Bork forces. Most importantly, the attack on the ''process'' soon encompassed the whole process—what went on inside the hearing room as well as outside—even though Broder's attack was only directed at the latter.

As the debate began to heat up during the first full week of October, Robert Bork was facing reality and a very difficult decision. With the committee's 9–5 vote against him and the increasing stampede against the nomination in the Senate, it was clear that he was not about to achieve his lifelong ambition. Should he withdraw or was his instinct right that something gravely wrong had occurred and that a matter of principle was at stake?

Robert Bork is not a sentimental man, nor is he one who acts out of anger or vengeance, nor is he particularly political. As the week wore on, it was clear that for the second time in his career, he had been placed at the center of the nation's attention, in the center of the maelstrom of the national media. Just as with the Saturday Night Massacre, Bork would be second-guessed, used by selfish politicians who purported to be his friends and by critics on the Left who would question his motives. For the second time in his career, Robert Bork made a difficult decision on the basis of a principle which he honestly believed was in the best interest of the nation.

As Bork saw his dream die, Washington increasingly became a city of sharks, friends and allies who had let him down, enemies who had, in his view, ruthlessly attacked him. As he struggled with his decision, Bork sought the refuge, the comfort and security of those in whom he could truly trust, his family.

He could not even completely confide in his close and loyal friend, Brad Reynolds. The Justice Department was, after all, concerned about whether they would even be able to fill the Powell vacancy. Time was running out, and some in the department were already looking for alternative nominees.

Regardless of motive, most of the advice Bork was getting from the Administration was the same: *withdraw*. As Reynolds recalls, ''There was an awful lot of pressure on Bob . . . from two quarters. One, from those who thought it was in his best interest; there was no way he could win, and he was being crucified. Two, from those at the White House who thought the President [didn't] need to go up in smoke on this: You magnanimously withdraw, and this takes the pressure off the President.''

But pressure was also being applied to Bork to stay in, from those who might not have had the purist motives or the best judgment.

In the summer of 1987, Leonard Garment was well on the way to becoming one of Washington's superlawyers. As a profile in a local magazine put it, Garment had gone from ''Richard Nixon's counsel in the early stages of his Watergate defense, . . . to become the premier 'power lawyer' of political Washington—the lawyer whom many public officials hire when their mistakes or misdeeds are splashed across the front page of the *Washington Post*.'' He had represented Ed Meese when the Attorney General had been investigated by an independent counsel while his nomination for Attorney General was pending before the Senate Judiciary Committee. His most recent success had been as attorney for Robert McFarlane, President Reagan's former national security adviser at the time of the Iran–Contra scandal.

Leonard Garment was a friend of Robert Bork's. He had recommended Bork to Nixon to be Solicitor General. They played in a regular poker game that often included such luminaries as Chief Justice Rehnquist and Justice Scalia. In late September he decided that Robert Bork needed his help.

Something was not quite right for Garment that fall, however. Reynolds found his actions ''bizarre'' at times. A reporter for the *Wall Street Journal* concluded that Garment seemed ''ready to fight to the last drop of Robert Bork's blood.''

Leonard Garment showed up at Robert Bork's home on the evening of the committee vote. The family was struggling over whether Bork should ask the President to withdraw his name. He was not anxious to meet with Garment, but Garment was insistent.

As he himself described the meeting for the *New York Times*, '' 'Bob said that he was tired, he was weary, he just wanted to get some sleep.' I said, 'You have an obligation. This transcends Robert Bork. You can't walk away from it. They've corrupted the process. By giving up before it goes to the Senate, you're conceding the basic accuracy of their case.' ''

Bork's description of the meeting, according to Reynolds, was somewhat different: ''Len Garment was bouncing off the wall with all sorts of proposals, all sorts of wild things he was going to do, that didn't make a whole lot of sense. . . . Bork was being polite. He sat there and listened and nodded his head, and Len went off and still did what he wanted to do.''

Before the week was over, Garment was making pronouncements about what terms Bork would or would not accept from the White House if he did not withdraw. He organized lawyers to attack the committee's negative report on the nomination and arranged the media attack on Bork's behalf against his enemies.

In the end, Garment acknowledged that he was "undertaking his pro-Bork crusade on his own and now has 'zero' contact with the secluded nominee." Finally, Bork himself publicly disowned some of Garment's tactics, and Garment was ultimately barred from the Senate press gallery for his overbearing behavior with reporters.

When Bork met with the President the next day, he was still ambivalent about withdrawing. As he was leaving the meeting, Tom Korologus told him that a group of Republican Senators wanted to meet with him on Capitol Hill.

Sixteen Senators, including the Republican leader Robert Dole and Senate Republican Whip Alan Simpson, were joined by hard-line conservatives like Jake Garn of Utah and Phil Gramm of Texas. The purpose of the meeting was to persuade Bork to stay in.

As Reynolds explained it, "Basically the Republican Senators were not at all unhappy with the prospect of him staying in." Reynolds explained that the Republicans could see some political advantage even if Bork lost. "They thought the Republicans could get more political mileage [from a vote] than the Democrats could. They liked the idea of Breaux and Heflin and Shelby having to vote. They wanted to put [Virginia Republican] Warner's feet to the fire and some of the others." Warner was one of the few Republicans who remained uncommitted to the very end.

The *Post* had carried a story that same day, saying that the White House saw "political benefits" from forcing a vote. As Robert Dole would say the next day to the *Wall Street Journal*, "Maybe that would not help him, but it would help Republicans."

Gordon Humphrey had made a similar argument to Bork's son on the phone. Alan Simpson, who genuinely cared about what was best for Bork and the price that Bork and his family had paid over the past few months, disagreed. His comment angered Garn: "If I'd known you were going to say that, I wouldn't have invited you."

Garn and fellow-conservative Phil Gramm were driven by anger and outrage more than by consideration for the Borks. Garn told a reporter after the meeting, "I've never been this angry before. It's a blot on the Senate. I've voted for liberal judges before. That will never happen again. If they [Democrats] win [the White House], there will never be another liberal judge as long as I'm in the Senate. The whole damn Senate will be tied up."

Gramm was more personal. Picking up on the We the People ad the day before, in an obvious reference to Biden and Kennedy, he charged, "The American people know what the people who cheated in college think. We want to hear from the straight-A student."

Dole announced that as a result of the meeting Bork "feels much better about it. If he was on the fence when he walked in I think [now] he's more determined to hang in there." Actually Bork was still very much on the fence.

On Thursday, Bork met with Reynolds and Meese at the Department of

Justice to tell them that he was inclined to withdraw. Indeed that very day, high-level aides at the Justice Department and the White House were telling the *Washington Post* that they sympathized with Bork but hoped he would withdraw.

However, when he returned to his chambers in the courthouse across the street, his family, and then he, had a change of heart. By the evening he was working secretly with his close friend, Ray Randolph, on a dramatic statement explaining why he would not ask the President to withdraw his name.

The next day he insisted on seeing the President privately. He did not trust Baker's White House staff. The issuing of the statement was to be Bork's moment. It was classic Bork, a declaration of principle that would infuriate his enemies and exhilarate his friends. Alex Bickel would have been proud. Robert Bork would once again "wreak himself upon the world."

"In the 100 days since [I was nominated], the country has witnessed an unprecedented event. The process of confirming justices for our nation's highest court has been transformed in a way that should not—and indeed must not—be permitted to occur again.

"The tactics and techniques of national political campaigns have been unleashed on the process of confirming judges. That is not simply disturbing, it is dangerous.

"Federal judges are not appointed to decide cases according to the latest opinion polls. They are appointed to decide cases impartially according to the law. . . .

"A crucial principle is at stake. That principle is the way we select the men and women who guard the liberties of all the American people. That should not be done through public campaigns of distortion. If I withdraw now, that campaign would be seen as a success, and it would be mounted against future nominees.

"For the sake of the Federal judiciary and the American people, that must not happen. The deliberative process must be restored. In the days remaining, I ask only that voices be lowered, the facts respected and the deliberations conducted in a manner that will be fair to me and to the infinitely larger and more important cause of justice in America."

The *New York Times* reflected the clear ambivalence of the White House about Bork's decision. One senior aide was quoted as saying earlier in the week that such an action would be "self-defeating." Liberal Sen. Dale Bumpers of Arkansas angrily defended opposition by himself and fifty-two of his colleagues: "Fifty-three Senators have found they don't believe he would do what they think ought to be done in interpreting the Constitution." In a comment obviously directed at the anger of Republican conservatives, he pointed out, "It's a curious thing. When you win around here, it's a great victory for the American people, and when you lose, it's a lynch mob."

Reagan had kept his distance from Bork. He did not, for example, appear with Bork when he announced his decision in the White House press room.

Pat McGuigan was in the White House when Bork spoke. McGuigan and other conservatives had held a rally in Bork's behalf on the Ellipse just beyond the White House grounds. Many had drifted onto the White House lawn after the rally, and some had smuggled pro-Bork placards through security.

McGuigan, like all of his conservative allies, was "fired up" by Bork's decision. Most of the demonstrators did not yet know it and were gathering around the presidential helicopter, awaiting Reagan's departure for a weekend at Camp David. Rebecca Range, a conservative ally on the White House staff, admonished McGuigan not to warn his friends. It would heighten the response when Reagan told them of Bork's decision as he got on the helicopter.

Earlier Morton Blackwell, the former Reagan aide and a conservative activist, told McGuigan that, with all the television cameras at the rally, Bork's speech, the crowd on the White House lawn, capped off with a Reagan "stemwinder," they would get excellent coverage that night on the news. Instead of a stemwinder, Reagan gave a lackluster six-minute statement.

As Reagan and his wife boarded the helicopter, Blackwell found McGuigan in the crowd and remarked angrily, "What an outrage! An incredible opportunity was just lost. He could have sent these people through the atmosphere if he'd said the right words."

Bork's announcement was met with varying degrees of enthusiasm from different quarters of the pro-Bork alliance. Garment's reaction was predictable. He called Bork up and told him "God bless you" and then volunteered his services. For Bork's friends in the Justice Department, it was not welcome news. They were already trying to select a successor, and they were worried time might run out.

To Culvahouse this kind of strategy—not withdrawing—was a "loser's strategy." "If you assume you're going to lose Bork," he said, "you make victory as painful as you can for Biden and the Democrats." But the White House was even more concerned than the Justice Department about filling the vacancy and the cost to Reagan's approval ratings in the polls. Most of Baker's staff saw the strategy as a mistake.

McGuigan and his allies in the conservative movement, especially Dan Casey, saw Bork's announcement as a last-ditch opportunity to turn the vote around. McGuigan targeted two groups of Senators, five Republicans who had not yet announced their position (Warner of Virginia, Roth of Delaware, D'Amato of New York, Murkowski of Alaska, and Heinz of Pennsylvania) and a group of ten moderate Republicans and conservative Democrats who had announced against Bork but might be won back (Stafford of Vermont, Bingaman of New Mexico, Heflin of Alabama, Chafee of Rhode Island, Chiles of Florida, Shelby of Alabama, Exon of Nebraska, Melcher of Montana, Graham of Florida, and Dixon of Illinois).

McGuigan coordinated lobbying and media toward these new target states. We the People ran a special Alabama version of their newspaper ad in Alabama, directed at persuading Shelby and Heflin to change their votes. In the words of the ad:

> It takes a certain maturity and sense of confidence for a person to reevaluate, and when appropriate, reverse a once taken position. This needs to be done by some Senators who have indicated they will oppose Judge Bork.
>
> It is our desire that Senator Heflin and Senator Shelby will take that leadership position and make Alabama and our nation proud.

The tone was much more dignified than the *USA Today* version of the ad with its personal attacks on Biden, Kennedy, Metzenbaum, and Leahy. However, the rest of the pro-Bork alliance was not nearly so polite.

Howard Phillips of the Conservative Caucus had criticized Reagan for not doing more to raise money for the fight for Bork. According to Phillips, "Conservative organizations have had less money available to them and have not been in a position to counter the expensive television and newspaper advertising underwritten by the Hollywood humanists, the big-profit pornographers, the multimillion dollar abortionists, and the others who had a selfish pocketbook interest in financing the unprincipled campaign of character assassination directed against the good and honorable Judge Bork."

Phillips also crafted ads along the theme "You Can Tell a Man by the Company He Keeps." The idea was to target Senators in a few states like Louisiana, Kentucky, and Montana, and remind the voters that the Senator was, in opposing Bork, taking the same position as the American Civil Liberties Union, Coalition for Lesbian and Gay Rights, the Feminists' Men's Alliance, and others.

Within minutes of Bork's announcement, Richard Viguerie sent out 350,000 direct-mail letters, attacking the "process" and "to raise money for 1988 campaign ads." As Viguerie had explained it earlier in the week, "Senators who thought they had a free vote will have to think again. We are going to make it the most expensive vote they ever cast. We will be able to take a vote against Bork and equate it with supporting the homosexual lobby agenda, the radical feminist agenda, with the AFL-CIO, Jesse Jackson, and Ted Kennedy."

Jack Kemp's campaign committed $50,000 for a pro-Bork television ad for cable television. The ad, not coincidentally, featured Kemp. Kemp was still, after all, a candidate for President.

There was even a classic dirty-tricks operation of sorts. An organization called Criminals Against Bork held a rally on the Capitol grounds. Holding handcuffs and wearing prison garb, they chanted, "More crime! More victims! No Bork! No Jail!'' Their message was, ''Welcome to the largest open meeting of alleged criminals since the Zaccaro family reunion early this week. . . . In decisions that Bork made he has shown the sort of 'firm but fair' [boos from the ''criminals''] application of the laws that the criminals here find so objectionable.''

It was certainly not the dignified kind of debate that Bork had called for when he announced his intention not to withdraw. Clearly some of his friends were not going to ''lower their voices.''

Much of the more extreme rhetoric, rhetoric which matched, if not exceeded, that of the earlier anti-Bork effort, was driven by anger. The anger was not just directed at the Democrats and the anti-Bork coalition. Howard Baker got his share as well.

In an October 9 op-ed in the *Washington Times*, Republican conservative stalwart John Lofton blamed Baker, whom he described as ''a dedicated lifelong anti-Reaganite mushy moderate.'' A week later Pat McGuigan was criticizing Baker specifically in interviews: ''They've already taken the high road and all it's gotten us so far is the defeat of Judge Bork.''

Howard Phillips and former White House communications director Patrick Buchanan were making a similar argument. They argued that Baker should have directed the GOP to make funds available for the Bork defense [presumedly for ads], that Baker erred in not using the ''right to life'' issue and for not using the White House to pressure Southern Democrats. According to *USA Today* on October 16, after a week of open calls for his resignation among these and other conservatives, Baker was not going to quit: ''I'm not leaving. I'll be here to lock the door and turn the lights out.''

Orrin Hatch, reflecting on Baker's mistakes two years later, commented, ''Howard was banking on the good graces of individual Senators up here. . . . The Senate was completely different from when he was here. He could count on twelve Democrats on almost any issue [when he was majority leader]. And on this case he couldn't. I don't think Howard could bring himself to admit that the Senate had changed so drastically, when the Democrats took back the Senate in 1986.''

As angry as they were with Baker, many were much more angry and disappointed with their hero, Ronald Reagan. In his October 9 column, attacking Baker, Lofton spoke for a significant number of conservatives when he concluded that the failure was ''Ronald Reagan's fault.'' His theory was that Reagan had, from the beginning, surrounded himself with staff like Howard Baker, and before him James Baker, who did not share Reagan's conservative views.

The problem may have been deeper than just staff. For Ronald Reagan's effort in the Bork affair was truly lackluster. He never threw himself into the fight. It's true that the Baker staff was concerned about not tying him to a losing cause, because of his flagging popularity numbers, but Reagan himself seemed strangely complacent about a struggle to control the Supreme Court—the nemesis of the conservative movement.

After the committee vote, the conservatives' greatest ire seemed to focus mostly upon whether or not Reagan would deliver a nationally televised address on behalf of Bork. On at least three occasions, Bork had asked the White House to have Reagan deliver such an address. On September 26, Griscom resisted the notion. Two of those times he specifically asked the President in his direct meetings with him. Reagan finally agreed on October 9, after Bork announced his determination to stay in the fight.

Terry Eastland and Mike Carvin spent weeks preparing drafts of a Reagan address on Bork, beginning in the second week of September, soon after Bork finished testifying before the committee. Mike Carvin had several bright young conservative lawyers working with him in developing drafts. All of the drafts were given to Reynolds and then seemed to "disappear into the White House."

As Eastland recalls it, "We were all throwing ourselves into this. We were all working so hard. I came in and worked three consecutive weekends and wrote three consecutive speeches. And what I was writing was whatever Brad wanted. I wasn't trying to put my spin on it. Whatever Brad said the White House wanted. . . . No one over there wanted to go forward."

Eastland knew that time was running out. The last weekend in September, as the hearings were coming to a close, Eastland remarked to his wife that it was already too late. Perhaps if the President spoke that weekend, it would make a difference.

The President did not, of course. Indeed he would not deliver the speech until over two weeks later.

Finally on the weekend of October 10, Carvin went home in disgust and disillusionment. Reagan delivered his address on Wednesday October 14, almost three weeks after Bork had asked for it. None of the networks were interested in carrying the speech in prime time, so he appeared at 3:15 in the afternoon. Only CNN carried the address live, and few Americans had their television sets on at that time of day. To Eastland, Ronald Reagan "was a trivial figure by then."

Ronald Reagan also did little personal lobbying of Senators until late September, and even that seemed half-hearted. His meeting with moderate Democrat Robert Graham of Florida is typical of the one-on-one meetings he held with uncommitted Senators. Graham walked into the Oval Office, where he and the President exchanged pleasantries. Reagan sat with his legs crossed and spoke from index cards that rested on his knee.

When Reagan asked Graham what his problem was with the nomination, the Senator expressed concern about Bork's views on civil liberties and civil rights. Reagan interrupted him with a long rambling story about how he understood race problems. It seems that, when he played football in college, the center on the team was black and was the subject of racial slurs by opponents. Sometimes this would rile the team up and spur them on to victory.

Graham was puzzled. How was this germane to his concerns about Bork? Reagan never addressed Graham's concerns or even seemed to understand them. Reagan was completely unpersuasive, and Graham ultimately voted against Bork.

DeConcini had a similar experience. In DeConcini's case, the President also seemed to have a rote presentation. The President argued that the ABA supported Bork, former President Ford, former Chief Justice Burger, and Lloyd Cutler supported Bork, and therefore DeConcini should, too.

DeConcini insisted on asking the President about Bork's views on privacy and constitutional jurisprudence generally. Baker, who had joined the meeting, answered DeConcini's questions. Ed Baxter, who sat through the meeting, recalled that after that, the President "sat there and didn't say anything else other than pleasantries."

Some conservatives blame Baker for Reagan's complacency. Others, like Pat McGuigan, believe that his wife Nancy was to blame. McGuigan believes that she never shared the conservative agenda, especially on abortion, and that she influenced the President's attitude, especially in the closing years of his term.

To the Washington press corps, Reagan had simply become a lame duck. As the *Wall Street Journal* put it on October 16, "The sound being heard around here is the sound of the Reagan Administration running out of steam." The story spoke of a "creeping paralysis" in the Reagan Administration. Conservative Congressman Newt Gingrich warned that President Reagan is "in some danger of becoming another Jimmy Carter." Republican political consultant John Deardourff was even more definitive: "It seems to me that at least in terms of domestic policy and domestic politics, the Bork chapter really does bring the Reagan years to an end."

Gingrich, a former history professor at West Georgia College, elaborated his Jimmy Carter point to Reagan in a letter on October 13. He laid out three models for the President:

> If you want the vast majority of Americans who share your values to join you in an all-out struggle to save the Supreme Court and the Senate from a left-wing lynch mob, you will have to systematically focus attention, arouse allies and encourage supporters. . . . The best historical example of a President who aroused his majority against a bitterly opposed Congressional leadership may be Andrew Jackson.
>
> Alternatively, if you want to wage a solid fight but gracefully accept the probable defeat of Judge Bork so you can get a judge approved this year,

> then you must follow [a] very different vision of White House Congressional relations. . . . [It] will require an insider strategy of accommodating power in Washington. The best historic example of a conservative President working with a liberal Congressional leadership may be Dwight Eisenhower.
>
> The worst possible course is for you to use the language and outline the vision of an assault against the corrupt left-wing lynch mob, but then to try to pull your punches so you and they can find an accommodation. That zig-zag policy will simply confuse your followers, enrage your opponents and cripple your presidency. The best historic example of the confused zig-zag approach is Jimmy Carter.

The next day Gingrich come to the sad realization that it was the last model that Reagan would follow on the Bork nomination. Appearing at a campaign rally in New Jersey, an angry Reagan departed from his prepared text and announced that, if Bork was rejected he would propose a nominee that the liberals will "object to as much as they did to this one."

The ad lib statement clearly was inconsistent with the Eisenhower model that Gingrich preferred him to follow. Three hours after the event, the White House staff circulated a toned-down version of the quip. Indeed Griscom had apparently spent the morning modifying the prepared text for the New Jersey event. Griscom removed a moving passage alluding to the movie *Mr. Smith Goes to Washington*:

"Remember . . . when Jimmy Stewart stands in the well of the Senate and says that lost causes are 'the only causes worth fighting for.' . . . Because of one plain, simple, rule, 'Love thy neighbor. . . .'

"And he added. 'I'm going to stay right here and fight for this lost cause even if this room'—he meant the Senate—'is filled with lies . . . and the [special interests] come marching into this place.'

"So will I."

As the *Post* explained, "The Baker forces appeared to have failed to reckon with Reagan's own strong views." Even though it had been dropped, Reagan did his own version of the Jimmy Stewart lines.

Gingrich was furious. Clearly the President seemed to be following the Jimmy Carter model. Gingrich wrote the President another angry letter that same day: "You must either impose your strategy of confrontation on your senior staff, or you must discipline yourself to stay within the bounds of a conciliatory strategy as designed by them. Either will work. The chaos and confusion exemplified by the [press coverage] is simply crippling your presidency."

In the week that remained before the final vote on the nomination, Reagan seemed to drift inexorably toward the Eisenhower model. Bork's more fervent allies continued to pursue the Jacksonian model, without, of course, a Jackson.

For example, two days after the New Jersey incident, NCPAC, the National Conservative Political Action Committee, launched an aggressive eighteen-state telephone fund-raising campaign. It was aimed at twenty-six Senators, all but three of whom were publicly opposed.

The plan was to use computers to make over 2 million phone calls. Each caller heard a taped message, which began with Senator Humphrey as honorary chairman of NCPAC: "President Reagan needs your support in his effort to have Judge Robert Bork confirmed to the United States Supreme Court." The tape next heard an excerpt from a Reagan speech: "[Bork] has been subjected to a constant litany of character assassination and intentional misrepresentation. Tell your Senators to resist the politization of our court system." The announcer then asked the listener to call a Senator, whose name was inserted—and to make a contribution.

Humphrey was not only the honorary chair of NCPAC but was leading the effort to delay a vote on the Bork nomination on the floor of the Senate. Within days Robert Byrd, the Democratic leader, was on the floor describing the NCPAC telecomputer program and accusing Humphrey and the conservatives of using the delay for fund-raising purposes. At the time, NCPAC had a $3 million debt. Byrd suggested that Humphrey would not agree to begin debate until NCPAC's fund-raising goals had been met. He asked sarcastically, "How much money do they need?"

Democrats were enraged by the tactic. DeConcini told UPI, "NCPAC, with the introduction of a member of the Senate, is attempting to turn around the vote of this Senator [himself]. . . . It's a waste of time, and quite frankly, an insult. I resent it."

Terry Sanford certainly spoke for all Democrats when he was chosen to respond to the President's speech on October 14. Sanford pointed out that Reagan had injected politics into the Supreme Court nominating process in the 1986 elections. Sanford reminded the audience that Reagan had come to North Carolina and elsewhere in the South to campaign against him and a Democratic Senate, which would, in Reagan's words, allow "drugs, thugs, and hoodlums" to reign by placing "a bunch of sociology majors on the bench."

According to Sanford, he and his colleagues made their decisions on the basis of a careful review of Bork's record and not pressure from outside groups or ads. Sanford angrily banged the table:

"We are tired of having our integrity impugned. We are tired of having our sincerity questioned. We are tired of having our intelligence insulted.

"It is at least imprudent that the President of the United States is fighting a rear-guard action against the clear mandate of the Senate to move on with the process of selecting a new Supreme Court nominee. One mark of a great leader is not only being gracious in victory but being gracious in defeat."

The Senate debate finally got under way on Wednesday, October 21. The first day continued the bitter exchanges on both sides about tactics. Proponents of Bork argued that the ads and the pressure tactics had "'smeared" Bork while Democrats who opposed Bork criticized the personal attacks, especially on colleagues by the pro-Bork coalition.

Some of the criticism of the process was even-tempered and telling. Specter criticized what he called the "rolling vote," by which members of the Senate off the committee announced their opposition before the debate even began. This he pointed out "short-circuited" the floor debate, making it "pro forma rather than substantive."

Republican John Danforth of Missouri, a former student of Bork's, gave the most eloquent critique of the process used to defeat the judge. Fellow Republican Alan Simpson said he had visited with Bork, who said he deplored the advertising in some states attacking Senators who oppose the nomination.

The debate also was quite substantive at times, especially between Hatch and Biden over Bork's jurisprudence. Republican Robert Packwood of Oregon gave a convincing presentation of the notion of unenumerated rights in our jurisprudence stretching all the way back to Magna Charta.

There was indeed still a struggle going on over a half-dozen undecided Senators. Sam Nunn of Georgia was undecided until the next to the last day, and two Democrats, Proxmire of Wisconsin and Stennis of Mississippi, and one Republican, Warner of Virginia, were undecided until the very last day. While he was managing the floor debate on the nomination, Biden spent hours in the cloakroom, or on the couches adjacent to the floor, personally lobbying the four undecideds. All four ended up voting against Bork.

The Proxmire and Stennis votes were particularly gratifying, because these men were retiring and not running for reelection. No one could argue that their votes were politically motivated. John Stennis had, of course, sat around that table with Richard Russell in the Old Senate Office Building. His vote was emblematic of how the South and John Stennis had changed.

Usually during a Senate debate, especially when the result is a foregone conclusion as it was with Bork, Senators don't show up on the floor until the last minute of the roll-call vote. But on October 23, 1987, the Senate was packed for most of the last hour of debate. Every member realized that he was participating in a historic event. You could feel the tension. Although we knew how almost every Senator would vote, all the staff and every member of the press in the gallery above the Vice President's chair had tally sheets in hand to record each vote as it was cast. There were no surprises.

The vote was announced at 2:00 P.M.—58 against, 42 in favor. The margin of defeat was the largest in history.

When the result was announced, there was a strange quiet in the room. There was no elation, just a sense of relief. Biden turned and walked over to Thurmond and shook his hand, and then headed out of the chamber.

I walked with him. We didn't speak. He looked somber and older. He seemed lost in his thoughts. We walked from the chamber through the Senate lobby, where the representatives of the groups mobbed us, but Biden kept walking and headed for the stairs to go to the radio and television gallery for the traditional victory press conference, which occurs after a major Senate vote. As we headed up the steps, we encountered Tim Ridley, manager of the then defunct presidential campaign.

He reached out and wished us both congratulations. He had a big smile on his face, but as he looked in my eyes, I saw the pain of defeat. I held onto his hand for a few extra seconds and thought about what might have been.

Larry Rasky, Biden's press secretary, grabbed my arm and urged me on, or we'd miss the press conference. With Rasky's nudge, Biden turned up the steps. He was ready to move on.

Across town in the Madison Hotel, Robert Bork ate a late lunch with his wife. He recalls the moment and his feelings about it in his book:

> We knew the vote was over when a reporter from the *Washington Post* interrupted our lunch by standing at the table and asking how I felt about being rejected. I told her I would like to have lunch in peace. . . .
>
> Only once since the day of the vote did I feel a pang of sadness. [Some months later his wife showed him a dress she had chosen for his swearing in.] The poignancy of that moment had nothing to do with my career but with her, and since I could not explain it, I said nothing and the moment passed.

CHAPTER 20

THE FINAL CHAPTER

THE FRUSTRATION, anger, and disappointment that conservatives felt about the Bork defeat continued to rise after the final roll-call vote on the nomination on October 23. The *Washington Times* editorial page surely spoke for most strong conservatives during this period when it warned that if the President did not appoint another Bork or take some audacious act like Bork had, "the executive will be utterly becalmed, without political or moral influence."

The defeat again ignited the struggle between Baker's pragmatists in the White House and Meese's "true believers" at the Department of Justice. Except that this time Baker, because of the criticism he had taken for "losing" the Bork nomination, was even more reticent than he had been during the weekend after the Powell withdrawal.

Again Baker sought consultations with Biden. By Tuesday October 27, the Administration search had focused on five finalists:

- Pasco Bowman, a member of the Eighth Circuit Court of Appeals, a former dean of Wake Forest Law School in North Carolina, where he ran an allegedly antilabor institute on labor law, a political protégé of the state's conservative Senator, Jesse Helms.
- Douglas Ginsburg, a member of the D.C. Circuit Court of Appeals on which Bork had sat, a close friend of Bork and Reynolds, a former assistant attorney general for antitrust in the Reagan Justice Department.
- Anthony Kennedy, a member of the 9th Circuit Court of Appeals, close to Reagan and Meese from his days as a lawyer and a lobbyist in Sacramento, where he had helped then Governor Reagan draft an unsuccessful statewide tax reduction initiative.
- Ralph Winter, a member of the 2nd Circuit Court of Appeals, formerly a fellow conservative colleague of Bork's at Yale Law School.
- William Wilkins, a member of the 4th Circuit Court of Appeals, a former staffer for and political protégé of Sen. Strom Thurmond.

As Biden prepared for his meeting with Baker, he reviewed extensive briefing books on each of the five and a half dozen more. The civil rights community seemed most concerned about Bowman, apparently because of his association with Helms. There were favorable reviews on both Wilkins, Thurmond's choice, and Anthony Kennedy. Professor Tribe, for example, pointed out that in a 1980 opinion, in a case called *Beller* v. *Middendorf*, Kennedy had written a balanced analysis of the application of the *Griswold* unenumerated right of privacy doctrine to a Navy regulation prohibiting homosexual activity. Although Kennedy upheld the regulation, he had recognized the contrary argument and had cited Professor Tribe to that effect in the opinion.

Winter, a friend of Kurland's, was described by many as a conservative but no ideologue. Wilkins had been researched by the staff immediately after the Powell resignation, but when Biden got into the meeting with Baker, it was fairly clear that he was not being seriously considered.

Biden explained that, of those remaining, Kennedy and Winter would be the least objectionable. Baker kept bringing the discussion back to Douglas Ginsburg, the candidate about whom we knew the least.

Biden emerged from the meeting to tell his staff, "We've got to find out a lot more about this guy Ginsburg." We explained that there was not much more in the public record, other than his opinions on the Court of Appeals, which seemed fairly innocuous.

Biden and his staff were not the only ones caught by surprise. Terry Eastland, who as press spokesman for the department would be expected to defend the nominee to the media, was not being consulted. Indeed, he was not allowed to review the FBI file or any background materials on Ginsburg.

As one Justice Department staffer pointed out, Reynolds and other conservatives were operating on "tunnel vision," only concerned with getting someone on the court they could trust. Baker on the other hand was looking to someone like Winter, and especially Anthony Kennedy, who might be acceptable to Biden and the Democrats.

Kennedy was becoming the front-runner, but on the Hill, a backlash against him was developing among conservatives. They were especially concerned about his opinion in the *Beller* case.

Conservative Republican Charles Grassley became an active participant in the behind-the-scenes lobbying. He called both Baker and Meese and encouraged fellow conservative Jesse Helms to help him block Anthony Kennedy. Although he was not enthusiastic about Ginsburg, he was adamant against Kennedy. Kennedy had, in Grassley's view, "too expansive a view of the Constitution and the judiciary" and apparently because of his *Beller* opinion Grassley feared that Kennedy supported a constitutional right to privacy.

On the evening of October 28, the three finalists, Ginsburg, Kennedy, and

Wilkins, were brought to the Justice Department for final interviews with Baker and Meese. By the end of the evening, Wilkins had been quickly eliminated. Meese was supporting Ginsburg and Baker was supporting Kennedy. The issue would be taken to the President first thing the next morning.

The conservatives orchestrated a very effective lobbying campaign on behalf of Ginsburg. William French Smith, Reagan's first Attorney General, called the President, and, only minutes before his meeting with Baker and Meese, Reagan took a call from Jesse Helms. Helms made it clear that he and other conservative Senators would oppose Anthony Kennedy. As he explained it to the *Los Angeles Times*, Helms told the President, "I have strong objections to one of the potential nominees . . . and that if he were nominated . . . I would openly oppose him. I said, 'No way, Jose, could I support him.' "

Reagan chose Ginsburg, and later that day Reagan introduced Ginsburg in a defiant press conference. He continued the theme that he had stressed leading up to the Bork vote, attacking the "process." He warned, "I hope we can all resolve not to permit a repetition of the campaign of pressure politics that so recently chilled the judicial selection process." Meese was greeted at the press conference with a round of applause by other Administration officials present. Meese had again dominated the selection process on behalf of conservatives.

The ideological battlelines were again drawn. An unidentified senior Justice Department official described Ginsburg as "one of us." Another Justice official said he offers a "level of certainty."

To Senator Kennedy, Ginsburg was "An ideological clone of Judge Bork . . . A Judge Bork without a paper trail."

Biden on the other hand was more cautious: "I assure the judge he will receive a full and fair hearing in our committee."

Among some liberal staff and representatives of the civil rights community, the mere fact that he was Meese's choice was an indictment. Conversely, on the Right, the fact that Meese and Reynolds were willing to certify him was enough to satisfy them that he would be a predictable vote on the Court.

However, his real views on the critical litmus test of social issues were anything but clear. For example, two law professors at the University of Chicago, his alma mater, painted an unexpected portrait. Prof. Jeffrey Miller, a friend of Ginsburg, explained, "Bork is a pluralist; he believes that the best outcome is that which comes out of the political process. Ginsburg is a libertarian, I believe—someone who believes that the government should stay off the backs of people in all areas of life—the privacy of the bedroom, rights of speech, even offensive speech, rights of the press."

Professor Kurland, who had taught Ginsburg at Chicago, drew the distinction on the basis of their approach to judging: "The difference lies in the fact that" Bork "has been outspoken in his commitment to extensive constitutional revision, with a judicial philosophy of restrained approval of civil rights and liberties." Kurland did not believe that Ginsburg had a judicial philosophy. "He's likely to do what good judges do, which is to rely on precedent, statutes and constitutional provisions, and to take it case by case."

Soon conservatives were expressing concern. *Human Events*, a conservative journal, published a article entitled, "Ginsburg a Mystery to Conservatives." Ironically it expressed the same concern Grassley had with Anthony Kennedy. The article speculated that Ginsburg might embrace a constitutional right to privacy and "thus refuse to vote to uphold curbs on homosexual conduct, pornography, and abortion."

Even some of his staunchest defenders in the Senate were shocked to learn that his wife, a doctor, had, while an intern, performed abortions. Reynolds privately vouched for Ginsburg's position on abortion. However, the severest shock came early the next week when Al Kamen of the *Washington Post* and Nina Totenberg of National Public Radio broke the story that Ginsburg had used marijuana with some frequency while a professor at Harvard Law School and in fact had done so in the presence of students.

Less than a week after he had been nominated, Republican staffers at the Judiciary Committee were furious about the situation and were explicitly blaming Meese and Reynolds for not adequately checking out Ginsburg's personal background. Bolton urged Reynolds to go to his friend and persuade him to withdraw.

By the end of the week, William Bennett, then Secretary of Education and one of the most outspoken conservatives in the Administration, took matters into his own hands. He called the President and asked if it was all right if he called Ginsburg and recommended that he withdraw. Although Reagan publicly defended Ginsburg, the President acquiesced in Bennett's call. Bennett announced what he had done to the press.

By the weekend Baker's staff had taken firm control of the situation, and it was clear that the message to Ginsburg was that he had no choice but to withdraw. Orrin Hatch, convinced that Ginsburg could survive the controversy, tried desperately to get to the President. But, according to Hatch, the Baker staff blocked the call. Obviously, they were not going to have a repeat of the William French Smith and Helms calls, which had gotten them Ginsburg in the first place.

Hatch was still angry about it years later. "They stopped me from getting to the President. That's one of the reasons I got so mad. I had never been stopped before. . . . I knew we could have confirmed Ginsburg. I knew it. I had already talked to a number of Democrats who were wiling to go with us."

Indeed, he was right that some Democrats, Biden included, would have given Ginsburg a fair hearing even on the marijuana allegation. ''There were only two or three Republicans—far right Republicans—who had any problem. . . . Ginsburg would have passed overwhelmingly. I was really offended that they wouldn't even listen to us. . . . They wouldn't let me talk to the President because he would be upset with them too.''

Ginsburg finally withdrew on November 7. Reagan had, within the space of two weeks, suffered two of the greatest humiliations of his seven years as President. Both were, in part, self-inflicted wounds. Clearly, however, the Ginsburg fiasco was the most obvious. The Administration was operating totally on ''tunnel vision'' on the Ginsburg nomination, unconcerned about the nominee's personal background, once they became satisfied he was ''one of us.'' In fact, *Human Events* may have been right; it's not at all clear that Ginsburg was even totally reliable on social issues. He had never really had an explicit discussion with any of the conservatives about his specific views on those issues.

When Ronald Reagan introduced Anthony Kennedy on November 11, the President's tone was completely different. He was unabashedly conciliatory. His statement was devoid of any of the rhetoric of the preceding month on the ''process.'' Instead, the President conceded, ''The experience of the last several months has made all of us a bit wiser. I believe the mood and the time is now right for all Americans in this bicentennial year of the Constitution to join together in a bipartisan effort to fulfill our constitutional obligation of restoring the Supreme Court to full strength.''

He even made a passing rhetorical nod to Biden's point about unenumerated rights, although he cast it in terms of ''unenumerated powers.'' ''Judge Kennedy is what many in recent weeks have referred to as a true conservative—one who believes that our constitutional system is one of enumerated powers—that it is we the people who have granted certain rights to the Government, not the other way around.''

Reagan's words echoed Judge Kennedy's in a speech less than a month earlier: ''[A]s the Framers progressed with their studies, [republican government] came to mean . . . a government that emanates from the people, rather than being a concession to the people from some overarching sovereign.''

Reagan even backed off his defiant statement in New Jersey that he would choose a nominee who his opponents would dislike as much as they dislike Bork: ''Sometimes you make a facetious remark and somebody takes it seriously, and you wish you'd never said it, and that's one for me.''

Still, some in the civil rights coalition felt that the Democrats had a perfect opportunity to delay the nomination until 1988 and perhaps even deny Reagan the chance to fill the slot, in the hopes that the Republicans would lose the White House. Others simply wanted more time to comb Kennedy's record. For example, Morton Halperin, Washington director of the ACLU, wrote to Biden asking more time to review Kennedy's record. Under Halperin's scenario, the Kennedy hearings could not begin until early 1988.

The LCCR agreed and argued strenuously for delay. Eventually they insisted on a meeting with Biden. He was reluctant to delay the hearings into 1988. The staff made it clear they could be prepared with summaries of Anthony Kennedy's full judicial record by the middle of December.

Biden announced that hearings would begin on December 14. The civil rights groups were furious. In a statement released immediately before the hearings, Ralph Neas accused the committee of moving in "haste" and later described the hearings as "ill-timed." Biden was unmoved.

Prof. Walter Dellinger's idea after the Powell resignation, for Biden to seek consultations with Baker, had finally worked. However, by acceding to Biden's request to "advise" on nominees, the Administration put a special burden on Biden to move the process of "consent" as fast as was reasonably prudent. They had chosen the one nominee on their list, who Biden had made clear to Baker was the least objectionable. Reagan had toned down his rhetoric and asked that the Senate proceed in a cooperative and bipartisan manner without delay.

As Biden explained in a November 20 press conference, "As much as I respect the input of the community, liberal or conservative, they do not run the committee; I do."

Kennedy testified for more than eleven hours over two days. His testimony was beyond what the Bork opponents could have legitimately expected.

Kennedy came across in the hearings as a nominee who was truly in the "mold of Powell," the marker Biden had laid down that first weekend before Bork was nominated. Unlike Bork but like Powell, Kennedy espoused no single comprehensive philosophy or ideology about the Constitution and how it should be interpreted. He would approach the job of interpreting the Constitution on a case-by-case basis.

In testimony on December 15, Kennedy insisted that he did not have "a complete cosmology of the Constitution. I do not have an overarching theory, a unitary theory of interpretation. . . . Many of the things we are addressing here are, for me, in the nature of exploration and not in the enunciation of some fixed or immutable ideas."

Much to the consternation of conservatives, Professor Tribe testified on Kennedy's behalf and agreed that the judge had "resisted the temptation to offer dogmatic, definitive answers to the most perplexing puzzles of our constitutional order." Former Solicitor General Erwin Griswold affirmed that it appeared that Kennedy "does not have an agenda."

Kennedy, like Biden, believed in a dynamic Constitution, that the "framers made a covenant with the future." "It would serve no purpose to have a Constitution which simply enacted the status quo." "The whole lesson of our constitutional experience has been that a people can rise above its own injustice; that a people can rise above the inequities that prevail at a particular time.'' And these were not simply recent sentiments expressed in anticipation of confirmation. Kennedy had said in 1980, ''[T]he constitutional system provides a dynamic mechanism for creative achievement in a framework that preserves our values.''

He also apparently believed in the notion of unenumerated rights: ''The Framers had an idea which is central to Western thought. . . . It is central to the idea of the rule of law. That is that there is a zone of liberty, a zone of protection, a line that is drawn where the individual can tell the Government: Beyond this line you may not go.''

Biden could not have said it better himself.

Tribe read this and other statements to mean that Anthony Kennedy believed that there were unenumerated rights deserving of judicial protection. It was a concept similar to Harlan's in his famous dissent in the case of *Poe* v. *Ullman*. For Kennedy, ''The concept of liberty in the due process clause is quite expansive, quite sufficient, to protect the values of privacy that Americans legitimately think are part of their constitutional heritage.''

Most important to Biden, Kennedy explicitly acknowledged that there was a marital right to privacy protected by the Constitution.

Biden was not the only Bork opponent to find satisfaction in Kennedy's answers. Kennedy reassured DeConcini that he embraced, without serious equivocation, the three-tier test for measuring gender discrimination under the Fourteenth Amendment. Leahy and Specter got the answers they were looking for on the First Amendment. Kennedy believed that the Amendment protects all forms of artistic expression, indeed that it applies ''to all ways in which we express ourselves.'' As for domestic dissent Kennedy embraced the ''clear and present danger'' test as well as the *Brandenburg* decision.

There was still room for serious concern about Kennedy from Bork's opponents. On the last day of the hearings, several prominent civil rights leaders, especially from the Hispanic community, expressed concern about Kennedy's views on discrimination on the basis of race or ethnicity. He seemed to toe the Reagan Administration line on remedying race discrimination by judicially vindicating the rights of individual victims, rather than classes of victims.

The LCCR expressed concern in a statement filed with the committee in January. It worried that Kennedy seemed to insist that a prerequisite to a judicial remedy for discrimination was evidence of intentional discrimination. In other words, a court could not act simply on the basis of evidence that some action—for example, some employment practice—has the effect of discriminating against blacks or women. The Leadership Conference was ''troubled'' by his ''constricted approach'' on race and gender cases. However, the LCCR did not oppose the nomination.

Indeed, the only groups in the former anti-Bork coalition to oppose

Kennedy were the National Organization for Women, the Americans for Democratic Action, and the National Gay & Lesbian Task Force.

Hard-line conservatives took a similar position. For example, Senators Grassley and Humphrey were dismayed by Kennedy's acceptance of an unenumerated right to privacy. "Judge Kennedy's readiness to endorse the legitimacy of the inherently subjective and standardless privacy doctrine is troubling," they announced in a joint statement. Senator Humphrey seemed peeved by the fact that Kennedy was reluctant to take a position on the constitutionality of the death penalty, whereas he was prepared to declare his support for the *Griswold* doctrine—both of which would surely come before him on the Court. Obviously, Kennedy's deliberate gesture to Biden and the Bork opponents did not go over well with Bork's most ardent defenders.

Nina Totenberg of National Public Radio probably spoke for many in the civil rights community when she interviewed Biden in a testy interchange, immediately after the hearings concluded on December 16. She pressed Biden with many of the specific questions that the civil rights groups had been asking. Why hadn't Biden sent an investigator out to California? Why didn't he ask for Kennedy's lecture notes from his law school class at McGeorge Law School? Biden explained that his general policy was to follow up on specific allegations, not to engage in general searches.

It didn't satisfy Totenberg. Finally, Biden, in exasperation, conceded that there were some who were "disappointed that" the Kennedy fight "was not as confrontational" as the Bork fight. In the end he felt that "one of the things that holds Judge Kennedy in best stead of all; and that is that no one's fully satisfied with his philosophy or how he would rule which means he in fact is as open-minded as I hoped he would be."

Apparently his colleagues in the Senate agreed. For on February 1, 1988, Judge Kennedy's nomination was reported out of the Judiciary Committee unanimously, and passed the Senate on a 97–0 vote three days later. On February 18, Anthony Kennedy was sworn in as the 105th Justice of the Supreme Court.

As the *New York Times* editorialized, "[T]he Constitution lives. . . . [H]e looks like a justice all Americans, whatever their politics, can respect."

Meanwhile, Robert Bork had not awaited Anthony Kennedy's confirmation to speak out on the way he felt he had been mistreated. In a speech to the American Jewish Committee in Chicago, Bork compared himself to "a man who had been tarred, feathered and ridden out of town on a rail." He was not shy about criticizing the Senate. "The vast majority of Senators have not thought much about constitutional theory."

In retrospect, Bork thought it was a mistake for him to have appeared before the committee and answered questions. "What I did is now being taken as a precedent for future nominees, and I feel that it should not be taken as a precedent."

Biden, Specter, and other members of the committee would indeed look at the Bork experience as an important precedent that should be preserved. Biden told Totenberg as much in his interview with her after the Kennedy hearings, and Specter would present the same case in a lengthy speech to New York University Law School in May 1988.

Unlike many of his allies, Bork was not simply preoccupied with the process but with defending the substance of his own jurisprudence. By contrast, the debate in the conservative intellectual community was increasingly bitter and preoccupied almost entirely with the process rather than with defending Bork's jurisprudence.

For example, *Commentary* magazine, the journal of the American Jewish Committee, in its January 1988 issue, published a scathing attack on the process, written by Suzanne Garment, Leonard Garment's wife. That in turn provoked pages of letters to the editor in response in subsequent issues.

''The War Against Robert Bork'' was to Suzanne Garment and most conservatives just that: a battle that must continue. She did not choose to engage the enemy on Bork's views but on the unfairness of the advertising campaign, the committee, and its reports.

Florence Ruderman, a conservative sociologist from New York City, was appalled by Garment's article. In a letter to me summarizing a response she prepared to Garment, she wrote, ''While Garment admits that there are 'intellectually respectable' questions about Bork and his views, she almost immediately forgets this admission. She discusses none of the issues, considers seriously none of the questions. Only the 'dirty tricks' are relevant; and all questions, all objections, indeed all analyses of Bork's expressed views, except avowedly friendly ones, are dismissed as mendacious, malicious, scurrilous.

''There was, and remains, on the part of neo-conservatism's major figures, a stunning inability to understand the extent of serious reservations about Bork among moderates and even conservatives, and the depth of distrust and hostility toward him among liberals. This is part of the pattern of self-deception and insulation from disagreement and dissent that I believe are now serious problems in this camp. . . .

''Somewhere along the way Bork's supporters stopped thinking. And now they refuse to hear.''

Ruderman had sent a longer version of her piece to *Commentary*, the most prominent journal for neoconservatives. It was rejected ''with a very nasty note.''

Other thoughtful conservatives agree with the thrust of what Ruderman is saying. Bruce Fein, for example, conceded that most of what Garment complains about did not make any difference. ''My own view is all of the brouhaha outside [the committee room], as much as I thought there were misstatements, it didn't make any difference. Bork lost it on television, and that was [where the opponents] carried the intellectual argument on television and that's where the people made [the decision to oppose Bork].''

Ruderman suggests that the Right does not want to face that fact. The easiest approach is to condemn the process. Linda Greenhouse explains that the ''Bork fight, for the Right, is what the Rosenberg case has been for the Left. Because of the emotional component, who-the-villains-are took on a life of its own. The facts [of the original controversy] have been subsumed by a focus on a system that was corrupt.''

To Robert Bork's credit he wanted to deal with the ultimate intellectual debate, and although he has been severely critical of the process, he has focused his intellectual energies on doing what he does best—defending his jurisprudential world view. For sure there have been times when he has seemed to sink into bitter self-pity. Apparently he did so at a Yale Law School alumni meeting, but it is almost forgivable in his case in that it was Robert Bork who had been at the vortex of an incredible and at times excessive national contest.

On January 14, 1988, Bork announced his resignation from the Court of Appeals. As he explained to the President in his letter of resignation, ''For several months various highly vocal groups and individuals systematically misrepresented not only my record and philosophy of judging but, more importantly, the proper function of judges in our constitutional democracy. This was a public campaign of miseducation to which, as a sitting federal judge, I felt I could not publicly respond.''

As he told the *Washington Post* in March 1988, ''The war is not over, and I want to be a part of it.'' The most important salvo that Bork has fired was his book, *The Tempting of America*, published in the fall of 1989.

His book was widely reviewed and became a best-seller. Although the last quarter, which rehashes the process argument, was often criticized in reviews, the first three quarters represented an eloquent and persuasive defense of his jurisprudence.

To Orrin Hatch, ''The Democrats had shot themselves in the foot. They have Kennedy on the Court and now have Bob Bork freed of judicial responsibility traveling all over the country making [his positions] understandable. He's going to have a more dramatic impact than if he were on the Court. Those who were his criticizers will end up being the goats of history.''

If the goal of the Bork battle was to influence the outcome of particular cases on the Supreme Court, almost as if it were a democratically elected body, Hatch is indeed correct. Many Bork proponents, and Bork himself, believed that was all the Bork opponents sought—to maintain a solid majority in favor of *Roe* v. *Wade*. Surely, that is what NARAL and Planned Parenthood wanted. But most members of the Senate meant what they said when they saw this as a battle over the basic elements of Bork's jurisprudence.

As Chris Schroeder pointed out recently, ''If one assumes that Senators are mere surrogates for litigants, caring only whether the judicial nominee will vote for the concerns of influential interest groups, then the Bork–Kennedy progression was an empty victory for Bork opponents.'' Schroeder points out that the Bork inquiry was, however, a serious jurisprudential exercise in that Senators were trying to understand Bork's view of ''originalism'' and against unenumerated rights. ''In voting against Bork, the Senate was voting against hidebound originalism and in favor of unenumerated rights.''

Again the freshmen Senators, who were voting for a Supreme Court nominee for the first time in their lives, helped to set the tone of the Senate debate. They spoke eloquently of the lofty principles of individual rights and liberties and a humane and less mechanistic approach to the law.

Brock Adams of Washington spoke of the need for a ''living legacy of the law'' and his fear that Bork would open old wounds; Kent Conrad of North Dakota was disturbed by Bork's ''narrow vision'' of the Constitution; Wyche Fowler of Georgia said he rejected the single issue analysis in voting against Bork; Harry Reid of Nevada was concerned about Bork's inconsistency in his philosophy and especially his ''confirmation conversions''; and Tim Wirth of Colorado found Bork's writings and decisions ''often to be morally bereft. For all of his legal scholarship and ability to dissect the letter of the law, I am unconvinced that Robert Bork grasps the spirit of our laws.''

None of these five Senators even mentioned *Roe* v. *Wade* in their explanations of why they opposed the nomination. The fact is that the opposition to the nomination in the Senate was not built around *Roe* but around the broader notions of unenumerated rights and not reopening old wounds by undoing the major civil rights decisions of the Warren era.

If the Bork struggle was over any one case, it was *Griswold* v. *Connecticut*. As Professor Tribe explains it, ''*Griswold* was a symbol of the notion of constitutional privacy and for the conception that the rights of individuals and minorities form a backdrop against which the Constitution must be interpreted. These rights are not ceded to them by the Constitution but that it presupposes them and that the Ninth Amendment affirms that vision. And that background of rights includes a number of basic rights of dignity and personality and privacy that are not to be found in the explicit words of the Constitution or its history. It was the referendum on all those things that made the episode so profoundly important.''

In July 1989, almost two years after the struggle had begun, observers waited anxiously for the Court to hand down its first abortion decision since Kennedy joined the Court. The case of *Webster* v. *Reproductive Health Services* presented a perfect opportunity for the Court to reexamine the *Roe* decision in that it involved a Missouri statute that would appear to violate the explicit terms of *Roe*.

There had been great interest in the argument, especially because of the attempt by Solicitor General Charles Fried to sway Kennedy against *Roe*. Practically the first words out of Fried's mouth were addressed to the *Griswold* case: "We are not asking the Court to unravel the fabric of unenumerated and privacy rights which this Court has woven."

Kennedy thought for a moment and then interrupted Fried: "Your position, Mr. Fried, then is that *Griswold* v. *Connecticut* is correct and should be retained?"

Fried was unequivocal: "Exactly, your Honor."

That argument would not have been necessary for Bork. Fried understood that Kennedy embraced *Griswold* and to reverse or modify *Roe*, Kennedy had to do so without disturbing *Griswold*.

Unfortunately, for the Pro-Choice movement, that is exactly what Kennedy did when the Court handed down its opinion in the *Webster* case on July 3, 1989. Although he did not side with Justice Scalia and Rehnquist who wanted to reverse *Roe,* he did join the majority, which substantially narrowed the rule in *Roe*. There is little doubt in the academic community that Kennedy will eventually vote to overrule *Roe*.

However, there is ample evidence that Kennedy does create the fifth vote for preserving *Griswold* as the high-water mark of Warren Court activism. Tribe and Schroeder point to the unusual *Michael H.* case for the proposition that a majority now exists to maintain a reasonably flexible notion of "fundamental rights"—the basic concept of the Warren era that Bork found so abhorrent.

At issue in the *Michael H*. case was an obscure California statute that presumes that a child born of a woman living with her husband is a child of the marriage. In this case the biological father of the child had an affair with a married woman. The biological father seeks custody. He argues that the statute infringes upon the constitutional rights of the child to maintain a relationship with her natural father.

What was striking about this case from Schroeder and Tribe's perspective was not so much the outcome—the court decided the case 5–4 against the biological father—but the debate that erupted between Scalia on the one hand and Brennan on the other as to how to analyze the case. Of greatest significance is where O'Connor and especially Kennedy fit into the debate.

Although he recognized the fundamental-rights analysis, Scalia insisted on the narrowest possible standard of review. The question for Scalia was whether society had traditionally protected the rights of a biological father in the circumstances of the case. As Linda Greenhouse pointed out, "To put the question that way was to answer it: clearly not."

Brennan said the question was whether "parenthood is an interest that historically has received our attention and protection." The answer to that question is clearly yes, based on *Meyer* v. *Nebraska, Pierce* v. *Society of*

Sisters through *Griswold* and even *Roe*. To Brennan the biological father was at least entitled to a hearing.

The center of the controversy was footnote 6 of Scalia's opinion, which O'Connor and Kennedy had joined. In that footnote, Scalia made his Borkian-type argument for the narrowest possible standard for review of fundamental rights. Scalia insisted that the Court should "refer to the most specific level at which a relevant tradition protecting, or denying protection to, the asserted right can be identified."

Specifically citing *Griswold*, O'Connor and Kennedy distanced themselves from the analysis in footnote 6 as sketching "a mode of historical analysis to be used when identifying liberty interests protected by the Due Process Clause of the Fourteenth Amendment that may be somewhat inconsistent with our past decisions in this area. . . . On occasion the Court has characterized relevant traditions protecting asserted rights at levels of generality that might not be 'the most specific' available." O'Connor and Kennedy were not prepared to foreclose "the unanticipated by the prior imposition of a single mode of historical analysis."

Clearly, what bothered O'Connor and Kennedy was that, under Scalia's analysis, you could never find a new unenumerated right. If the Court wished to protect a citizen's right to marry a person of a different race (especially in the South, where laws often prohibited such unions) or to marry while in prison—and it could look to no specific example in which a court had protected such a right—it could not do so. The same could obviously be said for the right to contraceptives, the technology of which did not even exist in "traditional" times, the right of criminals not to be sterilized involuntarily, and in fact all such "new" rights cited by Biden in his San Francisco speech of August 10 (see Chapter 7).

Tribe concedes that the Kennedy concurrence in *Michael H.* is an awfully slender reed. However, it is an important one because it goes to the heart of the controversy in the Bork hearings, and Kennedy seems to take the position for which most Bork opponents would have hoped.

Tribe certainly sees Kennedy as a profound disappointment on civil rights. On two major civil rights decisions in 1989, *Wards Cove Packing* v. *Antonio* and *Patterson* v. *McClean Credit Union*, Kennedy created the 5–4 majority to narrow the 1964 and century-old civil rights statutes. The civil rights community successfully led an effort to overturn the decisions in the Congress in 1991.

Whereas Tribe and others were clearly surprised by Kennedy's votes on civil rights, his position raised serious doubts among civil rights activists. But the Left could hardly have been any more surprised by these decisions than was the Right with Kennedy's vote in the case of *Texas* v. *Johnson* on June 21, 1989. Here Kennedy joined four of his colleagues in the majority and wrote an enthusiastic concurrence, striking down the Texas flag-burning statute. Bork has made it clear that he would have voted to uphold the statute. The *Johnson* case set off a political frenzy to amend the Bill of Rights for the first time in our history.

Clearly Anthony Kennedy is a very conservative justice, siding with Chief Justice Rehnquist and Scalia approximately 80 percent of the time. Terry Eastland writing in *New Republic* in January 1989 described Kennedy as an "80-percenter" who would "vote about 80 percent of the time the way Bork would have." He also predicted that one of the legacies of the Bork struggle is that a 100-percenter—that is, another Bork—is unlikely to be nominated, even by a Bush.

There are those who think that Kennedy may be more conservative than Bork. More conservative or not, there is little doubt that Kennedy is much more cautious than Bork would have been and on some issues, like the flag, more liberal than Bork. Bork made it clear that he would have joined Scalia in reversing *Roe*.

The continuing battle in the Supreme Court is going to be over the 20 percent or even the 5 percent of cases that remain, and Kennedy and O'Connor will be the pivotal votes. Bruce Fein, in an op-ed in the *New York Times* two days after the *Webster* decision, boasted that now the Supreme Court was a " 'Reagan Court' for the next generation in addressing criminal justice, social and civil rights issues. The day when the losers in the legislative process regularly captured success in the Supreme Court are over."

That is hopefully an overstatement. First, the losers in the legislative process never "regularly captured" the Supreme Court. It is true that, for almost fifty years, the Supreme Court was the only refuge against racist or hidebound legislative majorities. Surely, for every success, there were scores of failures, even in the halcyon days of the Warren Court.

Commenting on the controversy over footnote 6 in the *Michael H.* case, Linda Greenhouse questions whether Scalia has found some "magic potion" that makes for the more neutral analysis of what the due process clause of the Fourteenth Amendment means. Clearly, Kennedy and O'Connor are not yet in the Scalia and Rehnquist camp on these questions of when a fundamental right protects Bruce Fein's "loser in the legislative process." As Greenhouse points out, "Scalia and his allies are pressing on, and the future contours of constitutional law may depend a great deal on how they proceed."

So the battle will continue in the Supreme Court over the central issues that animated the Bork struggle, but its real legacy may be outside the judicial system and in the electoral process. The ultimate irony is that, although Bork and his proponents think that they had popular will on their sides for a narrower conception of the role of the Supreme Court and a repudiation of the Warren era, just the opposite was apparently the case. But this is dangerous and complicated waters for either side.

Michael Dukakis never really gained the offensive in the fall of 1988. For most of that time, he was on the defensive on the issue of the Willie Horton furlough for criminals and the pledge of allegiance and all of the powerful cultural issues that underlay the Bork effort a year earlier.

Terry Eastland explained that Dukakis had been "borked," which he defined as follows: "Your opponents take a matter involving a law and criticize you in terms of the policy outcome. You defend yourself by discussing the issue in legal jargon." That is what Eastland believed Ted Kennedy had done to Bork. Eastland smirked, "[W]hat goes around comes around." What the Democrats had done to Bork, the Republicans did to Dukakis by using against him so effectively his legalistic defenses of his positions on the pledge of allegiance and the furlough program.

What happened in this campaign is more subtle and important. The Dukakis campaign completely failed to seize the initiative. Ironically, several prominent players in the Bork opposition, Tom Donilon and Tom Kiley, had key roles in the campaign but could not persuade the Dukakis organization to use what they had learned about the vulnerability of the Reagan, now Bush, coalition.

The abortion issue was never a centerpiece of the Bork opposition yet it was, of course, the most salient manifestation of the personal liberty and privacy issues that drove opposition to Bork. Abortion did briefly become an issue in the first Bush–Dukakis debate. It was the only time Bush was on the defensive throughout the campaign. Yet Dukakis failed to press the attack as the campaign wore on, despite the fact that the Kiley and other polls clearly demonstrated that privacy, and especially Bush's abortion position, split young libertarian voters out of the Reagan–Bush coalition.

A black cab driver pointed out to me in frustration one afternoon after the election, "What I never quite understood is why Dukakis didn't turn to Bush and say, 'Mr. Bush if you're so concerned about the victim of that rapist, why do you think she has to have his child?' "

Tom Donilon's brother Mike was able to use the privacy and abortion issues to great advantage in the Virginia gubernatorial race the next year. As pollster for Virginia's black Lieut. Gov. Doug Wilder, Mike Donilon began to do some preliminary polling to determine whether Wilder could win the governor's mansion; he was discouraged by the declining fortunes of the Democratic Party in the Old Dominion. Since the last gubernatorial election young people were moving dramatically toward the Republican Party.

Despite two consecutive victories for the Democrats in the statehouse, those identifying themselves as Republicans were on the increase. In 1985, 45 percent of voters identified themselves as Democrats as compared to 40 percent as Republicans. By 1989, the numbers had reversed, with 45 percent saying they were Republicans and 39 percent Democrats. Fully 60 percent of people under the age of forty were now Republicans. The Democratic Party in Virginia was a paradigm of what was happening to the party nationwide.

But there were rays of hope. First, the far right was very unpopular in Virginia. Jesse Jackson had a higher favorability rating in Virginia then did Jerry Falwell or Pat Robertson, two Virginia natives. Second, abortion was a powerful issue that could work to Doug Wilder's advantage. Wilder's opponent, Marshall Coleman, took a doctrinaire Pro-Life position. Wilder espoused a moderate Pro-Choice position: He supported a woman's right to choose, but he also supported the requirement that parents consent to their underage daughter's abortion. Wilder's likely opponent opposed abortion even in cases of rape or incest.

In June, most polls showed Wilder behind by 10 points. Pro-Choice activists were concerned about his position on parental consent, and even after the *Webster* decision, when NARAL decided to make abortion an issue in several upcoming races, they had doubts about the Wilder race. Wilder was seen as a loser.

In Donilon's polls Virginians preferred Wilder's position on abortion to Coleman's by 65 percent to 25 percent. At the end of the poll, when voters learned of the two positions and then were asked how they voted, "Wilder went from 10 points down to 10 points up. It became the model for the campaign," Donilon explained.

After the *Webster* decision, the issue became even more salient. However, Wilder and his media strategists insisted upon using their own version of the message. Wilder wanted to put the emphasis on government and politicians interfering with a woman's right to choose. It was not going to be a classical liberal-versus-conservative definition of the issue.

As Donilon explained it, "What affected things in the Bork fight was this suppression of the standard liberal rhetoric, and it became couched in this libertarian language." The thrust of Wilder's message would be directed at meddlesome government and politicians. The ad also inadvertently picked up on another of the powerful Bork-campaign messages: Americans do not want to go backward.

The thirty-second television spot aired statewide: "On the issue of abortion, Marshall Coleman wants to take away your right to choose and give it to the politicians. He wants to go back to outlawing abortion, even in cases of rape and incest. Doug Wilder believes the government shouldn't interfere in your right to choose. He wants to keep the politicians out of your personal life. Don't let Marshall Coleman take us back. To keep Virginia moving forward, Doug Wilder is the clear choice."

As soon as the ad began to move, there were dramatic changes in Wilder's fortunes. Donilon's poll saw striking movement in all voters under forty, especially women. Soon NARAL was in the race with $400,000 of advertising money and organizers. According to Kate Michelman, NARAL contacted 200,000 voters in northern Virginia on Wilder's behalf.

Donilon saw the same thing as Michelman did in the Wilder race. As in the Bork fight, women under forty and blacks joined in the pursuit of the progressive agenda. Michelman looks back on the Bork fight with fondness and enthusiasm: "Bork forced us together and made us recognize how foolish it was for us to be divided as we had been in the past." In the Wilder race there was little formal coordination between blacks and women, as Althea Simmons and Kate Michelman had had in the Bork fight, but the same phenomenon was happening in neighborhoods throughout the state. In the age of television, that is a powerfully hopeful sign for the progressive agenda.

On September 24, 1988, Bork addressed the convention of the Concerned Women for America. He spoke of his battle in purely generational terms: "My nomination was in fact simply one battle, in a long running war for control of our liberal culture. That war is in turn part of a larger struggle for control of our politics and our culture at large. We are witnessing a revival on the national scene of the radical politics that savaged our universities in the late 1960s. We had thought the battles of the 60s generation was [sic] decisively won with the elections of 1980 and 1984; we were wrong. They are back and stronger and more determined than ever. . . . [In the battle over my nomination] they knew they were both in reality and perhaps more importantly, symbolically, they were facing a reversal of the trend that started with Earl Warren's court."

The Bork battle was not a rehash of the antiwar movement or of the excesses of the drug culture, but Bork was right. It was a referendum on the Warren Court, and it was clearly generational. As Richard Lacayo remarked in his article in *Time* magazine immediately after Bork was nominated, "All at once the political passions of three decades seemed to converge on a single empty chair."

Donilon, as Caddell's employee at the time of the Bork fight, had seen the dramatic generational divide in the polling numbers on Bork as young voters, especially women, learned of his opinions on privacy. He saw it again with Wilder. Once the abortion ad with its strongly libertarian message was on the airwaves, "you could lose voters over forty by 65 percent–35 percent and still win. It's purely generational."

Donilon also saw a fairly consistent philosophical thread through the Bork and Wilder struggles, and it was not purely generational. "The Reagan coalition is made up of fundamentalists and individualists. . . . The coalition that took Reagan from being this wacko to being this colossus" was made up significantly of individualists. "[T]hey say pull yourself up by the bootstraps; give us a shot at making some money; let this economic engine run."

The fundamentalists "want to tell you how to run your life"—what prayers you have to say, what books and magazines you can read, what living relationship you can have with friends and loved ones, whether you can use contraceptives and if you're a woman whether you can have an abortion.

There has always been, however, a "significant divide" in the coalition, because the individualists also believe government should ''stay out of my life.'' ''In the Bork fight the question was 'Are you going to stay out of my life or not?' ''

These individualists were voters under forty, and they were a powerful element of the Reagan coalition. In the Bork fight, they abandoned Reagan and Bork, and in the 1989 gubernatorial election in Virginia they abandoned Marshall Coleman for Doug Wilder. In so doing they elected the first black governor in our history and in a conservative Southern state at that.

On October 2, 1987, a little over a week after Biden withdrew from the presidential race, conservative columnist Charles Krauthammer wrote a column in the *Washington Post* celebrating the demise of Biden and Hart and Pat Caddell, who had polled for both of them. Most important Krauthammer relished the demise of ''generational politics'' which he said both espoused. He found it ''empty'' and ''unimportant.'' However, with the end of his presidential campaign, Biden was finally able to make the generational message substantive and win a stunning victory by dividing the Reagan coalition along generational lines. In so doing he denied for the time being the fundamentalist wing of the coalition their most prized goal, iron control of the Supreme Court.

As Howard Fineman, chief political reporter for *Newsweek*, remarked, it would indeed be ironic if it were generational politics that doomed Bork: ''[T]he Biden campaign founders and yet the Democrats connected with America on a generational message and Biden was the chair'' of the committee that did it.

Fineman is writing a book about the cadre of Republican strategists who have dominated Republican presidential politics since the late 1970s. A critical element of their victory strategy has been Baby Boomers.

''In the sixties there were two conflicting impulses. One of them was 'do your own thing' and the other was 'love is all you need.' Those things are fundamentally contradictory. And since this is America, politicians were shrewd enough to force people to make the choice between the two.

''Our generation is more likely to choose 'do your own thing'.''

Fineman agrees with Donilon that it was this fierce libertarian streak, especially as it related to the economy, that was the engine of the Reagan coalition. His extensive interviews with Republican operators tell the story of clever orchestration of young voters:

''Conservative hustlers are brilliant at manipulating the symbols of our generation, music, protests, literature and feelings of anti-ness. They've emphasized that and wedded it to the old Republican business notions of free enterprise. The fact that it doesn't fit so well is evoked by Bork's authoritarian moralism.''

However, Republican strategists are also clever enough to understand how fragile their coalition is: ''A lot of Republican strategists, even the ones adept at sucking up to the conservative social issue groups, know that they've got to stay on the libertarian side of that argument if they are going to keep the coalition together. That's why the abortion issue is so powerful and why you now have everybody from George Bush . . . to Dan Quayle saying the party is big enough to accommodate these interests.''

As Fineman describes it, Republican strategists should not relish another Bork fight. ''It reminds voters, baby boomers in particular, why there are things that they don't like about the Republican Party.''

To Patrick McGuigan the Bork fight is a tremendous missed opportunity and painfully sad memory, ''There are no words to express the sadness I felt personally for Judge Bork and his family at the end. The pain lingers in my heart more than a year later, as I close this text [of his book on the subject]. When I finally, intellectually accepted the inevitable before the final vote, I wept not only for Judge Bork, his family, his friends, his supporters; not only for myself and my colleagues in the cause of judicial reform—not only for these, but also for my country.

''Many of us are weeping still.''

Two years after the Bork defeat, the pain was still real as he spoke of those who bore real responsibility for the defeat. When in eight years did Ronald Reagan ever really put his presidency on the line for the social issues about which McGuigan and his colleagues cared so deeply? McGuigan looked away when asked the question and in a barely audible voice conceded, ''Maybe never.''

It has always been the case in the Reagan coalition. In the end it is the reason Ronald Reagan could never do what Andrew Jackson and Franklin Roosevelt did to get their first choices onto the Supreme Court. Unlike Jackson and Roosevelt, Ronald Reagan had to settle for ''80-percenters,'' and unless Robert Bork succeeds in his ''battle for the legal culture,'' so will George Bush and any Republican who succeeds him.

Kate Michelman was still exultant about the Bork battle two years later, despite Kennedy's votes. She not only still had hope for Anthony Kennedy on the Supreme Court, but she saw NARAL and the progressive coalition finally winning the electoral battles over these issues in the Wilder race and other contests.

However, as long as conservative Republicans control the White House and can set the national agenda and especially choose the members of the Supreme Court, many of these victories, especially the nomination battles are truly ephemeral. When reminded of that fact, Michelman got uncharacteristically somber and like McGuigan seems to get lost in her thoughts. After a short silence she agreed: ''It will not change until we elect a progressive President.''

Building a winning electoral coalition to regain the White House may indeed be as difficult for the Left as it is for a conservative President to nominate a "100-percenter" without jeopardizing the old Reagan coalition. Traditionally progressives have stood for an affirmative role for government, yet the pivotal libertarians are by definition antigovernment. At the center of the struggle are young voters who distrust government control of their personal lives and their personal fortunes. Whichever side gains their allegiance will gain the prize, the future of our jurisprudence, and maybe much more.

So the battle over the Bork nomination and the meaning of "liberty" in America continues. The final chapter has not been written. Hopefully, it never will.

EPILOGUE

MATTERS OF CHARACTER

ON JULY 20, 1990, Justice William Brennan, the intellectual architect of the liberal majority for over thirty years, resigned. President Bush nominated for his successor David H. Souter, a federal Appeals Court judge, who had been a state supreme court justice and attorney general for New Hampshire.

In Souter, Bush had chosen an obscure New Hampshire judge who—he was told by conservative chief of staff John Sununu—was safe on right-wing issues. He was, as Terry Eastland had predicted, an "80 percenter." He pursued the same cautious approach in his hearing as Kennedy had two years earlier—avoiding the pitfalls of Bork's testimony and clearly distancing himself from the Borkian approach to fundamental and unenumerated rights.

Biden focused on many of the same issues in the Souter nomination hearings as he had with Bork and Kennedy. At one critical point, Biden asked Souter directly about *Michael H.* and Scalia's footnote 6. Would the new justice side with the narrow view of Rehnquist and Scalia or would he side with the more generous approach of Kennedy and O'Connor? Souter was unequivocal. He "could not accept" the narrow view. "[W]e cannot, as a matter of definition at the beginning of our inquiry, narrow the acceptable evidence to the most narrow evidence possible. . . ." Once he gave that answer, I recommended to Biden that he support the nomination.

Biden had other concerns with Souter. Souter insisted that it was an "open question" whether *unmarried* persons have any fundamental right to privacy. But like Anthony Kennedy, and unlike Bork, he did recognize that there are unenumerated fundamental rights that are constitutionally enforceable, and he recognized a marital right to privacy. Biden supported the nomination.

With the exception of NARAL and a few other feminist groups, which focused entirely upon the *Roe* question, the civil rights coalition remained largely moot. Ultimately they opposed the nomination but did no grass roots organizing. Michelman, outraged by the *Webster* decision, fought a losing battle to make Souter's nonposition on *Roe* an issue. The nomination passed overwhelmingly.

By 1990 the White House had a new political team to handle nominations. Ken Duberstein and A. B. Culvahouse had both left the White House to pursue careers in the private sector. Both were recruited as outside advisers and strategists. Duberstein's basic strategy was to encourage Souter to be responsive but not expansive in the hearings. Culvahouse and Duberstein persuaded Souter to do what Bork refused to consider, extensive murder boards before the hearings. In the end Souter revealed just enough to distance himself from Bork. He was labeled by one reporter as the "stealth" nominee, with no past record for the committee to dissect and a strategy in the hearings to reveal as little as possible in his answers.

Within a few days of Souter's nomination, it was clear that something fundamental had changed in the process. By carefully choosing one of Eastland's 80-percenters and by using the Duberstein stealth strategy, the Administration made it tempting for opponents to focus on character. As soon as the press began sniffing around Souter's native New Hampshire, rumors began to spread, mostly by skeptical reporters, that there was something "strange" about a man who lived a lonely ascetic existence on a quiet road with his mother.

Two days after his nomination, Souter told the wily Duberstein that he wanted to go back to New Hampshire. Duberstein was naturally suspicious. He didn't know Souter all that well.

"David, why do you want to go right now? We have a lot of prep work to do."

"I don't have any clean clothes." Clearly anxious, Souter almost pleaded, "I've just got to get home."

This just piqued Duberstein's concern. "Why? What's the matter?"

"I just didn't realize, when I agreed to this, that the national media would be snooping around my house, looking in the windows."

Now Duberstein was really worried. "What's inside your windows?"

The private, shy Souter spoke haltingly: "I'm not very neat. I just don't want them taking pictures through my window."

Duberstein was alarmed. He pressed Souter to explain. Finally, the judge said, "A couple of weeks ago I was in Boston. Some friends of mine suggested I get this book, and I bought it, and I think it might be sitting on a table right inside my window."

Duberstein, expecting the worst, was almost afraid to ask: "What's the book about? What's its name?"

Souter gazed at Duberstein with a sheepish smile. "*The Tempting of America* by Robert Bork—you know, his book about his experience."

Limp with relief, Duberstein laughed. "Well, good! Just promise me one thing. You won't read that book until this is all over."

It's easy now, over a year later, to chuckle about the incident, but in the summer of 1991 the role of character in the process of confirming Supreme

Court nominees would no longer be a laughing matter for Duberstein, his charges, or for anyone for that matter.

On June 27, 1991, Justice Thurgood Marshall, the last of the unreconstructed liberals to be nominated by a Democratic President (Lyndon Johnson), resigned. Bush nominated Court of Appeals judge Clarence Thomas. Thomas, probably the most prominent black conservative, had served as Reagan's chairman of the Equal Employment Opportunities Commission. He had been appointed to the Court of Appeals for the District of Columbia barely a year before.

Thomas presented Biden and his anti-Bork allies, as well as Bork partisans, with a unique challenge. First, as a black conservative he immediately split the civil rights coalition. Older and moderate black leaders were willing to give Thomas the benefit of the doubt; others could not forgive his anticivil rights regime as chair of the EEOC.

Second, Thomas was no stealth nominee. He had written extensively on jurisprudential issues. He specifically presented Biden with a real dilemma. At the time he was nominated, both sides believed he fully embraced the notion of unenumerated rights and natural law. In a sense, though, he was Laurence Tribe's *and* Robert Bork's worst nightmare. In Thomas's words, "The best defense of limited government, of the separation of powers, and of the judicial restraint that flows from the commitment to limited government, is the higher law political philosophy of the Founding Fathers." But his view of natural law was very different from Biden's. He apparently saw it as the rationale for achieving an aggressive probusiness, antiregulation conservative agenda.

Some on the Right were still suspicious. In a conservative law journal, Thomas explicitly acknowledged Biden's argument in the Bork fight and concluded in almost Bidenesque language, "These rights are inalienable ones, given to man by his Creator, and did not simply come from a piece of paper." Some of Robert Bork's allies were not happy. Indeed, staunch conservative scholar Bruce Fein publicly acknowledged as much. Other conservatives said the same to me privately.

The disarray on the intellectual Right gave Biden cold comfort. What did Thomas really mean by his natural rights jurisprudence? He cited approvingly an article by another conservative using natural rights philosophy to justify reversing *Roe* v. *Wade*. Biden knew there were other conservatives who argued that natural rights reasoning should also be used to strike down economic regulation—in other words, a return to the jurisprudence of the "nine old men" who blocked the New Deal. In fairness, Bork had been just as forthright in his opposition to conservative, as well as liberal, natural rights advocates.

Biden decided to spend most of the summer studying Thomas's extensive writings, especially his forays into natural law. He also familiarized himself with the writings of prominent conservatives and libertarians on the virtues of natural-rights thinking in defense of greater economic liberty—writers like Steven Macedo of Harvard and Richard Epstein of the University of Chicago. Epstein believes that many of our welfare, social security, zoning, minimum-wage, and price-control laws are constitutionally suspect. He believes that they violate the Fifth Amendment's prohibition against taking private property "without just compensation." Thomas had said in 1987 that he "found attractive" Macedo's defense of "an activist Supreme Court, which would strike down laws restricting property rights."

While Biden was pursuing these questions of jurisprudential principle on the side porch of his home in Wilmington with teams of scholars and experts, the political maneuvering that had characterized the Bork fight resumed back in Washington.

On the Left, especially among feminists, the frustration with the nomination process was cresting. Although Michelman, for example, had acquiesced to Biden's strategy in the Bork fight to make the issue privacy and not abortion, by the time of the Souter nomination, she insisted upon framing the issue around the *Roe* case. After the *Webster* decision, NARAL and other feminist groups felt they could no longer work with the consensus-building approach of the Bork fight.

In May 1991, feminists suffered another large defeat in the case of *Rust* v. *Sullivan*. In that case the Supreme Court resisted a constitutional challenge to federal regulations restricting federal funding for abortion counseling. Souter joined Kennedy, White, Scalia, and Rehnquist in the Pro-Life decision. Although the Court did not directly address the constitutional issue underlying *Roe*, most feminists interpreted Souter's vote as meaning that a majority now existed to overturn *Roe*.

Almost immediately after Thomas was named, NARAL and NOW announced opposition. Feminist Florence Kennedy promised to "bork" Thomas. Of course, two important ingredients to a successful anti-Thomas strategy were missing. The mainline civil rights organizations, especially the NAACP and Neas's LCCR, were to withhold their decision to oppose the nomination until later in the summer. The Senate leadership, especially Biden and Ted Kennedy, had expressed no intention to oppose the nominee. The delay reopened the natural strains between the women's movement and the civil rights activists so skillfully bridged by Michelman and Simmons in the Bork fight.

The Right was taking no chances. Using the "borking" comment as a pretext, an organization called the Conservative Victory Committee announced an advertisement campaign designed to "neutralize" the opposition. Brent Bozell, its executive director, previewed for the press television ads containing personal attacks on Kennedy, Biden, and Alan Cranston. Bozell, a former top official of the National Conservative Political Action Committee, which had pioneered "attack" ads a decade earlier, worked with other conservative media experts who had made the Willie Horton ad in the 1988 presidential campaign. According to Bozell, "We learned a lesson in the Bork fight. If this is the way the game is to be played, it's important for conservatives not to sit back."

Sen. John Danforth, who was to become Thomas's chief patron in the Senate, condemned the ads as "sleazy." Eventually Bush's chief of staff John Sununu, his ambassador to the Right, and Bush himself asked Bozell to withdraw the ads. Bozell refused. By then it did not matter. As with the Gregory Peck ads, the national media attention achieved the desired result.

While Biden was immersing himself in natural law jurisprudence, the White House was building a case for Clarence Thomas that had nothing to do with his views but with his background, his character. It came to be known as the Pin Point Strategy, epitomized by the profile of Thomas in the *Washington Post* on the eve of the hearings. The thrust of the piece was Thomas's rise to the Supreme Court from poverty in the tiny community of Pin Point, near Savannah, Georgia.

Thomas's opening statement at the hearings on September 10 was an eloquent handwritten biography emphasizing his personal values and upbringing. It immediately prompted congratulatory comments from Republicans and Democrats alike. Biden made it clear as he opened his questioning that he saw Thomas's views, not his character, as the question for the hearings. Biden was prepared to "stipulate" to Thomas's character. He wanted to keep the focus on the direction President Bush's nominee would take the Court. Biden proceeded to cross-examine Thomas carefully on his prior expressions of support for the notions of "economic liberty" founded in natural law.

Thomas had been advised by Duberstein and his other handlers to follow three simple rules in his appearance before the committee: (1) stress his humble roots; (2) don't engage Senators in ideological debate; and (3) stonewall on abortion. At first, Thomas seemed stunned by Biden's careful questioning, even though Biden had made his concerns known in a lengthy op-ed in the *Post* the previous weekend. Thomas soon recovered and proceeded to disown his positions on this and other controversial conservative positions that had enamored him with the Right. One prominent conservative told columnists Evans and Novak, "I'm sick, my man is being confirmed, but he did not stand tall."

As frustrating as it was for conservatives to watch "their man" equivocate, the strategy worked. Furthermore, it was even more frustrating for Thomas skeptics and opponents. Biden was unable to articulate the natural law-economic rights argument in a way that average Americans could understand, as he had the privacy argument in the Bork case. By the time the hearings were over, many reporters seemed to agree with one *New York Times* reporter that Biden's natural rights concerns were over "esoterica."

It was far from irrelevant, for the economics rights agenda was an important new front the Right was intending to open in the Supreme Court and elsewhere in policy debates in Washington. Gordon Crovitz, the prominent conservative editorial writer for *Wall Street Journal,* admitted as much in a column aptly entitled "Biden's Nightmare." If the rest of the press did not recognize it, Crovitz admitted with satisfaction that Biden was "right to be worried."*

Although Thomas backed off his more controversial positions and deliberately distanced himself from Bork, Biden became increasingly angered by Thomas's coyness. Biden never asked Thomas directly about *Roe*, but Thomas deliberately frustrated Biden as he pursued other important lines of questions.

One favorite tactic—as when asked a question by Biden about a particular area of the law—was for Thomas simply to restate the current position of the Court:

> CHAIRMAN: You are going to take a philosophy to that Court with you, . . . and you are not limited . . . from reaching a conclusion different than that which the Court has reached thus far. . . .
>
> THOMAS: Well, I understand that, Mr. Chairman, but what I have attempted to do is to not agree or disagree with existing cases.
>
> CHAIRMAN: You are doing very well at that.
>
> THOMAS: The point that I am making or I have tried to make is that I do not approach these cases with any desire to change them, and I have tried to indicate that, to the extent that individuals feel, well, I am foreclosed from a—
>
> CHAIRMAN: If you had a desire to change it, would you tell us?
>
> THOMAS: I don't think so.

Liberal Democrats Metzenbaum and Leahy pursued the strategy suggested by NARAL and the other feminist groups, pressing Thomas time and again on how he would rule on *Roe*. Knowing full well that he would not answer the question, the Senators could justify a "no" vote simply on the basis of that refusal. The tactic contributed to cynicism in the press about the process. One *New York Times* reporter lamented that "silly trick questions were constructed, long-winded political speeches were delivered—all to score cheap points and maybe make the evening news." However, some of his answers were truly astonishing. For example, he told Leahy, in the most effective cross-examination on the *Roe* matter, that he could not "remember

* On November 19 after Judge Thomas was confirmed, the Supreme Court agreed to hear an important "takings" clause case involving environmental regulation. Although the *Washington Post*, in reporting the Supreme Court action, didn't even mention that it was an issue in the Thomas hearings, Crovitz wrote again in the *Wall Street Journal* to remind Biden he had lost on that issue and pointing out other areas where the Right was pursuing the economic libertarianism. A few weeks later, Vice President Quayle acknowledged that he intended to use the same theory to pursue his probusiness agenda at the controversial Competitiveness Council.

engaging in . . . discussions'' of the *Roe* case in law school and, indeed, he could never recall taking a position on *Roe* in private discussions during or after law school.

Feminists and other Bork opponents were angered by the failure of their strategy. They turned on their champions on the committee and the process the following week, when they appeared to testify. Holding up an issue of *Newsweek* magazine, which chided the committee for allowing the process to become a ''charade'' since the successful Bork encounter, Ellie Smeal pointed accusingly at Biden and the committee. ''You have given the benefit of the doubt to people, who, in their record and in their writings, have stood opposed. I plead with you: Do not give the benefit of the doubt yet again to a person whose record is replete with opposition to those very issues you stand for yourselves.'' It was not clear precisely what Smeal wanted other than simply to vote against every nominee who did not pledge allegiance to *Roe*. Biden reminded Smeal that she had testified in favor of Justice O'Connor even though O'Connor had stated that personally she opposed abortion. Even Thomas did not say that.

Biden was clearly troubled by the process, however, and did make it clear that he saw a new consensus emerging that the committee should give less latitude to a nominee who simply gave generalizations. Whereas Biden was troubled, Smeal and her allies were angry; ''basically there is a sense of hopelessness that is setting into the opposition.''

Harriet Grant is the tough, aggressive chief investigator for the Senate Judiciary Committee. On September 12, two days after the hearings began, a member of Senator Metzenbaum's staff called to tell her that a woman who had been sexually harassed by Thomas wanted to come forward to the committee. Grant told him to have the woman call her.

In two lengthy phone conversations that day, Prof. Anita Hill described her now famous allegations. Hill asked that the allegations be kept confidential and that Thomas not even be told. She wanted to ''remove responsibility'' and ''take it out of [her] hands.'' Grant explained that the committee would respect her wishes for confidentiality. But it was impossible to investigate the matter further without being able to confront Thomas or to seek corroboration without being able to use Hill's name.

On September 19, a week later, Hill called Grant to say that she wanted all committee members to know about her concerns, and she would allow her name to be used with the committee. Grant explained that it was committee policy not to pass on an allegation of this nature to the committee without giving the nominee an opportunity to respond. Furthermore, it was also committee procedure in this circumstance to ask the FBI to do a preliminary interview, especially when the witness is not close by. Hill taught law at the University of Oklahoma in Tulsa.

Hill was reluctant. She spoke with Grant several times in the next few days continuing to express her reluctance to be interviewed by the FBI. Finally, on September 23 she decided to draft and fax to the staff a personal statement and then would proceed with an FBI interview. Grant received the statement that afternoon and immediately instructed the FBI to interview Hill and confront Thomas. Both interviews took place that day.

The committee was scheduled to vote on the nomination on September 26. Biden immediately told Thurmond about the charges against Thomas and recommended that he brief the Republicans. Biden, either personally or through committee staff director Jeff Peck, orally briefed every Democratic member, allowing them to read the FBI report and Hill's statement. Even though Hill had not explicitly authorized it, Biden insisted that he and Thurmond brief the Senate leadership, George Mitchell and Robert Dole.

Under committee rules any Senator can automatically ask for a one week holdover on any matter on the agenda of the committee. Paul Simon called Hill and asked her if it would be possible to reveal her name. She insisted on her anonymity, although she would be prepared to allow the allegations to be distributed, without her name, to Senators outside the committee. Simon explained that that would be both unfair and tantamount to disclosing the name, since the press would eventually ferret it out. Simon told Biden of his conversation with Hill before the committee vote.

Clearly a ''holdover'' would ultimately have led to the disclosure of her name; the press would have pressured the committee and its staff relentlessly to find out what last-minute allegation would delay the otherwise inevitable vote. No Senator asked for a delay.

The vote was a surprising 7–7 tie. Every Republican, including Specter, voted for Thomas and every Democrat except DeConcini voted against. Biden was the last to announce his vote. He had been troubled until the very end about opposing Thomas. Thomas had answered many of Biden's questions and had, like Souter and Kennedy before him, clearly distanced himself from Bork.

Biden told me the night before the vote he was not willing to call Thomas a liar. It was not so much what Thomas did say as what he would not say. Biden was angered by the excessive ''handling'' and coaching that had gone on with Thomas and the Administration's ''hide the ball'' game. It was time to move the process to a new principled standard of opposition, based on the reluctance of the Administration and the nominees to engage the committee in revealing debate as had Bork.

When he announced his vote the next day, Biden cited as indicative of Thomas's general approach to the hearings his dialogue with Thomas, in which the judge acknowledged that he wouldn't have told Biden if he had had an agenda to change a line of cases. ''Perhaps Judge Thomas was advised that this approach was a sound political strategy designed to ensure confirmation. If that is the case, it is not a strategy I am prepared to accept.'' Biden repeated his now familiar caveat, ''I have no doubt about his character, credentials, competence or credibility.'' It was about his judicial philosophy—a matter of principle.

Biden and Ron Klain, my successor as chief counsel, felt that, with Biden voting against and with a 7–7 tie, they might in the end get as many as forty votes against the nominee. Klain told me the day of the vote that he thought that, although Thomas would win, the Thomas vote was like the Rehnquist fight in 1986. Thirty-three Senators voted against Rehnquist, the most in history for a successful nominee, laying the groundwork for the Bork fight in that it warned anyone in the Administration who was willing to listen that the Senate was moving toward a higher level of scrutiny on nominees. Klain felt that, with forty no votes, Biden could lay down a new marker for an even higher level of scrutiny than those for Bork, Kennedy, Souter, and now Thomas, insisting upon more candor from the nominees and the Administration. With that kind of vote, Biden and Senate Majority Leader Mitchell could go to Bush, as Biden had with Reagan through Howard Baker, and engage in prenomination consultations on nominees. They might be able to establish some ground rules on greater candor in the hearings and perhaps even agree on more moderate nominees.

Biden and Klain were not going to get the fight over principle they sought but something altogether different, something over which they would have little, if any, control. The disappointment and ''hopelessness'' Smeal expressed masked a deeper paranoia and suspicion, which exploded a week later with the public disclosure of the Hill allegations and the committee's handling of them.

Tim Phelps, a reporter for *Newsday* who claims he had heard allegations about Thomas's sexual harassment for months, broke the essence of the Hill allegations on Saturday, October 5. Clearly, someone who had seen Hill's statement, possibly even someone off the committee to whom she had shown it, revealed the contents to Phelps. One unnamed member of the committee told Phelps he thought it would affect the vote.

The next morning Nina Totenberg of NPR, who had brought down Ginsburg on similar personal allegations, broke the whole story in a lengthy interview with Hill. Totenberg quoted directly from the statement.

As far as Totenberg was concerned, the real culprit was Biden. She had written in the *Harvard Law Review* in 1988 that the ''Judiciary Committee was a disaster waiting to happen. They don't investigate serious charges.'' Many on the Left, especially the feminist Left, never cared much for Biden's principled attack on nominees. The investigation of character had worked so much more swiftly and effectively with Ginsburg.

Totenberg simply saw Biden as a sexist. ''Biden simply never got it—never understood that sexual harassment was a serious charge.''

She drove the point home that Sunday in her interview: ''Several Senators contacted by NPR say they are troubled by the Hill allegations and the long delay in investigating them by Chairman Biden.'' She then tried to draw Sen. Paul Simon of Illinois into the fight:

> SIMON: I did not know about it until after our vote, and—and I heard about it and then asked to see it.
>
> TOTENBERG: Do you know why nobody on the committee knew about it, or many on the committee didn't know about . . .
>
> SIMON: I think . . .
>
> TOTENBERG: . . . until after the vote?
>
> SIMON: I think that question you'd have to direct to the chairman.
>
> TOTENBERG: Are you mad?
>
> SIMON: No, it's—it's—it's a judgment call.

Totenberg did quote a ''Biden staff assistant'' that all the committee members had been told. Indeed, Simon admitted several days later that he had misspoken and that, not only had Biden shown him the Hill statement before the vote, but that he had spoken to Hill before the vote.

However, the damage had been done. The committee, led by Biden, had ''covered up'' a credible allegation of sexual harassment. As Smeal said the next day, ''It's back to what did they know and when did they know it. . . . It is shocking that he was not asked questions about it, at least.'' Never mind that Judy Lichtman, the most sophisticated feminist litigator in the city, told Biden in a private meeting after the story broke that he had handled Hill's request for confidentiality correctly.

Totenberg was not the only one who believed that Biden, like the rest of the ''sexist'' Senate, simply didn't ''get it'' about sexual harassment. Enter Biden's nemesis, of Kinnock fame, Maureen Dowd of the *New York Times*.

On Tuesday, in a front page article entitled ''THE SENATE AND SEXISM; Panel's Handling of Harassment Allegation Renews Questions About an All-Male Club,'' she explained that the Hill allegations and how they were handled ''offered a rare look into the mechanics of power and decision-making in Washington, a city where men have always made the rules and the Senate remains an overwhelmingly male club.''

Quoting activists like Ann Lewis, the issue was simply one of male insensitivity. According to Lewis the case ''had sent 'an electric current of anger through women'.'' As far as Dowd and the women she quoted were concerned, it was Biden and the ''old boys network'' in the Senate.

The problem was that the Senate had entered a ''unanimous consent'' decree ordering the vote on Thomas for 6:00 P.M. that evening. That meant that any single member of the Senate could object to a delay. Simon and other members of the committee now wanted a delay. Other members of the Senate were angered that they were not told. Hill held a press conference in

Oklahoma suggesting that Biden had mishandled the investigation. She apparently thought the Metzenbaum staffer who first relayed her allegation to Harriet Grant worked for Biden and was puzzled by the delay in the investigation.

It was clear that the White House would only agree to a delay in the vote if Democrats, who had announced for Thomas, threatened to change their vote without a delay. Working behind the scenes, Mitchell changed enough Democratic votes to force a delay. By 6:00 P.M. Minority Leader Robert Dole came to the floor, conceding that the nomination was at risk without a delay. A one-week delay was arranged.

John Danforth was furious and engaged in a tense dialogue with Biden on the floor that evening. Danforth had seen victory in his grasp, and he turned to the Democratic staff on the floor and looked accusingly at them, charging that the victory had been taken from him by the leak. Biden reluctantly agreed to proceed with the public hearing which would be, he said, "very difficult." Even he could not imagine how difficult.

It is impossible in this space to capture what happened in the next week. Democrats, traumatized by the charges of sexism and alleged mishandling of the investigation, forged ahead with a public proceeding that ought to have been held in private. Republicans, infuriated by the last-minute leak, set out to discredit Hill. Hill was a powerful, eloquent, and persuasive witness. For the feminists it was fourteen men against one woman. For Thomas and the Administration, it was fourteen white men against one black man, a "high-tech lynching." The committee lost both fights.

In the end the feminists who cheered Hill on made a terrible miscalculation. According to a national poll by the *New York Times* immediately after the hearings, most women sided with Thomas, not Hill. Jill Abramson, a savvy reporter covering the hearings for the *Wall Street Journal*, captures the complex currents of race and gender that the Administration politicians mastered and the rest of the Washington establishment totally misunderstood. "The morning after Hill testified, I was certain that Thomas was dead. And most of the national press at the press table with me in the hearing room agreed. I left the Senate at the lunch break and went to a cafeteria. As I paid for my lunch, I asked the cashier, a black woman, what she thought of Hill's testimony. She had not watched it but it didn't matter, her reaction was instinctive, 'They'll do anything to put him down'." And that was before Thomas even made his "lynching" allegation.

Biden was angered that the whole fight had taken this detour into an investigation of Thomas's character, obscuring the real question of the direction of the Court. He was also angered by Thomas's self-pitying "lynching" charge. On Saturday evening, as Thomas finished, Biden unburdened himself. He hated judging other people's character, "I did not sign on to this job or run for it to be a judge. . . . I hate this job."

He reminded Thomas and the committee that on scores of occasions he had had to make difficult decisions on whether or not to investigate further allegations not unlike the ones against Thomas. And in many cases I remember we reluctantly proceeded, and some nominations were quietly withdrawn. Now that this one had been forced into the open, Biden explained, we had to proceed to conclusion.

As to Thomas's attack on the process, which members on both sides had gleefully joined, Biden responded politely but firmly:

''I am getting fed up with this stuff about how terrible this system is. I hear everybody talking about how terrible the primary system is. We are big boys. I knew when I ran for President that everything was free game. Anybody who . . . is appointed to the Supreme Court . . . should understand, this is not boy scouts. . . . In the case of the President and the right to be leader of the free world, well, no one said it would be easy. And whoever goes to the Supreme Court is going to determine the fate of this country more than anybody.''

Three days later the nomination passed 52–48. The conventional wisdom was that it was a ''repellant spectacle,'' a ''degrading circus.'' Floyd Abrams, commenting in a television interview, did not share the Washington hand wringing. ''This is not so awful. Everybody proceeds as if we should be wearing black crepe over our arms. It's unseemly, but we live in a rich, textured, powerful country. We can take it. . . . It's not destroying anything.'' Besides, perhaps the Administration handlers learned something from this. If you are going to duck the main issue and make character the question, be prepared to live with the consequences.

To Klain, however, there was nothing enduring about a struggle over character. By its nature, it is sui generis, unique to the particular nominee. Even if Thomas has been defeated, the only message the Administration would have taken from it is that all they had to do was find another extreme conservative who had not engaged in sexual harassment. ''If the goal here is to shape the Supreme Court to protect individual liberties, more would have been accomplished with forty votes against Thomas, based on philosophy, than fifty-one votes against him based on the Hill allegations.''

Five years after the Bork summer I am sure that, to many, the whole effort seems for naught. The Court has moved inexorably to the right. Not only Kennedy but the subsequent nominees Souter and Thomas create a solid conservative majority. The committee, both Republicans and Democrats, and the process are the subject of constant ridicule in Washington.

However, on closer analysis the effect is both subtle and profound. Although a Court majority clearly exists for eviscerating or even reversing the *Roe* decision, this is not a Borkian Supreme Court. Robert Bork's jurisprudential agenda was to reverse the key decisions of the Warren Court, especially the high-water mark of Warren Court activism, *Griswold* v. *Connecticut,* with its open-ended notions of fundamental and unenumerated rights. Not only is *Griswold* secure but there is little evidence that this Court will undertake such a revolution.

That revolution should not occur if Democrats, moderate Republicans, and civil rights and feminist groups recognize what they did accomplish in defeating Bork. Important tactical mistakes were made by both the groups and sympathetic Senators in the Thomas–Anita Hill matter, and in retrospect perhaps they all should have insisted on more from Judge Souter.* The fact was that a political consensus did not exist among a majority of the Senate to do any more than confirm two justices who, like Justice Anthony Kennedy, forcefully rejected Bork's philosophy.

In the end, even as Kate Michelman admitted to me after the Bork victory, progressives will not save *Roe* or reverse the direction of the Supreme Court until a conservative President is replaced with one of their own. In Reagan and Bush we have two of the most conservative Presidents in almost seventy years. At best the process can only occasionally check the most extreme impulses of a determined executive. We did that. The Bork battle was not over *Roe*; it was over the legacy of the Warren Court, primarily privacy, fundamental and unenumerated rights—an enlightened and expansive notion of liberty.

The Republican strategists, savvy as they are, willing as they are to engage in the most aggressive form of hardball, from Willie Horton to the attacks on Anita Hill, know one fundamental truth about the Supreme Court. They cannot win on our battlefield. The American people agree with us, not them, about where the Supreme Court ought to be going. They reject the Borkian notion that the Warren court precedents, and especially the legacy of personal liberty, ought to be discarded.

By the same token, to the extent Senators get distracted by questions of character, either through the so-called Pin Point Strategy or even by focusing on negative questions of character such as sexual harassment, they are on much more dangerous ground. Ironically, it is a safer battlefield for a conservative President and his nominee, because it distracts the media and the public from his real agenda—quietly to implement Bork's jurisprudence. Furthermore, to the extent the media and the outside groups, rather than the Senators, seem to take control of the process, the more skeptical the public becomes of their motives. Although seriously undermined in the last five years by relentless attacks by the White House and the Right, the Bork process had credibility, at least at the time, because most Americans saw it as a question of principle debated by Senators acting on their own.

* I must acknowledge that, at least with respect to Senator Biden's actions in both the Souter and Thomas affairs, my advice was sought, and I agreed at the time with almost everything he did.

As progressive and liberal political experts consider both the presidency in this election year and the Supreme Court as part of the campaign, small as it may be, they should ponder this fundamental political truth. Even after the Thomas–Hill fiasco, the American people, when asked whether they wanted a moderate or conservative Supreme Court, chose the former by a stunning 55 percent to 21 percent margin. The American people have not forgotten what this struggle is all about, and that alone ought to be the ultimate legacy of the Bork fight.*

June 1992

* This manuscript was finished before the Supreme Court's decision in the Pennsylvania abortion case, as well as a number of enlightened First Amendment decisions and the emergence of a clearly moderate center on the Court, composed of Justices O'Connor, Kennedy, and Souter. These developments are further evidence of the point of this epilogue—that it is irresponsible to write off this Court simply because it has become more conservative.

NOTES

Some of the material in this book was obtained through a commitment to confidentiality, and therefore there is no acknowledgment of source. Other material is based solely upon my own recollection of events I witnessed. The following are specific sources.

INTRODUCTION

The description of Bork's comments at the White House are based upon my interviews with Tom Griscom and others present at the meeting. The quotations from Biden are from his speech to the American Bar Association that summer, transcripts of the hearings and conversations he had with me.

CHAPTER 1

The interchange between Eastland and Powell is recounted by Bob Woodward and Scott Armstrong in their classic on the Supreme Court *The Brethren.* (New York: Simon & Schuster, 1979). It was, however, legend at the Judiciary Committee when I first came there to work as an assistant counsel in January 1972.

Much of the information on Powell's role in the court came from the ACLU's summary of the 5–4 cases. The ACLU's list was probably one of the most significant things the liberal interest groups did that day or indeed for the first week. It tended to focus the debate on the reality of what the Powell resignation really meant. That, plus Biden's statement, kept the focus on the motives of the Reagan Administration in selecting a successor. I also found the *Washington Post* and *New York Times* articles on Powell's role extremely helpful. They tended to confirm the ACLU list.

Many of the quotations from activists on the Left and Right about the Powell resignation come from reporting by the *Washington Post*, the *New York Times*, the *Los Angeles Times*, *USA Today*, and the *Wall Street Journal.* The reactions of key Department of Justice officials is based on my interviews with Steve Markman, Mike Carvin, and John Bolton. Biden's reaction and the scene at the Los Angeles airport is based upon my interview with Tom Vallely.

Biden was not the only future opponent who had said positive things about Bork in 1986. Earlier that year Biden had joined civil rights and civil liberties groups in an unsuccessful effort to block the nomination of Daniel Manion to the United States Court of Appeals for the 7th Circuit. In the course of the debate, Biden and others made it clear that they were not opposing the nomination purely on ideological grounds and that several very conservative Court of Appeals judges had been acceptable, notably Antonin Scalia and Robert Bork. Biden was referring to a nomination to the Court of Appeals, not necessarily to the Supreme Court, although Biden did support the Scalia nomination to the Supreme Court.

It was in that vein that earlier in 1986 Anthony Podesta, the executive director of the liberal group People for the American Way, said to a meeting of the conservative Federalist Society that Scalia and Bork would be acceptable candidates for the Supreme Court.

I asked one of the conservative Bork advocates, intimately involved in his preparation and strategy, what his reaction was to Biden's ABA speech in August. In that, Biden had suggested that Bork might overturn important civil liberties and civil rights precedents and thereby, in effect, shift the balance on the Court. He laughed and answered, "My personal reaction was, 'Fuck yes!,' but I knew that the White House did not want us saying that. That wasn't their strategy."

CHAPTER 2

This chapter is based upon my interviews with Bolton, Carvin, Vallely, Linda Greenhouse of the *New York Times*, Ralph Neas, Ted Kaufman, and Dennis Shedd. A number of the quotes from Senators, Justice Department and other Administration officials, from Pat McGuigan and other activists on the Right I found in the reporting of the *Washington Post*, *New York Times*, *Washington Times*, *USA Today*, and other national media.

CHAPTER 3

The anecdote about President Reagan's meeting with Sandra Day O'Connor and the history of his abortion position are based upon Lou Cannon's *President Reagan: The Role of a Lifetime* (New York: Simon & Schuster, 1991). The Bruce Fein quote is from Lincoln Caplan's *Tenth Justice: The Solicitor General and the Rule of Law* (New York: Vantage, 1988). The McCellan quote is from his article in the March–April 1984 issue of *Benchmark*.

The Nofziger, Buchanan, Richard Cheney, Richard Lugar, Richard Viguerie quotes are from *Congressional Quarterly* and the *Los Angeles Times*.

The background on Meese and the "incorporation doctrine" is based on reporting in the *New York Times* and Sidney Blumenthal's *The Rise of the "Counterestablishment": From Conservative Ideology to Political Power* (New York: Harper & Row, 1986). The Bork quotes are from his Francis Boyer lecture in 1984 at the American Enterprise Institute and his 1971 *Indiana Law Journal* article.

The material on the Solicitor General's office, including a number of quotes from lawyers in the office, is based largely on Lincoln Caplan's excellent book on the subject (*Tenth Justice*, see above). Caplan also was the source of material on the Reagan Administration's general strategy for creating a more conservative jurisprudence. The quotes from Fein, Reagan, and Buchanan are from *Congressional Quarterly*, the *Los Angeles Times*, the *New York Times*, and the *Washington Post*.

I based much of my discussion of Jackson and Taney, including numerous quotes, on Robert Remini's *The Jacksonian Era* (Arlington Heights, Ill.: H. Davidson, 1989), Samuel Eliot Morison's *The Oxford History of the American People* (New York: Oxford University Press, 1965), Carl B. Swisher, *The Oliver Wendell Holmes Devise History of the Supreme Court of The United States*, Vol. V.: *The Taney Period* (New York: Macmillan, 1974), Laurence Tribe, *God Save This Honorable Court*, (New York: Random House, 1985), and Henry J. Abraham's *Justices and Presidents: A Political History of Appointments to the Supreme Court* (New York: Oxford University Press, 1974).

The section on Roosevelt and the Supreme Court, including numerous quotes, is based on William E. Leuchtenburg's extensive writing on the subject—e.g., an article in the 1986 *Supreme Court Review* and his book *Franklin D. Roosevelt and the New Deal* (New York: Harper & Row, 1963)—and Arthur Schlesinger's *The Politics of Upheaval* (Boston: Houghton Mifflin, 1967).

The quotes by activists on the Right about the Bork nomination are from the *Washington Post* and *USA Today*. The Dole quote is from the *Los Angeles Times* and the sarcastic columnist is Michael Kinsley in an op-ed in the *Wall Street Journal*.

CHAPTER 4

Numerous quotes by Senators and activists are from *Newsweek*, the *Washington Post*, and *USA Today*. Tom Donilon, John Bolton, Larry Rasky and Ralph Neas provided information and quotes for this chapter.

CHAPTER 5

The sources for most of the maneuvering within the Administration are extensive interviews with Terry Eastland, John Bolton, Steve Markman, Brad Reynolds, Ray Randolph, Tom Korologos, A. B. Culvahouse, and Ken Duberstein. I was also aided by excellent reporting in the *Washington Post*, the *New York Times*, and the *Wall Street Journal*. I was also fortunate to be given a copy of Brad Reynolds's notes of the pivotal meeting to organize the Bork defense on July 6 at the White House.

The tumultuous meeting of the Republican staff was described to me by numerous participants. Ironically, the suspicion that conservatives had of Senator Specter's staff was unwarranted. Manne and Robinson never discussed with Bork opponents any of their meetings with other Republicans or any confidential discussions with Specter or anyone in the Administration with respect to the Bork nomination until well after the nomination was defeated.

It was indeed ironic that Dennis Shedd was largely ignored by Administration strategists, since we definitely considered him one of our most dangerous and effective opponents. Shedd had been instrumental, for example, in crafting, along with Brad Reynolds, several successful Republican efforts to stymie the civil rights community's efforts to enact legislation to reverse the Supreme Court's decision in the *Grove City* case, until the Bork nomination, the primary civil rights priority.

CHAPTER 6

Much of the biographical information on Judge Bork came from thoughtful profiles in the national media such as Stuart Taylor's in the *New York Times*, Dale Russakoff's and Al Kamen's series in the *Washington Post*, and Tony Mauro's in *USA Today*. Bork's *New Republic* article was entitled "Civil Rights—a Challenge" and appeared on August 31, 1963. His *Indiana Law Journal* article was entitled "Neutral Principles and Some First Amendment Problems" and appeared in Vol. 47 of the *Journal* in 1971.

Insights into Bork's teaching and writing were provided by, among others, Deborah Levy, a former student and a member of the Judiciary Committee staff during the nomination battle, and Bork's friend, Ray Randolph.

The description of the struggle within the Administration over the preparation of the Blue Book is based on interviews with Steve Markman, John Bolton, Mike Carvin, Brad Reynolds, and A. B. Culvahouse.

Biden's speech on advice and consent appears in the *Congressional Record* of July 23, 1987. The quote by Biden summarized in the chapter is from *Federalist 76*.

The description of the Heritage Foundation meeting is based upon interviews with five participants in the meeting.

The reaction by the Right to the Blue Book is based upon interviews with Bolton and Eastland, press coverage, and an interview of Bruce Fein by Nina Totenberg on National Public Radio.

CHAPTER 7

This chapter is based upon interviews with Jeff Peck, Ted Kaufman, Larry Rasky, Tom Griscom, Will Ball, Tom Korologos, Brad Reynolds, and A. B. Culvahouse. One of the Will Ball quotes is from Ethan Bronner's excellent book on the Bork Struggle, *Battle for Justice* (New York: W. W. Norton, 1989).

The case referred to in Peck's list of cases pertaining to racially restrictive covenants is the case of *Shelley* v. *Kraemer* 334 U.S. 1 (1948). The so-called one-man-one-vote cases are *Baker* v. *Carr* 369 U.S. 186 (1962) and *Reynolds* v. *Sims* 377 U.S. 533 (1964). The 1966 case upholding the Voting Rights Act is *Katzenbach* v. *Morgan* 384 U.S. 641 (1966).

The ''dozens of cases'' quote is found in U.S. Congress. Senate. Judiciary Committee. Subcommittee on Separation of Powers. *Hearings on the Human Life Bill*, 97th Cong., 1st Sess., June 10, 1981.

CHAPTER 8

Bork's suggestion that *Meyer* and *Pierce* were wrongly decided appears in his *Indiana Law Journal* piece. In the case of *Pierce*, Bork suggested that perhaps it could be decided on other grounds but was wrongly reasoned. The Court never questioned the reasoning of *Pierce* even after the FDR justices were named. Bork's reference to *Skinner* being ''intellectually empty'' is also in the *Indiana Law Journal*.

Bork's criticism of *Griswold* appears in the *Indiana Law Journal*, a 1982 speech at Catholic University, and a 1986 interview in a conservative legal journal. His comment about the ''sexual privacy cases'' is found in a 1982 address to the Federalist Society at Yale.

William Coleman's prepared statement and testimony in the committee hearings contain a thorough discussion of Frankfurter's views of the due process clause. See also a letter from Stephen J. Schulhofer, one of Justice Hugo L. Black's former law clerks and now a professor at the University of Chicago Law School, reprinted in the committee hearing record. Also see Black's dissent in *Griswold*.

Frankfurter elaborated his views on due process in *Rochin* v. *California* 342 U.S. 165, 169 (1952). The two Cardozo opinions on due process are contained in *Snyder* v. *Massachusetts* 291 U.S. 97, 105, and *Palko* v. *Connecticut* 302 U.S. 319, 325.

Bork's critique of the fundamental rights jurisprudence also appears in the *Indiana Law Journal*. His comments on interpreting the Ninth Amendment were made at a speech at the University of Southern California in 1984.

The Frankfurter quote on ''freezing'' due process appears in his *Rochin* opinion.

I found Leonard Levy, *Original Intent and the Framers' Constitution* (New York: Macmillan, 1988) extremely valuable in coming to understand how the framers viewed natural rights. A number of the framers' quotes are found there. The longtime critic of Bork quoted on the difference between Bork and the framers' attitudes on natural rights is Stephen Macedo.

Edwin Corwin's classic article in *Harvard Law Review* 42:149 (December 1928) is an excellent history of the natural law roots of our jurisprudence.

CHAPTER 9

The three Supreme Court decisions discussed at the beginning of the chapter are *Brandenburg* v. *Ohio*, 395 U.S. 444 (1969), *Cohen* v. *California*, 403 U.S. 15 (1971) and *Hess* v. *Indiana*, 414 U.S. 105 (1973). Alexander Bickel's thoughtful articles on domestic dissent appear in issues of the *New Republic* in September 1969 and the following June and October and from *Commentary*. The excerpt from Bork's testimonial to Bickel is from Ethan Bronner's book.

The quotes by John Stuart Mill are from his classic *On Liberty*. Most of the quotes from Senator Specter are from two extensive interviews I had with him in 1989. The Neal Manne quotes are from interviews I conducted that same year. The Floyd Abrams quotations are from notes and memoranda prepared as a result of Abrams's briefing of Biden on August 6. The section on Senator Leahy is based on an interview with him and several members of his staff and a diary reflecting his preparation for the hearings reprinted in *Washingtonian* magazine in April 1988. The commentary on Leahy is from Michael Barone and Grant Ujifusa in *The Almanac of American Politics 1990* (Washington D.C.: National Journal Inc., 1989).

CHAPTER 10

The section on Senator DeConcini is based on interviews with the Senator and with staff members including Ed Baxter and Gene Carp. The material on the ERA defeat is from the *New York Times* and *Time* magazine. The commentator quoted on the original intent of the Fourteenth Amendment is Gerald Gunther in his casebook, *Cases and Materials on Constitutional Law* (Mineola, N.Y.: The Foundation Press, Inc., 1980).

Quong Wing v. *Kikendall*, 112 U.S. 59, is the 1912 Montana case in which Justice Holmes is quoted. *Radice* v. *New York* 264 U.S. 292, is the 1924 New York case on working hours for women, and *Goesaert* v. *Cleary*, 335 U.S. 464, is the 1948 Michigan case involving women bartenders. Much of the material on Ruth Bader Ginsburg is from an article by Judge Ginsburg "Women Becoming Part of the Constitution," *Law and Inequality* 6: 17, and from Kenneth Davidson, Ruth Bader Ginsburg, and Herma Hill Kay, *Cases and Materials on Sex-based Discrimination* (St. Paul, Minn.: West Publishing, 1974).

Marcia Greenberger in her interview explained the evolution of the Court's gender discrimination standards and the feminist legal strategy to change them. Orrin Hatch in his interview with me elaborated on his relationship to Senator DeConcini and his effort to persuade DeConcini to support Bork.

CHAPTER 11

Comments by Dean Clark and Paul Bator were made at a symposium entitled "A Discussion on Critical Legal Studies at the Harvard Law School" sponsored by the Harvard Society for Law and Public Policy and the Federalist Society for Law and Public Policy Studies, conducted at the Harvard Club, New York City, May 13, 1985 (transcript available from the Federalist Society, Washington, D.C.). Other material is based on an extensive interview with Prof. Chris Schroeder from Duke and an excellent article by Jill Abramson in a 1986 issue of the *American Lawyer* entitled "Right Place at the Right Time," one by Charles Bork entitled "Battle for the Law Schools" in the September 26, 1986, issue of *National Review*, and an article in the July 23, 1986, *New York Times*.

The summary of the July meeting at the White House is based upon interviews with participants at the meeting and the notes of one of those participants. The rendition of the early Administration efforts to organize the academic community is based on interviews with Ray Randolph, Steve Markman, and others involved in that project as well as memoranda prepared by Lee Lieberman and sent to key participants.

Interviews of Ricki Seidman and Bill Taylor provided the background for the anti-Bork effort to organize sympathetic academics.

The anecdotes about Barbara Black and Harry Wellington are from Ethan Bronner, *Battle for Justice* (New York: W. W. Norton, 1989).

CHAPTER 12

The material on the Carter campaign as well as much of the background on Paul Weyrich, Richard Viguerie, and the early organizing efforts of the political Right is based on Perry Dean Young's *God's Bullies: Native Reflection on Preachers and Politics* (New York: Holt, Rinehart and Winston, 1982), David Broder, *Changing of the Guard* (New York: Penguin, 1981), Alan Crawford, *Thunder on the Right: The "New Right" and the Politics of Resentment* (New York: Pantheon, 1981), and Richard Viguerie's *The New Right: We're Ready to Lead* (Falls Church, Va.: Viguerie Co., 1981).

I also relied on extensive interviews with Patrick McGuigan and Randy Rader. The material on right-wing organizing and fund-raising efforts is based on reporting in the *Washington Post* and the *Washington Times* as well as copies of actual fund solicitations by right-wing groups which I have in my files.

Ralph Neas, in several long interviews, provided me with extensive background on the history of the Leadership Conference on Civil Rights and its work in the summer of 1987. The material on the tension between women's groups and mainline civil rights groups is based on a number of confidential interviews with activists from both groups. I also relied upon Michael Pertschuk and Wendy Schaetzel, *The People Rising: The Campaign Against the Bork Nomination* (New York: Thunder's Mouth Press, 1989), and notes of interviews they conducted for that book, which they most graciously shared with me. I also found Herman Schwartz, *Packing the Courts: The Conservative Campaign to Rewrite the Constitution* (New York: Macmillan Publishing Co., 1985), an excellent source on much of the same material. Melanne Verveer of People for the American Way, Kate Michelman of NARAL, Mimi Mager, and Judy Lichtman were also helpful in their interviews on the organizing efforts in 1987.

CHAPTER 13

My interview with Jeff Peck enriched and refreshed my recollection of the preparation of the response to the Blue Book.

Tribe's book referred to in the text is entitled *God Save This Honorable Court* (New York: Random House, 1985). Tribe had spent considerable time writing about the parameters of the right to privacy. In 1986 he had argued the ill-fated *Hardwick* case in the Supreme Court to the effect that the *Griswold* right to privacy extended to private consensual homosexual conduct.

My interviews with Larry Rasky and Tom Donilon were invaluable in writing this chapter, both with respect to the Bethany Beach meeting but also in reminding me of what we had done in the editorial board campaign that summer.

My interviews of Pat Shakow at the *Post* and Jack McKenzie at the *Times* gave me great insight into how the two great papers arrived at their editorial judgments. A. B. Culvahouse and Brad Reynolds explained how the White House attempted to influence editorial opinion.

Ralph Neas was particularly helpful in describing his meeting with the *Post* editorial board. According to Shakow, Donald Graham is a weekly visitor to the editorial board, and Bradley does so on a less regular basis. As far as Shakow was concerned, the Bork nomination was probably the "most important subject of the year and it was really not surprising to see Kate Graham there." She would often come in for an editorial board meeting with a presidential candidate or on a major subject like Bork.

The civil rights community did attempt a coordinated effort to meet with other editorial boards but, according to Pertschuk and Schaetzel, it never really materialized. Neas and company did meet with the *New York Times* editorial board. Kate Michelman met with the *Philadelphia Inquirer*, and Judy Lichtman met with the *Atlanta Constitution*.

Linda Greenhouse, Adam Clymer, and Stuart Taylor gave me additional insights as to how the *Times* reacted to the Bork fight and Biden.

For the complete texts of the original White House Blue Book, the Public Citizen report, the Biden report, and the Justice Department response, see *Cardozo Law Review*: 9:1 (October 1987).

CHAPTER 14

Tom Korologos, John Bolton, Mike Carvin, Terry Eastland, Brad Reynolds, and Ken Duberstein were all helpful in understanding how Bork was prepared for the hearings and his attitudes toward the murder boards and the events leading up to them, including the ABA report. Reporting in the *Post* and *Legal Times* was also helpful here.

Most of Bork's comments are from his book *The Tempting of America* (New York: Macmillan, 1990). Comments by Weyrich and others on the Right are from Pat McGuigan and Dawn Weyrich's fascinating book, *Ninth Justice* (Washington, D.C.: Free Congress Research and Education Foundation, 1990). Ethan Bronner, *Battle for Justice* (New York: W. W. Norton, 1989), also provided good background, the Bork interchange with Boll in the first murder board, one Lloyd Cutler quote during the murder boards at Bork's house, and the discouraging interchange between Bolton and Culvahouse about the hearings.

Korlogos had been concerned about Bork's preparation for the hearings since July. He had said as much at early meetings with Judiciary Committee Republican staffers, according to interviews with Bolton, Shedd, Manne, and others present at the meetings.

My interview with Jeff Peck and Ken Bass and a memorandum Bass wrote to Biden on September 10 were useful in refreshing my recollection of the Biden mock hearings.

The interchange between McGuigan and Culvahouse is based upon McGuigan's book and my interviews with both men.

The events around the plagiarism allegations against Biden, and the internal deliberations of the Gephardt and Dukakis campaigns on how to take advantage of them, are based upon reporting in *Newsweek*, Christine Black and Tom Oliphant, *All by Myself: The Unmaking of a Presidential Campaign* (Chester, Conn.: Globe Pequot Press, 1989), Jack Germond and Jules Witcover, *Whose Broad Stripes and Bright Stars* (New York: Warner Books, Inc., 1989), and an interview with Mark Johnston of the Gephardt campaign.

Adam Clymer, Ken Bode, John Ellis provided valuable information about the other campaigns and the press coverage of the various charges against Biden.

Ted Kaufman and Tim Ridley reminisced with me about how the Biden campaign responded.

CHAPTER 15

The Markman quote about the Ford Administration judicial appointment record is from David N. O'Brien's *Judicial Roulette* (New York: Priority Press, 1988).

Dennis Shedd, Tom Korologos, Terry Eastland, Brad Reynolds, John Bolton, Ray Randolph, Bruce Fein, Ken Duberstein, and Randy Rader all contributed material for this chapter. Jack McKenzie did also. Ethan Bronner, *Battle for Justice* (New York: W. W. Norton, 1989), provided the interchange between Bork and his son the night after the first hearing.

Neal Manne spoke to me about Specter's strategy. Specter shared reactions to Bork's testimony. Hatch also told me his reactions and frustrations with Bork's testimony.

Michael Pertschuk and Wendy Schaetzel, *The People Rising: The Campaign Against the Bork Nomination* (New York: Thunder Mouth's Press, 1989) were the source for the Elaine Jones and Heflin interchanges.

CHAPTER 16

The discussion of the allegations against Biden is based largely on my review of the reporting in *Legal Times*, extensive reporting in all of the national newspapers plus my review of Biden's academic file that was released to the public at the time. Jill Abramson and John Ellis gave me great insight into how the allegations spread.

The Biden meeting with the committee, telling them of the allegations, is based upon my interviews with Senators Kennedy, Hatch, DeConcini, and Leahy.

My analysis of television news coverage of the hearings compared to coverage of the plagiarism allegations is based on my review of the daily TV news summaries available from Vanderbilt University.

Pertschuk and Schaetzel made available interview transcripts, which were particularly helpful in understanding how the civil rights group reacted to the allegations against Biden as well as their decision not to testify.

Diana Huffman described the nerve-wracking process of putting the hearings together and keeping them going as the crisis over the Biden allegations continued.

Senator Hatch and his then staffer, Randy Rader, described the failed effort to get Bork to come back later in the hearings to rebut allegations by the anti-Bork witnesses. Bronner provides details on Bork's activities after he finished testifying. Carvin described the preparation of the posthearing Bork letter to Biden.

Tim Ridley and Larry Rasky were helpful in reminding me of how the campaign reacted to the allegations.

CHAPTER 17

Bolton explained the White House's initial reaction to the hearings. Reporting in the *Wall Street Journal*, the *Post*, and other national papers provide considerable background on the polls, the Administration's reaction, and its change in tactics to begin to attack the committee and the hearing process.

The cost figures on the print and TV anti-Bork ads were supplied to me at the Senate Judiciary Committee at the time. Pertschuk and Schaetzel provided me access to interview notes on the same subject.

Bork's attempt to get the White House to become more aggressive is based on Ethan Bronner, *Battle for Justice* (New York: W. W. Norton, 1989), and interviews with Bolton, Culvahouse, Will Ball, Tom Griscom, Reynolds, and other high-ranking Administration officials. Carvin and Eastland described their frustration with getting a Reagan statement approved and the preparation of that statement.

The case in which Bork cited White's dissent in *Moore* v. *the City of East Cleveland* was *Dronenburg* v. *Zeck* 746 f.2d at 1396.

Bronner was also the source of some of the anti-Bork exaggerations that I did not know of at the time. Mimi Mager was valuable in providing other information on reckless anti-Bork allegations that she tried unsuccessfully to halt.

CHAPTER 18

The *Almanac of American Politics 1988* (Washington, D.C.: National Journal Inc., 1987) was very helpful on the politics of some of the Southern Democrats. Bronner is the source of the Dan Casey quote. Reporting in the *Post* was an important source on Reagan's effort to make judicial nominations an issue in the '86 elections. Mike House was invaluable in understanding how the Southern Democrats were evaluating the politics of the Bork vote.

Charles McBride, a confidant and former staffer, was helpful on how Bennett Johnston evaluated the nomination, and Michael Levy did the same with respect to Bentsen's approach to Bork. Levy provided background materials, including decades-old newsclips reflecting Bentsen's courageous stands on race in the late 1940s. A Bentsen interview with a staff member of Ralph Nader's Congress Project in John M. Ullman, "Lloyd M. Bentsen, Jr.," unpublished booklet compiled circa 1972 and supplied to me by Senator Bentsen's office, was also very helpful.

Earl and Merle Black, *Politics and Society in the South* (Cambridge, Mass.: Harvard University Press, 1987), and Merle Black's interview with me were very helpful in understanding the demographic and political trends in the South over the past few decades.

The 1985 essay in which Bork reiterated his criticism of the *Harper* decision was the "Foreward" in G. McDowell's *The Constitution and Contemporary Theory*, Vol. VII (Washington, D.C.: Center for Judicial Studies, 1985).

The Leroy Collins' conversation with Justice Black is from Senator Graham's speech on the Senate Floor on October 10, 1987. Ken Klein gave me insights into how Senator Graham analyzed the Bork vote and the Senator's background in Southern politics.

The instances in which Bork reiterated his concerns about the one-man-one-vote decisions are a 1968 *Fortune* magazine article, his 1973 Solicitor General confirmation hearings and the so-called Worldnet interview in June 1987.

The Cranston and Bolton quotes are from reporting in the *Times* and the *Post*.

Specter gave me his version of his final meeting with Bork. Bork's version of that meeting and his attitudes toward Specter are laid out in great deal in his own book.

Suzanne Martinez of his staff was helpful in background on Cranston and providing materials on Cranston, including press releases and other materials relevant to the story.

Pat Shakow described how the *Post* arrived at its editorial position.

Pat McGuigan's book is helpful in detailing other efforts on the Right to organize in favor of Bork after the committee's vote.

CHAPTER 19

Hatch's reaction to the ads run by the Right is from his interview with me. McGuigan describes in his book and his interview with me the efforts to organize for Bork and the events surrounding Bork's dramatic statement indicating his determination to see a Senate vote. Reporting in the *Washington Times*, *Washington Post*, *New York Times*, and other national publications were relied on for this portion of the chapter.

Bolton, Reynolds, Randolph, and Culvahouse all discussed with me the Administration maneuvering and Bork's own deliberations during this period.

The section on Garment is based on interviews with Bolton and Reynolds reporting in the *Times*, the *Post*, and the *Wall Street Journal*, and Ethan Bronner, *Battle for Justice* (New York: W. W. Norton, 1989). Bronner also was the source for a few other isolated incidents mentioned in this chapter and for the Garn quote.

Ken Klein of Graham's staff described to me Graham's meeting with Reagan. Ed Baxter, DeConcini's chief Judiciary Committee staffer, described the DeConcini meeting with Reagan.

The Gingrich letter to Reagan is reprinted in McGuigan's book. The NCPAC fund-raising campaign is described in reporting in the *Washington Post*, as well as Senator Byrd's statements on the Senate floor during that period.

Bork's reaction to the vote found at the end of the chapter is from his book.

CHAPTER 20

Confidential interviews with a high-ranking White House staffer and a top Justice Department official were invaluable for this chapter. I relied on reporting in the *Des Moines Register*, *Washington Post*, *USA Today*, and other national papers as well.

Interviews with Bolton, Reynolds, Hatch, and Steve Cannon (a former Ginsburg deputy and confidant) were helpful in developing the Ginsburg section.

Bruce Fein's comments are from his interview with me. Ruderman's comments are from her interview with me and a lengthy letter to me.

The Yale alumni incident was related to me by Walter Dellinger.

Professors Schroeder and Tribe discussed Kennedy with me at length. The Linda Greenhouse comments are all from her excellent reporting in the *New York Times*.

Mike Donilon gave me valuable background on the Wilder campaign. Howard Fineman discussed with me the generational politics underlying the Bork consideration.

McGuigan's closing comments are from his interview with me and his book. Kate Michelman's comments are from her interview with me.

EPILOGUE

The Souter incident is based on my interview with Ken Duberstein.

Two of the more disturbing Thomas comments on natural law are found in *Harvard Journal of Law & Public Policy,* Winter 1989, and his speech at the Pacific Research Foundation delivered in August of 1987.

The Bozell comments were reported in the *New York Times*, the *Washington Post*, and the *Washington Times*. Much of the material related to Thomas's preparation and the reaction to his testimony is found in similar reporting in the same papers.

Totenberg's comments are contained in a lengthy *Vanity Fair* article in January 1992.

The Hill allegations and the reaction to them are based upon extensive reporting in all the major newspapers relied upon elsewhere in the book. The Lichtman conversation with Biden and Klain was told to me by Klain. The Abramson material is from my interview with her. The *New York Times* poll was reported on October 15 in the *Times*. The Floyd Abrams comments are found in *New York* magazine on December 12, 1991.

The poll referred to at the very end of the Epilogue is a *Wall Street Journal*–NBC poll reported in the *Journal* on October 17, 1991.

INDEX